Known by many as "Russia's lost moral conscience" and hailed by the *New York Times* as "the bravest of journalists," **ANNA POLITKOVSKAYA** (born 1958 in New York City) was a special correspondent for the Russian newspaper *Novaya gazeta*. She received honors from many Russian and international groups, including Amnesty International and the Index on Censorship. In 2000 she received Russia's prestigious Golden Pen Award for her coverage of the war in Chechnya, and in 2005 she was awarded the Civil Courage Prize. She is the author of *A Dirty War; A Small Corner of Hell; Putin's Russia;* and *A Russian Diary*. She was murdered in Moscow on October 7, 2006.

ARCH TAIT translates from the Russian. His translation of Ludmila Ulitskaya's *Sonechka: A Novella and Stories* was shortlisted for the Rossica Translation Prize in 2007.

Also by Anna Politkovskaya

A Russian Diary
Putin's Russia
A Small Corner of Hell: Dispatches from Chechnya
A Dirty War: a Russian Reporter in Chechnya

IS JOURNALISM WORTH DYING FOR?

ANNA POLITKOVSKAYA

IS JOURNALISM WORTH DYING FOR?

Final Dispatches

Translated from the Russian by Arch Tait

MELVILLEHOUSE

BROOKLYN, NEW YORK

IS JOURNALISM WORTH DYING FOR?
Originally published in Russian as *Za chto?*
by *Novaya gazeta*, Moscow, 2007
© 2007 Anna Politkovskaya
© 2007 *Novaya gazeta*
Translation © 2010 by Arch Tait
First Melville House printing: March 2011

Melville House Publishing
145 Plymouth Street
Brooklyn, NY 11201

www.mhpbooks.com

ISBN: 978-1-935554-40-0

Printed in the United States of America

1 2 3 4 5 6 7 8 9 10

Library of Congress Control Number: 2011922469

This book was first published in Russian as *Za chto*—What For?—by *Novaya gazeta*, the newspaper to which Anna Politkovskaya contributed from June 1999 until her murder in October 2006. Her colleagues at the paper assembled the collection, and their reminiscences of Politkovskaya and investigation of her murder (including Vyacheslav Izmailov's "Who Killed Anna and Why?") are also included. Politkovskaya is one of four *Novaya gazeta* journalists murdered between 2001 and 2009.

CONTENTS

She represented the honor and conscience of Russia, and probably nobody will ever know the source of her fanatical courage and love of the work she was doing.

Liza Umarova, Chechen singer

Anna rang me at the hospital in the morning, before 10 o'clock. She was supposed to be coming to visit, this was her day, but something had come up at home. Anna said my second daughter, Lena, would come instead, and promised that we would definitely meet on Sunday. She sounded in a good mood, her voice was cheerful. She asked how I was feeling and whether I was reading a book. She knew I love historical literature and had brought me Alexander Manko's *The Most August Court under the Sign of Hymenaeus*. She had not read it herself. I said, "Anya, it is difficult for me to read. I have to read every page three times because I have Father before my eyes all the time." [Raisa Mazepa's husband had died shortly before.] She tried to calm me, "He didn't suffer. Everything happened very quickly. He was coming to visit you. Let's talk about the book instead." I said, "Anya there is an epigraph on page 179 which really moves me. It is so much a part of us, so Russian." I read it to her: "There are drunken years in the history of peoples. You have to live through them, but you can never truly live in them."

"Oh, Mum," she replied, "put a bookmark there, don't forget." I asked my daughter who the author of the epigraph was, and she told me about Nadezhda Teffi, a famous Russian poetess. Then she said, "Speak to you tomorrow, Mum." She was in a very good mood. Or perhaps she was in a bad mood and just pretending everything was fine in order not to upset me.

I was always very worried about her. Shortly before I went into hospital we had a talk. She was preparing an article about Chechnya, and I simply begged her to be careful. I remember she said, "Of course I know the sword of Damocles is always hanging over me. I know it, but I won't give in."

Raisa Mazepa (Anna Politkovskaya's mother), *Novaya gazeta*, October 23, 2006

SO WHAT AM I GUILTY OF?

This article was found in Anna Politkovskaya's computer after her death and is addressed to readers abroad.

"*Koverny*," a Russian clown whose job in the olden days was to keep the audience laughing while the circus arena was changed between acts. If he failed to make them laugh, the ladies and gentlemen booed him and the management sacked him.

Almost the entire present generation of Russian journalists, and those sections of the mass media which have survived to date, are clowns of this kind, a Big Top of *kovernys* whose job is to keep the public entertained and, if they do have to write about anything serious, then merely to tell everyone how wonderful the Pyramid of Power is in all its manifestations. The Pyramid of Power is something President Putin has been busy constructing for the past five years, in which every official – from top to bottom, the entire bureaucratic hierarchy – is appointed either by him personally or by his appointees. It is an arrangement of the state which ensures that anybody given to thinking independently of their immediate superior is promptly removed from office. In Russia the people thus appointed are described by Putin's Presidential Administration, which effectively runs the country, as "on side." Anybody not on side is an enemy. The vast majority of those working in the media support this dualism. Their reports detail how good on-side people are, and deplore the despicable nature of enemies. The latter include liberally inclined politicians, human rights activists, and "enemy" democrats, who are generally characterised as having sold out to the West. An example of an on-side democrat is, of course, President Putin himself. The newspapers and television give top priority to detailed "exposés" of the grants enemies have received from the West for their activities.

Journalists and television presenters have taken enthusiastically to their new role in the Big Top. The battle for the right to convey

impartial information, rather than act as servants of the Presidential Administration, is already a thing of the past. An atmosphere of
intellectual and moral stagnation prevails in the profession to which
I too belong, and it has to be said that most of my fellow journalists are not greatly troubled by this reversion from journalism to
propagandising on behalf of the powers that be. They openly admit
that they are fed information about enemies by members of the Presidential Administration, and are told what to cover and what to steer
clear of.

What happens to journalists who don't want to perform in the Big
Top? They become pariahs. I am not exaggerating.

My last assignment to the North Caucasus, to report from Chechnya,
Ingushetia, and Dagestan, was in August 2006. I wanted to interview
a senior Chechen official about the success or failure of an amnesty
for resistance fighters which the Director of the Federal Security Bureau,
the FSB, had declared.

I scribbled down an address in Grozny, a ruined private house with
a broken fence on the city's outskirts, and slipped it to him without
further explanation. We had talked in Moscow about the fact that I
would be coming and would want to interview him. A day later he sent
someone there who said cryptically, "I have been asked to tell you everything is fine." That meant the official would see me, or more precisely
that he would come strolling in carrying a string bag and looking as
if he had just gone out to buy a loaf of bread.

His information was invaluable, and completely undermined the
official account of how the amnesty was going. It was conveyed to me
in a room two metres square with a tiny window whose curtains were
firmly drawn. Before the war it had been a shed, but when the main
house was bombed its owners had to use it as kitchen, bedroom and
bathroom combined. They let me use it with considerable trepidation,
but they are old friends about whose misfortunes I wrote some years
ago when their son was abducted.

Why did the official and I go to these lengths? Were we mad, or
trying to bring a little excitement into our lives? Far from it. Open
fraternisation between an opposition-inclined gatherer of information

like me or another of my *Novaya gazeta* colleagues and an on-side government official would spell disaster for both of us.

That same senior official subsequently brought to the sometime shed resistance fighters who wanted to lay down their arms but not to take part in the official circus performance. They passed on a lot of interesting information about why none of the fighters wanted to surrender to the regime: they believed the Government was only interested in public relations and could not be trusted.

"Nobody wants to surrender!" The pundits will find that hard to believe. For weeks Russian television has shown dodgy-looking individuals declaring that they want to accept the amnesty terms, that they "trust Ramzan." Ramzan Kadyrov is President Putin's Chechen favorite, appointed Prime Minister with blithe disregard for the fact that the man is a complete idiot, bereft of education, brains, or a discernible talent for anything other than mayhem and violent robbery.

To these unholy gatherings squads of journalist-clowns are brought along (I don't get invited). They write everything down carefully in their notebooks, take their photographs, file their reports, and a totally distorted image of reality results. An image, however, which is pleasing to those who declared the amnesty.

You don't get used to this, but you learn to live with it. It is exactly the way I have had to work throughout the Second War in the North Caucasus. To begin with I was hiding from the Russian federal troops, but always able to make contact clandestinely with individuals through trusted intermediaries, so that my informants would not be denounced to the generals. When Putin's plan of Chechenisation succeeded (setting "good" Chechens loyal to the Kremlin to killing "bad" Chechens who opposed it), the same subterfuge applied when talking to "good" Chechen officials. The situation is no different in Moscow, or in Kabardino-Balkaria, or Ingushetia. The virus is very widespread.

At least a circus performance does not last long, and the regime availing itself of the services of clownish journalists has the longevity of a mouldering mushroom. Purging the news has produced a blatant lie orchestrated by officials eager to promote a "correct image of Russia under Putin." Even now it is producing tragedies the regime cannot cope with and which can sink their aircraft carrier, no matter how invincible it may appear. The small town of Kondopoga in Karelia, on the border with Finland, was the scene of vodka-fuelled anti-Caucasian race riots which resulted in several deaths. Nationalistic parades and racially motivated attacks by "patriots" are a direct consequence of the regime's pathological lying and the lack of any real dialogue between the state authorities and the Russian people. The state closes its eyes to the fact that the majority of our people live in abject poverty, and that the real standard of living outside of Moscow is much lower than claimed. The corruption within Putin's Pyramid of Power exceeds even the highs previously attained, and a younger generation is growing up both ill-educated, and militant because of their poverty.

I loathe the current ideology which divides people into those who are "on side," "not on side," or even "on the wrong side." If a journalist is on side he or she will receive awards and honors, and perhaps be invited to become a Deputy in the Duma. Invited, mind, not elected. We don't have parliamentary elections any more in the traditional sense of the word, with campaigning, publication of manifestos, debates. In Russia the Kremlin summons those who are irreproachably on side, who salute at the right times, and they are enlisted in the United Russia party, with all that entails.

Today a journalist who is not on side is an outcast. I have never sought my present pariah status and it makes me feel like a beached dolphin. I am no political infighter.

I will not go into the other joys of the path I have chosen: the poisoning, the arrests, the menacing by mail and over the Internet, the telephoned death threats. The main thing is to get on with my job, to describe the life I see, to receive visitors every day in our newspaper's offices who have nowhere else to bring their troubles, because the Kremlin finds their stories off-message. The only place they can be aired is in our newspaper, *Novaya gazeta*.

What am I guilty of? I have merely reported what I witnessed, nothing but the truth.

Published in a special issue of *Soyuz zhurnalistov*, October 26, 2006

1. Should Lives Be Sacrificed to Journalism?

A QUESTIONNAIRE FOR THE "TERRITORY OF GLASNOST" PROJECT

Circulated to journalists, editors, and columnists of *Novaya gazeta*.

1. *Surname and first name, or pen-name*: Politkovskaya, Anna.
2. *Topic of specialisation*: Anything of interest to our readers.
3. *Your professional credo, or motto*: What matters is the information, not what you think about it.
4. *What is your first priority as a journalist?* To provide as much information as possible.
5. *What do you think about the times you live in, the people, the country?* The people are remarkable; the country is Soviet; the times are another Time of Troubles.
6. *What do you find most difficult to write about (and which story most illustrates that)?* Our times.
7. *What do you most enjoy writing about (and story)?* People.
8. *Why and for whom are you doing your work?* For people, and for the sake of people.
9. *How do you rate the work of those in power today who take decisions at the highest level and shape Russia's reputation both inside Russia and abroad (the President, government, judiciary, parliamentary deputies, and business elite)?* Management of the state is extremely inefficient.
10. *How do you rate the willingness of people to regard themselves as representatives of civil society and to engage in open dialogue*

with the state authorities? Not highly. There is too much
fear in society and too little idealism.

11. *How do you rate the level of democracy and independence
    of the press? What do you think is happening in Russia to
    freedom of speech, and where do you personally obtain reliable
    information (not as a professional, but as a user)?* Freedom
    of speech is on its last legs. I only trust information
    100 per cent if I have obtained it myself.

12. *What recent events do you consider to have been a landmark
    for yourself, the country, and society (positive or negative)?*
    For the country, the occupation of Ingushetia; for society,
    the same; for myself, the same.

13. *What do you see as the main problems facing Russian society?*
    The fact that most people think it will never happen to
    them.

14. *What qualities most impress you, and which most disappoint
    you, in public figures and ordinary people? (Give examples if
    possible.)* I admire openness and sincerity. I am nauseated
    by lying and people who think they are cunning.

15. *Which politicians, economists, people in the arts and culture,
    and also private citizens could you nominate for Person of the
    Year, Hero of Our Times, or as iconic personalities in present-
    day Russia?* There are no heroes in sight. If we had one
    he would stop the war.

16. *How do you rate the quality of life in Russia? What factors
    should be taken into account?* Very low. The number of poor
    people is enormous and that is a disgrace.

17. *What can and should people (society), politicians, officials (the
    state), and journalists do to improve the quality of life in
    Russia?* Journalists should write; politicians should make
    a fuss and not wallow in luxury; and officials should not
    steal from poor people.

FSB OFFICERS CARRY OUT ANOTHER OF THEIR SPECIAL OPERATIONS AGAINST *NOVAYA GAZETA*

The Editorial Team of *Novaya gazeta*

February 28, 2002

As special operations go, this was a pretty dismal effort. For technical competence we award the Chekists three points, but for artistic merit, alas, zero.*

A statement issued by FSB representative Ilya Shabalkin claims that *Novaya gazeta* and its special correspondent Anna Politkovskaya are trying to exploit her assignments in Chechnya to "resolve their financial problems and disagreements with certain foundations." Shabalkin has declared that Politkovskaya's assignments are characterised by undesirable sensationalism and are hindering the counter-terrorist operation in Chechnya. He also baldly asserts that these sensations are part of an attempt to persuade the Soros Foundation to write off a grant of $14,000 which *Novaya gazeta* received for work in political hotspots.

Shabalkin claims that our newspaper has failed to provide the Foundation's Open Society Institute with an interim report, and that the Foundation has informed us in writing that it proposes to cease its financial support. Chekist Shabalkin additionally makes a particular point of claiming that Anna Politkovskaya lacked accreditation to work as a journalist in Chechnya.

All the pointers to a monstrous conspiracy are there: the link to American money, spreading disaffection among Russian troops on the orders of transatlantic fat cats, and absence of official permission to be operating in Chechnya at all.

The discovery of this plot against the Russian Federation was announced on all the main TV channels, distributed over the Interfax newswire, and gleefully published on the websites of the Effective Politics Foundation. It's a chore, but we have to respond. *Novaya gazeta*, like hundreds of other organizations, was awarded a grant, of $55,000, by

---

*The Cheka was a state security service established in 1917. It was the forerunner of the KGB, now the FSB.

the Soros Foundation for the purposes of establishing a database of individuals who have disappeared without trace in Chechnya; to facilitate the release of prisoners and hostages; and to provide support to an orphanage and old people's home. It is worth remarking that, although the grant was awarded last year, we have been doing all this work since 1994.

Our colleague Vyacheslav Izmailov succeeded in freeing more than 170 kidnap victims. Through the efforts of *Novaya gazeta*, and particularly those of our columnist Anna Politkovskaya, dozens of old people survived two winters in an old people's home in Grozny. With the aid of the Interior Ministry we moved the old people, who had completely lost hope, back to their relatives. The Soros Foundation appreciated these efforts and offered financial support, which we were glad to accept.

Of the $55,000 awarded, we have so far received only a first payment of less than $14,000. The reason is quite simply that for three months we had to hide Anna Politkovskaya outside the borders of Russia. When it was confirmed that an assassination attempt was being prepared against her, the law "On Protection by the State" was invoked until the suspect was arrested. She was granted a special status which we are not at liberty to write about.

For these reasons our report was submitted in February this year. The Soros Foundation has no complaint against *Novaya gazeta*, and in the coming 12 months we will be receiving the remaining $41,000, and will continue our work.

In the allegations of hype surrounding Politkovskaya's assignments, Chekist Shabalkin has excelled himself. It was not we, or Politkovskaya, but the Press Office of the Joint Military Command which on February 9–10 issued a statement claiming that Politkovskaya had left the Commandant's Office in Shatoy without informing the military. Politkovskaya had good reason to leave. The facts communicated to her by the Military Prosecutors were too serious not to.

We repeat that we issued no statements, generated no hype. That was entirely the work of the FSB using the Army as its mouthpiece. So who set the ball rolling?

The answer as to why the FSB got so exercised is to be found in

Novaya gazeta, Nos. II and I2. Using evidence from the criminal case and interviews with Military Prosecutors, Politkovskaya proved with facts and documents to hand that the shooting of six civilians, including a pregnant woman, and the subsequent burning of their bodies had been perpetrated by special operations troops of Military Intelligence. It is a unique case. Thanks to the courage of the Prosecutors and the public naming of the suspects, 10 military personnel have been arrested.

The FSB makes no attempt to refute these facts in its statement: it simply ignores them. The FSB is not concerned that this crime inflames and aggravates the war. The FSB is merely concerned that Politkovskaya did not have the requisite accreditation.

Actually, she did, and we print it here. Come on, Chekists! You will need to do better than this when preparing your disinformation.

In order to implement their highly intelligent campaign, the Chekists used some of our journalist colleagues as stooges. First the ultra-respectable *Vedomosti* carried an item to the effect that we had failed to provide a report to the Soros Foundation and that payment of our grant might be stopped. Why a serious business newspaper should suddenly start counting what by their standards is the small change in somebody else's pocket was baffling – until Shabalkin issued his announcement.

Statements were also distributed through Interfax, by then with our comments. At no point, alas, did our colleagues have qualms about printing private correspondence between *Novaya gazeta* and the Soros Foundation. You would think we were squandering taxpayers' money or the state budget.

How the correspondence was leaked is, however, a separate issue. One copy is in the possession of the Soros Foundation, and the original was received by *Novaya gazeta*'s editor through the post.

Neither the Foundation nor the editor of *Novaya gazeta*, needless to say, passed this to the press; so somebody has been intercepting our post, opening our correspondence, trying to monitor the newspaper's activity, and perhaps, also, the activity of the Foundation. It is gratifying to report that they found nothing more substantial than a delayed report.

As in our case, only the FSB's failures enable us to see what they are getting up to on taxpayers' money. As usual, they are trying to suggest a link between articles which tell the truth about the Chechen War and Western intelligence services, Western money, and so on.

The FSB likes to show how well informed it is about other people's affairs, especially when they are none of its business and not within its remit. So it is far easier for them publicly to point out problems in Russia which don't exist, than to find terrorists like Khattab or Basayev. Or perhaps it is Politkovskaya and our delayed reports which are preventing them from being able to do that. Perhaps this is how they justify their professional incompetence. The replies to these and other questions will no doubt be obtained in court. Our lawyers are preparing to sue.

Don't be in too much of a hurry, Mr Shabalkin, to spoil your jacket by making a hole in it for that medal you hope to receive.

WHAT NEXT?

March 4, 2002

First the Editor of *Novaya gazeta* requested that I, Special Correspondent Politkovskaya, should write an irate open letter to Mr Shabalkin. I thought about it and declined. Just too boring. Then the Editor said we needed to write an irate open letter to Shabalkin's boss, Mr Patrushev, who runs the FSB. I thought seriously about this but again declined. Someone who can't catch Basayev and Khattab with a team of many thousands is not of the slightest interest to me. He can't even make me irate.

Then write to Putin! But instead I wrote a letter to Major Nevmerzhitsky, Commander of Reconnaissance of the Shatoy District Military Commandant's Office.

Major Nevmerzhitsky was a witness of the Shatoy tragedy – the murder and burning of the bodies of six civilians by soldiers of the Central Intelligence Directorate (GRU), which occurred on January 11, 2002 and was officially described by Khankala as an operation to capture the injured resistance leader, Khattab. It was this atrocity I was investigating during my February assignment in Chechnya. This so irritated the FSB that they embarked on the campaign of disinformation described above. Why did I address my letter to him? Because I felt like it.

Dear Vitaliy,

See what they have been getting up to while we were trudging the tracks of Shatoy! They are saying we did it for money. Army Headquarters in Khankala claimed as much, and it doesn't really matter whose vocal cords they used. You were running around in the mountains; gazing down on the murder scene in horror from a cliff, trying not to fall off; discussing for days who had killed whom and burned their bodies; having to face 28 orphans. That kind of work, according to Officer Shabalkin, has a dollar value.

Of course we have nothing to prove to each other, and could now just keep quiet. But you actually saw what happened at Dai and Nokhchi-Keloy, and on the road to Barzoy where the bodies of two soldiers and an officer whom the Shabalkins of this world have no interest in have been lying in the river for over two months. You know that this is not about dollars.

At first I was very angry and thought that if Shabalkin had been in our shoes he would have had a different tale to tell. Then I calmed down and started to feel sorry for the man. "They" in Khankala have a hard life: they have to run around like servants whose masters are in a bad mood in the morning because their boots haven't been properly polished. It's really not that easy to talk about places you have never been to and things you have never seen, and to make it look as if you are doing a great job and do know everything that's going on. You and I would blow our brains out rather than jump through hoops like those but Shabalkin, poor sod, plods on. So we are more fortunate, having seen everything with our own eyes and not having to pretend. Although we are not happier when we think about what it is we have seen.

How are things in Shatoy? Have they given up sending helicopters from Khankala to catch wounded Khattabs? How is Victor Malchukov getting on, the Shatoy Military Commandant who long ago saw the reality of what is going on around him,

a man with haunted eyes? It must be difficult for you. I have
an easier time here in Moscow, deflecting the attacks of idiots.
It's a piece of cake by comparison with the mountains.
  Anna Politkovskaya

Around me my family are grim-faced. I am flying out to Chechnya
again, only I won't be meeting up with Vitaliy. I have other plans.

THE SAGA OF ANNA'S ASSIGNMENT IN SHATOY

February 14, 2002

*On January, 11 2002, in what Army Headquarters officially described as an
operation to capture the Chechen resistance leader, Khattab, soldiers of the
Central Intelligence Directorate (GRU) murdered and burned the bodies of
six civilians. Anna went to investigate.*

I take out the tape of my last assignment in Chechnya, and at the same
time read through the newspapers and the news agency tapes.

Well, well. My colleagues seem to have been competing to see who
could come up with the most unfounded stories. According to our
esteemed Interfax news agency, I was detained on February 9, by the
Shatoy District Military Commandant's Office during a special operation there because I did not have the necessary documents. It seems
to concern nobody that there was no special operation in Shatoy, either
immediately before, on, or after February 9.

As I read on, the tone gets more caustic. It seems I escaped from
the Commandant's Office and disappeared, thereby discrediting . . . I
should be punished just where it hurts . . . The Press Office of the
Joint Military Command in Chechnya fulminates that by my misconduct
I have brought disgrace upon all journalists.

What actually happened was that on February 8, the second day of
my assignment, having made my way from Grozny to Shatoy, my first
act, making no attempt at concealment, was to go directly to Sultan
Mahomadov, the Director of the District Interior Affairs Office, and

inform him of the purpose of my assignment: to investigate one of the most scandalous and tragic recent events in Chechnya, the extra-judicial execution and burning of the bodies of six civilians who were returning from Shatoy to their homes in the hill village of Nokhchi-Keloy on January 10, 2002. From the militia I went to the office of the District Administration and, as required, asked them to put a stamp confirming my arrival on my assignment papers. They duly did so.

From the District Administration I set off to the District Military Commandant's Office, to see the Commandant, Colonel Victor Malchukov. Why did I go to see him? Because, quite simply, I have known him for a long time, and respect his ability to talk to people in the villages, thereby resolving innumerable conflicts which arise between the Army and the civilian population.

We sat together and worked out a plan of how I could best do the job my newspaper had entrusted me with. The Colonel said that he had to fly to a meeting in Khankala the next morning, so alas there was a limit to the help he could give me.

My journalistic colleagues reported that I had been "detained," and had "escaped." This was complete nonsense, although admittedly only in respect of February 8, before the FSB piled in. By February 9, it was already clear that the massacre near the village of Dai in Shatoy District by soldiers of the elite special division of the Central Intelligence Directorate of the Ministry of Defence had its roots, as people in Chechnya say, in Army Headquarters in Khankala.

At 11:00 a.m. on February 9, I had arranged an interview with Colonel Andrey Vershinin, the Military Prosecutor for Shatoy District, who is presently conducting a criminal investigation into the execu-tions, and whose office is located within the headquarters of 291 Regiment, near the village of Barzoy, a few kilometres from Shatoy. The Military Prosecutor quite properly scrupulously checked all my documents, and then gave me a long interview in which he was as frank as it is possible to be while a case has yet to come before the courts. My sincere thanks to Colonel Vershinin. He is a terrific person to have in that job. We parted on friendly terms.

The surprises began immediately after this. During the interview,

I discovered, my militia security officers had been questioned by FSB agents about me. What were they after? Why? Who gave them permission? Officers I did not know approached me, said they were well-wishers, and quietly advised me to get out of the regiment quickly, warning that preparations were being made to detain me, and that the FSB was categorically opposed to journalists sticking their noses into this case, which involved military commanders right at the top.

This was the moment when my "disappearance" began; a change of cars, covering my tracks, searching for a place to sleep where no one would find me. There were many signs that this was far from a joke, and that it was vitally important to behave in just this manner. I very much wanted to stay alive and to get back home, in the face of a manhunt mounted by men armed to the teeth and with malice in their hearts. For this reason I had to dissolve in time and space, and not, as my press colleagues and the Khankala ideologists were shortly to write, in order to create a fuss and draw attention to myself.

Early in the morning of February 10, I slipped on foot into Starye Atagi, heavily disguised, avoiding checkpoints and the security sweep which was beginning in the neighbouring village of Chiri-Yurt. Moving very quietly, almost crawling on the ground, my main concern was not to attract any attention in order not to be killed. Escaping from Shatoy and from rabid FSB agents was only half the problem. Getting into Starye Atagi, which is now in the hands of the Wahhabis, was the next challenge. No federal soldiers or representatives of the new Chechen government walk the streets. They are very, very afraid of being killed. It's only journalists and human rights activists covertly collecting information who creep about like this, because journalists like me have no option, given how things have worked out in Chechnya, other than to keep a very low profile.

Perhaps you will think that this is playing at spies, that it amounts to militaristic thrill-seeking. Nothing of the sort. I hate this way of life. The situation created by the security agencies in Chechnya, and primarily by members of the FSB and Ministry of Defence, is so disgusting it makes me sick; a situation where a journalist's legitimate wish to be in possession of the full facts about an event results in direct threats to her life. What was I doing during those two days in Shatoy? My work, for heaven's sake, no more than that. Believe me, there is nothing more hateful than, in your own country, to feel that you are a target for shooting practice for parasites living it up, eating and drinking at your – a taxpayer's – expense. And then they have the gall to denigrate you.

Traditionally journalists do not write about how they get their facts. The reader's attention should be focused only on those facts themselves. That is entirely proper. Forgive me that today I have had to deviate from that ideal, reluctantly finding myself on the receiving end of a barrage of lies and conjecture.

A detailed report of my assignment in Shatoy will appear in the next issue. This will be the result of an investigation into the brutal murder of six civilians in Shatoy District, and I shall say no more about how I came by the facts. Only today, before I bring down the curtain, I will allow myself a few conclusions about the events which surrounded this inquiry.

In the first place, conditions for journalists working in Chechnya have been made completely impossible. I mean in terms of obtaining comprehensive information about an event.

In the second place, the unjustified, barefaced lies of the Army Command, passed on by most of the media without any attempt to check them out, are at the core of the world we now live in. More and more we are allowing ourselves to be brainwashed. It is a world where the Russian Army is encouraged to hunt civilians, including journalists, but not the terrorist leader Khattab.

And in the third place, many of my journalist colleagues, dancing to the tune of the state authorities and the Army top brass, are today prepared to do anything required of them, to report interviews without worrying about the truth, to write about scandals even when there are none, and all in order to avoid having to confront directly the fratricidal tragedy being perpetrated in Chechnya. That is what really matters about the mishaps which befell me on my last assignment, and which ended on February 12.

Anna Politkovskaya

FROM THE EDITORS

Novaya gazeta thanks General Victor Kazantsev, Plenipotentiary Presidential Representative in the Southern Federal Region, and many others for responding to our request to assist in the search for our special correspondent, Anna Politkovskaya.

We thank the Directorate of Personal Security of the Interior Ministry of the Russian Federation, and also the Secretariat of Presidential Aide Sergey Yastrzhembsky for helping to establish the whereabouts of our special correspondent after the incident in the Shatoy district of Chechnya.

IS JOURNALISM WORTH DYING FOR?

November 10, 2003

Is journalism worth dying for? Every time something like the events on the evening of November 3 in Ryazan happen – and in Russia attempts to kill journalists are no rarity – we, the servants and slaves of information, ask ourselves this question. If the price of truth is so high, perhaps we should just stop, and find a profession with less risk of "major unpleasantness"? How much would society, for whose sake we are doing this work, care? In the face of that, each of us makes his or her own choice.

On November 3, 2003, at approximately 2104 hours, at the entrance to residential block No. 26, Zubkova Street in Ryazan, an attempt was made on the life of 30-year-old Mikhail Komarov, Deputy Editor of the Ryazan edition of *Novaya gazeta*. As he was returning home he was struck from behind on the head with a heavy blunt instrument. Komarov's reporting is well known in Ryazan, and in recent years he has specialised in investigative journalism, some of it delving into the commercial activities of the local oligarchs.

At night all the dormitory districts of Russian towns are as alike as identical twins. Their kinship is in the darkness which descends on them, in which you can kill a person, unseen and unhindered, and then escape without repercussions.

It is not yet late on November 4, the day after the assassination attempt, but as usual you can't see a thing in the Ryazan suburb of Dashkovo-Pesochnoye. The district itself does not really seem to exist. Zubkova Street, "Broadway," can only be sensed, immersed in the darkness of non-being. You can only feel that somewhere nearby is habitation. All the conditions for a successful hit are there. We grope our way along, guided by Valentina Komarova, Mikhail's mother, who is shocked by what has happened. She has two sons. The younger, Dima, is 20 years old and a promising footballer. Her elder, Mikhail, "has turned out like his grandmother," Valentina explains, with a mixture of pride and fear. "She was a truth-teller too. She survived the war and is still fighting to this day, although she is 80. She doesn't give in, and she's penniless. Misha is the same. How many times have I begged him, 'Don't, son. Let them live their lives, and we will live ours.' At work people kept telling me, 'This is going to end badly.' There, we've arrived. This is our entrance, No. 14."

It was on these steps that two people in black woollen hats and leather jackets, the uniform of Russian hitmen, were waiting for Mikhail. The neighbours spotted them but, as is the way, thought nothing of it. "As long as I'm all right, as long as it's not me they're beating up, everything is fine." Here is the staircase the journalist crawled up, leaving a trail of blood, in order to escape his would-be killers. Today, just like yesterday, all the doors are firmly shut. The entrance is well adapted for murder, with dark corners in which you are your own rescue service, your own pyramid of power, prosecutor and militia.

Incidentally, the October District militia station is just round the corner. Actually, it is world famous because it was near here that, also in the darkness which is a friend not only of hitmen but also of the FSB, in the autumn of 1999 the Ryazan Directorate of the Federal Security Bureau was caught red-handed planting explosives in an apartment block just before the resumption of the Chechen War, the so-called hexogen "sugar" training exercise.*

"Have you heard that somebody made an attempt on the life of the

---

*Apartment blocks in Moscow, Buinaksk and Volgodonsk were blown up, apparently by the FSB, with the loss of many Russian lives. The Chechens were blamed as a pretext for re-starting the war in Chechnya. An attempt to do the same in Ryazan was foiled, and was subsequently represented as a "training exercise."

journalist Mikhail Komarov in your district yesterday?" I ask some young militiamen anxiously peeping out of the door.

"Yes. We've just seen it on television."

"This kind of thing must often happen here, since you're taking it so calmly?"

"No, this is the first time," Vitaliy Vyazkov, duty officer at the station, says, not turning a hair.

Early morning on November 5. On Wednesdays the October District Militia have an inspection parade. Some of the militiamen have not bothered to go to it and are smoking by the door, discussing the attempt to kill Komarov. "He should have kept his head down," a woman smoking a cigarette mutters. The others agree.

Their superiors arrive, the Acting Head of the District Militia, Alexander Naidyonov, and his deputy Yevgeny Popkov. "We have nothing to say," is their curt joint communiqué.

"Can you at least tell me whether you are instigating a criminal investigation? It is already November 5."

Colonel Naidyonov almost runs away from me, his eyes darting all over the place.

What's the problem? Isn't it straightforward: if there has been an attack on someone it should be investigated? Or might the militia's skittishness relate to the fact that in his statement Komarov named as his own prime suspect the Ryazan oligarch, Sergey Kuznetsov, one of the ten wealthiest locals, the owner of a large shopping center and much else besides, about whose business methods Komarov frequently wrote?

This explanation seems to be confirmed when Investigator Mikhail Zotov, accompanied by Colonel Naidyonov, arrives to question the victim for the first time in the provincial neurological clinic. He is persistently curious to know why Komarov wrote so much about Kuznetsov. Was it, perhaps, Zotov suggests insistently, because he had been taking bribes to write "good" articles about him and then, when Kuznetsov stopped paying, he started writing critically about him? This is what Kuznetsov is saying. No doubt everybody judges by their own standards. "Give us what we want and we're on your side. Don't, and we're against you." That is the sickening creed of the militia.

It is almost noon but the enforcers of law and order are in no hurry to get on with their work, and are plainly not on Komarov's side. We rush around Ryazan, putting together a criminal case: from the October District Prosecutor's Office to the Ryazan Provincial Prosecutor's Office, from there to the October District Militia on Yesenin Street and finally, forcing our way into the office of the indignant Colonel Naidyonov, encounter a very amiable Georgian who will subsequently tell us, "I am a Georgian, and accordingly the man has not yet been born who can bribe me."

This is the Head of the Provincial Criminal Investigation Department, Militia Colonel Dzhansug Mzhavanadze, and he informs us with some ceremony that a criminal investigation was opened on November 5 at 11:30 a.m.

"What work is being done on the main line of inquiry, involving Kuznetsov? Are Komarov's articles being attached to the file, and his statement to the FSB two weeks ago that he was being threatened?"

"I am not at liberty to tell you about the means and methods we are employing to solve the crime."

We fully understand, and carry on crisscrossing Ryazan to try to ensure that these do not turn into means and methods of covering up a crime. Oligarch Kuznetsov is everybody's daddy.

The oligarch is unflustered, and very democratic in his ways, as you would expect of a major financial supporter of the Governor of Ryazan.

"What sort of an oligarch am I?" Sergey Kuznetsov asks coyly. In an earlier life he was the Secretary of the District Committee of the Young Communist League. He radiates civilised behaviour, bonhomie and modesty. "I borrowed $5,000 from my mother-in-law yesterday. I have invested my last copeck in my business. I don't have a home of my own. I should have emigrated to Israel long ago. My mother, Galina Abramovna, is there and here I am struggling for a better life. I am a builder. By nature I am a creator. On the old rat-infested city rubbish tip I built a retail center with 600 shops. I opened the best beauty parlour in Ryazan, which has an excellent surgeon. He gave my wife's breasts a lift, and removed my moles. Everybody without exception is pleased. Only Misha Komarov is dissatisfied. He writes endlessly that the plastic surgery operations are performed without a licence. He's just trying to settle personal scores with me. I am getting tired of his articles. I decided to teach him a lesson."

"To teach him a lesson? Do you know that on November 3 someone tried to kill him? Just after he had left another court hearing against you?"

"You won't believe me but I've only just heard about it, immediately before our meeting." The oligarch calls in the head of his security service, a large fellow in a black leather jacket. "Have you been to the hospital?" he asks him.

The bodyguard relays in detail what the doctor told him about Komarov's state of health.

"Isn't it strange that the doctor has passed all this information – confidential medical details – to your Viking?"

Kuznetsov is pleased with the effect he is having and smiles masterfully.

"What confidential details are you talking about? I was treated in that very same neurosurgery department after somebody lobbed a grenade at me. But Misha never seems to learn."

"What right do you think you have to 'educate' Komarov as if you were his father?"

"In Ryazan I am everybody's father, and it seems to me I am having some success. Komarov thinks more carefully about what he writes, he weighs his words now. Personally I think *Novaya gazeta* is great. And don't be afraid for Misha; he has been hit on the head many times before because he doesn't know when to give way."

We part, having got nowhere.

During the afternoon Victor Ognyov, the Deputy Prosecutor of Ryazan, makes a surprising announcement: he says a criminal investigation was launched yesterday, November 4, at 19:10 hours, rather than at 11:30 on November 5 as Colonel Mzhavanadze was assuring us just a couple of hours ago.

"The militia are saying something quite different. Who should we believe?"

"They simply did not know." Ognyov imperturbably shuffles the papers in his file, where two separate directives about instigating one and the same case are visible to the naked eye. "We intervened operationally so that everything would move along more effectively. First we appointed Skrynnikov, a junior investigator, but now at my request a more experienced official will investigate the matter (Mikail Zotov, who was defending Kuznetsov against Komarov). We're about to send a special report on all this to the Prosecutor-General's Office in Moscow since, as you will agree, this is not a routine case. We are observing all the requirements of the Criminal Procedure Code."

"But why is the charge merely 'disturbing the peace'?"

"Because Komarov was neither killed nor robbed. There was no intention of killing him."

"How can you be so sure? Do you know the person with the intentions?"

"We know if they had meant to they would have killed him, but they were merely giving him a fright. It will be a matter of minor physical injury affecting the victim's health for a short time."

"He hasn't recovered yet!"

"You will forgive my remarking that there is no article in the Criminal Code relating to beating up a journalist." Ognyov smiles sardonically.

Evening falls once more. Misha is lying in one of the narrow beds typical of an underfunded Russian hospital. His head is bandaged and he looks pale. His mother has brought in all the medicine, bandages and syringes he needs because as usual there are none in the neurosurgical department. No doctors or nurses in the evenings either, but luckily Valentina is a nurse herself. Komarov is holding forth to his neighbours about democracy, the duty of the mass media, and the need to be unflinching in the fight against corruption which spoils life for everyone. His neighbours listen sullenly, either because of their own ailments or because they have little faith in the victory of democracy or in the need to make the effort Misha is describing. Sitting on the edge of the next bed, Valentina lectures her son.

"Yes, I understand what you are saying, and I am not against your being a journalist, but you do need to be more careful."

"We can't give in, Mum," Mikhail answers with the passion of one who will brook no compromise in the fight for good. He is in a state of post-traumatic euphoria, ready for the worst, fearing nothing. "Let them be afraid every week of what we are going to write about them, not we of them!"

"What are you going to do now, Misha?" I ask in parting.

"Carry on writing articles," Komarov replies unyieldingly.

So, is it worth sacrificing your life for journalism? How does each of us make our choice?

Every successive attack on a journalist in Russia – and by tradition nobody ever gets caught – relentlessly reduces the number of journalists working because they want to fight for justice. The risks are very great and not everyone is up to the unremitting tension which accompanies this kind of work. As the numbers of one kind of journalist fall, so there is an increase in the number of those who prefer undemanding journalism, reporting which doesn't involve prying where you are not welcome.

Undemanding media cater for an undemanding public, ready to agree with everything it is told. The more there is of the former, the more monolithic the latter becomes, and the less opportunity society has of seeing what is wrong with the circumstances in which it lives.

In the last few months the situation has been deteriorating rapidly. It seems we are at a tipping point, and that soon the Government (the oligarchs, the FSB, the bureaucracy) will no longer be breathing down our necks, because they will have achieved what they want: there will be nobody left prepared to lay down their life in order to get at the truth about other people's lives. If there is no demand, there will be no supply.

More than three years later, the criminals still have not been caught: neither those who attacked Mikhail Komarov, nor those who paid them to do so.

2. The War in Chechnya

The Chechen War was re-started in 1999, supposedly in response to a Chechen attack on neighbouring Dagestan and the blowing up of apartment blocks in Russian cities in which over 300 citizens died. It is widely believed that both these pretexts were stage-managed by the Russian Government itself, which would mean it was responsible for the politically motivated mass murder of its own citizens. The former Director of the FSB Vladimir Putin came to power in the 2000 presidential election as a would-be saviour of the nation on a wave of anti-Chechen hysteria. Anna Politkovskaya reported uncompromisingly on the war and on its accompanying atrocities.

Part I: Dispatches from the Frontline

LIBERTY OR DEATH? SOMETIMES THEY ARE THE SAME THING

March 27, 2000

These are appalling stories. Sometimes people say that to be on the safe side you should divide them by 10, or 100 or 200; but divide them as we may, they are still stories about atrocities.

On grey UN humanitarian aid blankets covering concrete barricades, a boy and girl are sitting, hunched and huddled. We try to talk about the future. I keep going on about prospects, the larger issues, the international dimension: "What plans do you have? What are you going to do with your lives?" Their replies relate only to the specific, the here and now: "Tomorrow we are going to the mountains to look for wild leeks. That is all there is to eat."

I try again, about when things get better, what they hope for, about ordinary, human things: "Are there wild flowers already blooming in the mountains?" "There are unexploded bombs there, and a lot of soldiers," comes the response, unhurried and unemotional, but behind the words hatred flutters like a banner.

These are Aslanbek and Rezeda, a brother and sister aged 18 and 20. In the First War they were in their early teens, in the Second they have hardened. If Rezeda still manages a fleeting smile, Aslanbek is as gloomy as the dirty concrete surrounding him. They both sat through all the bombing and shelling in cellars, until February 5 when their personal drama came to a head with the brutal killing by federal soldiers of their father, Salman Bishayev. He was 54 and was killed by federal troops in the courtyard of No. 3, Kislovodskaya Street in Grozny during a security sweep in Aldy, Chernorechiye District. They killed him and dragged the body away, and only after a 13-day search did Aslanbek and Rezeda's elder sister, 30-year-old Larisa, find what they were dutifully looking for. It was she who scraped Salman's brains from the walls into a bag in order to bury them. Then they all fled to Ingushetia.

Now home is a quarry on the outskirts of Karabulak, where a building materials factory once flourished and where there are still many half-ruined stone storehouses. Along with 30 housemates, 23 of whom are children or young people aged between 15 and 22, Aslanbek and Rezeda have taken up residence in one of these boxes in this concrete waste-land. They jokingly call their shack "The Disco," but there is no music or dancing here. The furniture consists of plank beds, and the 23 boys and girls sitting on them have no light in their eyes, and their arms hang listlessly by their sides. The Disco's inhabitants have bonds of distant kinship and the shared experience of recent security sweeps in which their fathers and grandfathers, brothers and sisters, aunts and uncles were tortured and shot.

"What do you usually talk about?"

"For days at a time we talk about who has been killed and how it was done, and where someone's grave has been found. It is dreadful," 17-year-old Fatima Doldayeva tells me. She graduated from Grozny No. 2 High School in late 1999 with a gold medal. What Fatima says is true. By evening the talk is more than you can take. In the refugee camps of Chechnya and Ingushetia what people mostly talk about nowadays is death.

A Woman's Head in a Red Scarf

Sultan Shuaipov hastened to Magas Airport in Ingushetia very early in the morning, even though everyone told him he was wasting his time. He had heard on the radio that a Council of Europe delegation would be stopping off briefly in Ingushetia, and was determined to meet these solicitous foreigners the moment they got off the plane and tell them *everything*.

Sultan looks very old although he turns out to be only 45. His head of grey hair twitches, a nervous tic which keeps his eyes on the move, and his body jerks periodically. He is profoundly disturbed. On February

20, having spent the entire First War in Grozny guarding his house, he had to gather up 51 bodies from Shefskaya and the neighbouring streets, Lines 3–8. Twenty-one of the bodies he managed to bury, after first giving each an individual tag. When he was physically incapable of burying any more he laid the remaining 30 in the inspection pit of a car maintenance business on Line 3.

All 51 had been brutally murdered in a so-called security sweep in the suburb of Novaya Katayama during the night of February 19. Most of them were Sultan's friends and neighbours. This is believed to have been the doing of the notorious 205 Brigade, retaliating for losses in the previous war.

On February 19 soldiers had come to Sultan's street, Line 5, and warned local people who emerged from their cellars, "Get away as quickly as you can. The bunch coming after us intend to kill the lot of you."

"The soldiers moved on," Sultan relates, "but we, my neighbours and I, just laughed at them. Very clever! They want us all to run away so they can take their time looting our houses. Behind these soldiers came a rapid reaction squad. They were very decent lads, and again nothing happened. We relaxed. The nightmare began as night was falling. Federal soldiers of some description entered our streets in the twilight. My neighbour, Seit-Selim from Dunaiskaya Lane, was one of the first to be shot. He was about 50. He just asked a soldier what kind of troops they were. In the morning, when we were burying Selim in his courtyard, the same troops came by. They said, "What did he die from?" The soldier who shot him was the one who asked us that. We replied, "Shrapnel." We knew by then that if we told the truth they would shoot us too. The one who had killed Seit-Selim burst out laughing at our lying. He was a young fellow, and he really enjoyed the idea that we old men were scared of him.

"But to return to the previous evening. When 74-year-old Said Zubayev came out of No. 36 on Line 5 he ran into the federals and the soldiers made him dance, firing their rifles at his feet to make him jump. When the old man got tired, they shot him. Thanks be to Allah! Said never knew what they did to his family."

Sultan falls silent, raising his head very high, not wanting the

treacherous tears to run down his cheeks. Nobody must see his weakness. With a toss of his head he drives them back into their ducts and
continues.

"At about nine at night, an infantry fighting vehicle broke into the
Zubayevs' courtyard, taking the gates off their hinges. Very efficiently
and without wasting words the soldiers brought out of the house
and lined up by the steps 64-year-old Zainab, the old man's wife, their
45-year-old daughter, Malika (the wife of a colonel in the Russian
militia); Malika's little daughter, Amina, aged eight; Mariet, another
daughter of Said and Zainab, 40 years old; their 44-year-old nephew,
Said Saidakhmed Zubayev; 35-year-old Ruslan, the son of Said and
Zainab; his pregnant wife Luiza; and their eight-year-old daughter Eliza.
There were several bursts of machine-gun fire and they were all left
dead in front of the family home. None of the Zubayevs survived except
for Inessa, Ruslan's 14-year-old daughter. She was very pretty, and before
the massacre the soldiers carefully set her to one side, then dragged
her off with them.

"We looked desperately for Inessa but it was as if she had vanished
into thin air," Sultan says. "We think they must have raped her and
then buried her somewhere. Otherwise she would have come back
to bury her dead. That same night Idris, the Headmaster of School
No. 55, was killed. First they battered him against a wall for a long
time and broke all his bones, then they shot him in the head. In
another house we found, side by side, an 84-year-old Russian woman
and her 35-year-old daughter, Larisa, a well-known lawyer in Grozny.
They had both been raped and shot. The body of 42-year-old Adlan
Akayev, a Professor of Physics at the Chechen State University, was
sprawled in the courtyard of his house. He had been tortured. The
beheaded body of 47-year-old Demilkhan Akhmadov had had its arms
cut off too. It was one of the features of the operation in Novaya
Katayama that they cut people's heads off. I saw several bloodstained
chopping blocks. On Shevskaya Street there was a block with an
axe stuck in it, and a woman's head in a red scarf on the block.
Alongside, on the ground, also headless, was a man's body. I found
the body of a woman who had been beheaded and had her stomach

ripped open. They had stuffed a head into it. Was it hers? Someone else's?"

What did people do the morning after the pogrom? On February 20, the men who had survived tore strips of clothing from the victims and tied them to branches of the trees under which they had buried them, so that later, after the war, people would be able to find the graves of their kinsfolk. Novaya Katayama, where so many trees are festooned now with scraps of cloth, wholly lives up to its strange Japanese name. In Japan they tie colored ribbons to branches as a sign of remembrance of someone they loved and still love.

"But why didn't you flee Grozny when you had the opportunity? Why didn't you get out to Ingushetia, you, and the Zubayevs, and Professor Akayev, and Idris, and Larisa the lawyer, and all the others who died?"

Sultan's answer is devastating: "We often talked about it in the cellars while we were being shelled. We really believed the generals were telling the truth when they said that after the federal troops came, life would get back to normal. That gave us hope that things would get better, that is why we guarded our houses. We wanted to be first in line to get back to work after the liberation."

They believed *us*! They trusted *us*! So we killed them!

Sultan went to the airport to do his bit but no delegation from the Council of Europe arrived. Instead some senior officials from Moscow emerged from their plane and right there, on the runway, got into cars sent to meet them, and that was that. Nobody listened to what Sultan had to say. "I suppose I should have doused myself with petrol to get their attention," he says seriously, and slouches off, a lonely old Chechen who buried 21 bodies and hadn't the strength to bury the other 30. His head bobs about more than ever, and every few moments he has to raise his hands to stop his hat falling off.

Bullet Holes in a Passport

"How am I going to get through the checkpoints and back to Chechnya now? With a passport like this the federals will see immediately that somebody has tried to shoot me and are bound to arrest me. If I tell them the truth, they are even more certain to shoot me." Kheyedi Makhauri, a refugee from Grozny, can barely speak and talks haltingly, but she desperately wants everyone she meets to see her red booklet. It really is an extraordinary sight: you can view the world through two bullet holes shot in her passport. The young Georgian woman who looks out at you from page 2 of the perforated ID has such delicate features, such an interesting face and exotic slant to her eyes, that you can hardly bear to look from the photo to the original standing in front of you today.

Kheyedi is crying. She knows exactly what you are thinking, and is certain she is doomed, that she will never be able to return to Grozny. She is afraid of people in uniform.

Her story is straightforward and appalling. Throughout the war she and her five children have lived far from home, in the hill village of Nesterovskaya in Ingushetia, under someone else's roof. When she heard on television that Grozny had been liberated, she decided to return and see how her house at No. 201 Pugachev Street had fared. She wanted to see whether it would be possible to move back. She set off with Larisa Dzhabrailova, a Russian and mother of four who had been her friend and neighbour both in Grozny and Nesterovskaya. On the way they were joined by Nura, a Chechen acquaintance on a similar mission. They reached Kheyedi's house the next day and found it was now a mere shell. They were on their way to look at where Larisa had lived when the thing which people most dread in Chechnya today happened: the three of them stumbled upon soldiers who were in the course of looting. The soldiers were loading mattresses, chairs and blankets into an infantry fighting vehicle, and when the women unexpectedly came out of a side street they came face to face with the marauders.

Kheyedi, Larisa and Nura were promptly arrested, blindfolded and bundled into the vehicle. A little later they were set down and ordered to walk forwards, holding hands. Then they were ordered to remove the blindfolds and found themselves against the wall of a ruined house. They knew immediately what was going to happen. First the federals shot Larisa. She pleaded for mercy, shouting, "I am Russian, I was born in Moscow Province! We saw nothing! We won't say anything!" She was 47 and died instantly, without suffering. Next they shot Nura. She too pleaded, "I'm only 43! I have three sons like you!"

"I was third," Kheyedi concludes her story. "They pointed a rifle at me and everything stopped. I came to when I felt a sharp pain, and only later realized what had happened. They had shot but failed to kill me. I'd been unconscious and the soldiers must not have checked if I was still alive. They dragged our bodies together, threw a nearby mattress over us and set it on fire. They wanted the bodies burned so nobody would know what had happened, and that was the pain which woke me. It was the fire licking at my leg. The soldiers had gone. I crawled out from under the mattress and just lay there for a long time before deciding to crawl away. I was found unconscious in the road by two Chechen women going to milk their cow, and came to in a cellar. There were other wounded people there and somebody found a bus for us and sent us all to Ingushetia."

I met this woman who had faced execution in Ward 1 of Sunzha District Hospital, in Ordzhonikidze on the border between Chechnya and Ingushetia. Kheyedi is very ill now. Her body was riddled with bullets and she has a lot of pain from where a bullet passed right through her back, damaging the nerves. The upper part of her body is completely paralysed and she has no sensation in her arms. It is too early to make any prognosis.

"Why did they do it?" asks Kheyedi's 13-year-old daughter, who is looking after her. "She is so kind and gentle. She just really wanted to go back home."

A nurse comes in and begins bandaging Kheyedi. Her belly is covered with scabs over the holes left by her "passport" bullets. She does not remember what happened, unconscious as she was after the shooting, but guesses that before they left the soldiers riddled her stomach with bullets. That is where the bag containing her passport was hanging.

Nightmare in Aldy

It is time to return to the quarry, to Aslanbek and Rezeda. I am sitting with them on those concrete blocks again and the boy is telling me about atrocities the soldiers committed in Aldy. They didn't just murder, they desecrated the bodies. His father had every one of his gold teeth pulled out, along with all the others. During the "security sweep" their neighbour, old Grandmother Rakiat, had her mouth ripped open to her ears as they tried unsuccessfully to tear her jaw out.

Rezeda sketches a map of their street to show how the troop detachment advanced. "This is our house," she says, "and this one belonged to our neighbour, an old-age pensioner called Sultan Temirov. Contract soldiers decapitated him and took his head away. Somebody told us they usually take the head if they suspect someone is related to resistance fighters. Before the war Sultan's brother was the Speaker in the Chechen Parliament. That is why they threw the rest of his body to the dogs. After the federals had moved on to other houses, the neighbours managed to save his left leg and groin from the frenzied dogs. That is all they were able to bury."

Witnesses believe more than 100 people were killed during the security sweep in Aldy. These are the only available figures so far. The greatest suffering was visited on those still living in Voronezhskaya and Matasha Mazayev Streets. (Matasha Mazayev was a Hero of the Soviet Union during the Second World War who was born and grew up in this village.) It befell them entirely by chance, simply because those are the first streets you come to when entering Aldy.

Rezeda continues, picturing the soldiers' progress through the houses. "They did us, then Granny Rakiat and Sultan Temirov. Then they moved on to the Khaidarovs and shot the father and son there, Gulu and Vakhu. The old man was over 80. Beyond them was Avalu Sugaipov, an elderly man who had refugees living with him. We hadn't even had time to learn their names, but they were two men, a woman, and a five-year-old girl. All the grown-ups they burned alive with a flame-thrower, including the mother in front of her daughter. Before executing them the soldiers gave the little girl a tin of condensed milk and said, "Run off and play." I imagine she has lost her wits. The Musayevs lived at No. 120 Voronezhskaya Street; they shot old Yakub, his son Umar, and his nephews, Yusup, Abdrakhman and Suleiman. The only one they didn't kill was Khasan, an old man who owned the house. He was considered the Elder of the whole of Chernorechiye, but they didn't just leave him alone. The federals kicked the bodies of the Musayevs together and forced the old man to lie across all five of them and not to move. Then they fired a burst of semi-automatic fire and wounded him. They told him if he got up they would kill him, and then they stood around smoking. Khasan didn't move and they went off, pleased with themselves. I can't go on!"

Rezeda runs outside. Aslanbek crawls over the bunks into a far corner and turns away. Their elder sister, Larisa, takes up the story. She tells of deeds beyond the imagining of anyone but a psychopath. She tells how the trees in their street are now decorated with monstrous bloody blotches where neighbours were put up against them and shot. "You can't clean it off! That's why I will never be able to go back there. I just couldn't live beside those trees where they murdered people I knew and loved. When we left Aldy we saw the men who had survived crying like women; young men's beards had turned grey. When we were in Ingushetia I saw a television report on the security sweep operation in Aldy. They showed a female sniper they said was Chechen who had supposedly been shooting at the federals from houses in Aldy. They claimed that was why the reprisals were so severe. I couldn't believe it. It was Tanya Ryzhaya. Everyone in Chernorechiye knows she is an alkie, and, incidentally, Russian. For more than two years her arms have been shaking so violently she couldn't hold a spoon. We had to feed her, and here they are saying Tanya Ryzhaya was the justification for this whole nightmare in Aldy!"

A boy of about seven jumps down from the bench. He points a wooden rifle at me and shouts, "Are you a Russian?" The grown-ups shush him, but he yells, "You are a fascist!"

The war we are waging in the Caucasus dishonors our nation from top to bottom. Do you wonder how we can ever atone for this? How long it will take? Remember, Germany spent half a century trying to free itself from the tatters of its national disgrace. Throughout those decades, Russian children were playing games of fighting the Germans, and the grown-ups encouraged them. Are not we the Germans now? How long will it be before Chechen children stop playing games in which the most unpopular boy is the one who has to be the Russian?

CHECHNYA BELONGS TO RUSSIA, BUT WE DON'T WANT THE CHECHENS

January 31, 2000

The crusted wounds look painted on. The shaven head of a semi-conscious child moves feverishly to and fro on an over-laundered greyish-brown institutional pillow. No groaning or whimpering, only a silence deeply unsettling in someone so seriously injured.

"She has small shrapnel fragments in her head, but don't waste your time on that," the emotionless voice of a middle-aged woman instructs me from a dark corner of the ward. "Much worse is that now she is an orphan. And take a look under the blanket!"

The shaven skull stubbornly continues trying to dispel its delirium. The little girl is five, her face jaundiced and sallow. Her name is Liana Shamsudinova, and from time to time her eyes flicker half open and stray disapprovingly over the ward without coming to rest on anyone. Her left hip is not covered by the blanket and is worryingly streaked with pus leaking from beneath an enormous dressing.

"You Russians count her as another resistance fighter," the monologue from the corner goes on. "The girl needs specialist treatment if she isn't to be crippled for the rest of her life, but she isn't going to get that here, and we don't get sent to clinics anywhere else in Russia, because we are Chechens."

My invisible informant had correctly identified the most important issue that day. The setting was Sunzha District Hospital No. 1 on the Chechnya–Ingushetia border. Until recently every day saw a steady inflow of those most severely injured in the war zone in the security sweeps, raids, repeat raids and repeat security sweeps. Hundreds of people with amputated limbs: women, children, the elderly, Ingushes, Chechens and Russians. The wounds of most were neglected and festering because they had had to shelter two or three days in cellars waiting for the bombing to stop, unable to leave their villages. Then they had to wait as long again for soldiers at the checkpoints to relent and let them cross over into Ingushetia.

The result has been a wretched carnival of infection in the Sunzha hospital, destroying any remaining nerve endings. Along the corridors, spectral young girls swathed in bandages shamble with unfeeling, lifeless arms and legs. The nerves in some limbs have been severed, while others have succumbed to gangrene.

Who will pay for the intensive courses of treatment they will need for years to come? The same state budget which today is funding the war that crippled them in the first place? Where is our valiant state, conducting this war in accordance with its "overall plan," expecting to find the money to provide artificial limbs for the hundreds of newly disabled it has created? Which of its plans contains the budgetary provision for that? Who is going to accept responsibility for the thousands of civilians whose health has been taken from them in the course of this fighting?

Millennium Celebrations Caused this Tragedy

I hate battle-pieces. In paintings, as in life, detail is what matters most. It is the detail which gives the measure of our humanity. How we react to the tragedy of one small person accurately reflects our attitude towards a whole nationality; and increasing the numbers doesn't change much. Little Liana Shamsudinova was born in 1994 in Martan Chu, Urus Martan District, and the recent details of her life are entirely typical of today's Chechnya.

Fleeing the bombing, her family lived from October to December 1999 in a refugee camp in the hill village of Assinovskaya. From mid-December the refugees came under increasing pressure from Migration Service officials, who did not want them concentrating in one locality and urged them to return to their home villages, assuring them that peace had returned and their area was secure. On December 29 Liana's mother, Malika Shamsudinova, finally fell for these lies, the family went back to Martan Chu, and just four days later Liana was orphaned. On January 3, 2000 at 8:20 p.m. their home on Pervomaiskaya Street suffered a direct hit from a tank shell.

There was no military engagement at that time in Martan Chu, but the soldier who fired the shell knew perfectly well what he was doing. He fired just for the hell of it. By current standards in Chechnya 8:20 p.m. is late at night. The federal command has ordained that absolutely everybody must remain in their houses. They are not even allowed out into their own courtyards to relieve themselves, on pain of being shot without warning. This actually happened in Novy Sharoy to Mahomadov, a refugee from Naur, who ventured out just as dusk was falling and was shot in his doorway by a sniper.

Liana's house was wilfully targeted by someone well aware that it was inhabited. A lit oil stove, that surest sign of life, was visible through the windows. There is every reason to suppose that the shelling was an expression of drunken exuberance on the part of the tank troops deployed on the outskirts of Martan Chu. There was no other firing on the village that night. The soldiers simply loosed off a shell and their unruly emotions were placated.

"They were celebrating the New Year," Liana's aunt, Raisa Davlet-murzayeva, surmises. This is what the villagers also concluded.

The result was that Liana's mother, Malika, was killed. She was 28 and was breast-feeding her youngest son, Zelimkhan. The shrapnel split her head in two, and the neighbours who ran to the Shamsudinovs' house found her body cooling, her breast exposed, and Zelimkhan pressed to it.

The little boy's position was unchanged in death, firmly clasped in his dead mother's arms. From beneath the remains of the roof the neighbours retrieved the bodies of Liana's elder sister, seven-year-old Diana, and, next to her, of her 18-year-old aunt, Roza Azizayeva, who had come to help about the house. The neighbours carried Liana out, alive and crying. There were no other survivors and today she is an orphan, her father having disappeared somewhere in Ukraine after going to Belaya Kalitva in search of work a year ago.

Since then Liana has not spoken to anyone, and she was certainly not going to speak in Russian to me. She has been in shock since January 3, and only calls out from time to time in Chechen for her mother. In her lucid moments fellow patients have tried to communicate that her mother is dead. It is a Chechen tradition not to conceal misfortune, to teach children to be brave, even when a very young child is facing a lifetime of having to be brave.

"I will look after her of course," Raisa tells me, "but there is a limit to what I can do. In the Sunzha hospital we had to buy everything ourselves, hypodermic syringes, drugs, drip-feeds. She needs a lot of medical care. Where am I to find the money for that?" By now we are talking in a different hospital, in Galashkino, a tiny primitive facility with only 40 beds. Nearly all the wounded have just been transferred here from Sunzha, which is closed for a thorough disinfection. Contagion spreading from neglected "Chechen" wounds had reached crisis levels.

Liana, although blameless, is also a carrier of infection, and now finds herself in the markedly worse conditions and reduced nursing care of Galashkino Hospital. The wards are cramped and overcrowded, there is little equipment, and it is freezing cold because the heating system is useless. With her major gangrenous fractures, Liana is unlikely to recover in such conditions. How can people survive when the Empire, sweeping aside all in its path, declines to rest its baleful gaze on those who happen to be in its way?

On January 4, the Shamsudinov family funeral was held in Martan Chu. In full view of the tank crews basking in the Caucasian sunshine, all the women and children they had murdered were borne to the cemetery. Not one of them even came to apologize for their New Year high spirits.

Similarly vile, but even more cynical behaviour was displayed in Shali. On January 9, the administration of this district center assembled people in the central square to issue the first pensions and benefit payments from the Russian-installed government of Nikolai Koshman.

There is a school facing the square and Zarema Sadulayeva, its Deputy Headmistress and maths teacher, had also gathered the children to finish giving out New Year and Kurban-Bairam (Eid ul-Adha) presents.

They had no idea that at that same moment resistance fighters were entering the far end of this very large village. A tactical missile came crashing down, not on the enemy detachment but straight into the crowded central square. The fighters melted away, but in the square many people died or were severely injured. How many? Dozens? Hundreds? There is a large discrepancy in the figures given for the simple reason that the surviving villagers could not dig graves fast enough and many buried their relatives together, so that there were fewer graves than casualties. It was another Guernica, comparable in horror to the infamous missile attack on the central market in Grozny last October.

The nightmare was repeated in Shali the following day. Ali-bek Keriev, Zarema's husband, took his severely injured wife away from the hospital, fearing that it too might be targeted. He asked his sister, a doctor, to come and care for her. Alas, 40-year-old Kisa was killed during an ensuing mortar bombardment, and since January 9 Ali-bek has been unable to sleep. He maintains a full-time vigil at his wife's bedside. On January 13, he managed to move her, pregnant and close to death, to the central hospital in Nazran but the outlook is not good. He can't bear to look at her dreadful wounds and watch her convulsions. She desperately needs powerful, intensive-care drugs but as usual they are in short supply. In his sleepless nights Ali-bek writes poetry, a personal appeal to the Being who may or may not be sitting on high observing everything that happens here below. All Zarema had done was to go out to distribute presents to children.

Whatever appeals may be addressed to the Almighty, relations between civilians and federal troops are just as soulless in Shali as in Martan Chu. There will be no inquiry into the killings in Martan Chu, the massacre of a family not meriting a criminal investigation. No prosecutor will question the shameless lies which tricked the Shamsudinovs into returning to their village. The implication is that the aftermath of the New Year crime is the personal problem of this luckless little girl and her Aunt Raisa, who now faces the task of trying to bring her up. Raisa views the future with unconcealed foreboding; in order to treat the child's injuries adequately she would need a lot of money for the proper drugs, a top-class clinic and consultants, things she is not going to find in Martan Chu or anywhere else in Chechnya or Ingushetia today. Be that as it may, the Empire refuses to make an exception: Chechens are not allowed beyond the borders of Chechnya and Ingushetia. Not a single general is to be found with the decency to admit that he bears any guilt for Liana's suffering, or that it is his duty to help her.

The situation is identical in respect of Shali: no half-witted gun-layer has been blamed for devastating the central square, no criminal charges are being brought for the murder of civilians. Nobody has so much as apologized.

Madina and Alikhan: A New Generation Consigned to a Hospital Bed

Madina and Alikhan Avtorkhanov are cousins. Their mothers Khava and Aishat are sisters. Khava lived in Samashki and Aishat in Novy Sharoy in Achkhoy-Martan District. They were not far from each other, but the shelling left them separated by a whirlwind of deadly lead flying in all directions.

In this war family reunions take place outside operating theatres. The sisters met in the treatment unit of Sunzha Hospital. Khava was at the bedside of 22-year-old Madina, while Aishat was looking after her younger son, 18-year-old Alikhan. (Her elder son died during random shelling of their village during the First Chechen War.) Madina, only recently a beautiful young girl but now worn out by operations and pain, her parchment-colored face and body a shadow of what they were, has almost certainly been permanently crippled by the injuries she sustained on October 27. Some of her bone has been cut away and they need to find somewhere for her to have an operation, and then somewhere for her to convalesce because their house at 27 Kooperativnaya Street has been destroyed.

The history of Alikhan's illness is no less grim. One leg has already been amputated above the knee as a result of the curse of gangrene. For several days the soldiers refused to allow the wounded to be taken out of their village. He has already lost the big toe on his other foot and so far attempts to stop the gangrene from spreading have been unsuccessful. Alikhan is a quiet, thoughtful young man who holds Russia responsible for destroying his life on October 23, the day he was injured. He has no plans for the future now. His only distraction is when one of the men visiting the hospital picks up his stump of a body and takes him for a "walk" along the corridors.

Alikhan tells me that none of his classmates are still alive. He left school along with eight other boys and eight girls. All the boys have since been killed. He is alive, but crippled. Everybody was sheltering in their cellars during relentless shelling of Novy Sharoy. When things quietened down at around nine in the morning Alikhan's classmates quietly came together beside his house at 12 Tsentralnaya Street to discuss what they should do. Mortars were fired at them and all except Alikhan were killed. Who is going to provide the complex, expensive artificial limbs he now needs?

"Nobody, of course," Alikhan says. "I am a Chechen. I can just crawl from now until the day I die."

"Why do you get so het up about them?" the officers demanded when I tried to find out who would be responsible for supplying the artificial limbs and treatment required after these wicked acts against the civilian population. "They are not human beings, they are little furry animals. Don't worry, they'll soon give birth to plenty more new little furry animals."

My present assignment to report on the war in the North Caucasus has immersed me in the suffering of our people, interspersed with this kind of insolent frontline and near-frontline cynicism. The war-zone slang is little better than what is going on there. They refer to Chechen men, even the resistance fighters, with the more or less respectable label of "Chechies." All other Chechens, particularly boys, children, and young people generally they call "little furry animals." Who does? The entire military and administrative infrastructure waging and servicing the present war. Even the hospital doctors have this wretched expression on the tip of their tongue. It is bad enough coming from sergeant majors, but a complete disgrace coming from the intelligentsia.

When this nightmare was inaugurated in September 1999, one did secretly hope in the depths of one's heart that the state would catch terrorists and refrain from waging war against everyone in Chechnya. Some hope! Today it is obvious that the policy from the outset was genocide. The genocide of one people, however, soon leads to the genocide of another, a truism borne out through the centuries by successive generations of invaders and those invaded. For the totalitarian empire being constructed in front of our eyes, punitive expeditions give life meaning. Today one group is sent to the guillotine, tomorrow a different one. The day after tomorrow it will be the turn of little Liana, and later still, we need have no doubt, it will be our turn.

Perhaps the genocide would be justified if the villains who grew rich by holding hostages to ransom and selling oil illegally were totally eradicated? There is no chance of that happening. The kidnappers are quietly resuming their business under a different guise. Petrol tankers from the liberated regions of Chechnya are again turning up in Plievo in Ingushetia. Refining continues at full tilt. The Chechen oil irregulars have sat out the cataclysm and are back in business.

But what about the so-called Wahhabis, the Islamist extremists? Perhaps they have been melted down by the flamethrowers, or have slunk away to caves in the mountains? Wrong again! On January 18, Idris Satuyev, a Chechen refugee, Headmaster of the school in Alkhan-Yurt, was shot at point blank range by unidentified individuals in Maiskoye, Ingushetia, just for wearing a tie. "I told them that had been my custom throughout a long working life in the school. My lifestyle is European and secular," the headmaster wheezes. He has survived but is now very ill in the overcrowded Nazran Hospital, in Ward 3 of the accident department. Idris lies there dreaming of the only way out of his situation: to emigrate once and for all from our sixth of the world's land surface; no longer to be a Chechen obliged to live anywhere near us Russians.

HOW TO RECRUIT A DISPOSABLE WOMEN'S BRIGADE

June 9, 2003

On June 15, 2003, 17 people died and 16 were injured as the result of an explosion on a bus transporting military and civilian personnel to the military air base at Mozdok. The attack was carried out by a female suicide bomber. On August 1, as the result of another terrorist attack at the Mozdok military hospital, 51 people died and more than 100 were wounded.

Once again, words flood from the television screen . . . "suicide bomber," "that bastard Basayev," "Maskhadov knew," "zombified by centers of international terrorism beyond the borders of Russia . . ." Instead of analysis, primitive ideological war cries: "Enemies of the political process, trying to keep it from developing"; "We will deal with Basayev and there will be no more suicide bombers." Oversimplification of the problem to a level which only moves us further away from taking a sensible decision on how to deal with this new phase of Russia's Chechen tragedy.

So, what is really going on? What is happening to Chechen women in this fourth year of the Second Chechen War? Do they really need to be brainwashed and "zombified" by centers of international terrorism?

No, actually they don't. No external input is required to make a Chechen woman decide to become a disposable terrorist bomber, because the work has already been done. A typical Chechen woman today really is a zombie: she has been turned into one by the grief in which she has been immersed for year after year, by the environment surrounding her family. She has been trained to be a suicide bomber not in foreign training camps but by the brutality shown by the warring sides towards the civilian population in Chechnya. This is what has engendered an overriding desire in thousands of mothers, wives and sisters to take their own cruel revenge for their disappeared sons, husbands and brothers.

She does this not because of the dictates of a Chechen form of Islam or the traditional *adats* or laws which govern life in her country, but out of despair. The Constitution adopted by referendum on March 23 has only increased the numbers queuing up to join the women's brigade for these special operations because there were high hopes that it might change something. Alas, the new Constitution has proved to be just so much paper. It has not stopped the Army's anarchy and is protecting nobody.

The number of civilian men and women "disappeared" by the federals during the spring of 2003 has been far higher than during the same period last year. Worse, the authors of the fake political process leading up to March 23 unforgivably promised those searching for their abducted relatives that if they would just vote, some of the disappeared would return home; they would be released from prison. "The Kremlin has given the go-ahead," they lied. "Just vote!"

Nobody returned, so let us not delude ourselves that the increase in terrorism since the referendum is a coincidence which Basayev is exploiting. It is all far more complicated than that.

Who is she, today's Chechen woman? The traditional upbringing of a Chechen woman is ascetic in the extreme. Her obligation is to endure everything without complaint. She should not speak of her personal feelings. For her, virtue is concealment, the ability to hide her feelings deep down, not to show them – not only publicly but even at home in front of her closest male relatives. All her turbulent emotions are bottled up. But can that last for ever?

The devotion and love of a Chechen sister for her brothers, and especially of a Chechen mother for her sons, is passionate and absolute. The strength of feeling is volcanic, and most Chechen women believe that with the loss of a brother, a son or a husband their own life comes to an end.

During the first and second years of the war these private volcanoes did not erupt. The Chechen women were waiting in the hope that everything would come right. They said they had faith that their menfolk would fulfil their traditional role. A Chechen boy is brought up to believe that a man's first duty is to defend woman and home. Unlike a girl, a boy can be spoilt; much can be overlooked by a woman in return for his willingness to die protecting her, if that should be required.

That is not what happened. The war dragged on, until finally all the traditions collapsed under the pressure of the style of war so mercilessly imposed by the federals. Chechen men found themselves having to be defended by the women. It was the women who haggled in bazaars in order to feed their families, and threw themselves under Army vehicles in an attempt to stop them kidnapping their men; while the men mostly stayed out of sight in cellars in order not to be abducted, "swept" or blown to pieces.

This is how Chechen women were propelled into the foreground of the struggle. They were radicalized more quickly than the men hiding behind them, even if the men continue to believe they still have at least some measure of authority. The Chechen woman finally found a way of letting her powerful emotions burst out. The volcano erupted with molten lava whose bounds are only those it sets itself, vigilante justice as the only effective response to unbridled violence. Women rose up to defend their families, inflicting personal retribution on those they themselves pronounced guilty of murder. They chose to die rather than go on living, unable to defend their sons, brothers, or husbands.

I can already hear my opponents protesting, "But Basayev claimed responsibility."

Of course he did. He will claim responsibility for anything he can. The terrorist mantle of Salman Raduev, who "died" in prison, had to be inherited by somebody. Far more important is not who claims responsibility, but that there are women prepared to carry out the acts for which somebody else subsequently claims responsibility. There is no shortage of women prepared to blow themselves up, and their ranks are growing the longer the Army's atrocities continue.

But what about the Chechen men? After the suicide bombings in Znamenka and Iliskhan-Yurt on May 12 and 14 many spoke harshly against the women who carried out those attacks. "They have humiliated us," they said. "They have shown us we are impotent."

And so they did. They did humiliate the men and show them they were impotent. The reversal of traditional roles was complete. The women had independently dotted the i's. They would no longer rely on the men, discuss matters with them first, ask their advice. Instead, they would decide things for themselves, very quietly and privately, and the world would see only the result.

That's the reality, but everybody keeps prattling on about al-Qaeda, that lifebelt for failed politicians.

What is to be done now? We really cannot take seriously the security agencies' assurances that they are reinforcing checkpoints and sealing the administrative border of Chechnya, and that everything is "under control."

In the first place, nothing is under control other than the sloshing of black market currency through the checkpoints. In the second place, imposing even more severe restrictions will not stop women participating in terrorist attacks. In the third place, it is absurd to demand that Maskhadov should call upon the women to abandon these tactics: the women have reached boiling point because of the actions of many men, including Maskhadov. They will simply ignore him.

In the fourth place, finally and most crucially, the mind of someone bent on retribution functions extremely efficiently. You will not keep up with it or be able to guess which weak point it has identified. Checkpoints and checking everybody's documents will be ineffective against women carrying explosives on their person. "We will pass through your checkpoints 'pregnant,'" some of them say. "Your lot are not going to look under our skirts, and you can't keep a gynaecologist at every checkpoint."

The only solution is to overhaul Russia's policy towards Chechnya. We need to take a step in their direction if we want to survive. This means a complete clamp-down on the Army's anarchy. It means beginning peace negotiations (nominally between Maskhadov – if you can talk to Arafat you can talk to him – and nominally the Kremlin), under the watchful eye of authoritative international observers, in order to effect a rapid demilitarisation of the Republic, cessation of hostilities, and bringing of war criminals to justice. The sole result of the referendum was to tack the title of "Acting President of the Chechen Republic" on to Akhmat-hadji Kadyrov. It is self-evident that Kadyrov, as someone incapable of anything other than feathering his own nest, should be removed.

The future political status of Chechnya? There will be time to think about that later. First, let's survive.

Nobody can doubt that it will take a hero to disentangle this mess, and heroes are currently in short supply. We need, nevertheless, to find such a hero, because we have already burned every other bridge.

A WEIRD BATTLEFIELD FOR THE PRESIDENT'S IMAGE

February 16, 2004

By March 1, officials promised Putin, there would be no refugee camps outside Chechnya. Anybody who persisted in their reluctance to move from a camp in Ingushetia to a camp in Chechnya would be "entitled" under the Government's Guarantee to have their water, electricity and gas cut off, and would lose the right to medical care and education. Glory be to the Guarantee! That stout defender of the Guarantee, Ella Pamfilova, Chairwoman of the President's Commission on Human Rights, has been appointed to oversee this massive violation of human rights and of the Constitution.

It would be difficult to call Okruzhnaya a township, a suburb, or even a farm. The most truthful name for it is simply a camp, consisting of unpainted huts hastily knocked together. There is no gas, no water, and there are no amenities, not even in the courtyards. The workers look at me warily for reasons which become apparent later. The so-called Renovation Board, which rules the roost here, is chronically incapable of paying them for their work, but takes the ideological approach: "Build a settlement! Just do it! Putin has spoken!"

"What work is that?" I ask Supian Sambayev, who introduces himself as the site foreman. He and I walk over an area strewn with wooden structures and a defunct lattice of rusting pipes which is the battlefield for the image of the President as Architect of Peace in Chechnya.

"For the houses," the foreman insists grumpily. "They ought to pay us for them."

"But what houses?"

Supian looks away. These half-finished shacks on the outskirts of Grozny have a history. They were hastily erected along the road shortly after last year's flooding and were the material evidence of the budget resources allocated to aid the flood victims. Despite their desperate situation, the flood victims refused as one to move to this out-of-the-way site with no infrastructure. They decided they might as well stay in the ruins of their houses as move to a bare field.

Then the Chechen Government; Kadyrov's Administration; Stanislav Iliasov, Minister for Chechnya; the Interior Ministry of the Russian Federation as represented by its Migration Service, which is responsible for forcing refugees out of Ingushetia and back into the zone of what the President calls the continuing "struggle against international terrorism"; two Boards for rebuilding, one in Grozny and the other in Moscow; all of them held a great big meeting and dreamed up a proposal to the Russian Government to turn this camp which the flood victims had spurned into, in Iliasov's expression, an "excellent location for refugees choosing to return from Ingushetia." It was a moment of pure bureaucratic black magic, although they didn't tell you afterwards how they had done it. Commissions came from the capital and the Southern Federal Region. Grave gentlemen furrowed their statesmanlike brows, condemned the concrete floors which, according to the specification, were already covered with linoleum, and resolved that there should at least be floorboards.

They then pronounced the shacks (costed at 775,000 roubles apiece!) suitable for well-appointed occupation. Reports were sent to the Kremlin that everything was ready and only the wicked refugees, reeling under Maskhadov's propaganda, were continuing to persist in refusing to enjoy their good fortune. The Kremlin set a deadline, March 1, before the election. The issue of the consequences of a war that had been started before the previous election was to be laid to rest. In January, Ella Pamfilova was sent here on behalf of Putin's Administration to give her deeply sincere verdict.

"Pamfilova liked it. Why are you trying to stir things up?" the workers mutter darkly.

"Would you want to live here permanently yourselves?"

"What do you mean, permanently?" the foreman says. "It's only for a time, until their own houses are rebuilt."

"But you know yourself how things get rebuilt here! Has anybody gone back to their rebuilt houses yet?"

The brigade don't reply. Nobody has gone back at all, and everyone knows it.

There are supposed to be two approaches to rebuilding in Chechnya. The first is to transfer money to people's bank accounts and let them organise it themselves. The second is for the work to be done for you up to a set value, but for no money to pass through your own hands.

In reality these approaches merge like the confluence of two rivers. You don't have to go far from Okruzhnaya to see the evidence. In fact, you only need to cross the road. The people living on Transportnaya Street are not those whom officialdom tried to force into the camp in Okruzhnaya after the River Sunzha burst its banks last year. The people here have experienced both the first and second approaches to "rebuilding." They were supposedly paid compensation by the Government, and the relevant sums of money, to judge from the documents, were transferred to the citizens' personal bank accounts so that they could repair their houses. But . . .

What do we see? The hovels are unchanged, only they have dried out. The occupants have patched them up themselves. The whole of Transportnaya Street looks like that. How were the payments to personal bank accounts made? Brigades arrived from the Grozny Board and said, "You are required to undertake work to a value of 771,000 roubles (the actual estimate by the Commission of the repair bill for a family whose name is known to *Novaya gazeta*), but we have to give the Kadyrov Administration a kickback, and also the Moscow Board, so we have had only 30 per cent of your money paid to us, and with that we can only put your roof back on." Which they then did. The family signed for 771,000 roubles.

Things will be no better with the "rebuilt accommodation" for refugees returning from Ingushetia. Nobody doubts that the temporary huts in Okruzhnaya will become permanent dwellings the moment the refugees cross the threshold.

The foreman continues:

"Stop worrying. They will come and sort everything out themselves. Our people are hard workers. They have spent their lives doing casual labor elsewhere in Russia. We have knocked these houses up and they will take care of the rest. What's wrong with that? Every family likes to do it their way. Isn't that right?"

"Absolutely right, but it says here on the plan that there is a kitchen. Where is there any sign of that? A cooker?"

The foreman responds with a question of his own:

"And if there is a toilet here on the plan, does that mean we have to put in a WC pedestal even if there is no water?"

I hear the regular sound of hammering. Some way off a laborer is knocking together a chicken coop which is to be the refugees' communal toilet.

"Excuse me, but you said yourself that there was going to be water."

"Oh yes . . ." the foreman falters. "Only nobody knows when."

"And when will they be getting a floor?" I ask, standing in one of the houses which is "completely finished."

"That's it," he says, and points at what appears to be bare earth, or concrete. It's difficult to tell under the layer of mud.

"But that's just earth."

"Well, what do you think they've got in their tents?"

The telephone is ringing and I know who it is. Vera, a Russian refugee from Grozny who is married to a Chechen. Her family, having lost their toehold in Grozny, have been languishing for over four years in a tent on the outskirts of the Ingush hill village of Ordzhonikidzevskaya.

"They drove us out of one camp," Vera shouts through the "anti-terrorist" electronic jamming. "Now we are in another called Satsit, but they cut the water off here too yesterday. How are we supposed to live? Do they call this voluntary repatriation? Where are we supposed to go? To a new camp? Please, do something about it."

"But Pamfilova came to see you," I shout back in reply.

Our conversation is cut off, but I know that the travels through the North Caucasus of the Chairwoman of Putin's Commission on Human Rights succeeded in bringing back to Moscow just one thing: legitimisation of the travesty being perpetrated, and an opportunity for the state's leading lights to tell their VIP Western colleagues they have the situation under control, while continuing to trample all over the Constitution. Madame Pamfilova is a good-hearted woman, but she is now part of a state system insisting, against all logic, on sending refugees back to Chechnya. The bureaucrats are not prepared to listen to common sense. They want everyone out by March 1, so that before March 14, the date of the Russian presidential election, they will have had time to remove the tents, and their problem will have been solved. Why does it have to be like that?

One of the most persistent stereotypes of the Second Chechen War is that the refugees are enemies of Russia. They are not seen as living in tents because their own warm houses were bombed. They are not seen as having been deprived of their rights. They are not seen as innocent people unjustly accused.

They are enemies who must be crushed. They are part of Maskhadov's power base, accomplices of the "international terrorism" which Putin has been fighting, is fighting now, and will continue to fight. To listen to the Army and the officials, you would think the refugees' reluctance to return to Chechnya was solely because they want to be able to continue their propaganda against Putin's policies to foreign journalists and human rights activists, who find it easier to get into Ingushetia than the closed zone of Chechnya.

This is the thinking behind the solution of the refugee problem whose apotheosis we are now witnessing. Victory at all costs. No negotiations or understanding. Cut off their gas and water and send them back to the security sweeps and the war. If they don't do as they're told, that's their lookout. You don't pussyfoot with the enemy.

A program of repression is being rolled out across Russia, sweeping aside everything in its path. It engenders resistance. Everything seems to be done in order to spite someone; everything is directed against someone. But against whom? Is it only against the refugees? No, it is directed also against you and me. History tells us that children from the reservations never forgive children from warm houses for their humiliating childhood.

YELTSIN AND DUDAYEV SHARE FIRST PRIZE. THE SILVER GOES TO PUTIN, BASAYEV AND LEONTIEV

July 5, 2004

First, the profiles of the candidates for the War Prize, awarded for unleashing and fomenting the Chechen tragedy of 1994–2004. It has been founded by *Chechenskoye obshchestvo*, unquestionably the best newspaper today published in Chechnya and Ingushetia, and the one most dynamically increasing its circulation. Its editor is Timur Aliev. Announcing the War Prize, *Chechenskoye obshchestvo* showed that it is also more in touch with the public mood in the North Caucasus than its competitors. The question, "Who bears the guilt for all this horror?", is one people ask themselves when they wake, when they go to bed, and which they ask each other constantly.

The rules were that anybody could nominate a candidate, and also vote, the winners to be decided by a simple majority. The results of this popular poll exceeded all expectations in the accuracy of the choice, which testifies to high public awareness of the true nature of events. But of course, who else could the winners be if not Yeltsin and Dudayev? And who could be awarded the second prize, if not Yeltsin's worthy successor, Putin; that No. 1 ideologist of blood-letting, journalist Mikhail Leontiev; and that lover of personal power and big money, Akhmat-hadji Kadyrov? Also, of course, Basayev who has given all the above invaluable assistance in discrediting the Chechen resistance and reducing it to the status of "forces of international terrorism," thereby effectively eliminating any chance of its cause being espoused.

And the prizes? Those in second place, alas, get nothing but their negative rating. The winners of the first prize, however, receive certificates which they can collect from 52 Mutaliev Street, Nazran; a year's subscription to *Chechenskoye obshchestvo* (very good analysis, we recommend it); and, most importantly, an all-expenses-paid three-day tour of the war zone in Chechnya. As Djohar Dudayev is no longer with us, Boris Yeltsin is duly awarded a six-day extreme memorial tour with an itinerary in whose construction he was actively involved.

THE SOLDIERS' MOTHERS GO OFF TO THINK ABOUT PROPOSALS FROM THE CHECHEN SIDE, BUT WILL IT STOP THE TERRORISM?

February 28, 2005

The latest development in Russia's history is that in the sixth year of the Second Chechen War the first Russo-Chechen declaration of intent to restore peace in the North Caucasus has been signed in London. It is in English, and is not available in Russian. It is called "The Road to Peace and Stability in Chechnya (the London Memorandum)." The signing took place on February 25, 2005 when women representing the Union of Committees of Soldiers' Mothers of Russia, after several unsuccessful attempts to find somewhere in Europe to discuss a peace settlement with Maskhadov's representatives, finally came to London, the capital of the new Russian emigration. There they met with those whom Aslan Maskhadov had delegated to meet them on behalf of the Chechen resistance (Amina Saiev, Deputy Minister of Foreign Affairs of Ichkeria, Akhmed Zakayev, Maskhadov's Special Envoy in Europe, and Yaragi Abdullayev).

[The following account of the prehistory is taken from Anna Politkovskaya's article, "The Struggle for Peace Is Deadly Dangerous," *Novaya gazeta*, October 25, 2004.]

On October 9, a Saturday, when it usually becomes slightly quieter in the cramped Moscow office of the Union of Committees of Soldiers' Mothers of Russia and it is possible to think about something other than the immediate concerns of receiving soldiers, conscripts and their parents, Valentina Melnikova, a member of the Union's Co-ordinating Committee, and Ida Kuklina, a member of the President's Commission on Human Rights, sat down together. They discussed what is preoccupying nearly all the human rights organizations: the state authorities' manifest inability to cope with the Chechen crisis, the continuing acts of terrorism, and what the Soldiers' Mothers movement could do to change the situation. It was time to act.

Thus did the idea of writing an open letter to the field commanders of the Chechen resistance come into being. A further three days were spent revising and discussing it with members of the Committee, and on October 13 the following brief text was released to the news agencies:

We understand the cost of the armed violence in Chechnya; it involves immense and irreparable losses for the Chechen people. Hundreds of thousands have been killed or have disappeared without trace. There are refugees; ruins in place of cities and villages. Thousands of our sons, both soldiers and officers, have died. There have been hundreds of innocent victims of terror. A whole generation of young Chechens and Russian servicemen has been crippled by the experience of violence and lawlessness. Thousands of impoverished invalids are doomed to a life of penury. Tens of thousands of families grieve over the loss of those dear to them. Such is the cost of this war, which long ago exceeded the losses incurred during the Afghan War. Ten years of war have not brought the desired results either for you or for the federal authorities. Terror engenders anti-terror, and vice versa. Neither in Chechnya nor in Russia do people feel safe.

Commanders of the Chechen armed groups! You will kill or be killed without end. You will not be able to change anything until you are recognised as negotiating partners. The Soldiers' Mothers appeal to those of you who truly seek the good of the Chechen people with a proposal to give peace a chance and open negotiations for a peaceful settlement. We are willing to travel anywhere, to meet those you authorise anywhere, in order only to halt this deadly race. In coming forward as the initiator of negotiations, we will make all necessary efforts to involve in the negotiation process representatives of the leadership of the Chechen Republic and the Russian Presidential Administration, inter-governmental and peace organizations, and influential and respected public figures. We await your reply.

Members of the Coordinating Council of the Union of

Committees of Soldiers' Mothers of Russia, Valentina Melnikova, Maria Fedulova, Natalia Zhukova.

The reply was not long in coming. The very next day Aslan Maskhadov communicated through Akhmed Zakayev, his envoy in Europe, that he and the fighters of the resistance welcomed the Soldiers' Mothers' initiative: for their part, they were willing to attend such a meeting. A day later, Zakayev rang Melnikova and their communications ceased to be only in writing. "We agreed that the meeting should take place in a European country in November," Valentina explains briefly.

The Mothers flew to London on February 24. Their accommodation was decidedly acceptable: the Waldorf, one of central London's most luxurious hotels, near the famous Waterloo Bridge across the Thames. They came down to the hotel lobby at about 5.00 p.m., at first behaving like secret agents behind enemy lines. They were very nervous. On this note the meeting began between Ida Kuklina's group (and it was she, a colleague of Pamfilova and member of President Putin's "Committee to Promote Civil Society," who was running the Mothers' show) and Zakayev's team. The meeting was held in the hotel's conference room from 5:00 p.m. until midnight. At first the Mothers demanded secret negotiations, which suggested that these representatives of civil society had secrets they wanted to keep from civil society. At 7.00 p.m., however, at the Chechens' insistence, observers representing *Novaya gazeta* and Radio Liberty were admitted. It was clear that journalists, unlike politicians, just wanted to see somebody at last agreeing to seek peace in Chechnya, and doing something to make it happen. Yet it soon became apparent why the Mothers were so reluctant to admit outsiders. They had come to London without any proposals other than that "a Multi-Lateral Working Group should be set up to to begin considering preliminary steps for the negotiating process," as Ida Kuklina put it.

"What, in your view, should be the mechanism for a ceasefire?" the Chechens asked.

"That is for the Working Group to decide," the Mothers replied.

"But the Working Group cannot work while the war is continuing," one Mother said doubtfully. "We need a ceasefire. That is the main thing."

"That is a matter for the Working Group, not us," other Mothers corrected her.

"We would like to propose two groups of delegates, one from each side, to establish their own ideas about the mechanism for a ceasefire, and then to bring them together."

"No. Only a Multi-Lateral Working Group with everybody in it. With third-party observers."

It was fairly pointless trying to discuss anything, and that looked decidedly odd. They had been moving towards this meeting for such a long time, and had presumably been preparing for it. Alas, I cannot write in detail about what was discussed at the Waldorf Hotel. The Mothers insisted I should convey only the gist, which I now do because it is particularly important for anybody who had high hopes for peace resulting from this meeting. The gist was that all proposals from the Chechen side were rejected. Not one made it into the final memorandum. As Ida Kuklina explained afterwards, "We will take them back with us and consider them."

"And what action will you take?" *Novaya gazeta* asked.

"I don't know," Ida Kuklina replied.

"Why do you keep going on at us?" Valentina Melnikova added. "We are ill old-age pensioners."

"So as to be able to write about this."

"Write anything you like."

This too seemed very odd. What had been the point of seeking this meeting if there was no sense of urgency? They had evidently come to London for some other purpose.

In fact, at the Waldorf Hotel flaccidity alternated with bursts of hyperactivity. "We cannot wait for Russian society to reach a consensus," the Mothers declared. "We have been at the forefront for the past 16 years. We do not wait, we act as the situation requires. The only place where people can come for help is to the Committees of Soldiers' Mothers." That is an exaggeration. They are not by any means the only place people can go, even in Moscow. It was followed, however, by a truly absurd exaggeration: "The generals will do what we tell them to."

The Chechens were amazed. In that case, why had they not told them to stop the war long ago? Or was that not what they meant?

Zakayev's group tried consistently to hurry the Mothers along. They tried to persuade them of the need for momentum. Time was not on our side: they explained that radicalism in their ranks was increasing, which it might soon no longer be possible to contain. The overall situation in the North Caucasus was highly volatile. The Mothers, however, were not budging. One thing at a time. "People are expecting a miracle from us, but there is not going to be one." We heard that repeated again and again.

The Mothers' belief that taking things slowly was a fundamental principle of popular diplomacy was supported by the observers from European institutions: "We are prepared to provide a venue for further meetings with the same participants somewhere in Strasbourg or Brussels, and we will continue the dialogue." The European representatives who had flown in specially to London were Vytautas Landsbergis, the former President of Lithuania and today a Member of the European Parliament; and his Belgian colleague Bart Staes. Later, on February 25, they were joined by Andreas Gross, a member of the Parliamentary Assembly of the Council of Europe (PACE); Lord Judd, former rapporteur to PACE on Chechnya, and Baroness Sarah Ludford, the main organiser of these Chechen–Russian meetings in London.

They broke up on February 24, having agreed the draft text of a joint London Memorandum which acknowledged the thousands of victims and the fact that the conflict cannot be resolved by military means.

*   *   *

Queen Anne's Gate is the name of a London street near St James's Park and here, on the morning of February 25, the parties met in the presence of European observers for a concluding two-hour discussion and press conference, which as a matter of principle was to take place on neutral territory, in the British office of the European Union.

Baroness Ludford presided, firmly and constructively. The aim of the meeting was to finalise a joint statement, the London Memorandum: "The Road to Peace and Stability in Chechnya." Thanks to the superhuman efforts of the Baroness, it did eventually materialise. The main reason why the London Memorandum was adopted in English is because this was the Baroness's native tongue and there was no time left to translate it. It was accordingly in the English language that the London Memorandum became part of the history of the Russo-Chechen War of the twentieth and twenty-first centuries.

Incidentally, as regards the Russo-Chechen nature of what is going on in the North Caucasus, and the complicated and paradoxical climate of the London meetings, the Mothers spent an inordinate amount of time attempting to lower the emotional charge of the Memorandum's language. They wanted to make sure that nobody officially labelled the war "Russo-Chechen," but only, blandly and inoffensively, "this conflict," in accordance with the Kremlin's official position to characterise it as an "internal armed conflict." The fact that the Memorandum will go down in history in a foreign language itself demonstrates that the conflict amounts to something more than an internal matter.

Queen Anne's Gate closed at 1400 hours Greenwich Mean Time on February 25, 2005. The greatest positive result was that a meeting had at least taken place. For the time being, that is all. The Mothers saw that the other side are not devils with horns, don't bite, are entirely reasonable and moderate. If on the 24th everything had got off to a nervous, edgy start, it concluded on the 25th with a joint photograph, although even that took some organising. It is to be hoped that these new insights will be taken back with them to the Kremlin. And then? Who knows?

Finally, who was paying for all this? People in Russia traditionally take an interest in that aspect whenever anything is happening in London. Was, perhaps, Berezovsky paying for this junket? Well, this time you can be reassured. I checked. All costs were paid by the European Parliament. The Mothers even handed its representatives their air tickets as proof of expenses. For that we owe the European Parliament a big thank-you, for saving us from damaging rumors.

The text of the proposals of the Chechen side, presented to the Soldiers' Mothers, was:

Step 1. Ceasefire and fight against terror. The opposing sides, via special representatives, create a mechanism for an immediate ceasefire without preconditions. The Chechen side is ready to co-operate in combating terrorism, both within the framework of bilateral relations and as a part of the international coalition to fight terrorism.

Step 2. Demilitarisation. After an armistice is reached, the removal of Russian troops from the Chechen Republic and the disarmament of the National Militia take place simultaneously. The functions of providing safety are transferred to a temporary peacemaking contingent in connection with this.

Step 3. Transition period. During the period between the ceasefire and elections, the state functions are assumed by a temporary coalition government, created under international control. In questions of providing safety the Provisional Government relies on the peacemaking contingent. (The "Kosovo" option – AP) The legal basis for the creation and working of the temporary coalition government of the Chechen Republic of Ichkeria is the agreement of 12 May 1997. ("Agreement on Peace and Principles of Mutual Relations between the Russian Federation and the Chechen Republic of Ichkeria," concluded in accordance with the Constitutions of the RF and ChRI. – AP)

Step 4. Elections. Based on the Agreement of May 12, 1997, the Provisional Government prepares and organises direct democratic elections with participation of all political forces of the Chechen Republic under the observation of international institutions.

Step 5. Economic reconstruction. The European Union is
called upon to grant large-scale, direct economic aid
for the reconstruction of Chechnya.

THE SECRET OF MASKHADOV'S ASSASSINATION. HOW AND WHY THE SECOND PRESIDENT OF CHECHNYA WAS KILLED

September 19, 2005

In the Chechen Supreme Court in Grozny the trial begins this week of
those who were with Maskhadov at the moment of his assassination.

Was he killed? Did he commit suicide? Was the body planted? Was
it a planned operation or did they happen upon him by chance? It is
still debated how and why it was that on March 8, 2005 in the village
of Tolstoy-Yurt death came to Aslan Maskhadov, elected President of
Chechnya in 1997 and 1999. With the outbreak of the Second Chechen
War, it was Maskhadov who led resistance to Russian federal troops
and who gradually became the personal enemy of Vladimir Putin.

Before March 8 any conversation with Russian soldiers in Chechnya
about Maskhadov and Basayev would conclude with them claiming that
everybody knew where Maskhadov was, only the order had not yet been
received to bring him in, and that was the sole reason why neither of
them was already in prison.

Does that mean that on March 8 the order was finally given? After
the killing, both the federals and indeed everybody else started
concocting increasingly bizarre and contradictory accounts. He had shot
himself. He had ordered his bodyguards to shoot him. He had been
killed in a different place and the body had been moved to Tolstoy-Yurt.

Novaya gazeta is in possession of the case files of Criminal Case
No. 20/849, relating to the circumstances surrounding Maskhadov's
assassination. The investigation was conducted by the same team from
the Prosecutor-General's Office as the Beslan cases. Four individuals
were held from March to September in the Vladikavkaz pre-trial detention facility and gave evidence in the Prosecutor's Office of North
Ossetia. They are now in the dock in Grozny.

The four accused are: Ilias Iriskhanov, one of Maskhadov's body-guards who arranged his accommodation in Tolstoy-Yurt; Vakhid Murdashev and Viskhan Khadzhimuratov, Maskhadov's bodyguards; and Musa (Skandarbek, according to his passport) Yusupov, owner of No. 2 Suvorov Street, Tolstoy-Yurt where Maskhadov stayed without leaving the house from November 17, 2004 to March 8, 2005). All four are charged under the Russian Criminal Code, Article 209, Part 2 ("banditry: membership of an established armed group"); Article 222, Part 3 ("illegal acquisition, storage, or bearing of firearms, explosive devices, military supplies, under the aegis of an organised group").

The main question is, why was Maskhadov killed in March 2005, and neither earlier nor later? The whole of the last winter of his life was spent in the expectation that peace feelers were about to be put forward. We now know this is not speculation but a fact.

From the evidence of one of the witnesses: "He (Maskhadov) told me that negotiations with Putin were about to begin. On January 23, Aslan Maskhadov told me he had suspended the war on the Chechen side." Similar testimony is scattered throughout the case. What were Maskhadov's hopes based on? Who instilled and fostered them right up until his last day?

We know the answer to that. Mainly it was Andreas Gross, a Member of the Swiss Parliament and former rapporteur on Chechnya to the Parliamentary Assembly of the Council of Europe, who visited the Republic under the vigilant monitoring of the Special Operations Executive of the Russian FSB, and accordingly became convinced by the winter of 2004 that he knew all there was to know about Chechnya. Also Akhmed Zakayev, resident in Great Britain, Maskhadov's Special Envoy in Europe. Also members of the Committee of Soldiers' Mothers.

Beginning in November, the very time when Maskhadov moved to Tolstoy-Yurt, Mr Gross began shuttling back and forth between Euro-pean capitals and Moscow, preparing the ground for round-table discussions on Chechnya. He met a number of highly placed individ-uals, members of the Presidential Administration, and they assured him they were "ready for peace." The only condition they put to Gross was that he should cut out all undesirable contacts, by which was meant that his shuttle diplomacy for peace should exclude all those who had been insisting on peace from the inception of the Second Chechen War. Among those deemed unacceptable were most civil rights activists, including the author of these lines. Those who were acceptable were the officials of pro-Moscow Chechnya: Khanid Yamadayev, Alu Alkhanov, even Ramzan Kadyrov, and Mahomed Khambiev, the former Defence Minister of Ichkeria who had defected from Maskhadov to Kadyrov.

Gross was completely sincere and committed to the tasks for "peace" which he had been set by Putin's Presidential Administration, and to the whole business of shuttle diplomacy entrusted to him. He told me all about it himself in Helsinki during those winter months. The main stopover in his shuttle trips was London, where he assured Akhmed Zakayev that this was the best way to proceed. Zakayev was in constant contact with Maskhadov and it was he who passed on all these hopes of peace and encouraged Maskhadov to believe that the long-awaited negotiations with Moscow might soon start.

In the meantime, the London negotiations of the Union of Committees of Soldiers' Mothers with representatives of one of the belligerent parties collapsed. They collapsed for the very good reason that the Soldiers' Mothers suddenly started adopting a hardline position in London, as if blithely unaware that failure was precisely what Moscow wanted from them.

This left Maskhadov with only one potentially promising, but in fact disastrous, way forward to peace: the "path of Gross." He took the bait. Reassured by Gross's blandishments, which he heard about from Zakayev and over the Internet, Maskhadov let down his guard and began regularly using a mobile phone. Russia had succeeded in killing his predecessor, President Dudayev, by locating him through his use of a mobile phone, and during all the previous years of the war Maskhadov had never touched one. Now his main method of communication became text messaging.

As one of the witnesses testifies: "Aslan Maskhadov used his mobile telephone for sending text messages. When I asked him why he didn't ring anybody, he replied, 'The whole world knows my voice. They would work out where I am instantly.'"

It was through mobile telephone traffic that Maskhadov's whereabouts were established. More precisely, the intelligence services registered the fact that the source of the traffic was in Tolstoy-Yurt.

If we try to summarise what happened in the last months of Maskhadov's life, we find that he was weary of the war and of living in hiding. He did his utmost to achieve peace by making major compromises; he accepted the need to take extremely radical steps, and, to demonstrate his willingness, announced a unilateral cessation of military operations on January 14, with an extension on February 23. In other words, throughout the winter of 2004–5 Maskhadov was, on the one hand, being drawn into the Kremlin's games, but on the other was clearly outsmarting Moscow in the management of the peace process. "Management" is perhaps not the ideal expression, but it best approximates to what was going on during the winter on the Tolstoy-Yurt–Moscow–Helsinki–Brussels (where Gross's round table was conducted)–London axis.

By March, Moscow was finding Maskhadov's activity intolerable and the process moved beyond Gross's control, even though he is an influential individual. "Maskhadov's peace initiatives' were a constant topic of conversation in the political salons of Europe: the European Parliament, the Parliamentary Assembly of the Council of Europe. I know what I'm talking about because I was there. In the continent's highest diplomatic circles Putin began to recede into the background, acquiring the reputation of a man who 'would not compromise despite what common sense dictated," a man "moving matters towards the next Beslan." A moment came when Putin was clearly under considerable pressure from Western leaders as a result of Maskhadov's peace initiatives.

So, what are we talking about here? About the fact that Maskhadov's assassination was a direct result of his peace efforts last winter. He signed his own death warrant by seizing the peace initiative, if only briefly.

To all appearances, Maskhadov was very seriously preparing to declare a unilateral ceasefire, which he believed should be timed for the beginning of contacts between Akhmed Zakayev's group and the Soldiers' Mothers in London, as a sign of goodwill on the part of one of the warring parties. The ceasefire would be extended to coincide with Gross's round table in Brussels.

In order to achieve a real armistice, however, Maskhadov needed to reach agreement with the principal actor in the Chechen War, Basayev. Accordingly, on November 13, 2005 Basayev, summoned by Maskhadov, appeared at No. 2 Suvorov Street and stayed for six days. There is some lack of clarity about dates in the case materials, where it is asserted both that Maskhadov moved to Tolstoy-Yurt on November 17, and also that on November 13 Basayev came to visit him there. Our information is that Basayev stayed in Tolstoy-Yurt from December 13 .

He stayed for six days, and the amount of time they spent together is very important. In the first place it refutes rumors that Maskhadov and Basayev never stayed in the same place, let alone for so long, in order not to be killed simultaneously. But the fact is a fact: they remained together in a very small residence.

From the testimony of one of the witnesses: "He (Basayev) stayed for about six days in the old house (at that time the owner, Musa Yusupov, had two houses standing on a plot of 1,500 square metres: an old adobe house, and a new stone house). He and Maskhadov were together all the time and talked at length. When they were together they did not allow anybody else near."

In the second place, those six days spent in conversation are clear proof that Basayev had no wish at all for a truce. Maskhadov did not let him off the hook and succeeded in bringing him round; Basayev deferred to Maskhadov and the truce was more or less observed by Basayev's men. As even the official media later stated, explosions in early summer 2005 were the work only of malcontents taking revenge. These had long been a third, and very serious, force in Chechnya, taking orders neither from Maskhadov nor from Basayev.

Agreement to observe a ceasefire was achieved between Maskhadov and Basayev. This raises an agonising question, to which for the present we have no answer: if Maskhadov was able to influence Basayev in this matter, why did he not do so over Beslan? Why did Maskhadov not use all his influence to prevent the seizure of the children?

As the evidence of one of the witnesses relates: "Maskhadov also told me in conversation that the seizure of Beslan had been a mistake. He was very displeased about it." A "mistake"? Not a catastrophe?

Now, some accompanying detail about the last months of Maskhadov's life, which also tells us a lot. Would it have been possible for the federal forces to have arrested Maskhadov and Basayev earlier? Were they within their reach? Judge for yourselves, for instance, from the manner in which both were travelling around Chechnya last winter when, supposedly, everything had long ago been brought under control and, supposedly, operations were "constantly being mounted to track down those guilty of the Beslan tragedy."

This from the testimony of one of the witnesses: "November 17, 2004. During the night we went to a meeting (with Maskhadov, near Avtury). We drove into Soviet Farm No. 4 at approximately 2130 hours. Some 200 metres from the bus stop we stopped the car, flashed the lights two or three times, and approximately two minutes after this a car standing at the bus stop drove off in the direction of Mozdok. (At the bus stop) stood Vakhid and Viskhan, who are distant relatives of Maskhadov, and Maskhadov himself. Beside them were five or so large bags. They had at least three rifles and one sniper's rifle, black with a thick barrel. They also had three pistols. Maskhadov's was much longer than those of his bodyguards. The three of them were wearing green combat uniforms. In one of the bags I could see a military combat uniform."

There follows a description of how all this baggage was casually loaded by Maskhadov and his bodyguards into the boot of the car and the back seat, and they headed off towards Tolstoy-Yurt. Through all the checkpoints, through localities riddled with nocturnal secrets and patrols. Avtury, where Maskhadov and his two bodyguards were standing at a bus stop, is completely under the control of one of the regiments of the Interior Ministry's troops, and there are legions of Kadyrovites there around the clock. Or at least, that is what the Kadyrovites claim.

These details give support, if only indirectly, to the belief that in November 2004 no order had been issued to kill or even arrest Maskhadov. In late February 2005, however, it was.

Even more startling is the testimony regarding Basayev's trip to Tolstoy-Yurt to meet Maskhadov: "Halfway to Farm No. 4 (again, in closely monitored Avtury) there was a vehicle. Some 200 metres before we reached it, the vehicle drove off and we approached Shamil Basayev. He was alone. Shamil Basayev had a plastic sack and a large sports bag. He was armed with a rifle. When I asked him what he had in the sack, he replied, 'a sleeping bag.'"

If Maskhadov's voice may not, in fact, be known to the whole world, Basayev's face is surely familiar by now to everybody on the planet. Here he was, standing at a bus stop, completely alone, with no mask, carrying a rifle and a sleeping bag.

Let us recall the official version of why Basayev supposedly could not be caught. He was said to be hiding all the time in the mountain forests, lurking in a network of caves, and if he moved he was invariably surrounded by a host of men armed to the teeth, so that to capture him would cost too many of "our" lives. Does that mean that as of this date there were no orders for Basayev's arrest? We have no answer to that question.

Maskhadov spent almost four months in Tolstoy-Yurt, hemmed in virtually the whole time, at first in the old adobe house, but then from the end of December he and his bodyguards went down to the cellar. The case materials give its dimensions as 2 x 2 x 2 metres. A cramped vault.

From the testimony of one of the witnesses: "They only came out of the cellar to pray namaz, at dawn and in the evening. Aslan Maskhadov, Vakhid and Viskhan (Murdashiev and Khadzhimuratov) had three computers which opened like a book, and two video cameras. Maskhadov spent practically the whole day at his computer. They sometimes videoed themselves with the cameras. In approximately early February 2005, a man who appeared to be about 40 years old came to the house. He had a short beard and was wearing civilian clothes. In conversation with Maskhadov they called this man Abdul

Khalim (Sadulayev, Maskhadov's successor. He just walked in, and equally easily left).

"On March 8, at about 9:00 a.m. armed men ran into the court-yard of No. 2 Suvorov Street shouting 'Come out one by one with your hands up!' They asked Musa Yusupov whether his house had cellars. 'I showed them the cellar area beneath my new house. Then they started conducting a search and in the old house found the entrance to the cellar in which Aslan Maskhadov, Vakhid and Viskhan were living. The soldiers blew up the entrance to the cellar and after that one of them shouted, 'I can see a body.' They shouted through the opening they had made to ask if anybody was alive in the cellar, and shortly afterwards took Vakhid and then Viskhan out of the old house."

At the moment the entrance to the cellar was blown up, according to the case materials, Maskhadov was closest to it and took the full force of the blast. That is why he died instantly. His bodyguards survived only because Maskhadov died.

Do you remember the television images of the dead Maskhadov, stripped to the waist, lying on concrete in a courtyard? That was the Yusupovs' courtyard, despite all the official fairy tales suggesting it was Kadyrov's.

The Yusupovs' courtyard no longer exists. The adobe house collapsed during the operation on March 8, and some four days later federals arrived, laced the Yusupovs' new house with ribbon explosives and destroyed all the evidence, thereby ruling out any tests or the possi-bility of an independent inquiry. One important question is: how sure were the soldiers that it was Maskhadov in the cellar?

Some three days before the operation they knew only that an import-ant figure of some description was in this part of Tolstoy-Yurt. Maybe Basayev, maybe Umarov [Doku Umarov, a later President of Ichkeria], or maybe Maskhadov. That was all. By late in the evening of the seventh, however, from tracing the text messages it was evident that, with a high degree of probability, it was Maskhadov living on Suvorov Street. The information was sent to Moscow, and overnight a special Russian unit, answerable directly to the Director of the FSB, flew out. The reason why the culmination of the operation was not entrusted to soldiers of the Special Operations Center of the FSB, which is permanently deployed in Chechnya, was simple: mistrust even within a single Ministry, and particularly of officers who are permanently stationed in Chechnya. The problem of the selling of information is acute.

The special flight of Moscow troops, and the fact that they were waited for in Chechnya for several hours without anybody else moving to the concluding phase of the operation, is further evidence that they knew it was Maskhadov they were dealing with. The Moscow agents who flew to Tolstoy-Yurt were a group of Russia's best commandos whose only task is to kill. And kill they did, because this time the order had come.

What resources did Maskhadov have for defending himself, if, indeed, he was intending to defend himself at all? What was found in the cellar?

It has to be said that there was precious little. He had a typical Chechen array of four assault rifles (between five men). Three of 5.45 mm calibre, and one of 7.62 mm. There were three home-made grenades, and one F1 grenade for blowing himself up. There should also have been the renowned Maskhadov Stechkin, his personal Army officer's pistol. The Stechkin, however, disappeared. We find the papers of the criminal case peppered with the investigators' questions about where the Stechkin had gone. Nobody kept an eye on it at the time.

Death, of course, is no laughing matter, but the morals among the Army in Chechnya, where looting has become ingrained over many years, make it difficult to suppress a wry smile. Even the operation to liquidate Maskhadov was not free of a spot of looting. To put it politely, the Stechkin was filched by the killers. Maskhadov had it when he was in the cellar but after the operation it was nowhere to be found. It's not difficult to imagine the details: the Stechkin is now hanging on a wall, or perhaps it is in a safe, belonging to a member of the FSB's special operations unit, and when he has had a drink or two its new owner shows off his trophy to his comrades-in-arms, or girlfriends, or, heaven knows, perhaps even to his children. The Stechkin will turn up at auction 50 years or so from now. It is the sort of thing that has happened often enough in the past.

So where does that leave us, in September 2005, as a trial begins at which the circumstances of the last months of Maskhadov's life will be under scrutiny, full as they were of peace initiatives, the Internet, and text messages bleeping from morning until night?

Basayev and Sadulayev want to hear nothing about peace. Their answer to the assassination of Maskhadov is only a long war, a parallel clandestine government, and explosions, armed conflict, and people dying on all sides every day.

And against this background, we have the constant bluffing by government officials about how wonderful it is in the newly Chechenised and Kadyrovised Chechnya. Mike Tyson, a semi-naked Miss Sobchak, an aquapark, a Disneyland, free parliamentary elections, Zhirinovsky and the rest of them posing against the backdrop of Grozny to which peace has supposedly returned. In fact they are all in a bunker, in a besieged city within a city, a government complex where they have now even built houses for the bureaucrats so they don't ever have to risk taking a step outside the confines of this stronghold. The reality – not the politicians' virtual reality – is that there is a total absence of even elementary control of the country, and an equally total absence of security for people who have nowhere to run to, and are forced to survive by fair means or foul.

Could not peace have been given a chance?

THE "MARCH 8" CASE: THOSE WITH MASKHADOV WHEN HE WAS LIQUIDATED ARE SENTENCED

December 5, 2005

The Supreme Court of the Chechen Republic has sentenced Vakhid Murdashev to 15 years' imprisonment, Viskhan Khadzhimuratov to seven, Musa Yusupov to six, and Ilias Iriskhanov to five and a half. By recent Chechen standards these sentences are considered light. The young lads the security services seize, torture and force to confess to "terrorism" usually get 17–24 years.

Why this should be one can only guess. In throwing the book at boys nobody knows anything about, judges are taking no risks and ingratiate themselves with the authorities. In the case of Maskhadov's associates the risk is obvious: there are plenty of pro-federal officials in Chechnya who continue to pay Basayev a "resistance levy" to buy their way out of trouble and avoid execution as collaborators.

That, however, is not the main reason. It did not become clear in the course of the trial who actually killed Maskhadov. The state prosecution, without producing a single witness, made public the conclusion of a ballistic test which claimed that Maskhadov was killed by a bullet fired from a Makarov pistol belonging to Khadzhimuratov, Maskhadov's bodyguard and nephew.

Why should the court suppose he was killed by a bullet? The results of the post-mortem were not published, so the cause of death remains unknown and you can bandy about whatever ballistic "evidence" you choose. Khadzhimuratov did not admit responsibility for the killing and the court ended up falling between two stools, apparently accepting the claim that Khadzhimuratov had fired the shot, but not finding him guilty of murder.

The obvious conclusion is that the purpose of this trial was to create a myth about how Maskhadov died. The verdict makes clear what legend was required for public consumption: the federals had virtually nothing to do with the assassination, it was the Chechens themselves who killed their leader. Moreover, it was all within a single family: Maskhadov was killed by his nephew, so if there is to be any settling of scores it will be contained within the family.

Is this what we expected from the Maskhadov trial? Of course not. We expected to learn the truth about his death, but that has been kept secret, so we can look forward to endless rumors, inventions, gossip and myths for years to come, as was the case when Maskhadov's predecessor, Djohar Dudayev, was assassinated.

THE MAN WHO RE-EDUCATED FEMALE SUICIDE BOMBERS

September 21, 2006

On September 13, in a now notorious border checkpoint battle between the Chechen and Ingush militias, the Deputy Commander of Chechnya's OMON Militia special troops, Buvadi Dakhiev, was wounded in the head and died shortly afterwards. The causes of the battle are clear enough and have been much debated and publicised. I want instead to describe some aspects of Buvadi's character which could not be written about while he was alive. It is more than a tribute to the memory of a man who on a number of occasions helped me in my work during the war, at times probably saving my life.

Buvadi was a special person, riven by contradictions and with a split personality. He used to remind me of the monument on Khrushchev's grave in the Novodevichy Monastery cemetery in Moscow, half of which is pitch black, while the other is white as snow.

On the one hand he was an archetypal member of the security services, like so many others in Chechnya, an officer of the pro-Moscow Chechen militia; but he dated from well before the present times, when criminals and former resistance fighters have started running at Kadyrov's beck and call. He was typical of those who opposed President Djohar Dudayev, and from 1995 dedicated himself to serving in the Chechen OMON special operations units, which marked him out as a wholeheartedly pro-Russian officer when Chechnya was only a part of Russia. For this he received medals and the Order of Courage, and was promoted to Lieutenant-Colonel. Buvadi refused to live in Chechnya while Maskhadov and Basayev were in power, and when the Second War began, he was in the foremost ranks of those opposing them.

At times the things he was involved in were extremely cruel. Let us not beat about the bush: those working in the Chechen OMON are not children in ragged trousers sharing sweets. The people who work there do so in order to shoot, and they shoot to kill before someone kills them. The units arrested people who were sometimes never seen again. They beat them, and worse.

My last meeting with Buvadi was in August in Grozny. He wouldn't look me in the eye and bit grimly and guiltily into a watermelon. He was on edge and devoured the red fruit as if he was starving, doing his utmost to move the conversation away from a Chechen student who had been "swept" by his units and was thought to have been in their custody before simply disappearing. Now Alikhan Kuloyev's mother, Aminat, an old-age pensioner, had joined the ranks of other mothers frantically searching Chechnya, and was begging anyone she met to at least put in a word with Buvadi. Perhaps he would tell her where her only son was.

I did put in a word, but Buvadi was saying nothing. He had nothing to say. There had been that student and now there wasn't. Buvadi said, "He wasn't guilty of anything."

"Well, why hasn't he been released?"

Buvadi said nothing, tearing at the melon's skin.

On the other hand, Buvadi could just as often be kind as cruel, where many others were never kind. Everyone working in the Chechen security agencies can be divided into those who think before they kill, and those who long ago ceased to think. Buvadi did at least try to establish who he had in his sights, and that saved the lives of many, including some who would ordinarily have seemed doomed under the rules of the Chechen meat-grinder.

A few people in Chechnya knew that Buvadi tried to rescue the widows of commanders, women who were supposed to be slaughtered out of hand as "black widows," likely future suicide bombers. How did he rescue them? After the widows were abducted, Buvadi would take them to his own home, which was completely against the rules.

And then what? They were in a kind of custody, a kind of quarantine. Buvadi would return home from work and talk to them for nights at a time. His house resembled a barracks, and Buvadi would hold women there for many weeks who, without any exaggeration, were potential suicide bombers. They were entirely ready for the job because, before they ended up with Buvadi, they had been trained by their husbands and their comrades in the handling of explosives and driving a bus, so that when the order was given they would crash it into whatever they were instructed to.

"Why did you take them in?"

"They all had children."

"And did their children live with you?"

"Yes, they were here with their children. I wanted to see whether they were lost souls, whether they were still capable of bringing up their children, or were out of it already."

In fact, none of the black widows left his house as a lost soul. The result of this odd re-educative work by Special Operations Agent Buvadi among the most spurned section of Chechen society was that mothers, often under-age mothers, were saved to bring up their own children. Buvadi's processing really helped them to understand that their first duty was to be a mother.

"They would start by saying, 'Just let me die for my husband.' They wouldn't accept a crust of bread from me," Buvadi told me, "because it was infidel bread. They wouldn't touch their children, as if they didn't exist. They would just sit in their hijab as if they were dead, and that was it."

"And then what happened?"

"Later they would talk, and after two or three days they would start to eat. A few even took off the hijab and just wore a headscarf in the Chechen manner. There was one who robbed us – she was a real Wahhabi! – but she was the only one. Later, when they had come back to life, I would fix them up with somewhere to live, either abroad or here in Russia. I looked for relatives they could live with, as far away as possible from big cities. I made phone calls, got agreements."

I asked him about his motives: why did he do all this?

"What do they know, these girls?" Buvadi explained. "At their age we were in the Pioneers, going to Pioneer camps, going to the cinema, eating ice-cream. They have had none of that and that's how they have ended up in this state. I feel guilty about them."

"What is your conclusion about suicide bombers? Are they a lost cause?"

"No, for most becoming a Wahhabi is not the end of the story. It's just that their empty minds have been messed with."

I won't name the names of young widows Buvadi saved. The point is that they know themselves who they owe their second life to. Having been sent far away from the Caucasus by Buvadi, they carried on phoning him, asking his advice on how to deal with particular situations, for example, right up until September 13 this year.

I think back to 2002, or perhaps the very end of 2001. It is the depths of winter and there is shooting and explosions, but at least Kadyrov Junior is still standing quietly in the corner while the grown-ups are talking. Grozny is teeming with underground jamaats, most of them consisting of people who are just kids aged between 14 and 16.

"I feel so sorry for them," Buvadi told me. On more than one occasion he was in charge of operations to eradicate them. "We surround them. They know they're about to die, and I can hear what they're talking about over my radio."

"Why are you sorry for them?"

"It's the same as with the black widows. They've never had a life, never seen anything. I feel personally guilty that their childhood has been taken from them. How many times they have asked me, shouting from houses we had surrounded, 'Uncle, let us die!' I let them blow themselves up, because I know what would happen to them if we took them alive. There have been occasions when I passed on their final words to their parents."

For some reason, this past August we spent far more time than usual recalling stories about the boys from the jamaats he had killed. Buvadi was glad that at that time the idiotic law had not yet been passed which forbade the return of their bodies.

"I gave their bodies to the parents myself. How could I do that now?"

In 2002 or 2003 we were discussing who he thought the Wahhabis were, and what should be done with them. At that time pro-Russian Chechens had only dreadful things to say about the Wahhabis, and killed them without a moment's hesitation. Buvadi, however, took the liberty of saying out loud:

"There were some villains among them, but some were completely pure people. We killed them all indiscriminately."

I remember exactly where it was he told me that: the second floor of the "white box," the headquarters of the Grozny OMON Unit, in the office of the Commander, Mussa Khazimakhomadov, who was later killed. There were drunken officers from the Russian intelligence agencies, staggering around incoherently with the vacant eyes of killers. They were from the death squads of the Special Purposes Center of the FSB, and the GRU – Buvadi's colleagues in the war. He set out some snacks, some bottles, and was telling this to them too.

"Pure people? How can they be pure if, as people say . . ." I repeated something monstrous about the doings of those they called Wahhabis.

Buvadi stopped me.

"My brother was a Wahhabi. He was completely pure. I never met anyone so pure before or after him. He was pure in every respect, in his thoughts and his deeds. He didn't drink, didn't smoke, didn't swear, did nothing evil."

"Did he try to recruit you?"

"Never. He never tried to impose anything on me."

"Where is he now?"

"He was killed."

After a long pause, smiling, with immense pride, even joy, as if he was telling me his brother had been awarded the Nobel Prize, he said,

"He died in battle. As was right."

Those who were eating and drinking at that moment, stopped. Showing that kind of pride in a Wahhabi in the center of the anti-Wahhabi movement he might quickly have followed his brother.

Then it was the turn of Kadyrov Junior. How he hated Buvadi! He kept trying to nail him as a resistance fighter. "You are helping them!" For the whole summer he was trying to get Buvadi kicked out of the OMON, to drive him out of Chechnya. That was when the disgusting process of "Chechenising" the war was instigated, and being vile started to be considered as honorable as being courageous. People would remind Buvadi, this soldier to the marrow of his bones, about his brother, and accuse him of being soft on the fighters because of his efforts to redeem black widows.

But Buvadi never did cease to be proud of his Wahhabi brother's purity, or of his private campaign to rescue mothers for their children. He never even attempted to hush it up. A lot of people in Chechnya are today in Buvadi's situation, with brothers on opposing sides. The civil war so undermined family morality that it became acceptable to publicly denounce your brothers if they failed to surrender to the right flag.

There are two versions of how Buvadi died. The "black" version asserts that he came to a place where Chechen and Ingush militiamen were having a violent disagreement, punched an Ingush militiaman, and was promptly shot. I don't believe that. He might have shot someone, but I don't see him punching anyone in the face. That was not his style, and he would in any case have known only too well what would come next in an argument between the two Vainakh peoples.

The second version is that Buvadi was not there when the alteration started, but was nearby and moved in to calm things down. He got out of his car, tried to persuade them to cool it, and somebody fired a round at him from an assault rifle.

I think that is far more probable, and would like to believe that Buvadi was his own man to the last, trying to prevent bloodshed. I know he was an expert in firing at living targets, but I believe Buvadi nevertheless spent his last moment in his white half. "Everybody is completely fed up with the war," he told me a month before he died. "We should all just make peace."

There is a desperate shortage of men like him in official Chechnya today: not angels, but human beings who agonise and suffer. In Chechnya there are ever more people who are as rudimentary as amoebas, for whom killing is no different to sipping a glass of tea. Amoebas are incapable of understanding another person who has been declared an enemy simply because he lives his life in a different way.

What does "understanding" mean in Chechnya? It means, not to kill. That is how you recognise tolerance, and for the present there is no other way. Even now there are those who continue to believe that playing at amnesty games is an indication of tolerance on Kadyrov's part as he supposedly saves fighters' souls and preserves the nation. Stuff and nonsense! They are binding people together through even more bloodshed, and see that as fettering them to their cause. Buvadi wanted to bind people by offering them a chance to live without his involvement. That was fundamental. He gave them a second life, although his job was to terminate their first. He gave it from the goodness of his heart, and there is no one to replace him.

The last time I saw him, we took a long time saying our goodbyes.

"I hope they at least have a rifle in the house where you are going to sleep tonight," Buvadi grumbled.

"There is no rifle there. I don't want one," I muttered. "I'm tired of guns. We have had them for seven years already. Are you really not tired of them yourself?"

Buvadi said nothing, but I felt his solidarity. He too was fed up with guns, with the constant fear. He was terribly weary of never being parted from his weapon, sleeping in combat fatigues, and living in a house that resembled a barracks. They say it is when people grow weary that they die.

Part II: The Protagonists

CHECHNYA IS THE PRICE YOU PAY TO BE SECRETARY-GENERAL OF THE UN

May 21, 2001

The past week has brought striking evidence of how enthusiastically we have got stuck into bringing back the Brezhnev era.

The influential Human Rights Watch group timed publication of its report about just one of the hundreds of civilian mass graves in Chechnya to coincide with the arrival in Moscow of UN Secretary-General Kofi Annan in an attempt to demand support from the international community, and in particular, of course, from the United Nations, for a proper inquiry. A great barrage of irate Kremlin comment, refutation and repudiation ensued.

Why were the state authorities squirming so nervously on their chairs, as if someone had put drawing pins on them? Can Secretary-General Annan's visit be seen as a drawing pin? And why, finally, did the UN's top diplomat remain silent – disgracefully so for someone in his position – when at least some human sympathy was called for, 'and a few words, even if couched in diplomatic terms, at least referring to the need to rein in the ongoing war crimes in Chechnya?

There is no doubt that we have observed the conclusion of a business deal on a podium of human bones. It was the signing of a contract between two major players, the Kremlin and the most senior official of the United Nations. So why all the edginess? Why this nervous burst of commentary from Putin's court liars? It was all perfectly logical: the Russian side was not completely sure it had the upper hand and was very concerned that in the wake of the Human Rights Watch report the deal might be called off at the last moment.

But first things first. Let us look at the main points of the report, a highly detailed, almost forensic document about a mass grave discovered in January–February this year not far from Grozny and just across the road from Khankala, the main Russian military base in Chechnya. A total of 51 bodies were unearthed, and the way the mass grave was identified is entirely typical. The information about the first of the bodies, that of Adam Chimayev who disappeared on December 3, 2000, was obtained by the Chimayev family after a commercial deal: the relatives paid an officer who had been guarding Adam while he was held at the military base the rouble equivalent of $3,000 for information about the location of the burial site. After payment had been made, the family was allowed to collect the body.

The news rapidly spread through Chechnya, and the relatives of other Chechens who had vanished without trace flooded into Dachnoye. As a result 19 bodies were identified, leaving 34 unidentified. On March 10, 2001, without warning, the unidentified bodies were reburied by military personnel, who failed to retain biological specimens as is required in such cases. In its report, Human Rights Watch cites numerous accounts by witnesses about the behaviour of the Prosecutor's Office and the relevant Russian government and presidential institutions at that time. It characterises it as "unsatisfactory."

In essence, the behaviour of the Russian authorities proved that they wanted no investigation of the mass grave; they flatly denied it was anything to do with military personnel. But the human rights activists have also put the international community on notice for turning a blind eye to the Dachnoye scandal. The USA, the European Union, the European Parliament and the Organization for Security and Co-operation in Europe (OSCE) in effect did everything they could to hush the story up. Alvaro Gil-Robles, the Council of Europe's Commissioner for Human Rights, who was flying on February 27–29 on an inspection tour of Chechnya immediately after the discovery of the graves, did not even visit Dachnoye to meet the relatives of those who had been identified.

The report concludes that it is essential for the inquiry into the mass grave to be resumed, and that a special international commission should be created as a matter of urgency. Its first task will be to exhume the 34 hastily reburied unidentified bodies under the supervision of the International Red Cross, the OSCE Support Group, experts from the Council of Europe, and representatives of the UN Commission on Human Rights.

In order to understand what was behind the reactions of the Kremlin and Secretary-General Annan to all this, let us take a look at what is going on in the United Nations in spring 2001, primarily as regards Kofi Annan himself. We need to establish whether it is in principle possible to have an international protectorate in Chechnya under the aegis of the United Nations, and what the powers of the Secretary-General are.

It is worth mentioning that before anything was heard of the Human Rights Watch report, or any scandal had been raised in relation to it, *Novaya gazeta* was already trying to get answers to these questions in New York and, moreover, directly from UN headquarters. We were doing so in highly diplomatic, terribly behind-the-scenes centers of power, namely, the Security Council's lounge where so-called international humanitarian policy is cooked up. Needless to say, *Novaya gazeta*'s correspondent was conducted to this privileged enclave, which is shielded from prying eyes, and introduced to the right people "unofficially." I am immensely grateful to the person who acceded to my request, because he knew exactly the questions I wanted to raise and the real purpose of my raid on the Security Council: to discover what the United Nations could do to resolve the dreadful crisis in Chechnya.

My view, arrived at after discussing dozens of approaches to a peaceful settlement of the conflict with hundreds of people living in Chechnya – ordinary people and people in various official positions, people in Grozny and in villages, in the valleys and the mountains – is clear: given the way the situation has evolved up to the present, it is impossible to get by without an international protectorate. Third-party involvement is imperative. It is needed to temporarily separate the parties to the conflict, and today these parties are not by any means the resistance fighters and federal forces, as official Kremlin propaganda would have us believe. The conflict is between the federals and the civilian population. Intervention is needed to cool passions as far as possible, and to move towards a softening of positions.

But let us return to the UN in Manhattan. Most of the UN Security Council diplomats I questioned agreed that it would be practically impossible to get a resolution passed. Before the Security Council can mandate peacekeeping troops, the consent of both sides in a conflict must be obtained. In this case, the civilian population of Chechnya, daily bearing the brunt of violations of their human rights, cannot be recognised under UN definitions as such a party to a conflict. As for obtaining the consent of the Russian Government, that is out of the question.

There is, however, another approach for obtaining a UN mandate for peace enforcement, and it was under this protocol that events in Iraq and Yugoslavia proceeded, which later entailed major unpleasantness for the United States when it lost its place on the UN Commission on Human Rights. If we could have the Chechen crisis considered in terms of peace enforcement, the Security Council diplomats assured me, there would be no need to obtain the consent of the parties to the conflict.

But Iraq and Yugoslavia are not Russia. They are only members of the United Nations, while Russia is a permanent member of the Security Council and holds a veto. A decision under Article 7 [which covers crimes against humanity] is taken by the Security Council, and this meant that while such proposals could be introduced, the result, after protracted discussion, would be a foregone conclusion dependent on the viewpoint of the Russian Government. Most of the diplomats advised me that UN peacekeeping in Chechnya was out of the question, and that had to be faced as a given fact. The only means of influencing the situation and finding a way out of the deadlock would be the personal intervention of the Secretary-General of the UN.

So then we turned to Kofi Annan. Could we pin our hopes on him? Back then, in late April, Security Council diplomats already foresaw events taking the turn we have seen in Moscow in the last last few days: Kofi Annan, they felt, turns a blind eye to the human rights situation in Chechnya and, accordingly, also to the Human Rights Watch report. These, incidentally, were high-ranking diplomats working immediately under Kofi Annan, and they assured me that today he does not want to focus on the suffering in a tiny spot on the planet which is situated on the territory of the Russian Federation. After all, his prospects of getting a second term as Secretary-General are nil without Russia's help.

What does all this add up to? There are occasions in life when everybody distances themselves from you. When the going gets really tough, even close friends slip away. You find you have no real allies, so you just have to go it alone. This is exactly what is happening with Chechnya: we must stop the war ourselves. Nobody is going to help us. Remember, we have been here before. It was the tacit willingness of the international community not to challenge the authenticity of the Chernokozovo "model" pre-trial detention facility in Chechnya, which gradually acquired the status of a sham Potemkin Village for receiving international VIPs, that led to later disgraceful developments. By the dozen, and later in their hundreds, people began not to be imprisoned but simply to disappear, after which their bodies might be found only by chance, buried in unspeakable circumstances.

Even if Moscow gives in to the pressure from Human Rights Watch and agrees to resume the inquiry into the mass grave in Dachnoye, it too will go the way of Chernokozovo. No matter how obscene it may sound, Dachnoye would become a model mass grave. The state authorities would find a way to wriggle off the hook. Before you knew it, foreign journalists and parliamentarians would be transported in droves to visit Dachnoye. That would be the end result of the report Human Rights Watch produced with the intention of putting pressure on the Secretary-General of the United Nations. Sad but true.

Meanwhile, what is going on in Chechnya? More of the same: a wave of atrocities, lies and terror. There are rumors that on May 13 in Urus Martan, Arbi Barayev himself – a field commander and brutal murderer – was detained but released the same day by the Commandant of the Urus Martan District, citing orders from his superiors. On May 14, also in Urus Martan, an unmarked infantry fighting vehicle drove up to the home of the Bardukayev family. Six men had been taken from this house during a security sweep in January. Three were released shortly afterwards, but for almost half a year the family knew nothing about the fate of the others. The officer who climbed down from the vehicle, using exactly the same methods as Arbi Barayev (you remember the severed heads of Western engineers lying in the snow?), showed photographs of the bodies of the Bardukayev brothers to their relatives, who confirmed their identity. The officer demanded $1,500 to disclose where they were buried. Exactly the same routine as with the body of Adam Chimayev in Dachnoye. Only here fewer bodies were involved, so the price was lower: not $3,000, only $1,500.

A FUGITIVE FROM HIMSELF. WHY THE INTERVIEW WAS CENSORED

May 21, 2001

Man as he is rarely suits us. Like life itself. You keep wanting to substitute what you would like to believe for reality and either view it through rose-tinted spectacles or give it horns and a tail, depending on your personal inclinations.

Aslan Maskhadov today is a virtual person. He is neither really there, nor not there. Society has seen and heard nothing of him for a long time, so when the President of independent Ichkeria surfaces out of the blue with something to say, the majority take exception. The Maskhadov of late May 2001 is very different from the Maskhadov of the beginning of the war, let alone the President of Chechnya in 1997–8. Today he is an irreversibly exhausted, ageing officer, boxed into a corner, who understands a lot but can't do much about it. He no longer has all the information at his fingertips and his conclusions tend to be vague. He is trying to retain his place in the history of his people but, tragically, does not know how to go about it. He is a fugitive from his former self.

But then, so are we all, we members of society who want our information objective. Some are keen to defend today's Maskhadov, others to act as his prosecutors. The former paint him in rosy colors, while the latter portray him with scary horns; what they should do is just listen and take in everything he says in order to know the real situation, to understand what "they" on the other side are thinking, and how deep the gulf between us is.

As you may have guessed, there has been a debate at *Novaya gazeta* about whether this interview could or should be published. What people wanted to believe outweighed reality, and the text was emasculated. It was argued on the one hand that Maskhadov does himself no favors in the interview and we don't want to make things worse for him by publishing it.

On the other hand the interview was seen as straightforward mischief-making by both interviewer and interviewee, because publication would lead immediately to sanctions from the state authorities on the grounds of seditious libel. Russia's leaders have got so carried away by their own black propaganda, the argument went, that they no longer want to know the true situation in Chechnya and prefer to stick with the "Maskhadov with horns" invented by their own propaganda.

It was decided that the following paragraph should be cut from the interview. We offer it here instead, outside the interview, along with comments which would have been impractical within the context of the interview itself.

Neither Chechens nor the Chechen leaders would ever give orders, no matter what political benefit it might bring, to shoot their own citizens. It is contrary to our whole way of thinking, especially in our own village, especially our own relatives. That is the sort of thing you in Russia are capable of. We are not. As an excuse for military aggression, or in order to dub someone a terrorist, you in Russia can calmly give orders to blow up multi-storey apartment blocks full of your own citizens or commit all manner of terrorist acts in crowded places. These are timed to take place immediately before the opening of the Parliamentary Assembly of the Council of Europe, sessions of the Organization for Security and Co-operation in Europe, and so on. Our culture is completely opposed to that sort of thing. The Chechen President does not wage war against his own people; neither does he wage war against the women and children of Russia. It is the President of the Russian Federation who indulges in that

sort of thing, and takes satisfaction from it. Yes, satisfaction. We
are fighting aggressors, mercenaries, contract soldiers, your
General Shamanovs [accused of war crimes] and Colonel
Budanovs [a rapist and murderer, supported by Shamanov but
convicted after a long press campaign]. Those are the people we
are fighting, and will continue to fight until we have destroyed
them without pity.

What is this? Typical war paranoia? Maskhadov is profoundly affected
by this, perhaps to the exclusion of all else. The censored paragraph
only emphasises, however, the tragic nature of a situation where, on
the other side of the conflict, the federals are no less paranoid in their
determination to believe Maskhadov is the devil incarnate. Meanwhile,
what is to become of those caught in the crossfire? The tragedy of
Chechnya grinds on, and until we stop lying we are all complicit in
the persecution of the guiltless.

[The agreed text of the interview with Aslan Maskhadov now follows:]

ASLAN MASKHADOV: "WE TOO ARE WONDERING
HOW TO BREAK THE DEADLOCK"
May 28, 2001

Our country is limping into the third successive summer of the Second
Chechen War. There are thousands of victims on both sides, and perhaps
one million damaged souls. Why is this war lasting so long? Are we
really to believe that a large, well-equipped army continues to pursue
a dozen field commanders through little Chechnya and for some reason
can't catch them? With the coming of spring the television brainwashing
will start up once again, explaining how it is "leaf cover" which is the
main obstacle to bringing the war to a victorious conclusion. As a
country we have plainly lost our way.

Here we offer the viewpoint of the other side: an interview with
Aslan Maskhadov, given at a time when every highly placed official in
Moscow would claim it was impossible to meet him, in the very area

where "everything is under control." That is, in the very thick of the federal troops' fortified positions.

What do you think comes next? How can the war be ended?
We are also wondering about this. Where do we go from here? How do we get out of the current stalemate? After all, we too recognise that there is a stalemate, and that the war is just useless, senseless slaughtering of each other – murder carried out with exceptional brutality, fuelled by extraordinary hatred.

There is no point trying to pretend that the military operation has ended, let alone been brought to a successful conclusion, and that now the FSB under the leadership of Patrushev will proceed to catch terrorists. That is laughable. The outcome of the military operation is that Marshal Sergeyev, the Russian Minister of Defence, has been removed from his post. Victors are not sacked, they are promoted.

Russia has lost the war. That much is clear even to the hawks in the Kremlin and to Russia's leaders. The victorious blitzkrieg which the generals promised Putin has not come to pass. The Russian Army is exhausted, demoralised and disintegrating.

I have worn a soldier's uniform for 25 years. I served in the Soviet Army, helped raise its fighting capability, was proud of it, and put my soul into it. I too wonder where all these psychopathic Kvashnins [General, Chief of GHQ] and Budanovs in this Army – which, at one time, we were all proud of – have come from. Where have all the criminals who serve in it appeared from? The labor camps? Are they contract soldiers? Are they looters?

Well, where have they come from?
An enormous military machine is now beyond the control of its generals. So what is to be done? Moscow has started flirting with "good" Chechen field commanders and "bad" Chechen field commanders, and is openly talking about who it is prepared to conduct negotiations with and who it isn't. It is recruiting to its ranks puppets and traitors to their country.

From the experience of the last Chechen War we know that this is a dead end. Remember the incident with the former Minister of State Security, Geriskhanov. Anybody, no matter how great a celebrity he might be, commanding officer or field commander, has only to cross the line of what is permissible to find his status has changed to that of a traitor. He crosses that line today, and tomorrow he finds he has no one behind him, he is on his own. When that happens the traitor is no longer any use to anybody. Neither to us nor to our opponents.

How do you regard the possibility of peace negotiations conducted by the federal side with Field Commander Gelayev? You must know that recently the federal side has been publicising precisely such negotiations. Presidential Representative Victor Kazantsev made an announcement about it.

Gelayev, you say? Well, what of him? Anybody, including Gelayev, who oversteps the mark of the permissible must expect the same fate as befell Geriskhanov. For the Chechen side it is quite clear the war needs to be stopped. Chechens do not need it – it is mainly civilians who are being killed – but we are also aware of what awaits our people if we do not persist, if we give in, if we are brought to our knees. One Russian general, I do not know his name, said, "We need to destroy them all, down to the five-year-olds, then enclose them behind barbed wire and re-educate them." I have heard other things said: "We should pass them all through filtration points, from ten to sixty years old." That is, break everyone's ribs and cripple everybody. Even "intellectual" people have said, "We need to build a Great Wall of China along the Baku highway."

That is the fate facing my people. God forbid that we should lose. In order to save our people from genocide our only option is to defend ourselves. Only that. And defend ourselves we shall.

Who, in your view, is the principal enemy of peace negotiations between you and the federal side? Are negotiations possible at all? What might they yield?

My representatives are constantly putting out feelers to the Russian leaders, to the top officials, and my people tell them, "There's been enough fighting. It's time to sit down at the negotiating table." Immediately we hear triumphalist yelling: "What do you mean negotiations?!

Negotiations spell political death for us! How could we explain it to our people?" and so on.

My representatives then say, "But the war has to be stopped. Do you not realize that?" They reply, "Yes, the war needs to be stopped." And the next question is, "But how?"

... In my view the overriding problem is that there is no official in the Kremlin we can talk to soberly and reasonably. Not even about the interests of Russia, about things that are primarily of benefit to Russia. You need to understand, there is nobody there to negotiate with!

But do you believe that negotiations are nevertheless possible? Or has the train already left the station and all that remains is for you to fight it out with each other to the bitter end?

Negotiations are both possible and inevitable. Wars are ended only by negotiation, and I am sure that is how this war will be ended too. Our proposals for a peace settlement are clear to everybody: sit down at the negotiating table without any preconditions and there, at the table, decide what to do next, how to improve relations. I believe it is crucial to found our mutual relations on the basis of the Peace Treaty signed on May 12, 1997. The second point in it states, "Mutual relations between the Russian Federation and the Chechen Republic will be built on the universal norms and principles of international law." That is the most important requirement. Lack of clarity about mutual relations is the cause and excuse for all sorts of provocations and wars.

This defines my approach to the supposed negotiations and contacts with Nemtsov [Leader of the Union of Right Forces political faction]. I know nothing about them. I have given no authorisation for them to anybody for the very good reason that you cannot conduct negotiations with Nemtsov if he would like to build a Great Wall of China on the Baku highway.

What do you know about the causes of the recent much-publicised murder of Adam Deniev in Avtury? From early spring this year Deniev was presenting himself as the Deputy Head of Akhmat-hadji Kadyrov's Chechen

Administration, but after his death even members of the personnel depart-
ment of the Administration were unable to find documentation of any such
appointment.

I have no idea whose deputy Deniev was supposed to be among that
lot. It is of no interest to us. The first possibility that comes to mind
is that, realising the war is already lost, the Russian intelligence services
are doing away with unwanted witnesses, as happened in the last war.

Another possibility: Deniev had 11 blood feud enemies in his native
village of Avtury alone. They were likely to take revenge on him at any
moment.

The Chechen side had no particular need of Deniev's murder,
although our intelligence services have him listed as a traitor and for
that he would at some point have had to stand trial before a sharia
court, in accordance with the Criminal Code of the Chechen Republic.

I see no sense in shooting at these people from the shadows or carrying out terrorist attacks on them. As regards the financial dimension,
which the Kremlin has been making great play of, I have no knowledge
that Deniev was preventing financial resources reaching our side.

One other recent accusation levelled against you is that you were involved
in the brutal murder of a shepherd and three of his assistants on April 17
in your native village of Alleroy in Kurchaloy District.

I did receive operational intelligence that a reconnaissance group of
Russian troops brutally murdered a shepherd and his three assistants
in broad daylight on April 17, 2001 in Alleroy. They were murdered
between noon and 4:00 p.m. hours beside the ravine where their bodies
were discovered, and there were numerous prints in the mud from
soldiers' boots and gumboots. It appears that before they were shot
they were forced to lie face down on the ground, and afterwards shot
once more in the head.

The names of the murder victims are Khozhakhmed Alsultanov,
a shepherd, 44, the brother of Saidakhmet Alsultanov who was a
bodyguard of the President of Chechnya assassinated in 1998;
Khozhakhmed's son, Islam; and two nephews, Shamkhan and Shakhid
Umarkhadzhiev.

Our preliminary investigation has revealed that on the afternoon of April 17 Kadyrov's elder brother-in-law was celebrating a housewarming. Kadyrov also attended, with numerous bodyguards. Russian reconnaissance troops were observed in the south-east and north-east outskirts of the village and we imagine that the group which shot the shepherds did so at that time.

A WITNESS FOR THE PROSECUTION BECOMES A WITNESS FOR THE DEFENCE. THE ZAKAYEV CASE: THE LATEST SENSATION IN A LONDON COURT

July 28, 2003

There were few people in Court 3 of Bow Street Magistrates Court, London on the morning of July 24, 2003. Although hearings were resuming in the case of The Government of the Russian Federation versus Akhmed Zakayev, the Russian side had already indicated that the day would be of little interest, as they always do when there is to be cross-questioning of a witness for Zakayev's defence. This time there was a noticeable lack of members of our Prosecutor-General's Office, who are usually only too eager to come to London. Sergey Fridinsky, Deputy Public Prosecutor for the Southern Federal Region, charged with ensuring the extradition of Maskhadov's Special Representative, had decided not to fly in. Igor Mednik, Investigator of the Southern District Prosecutor's Office and second-in-command of the Zakayev case, had also decided to ignore Zakayev's defence witnesses.

How unwise. Mednik and Fridinsky would have been surprised to discover that a witness for the prosecution, a supposed victim of Zakayev, was instead appearing before Judge Timothy Workman as a witness for Zakayev's defence. In the case materials sent from Moscow and prepared by Investigator Mednik, Duk-Vakha Dushuyev figures as Zakayev's former bodyguard, who in December 2002 testified that in January 1996, on the orders of the individual whose extradition is sought, his other bodyguards had taken hostage two Orthodox priests, in Chechnya on a peacekeeping mission, in order to hold them to ransom. These were Father Anatoly Chistousov, who subsequently died

in captivity, and Father Sergius Zhigulin, whose monastic name is
Father Philip and from whom the court had already heard evidence.

Background

> Akhmed Zakayev, born 1959 in Kazakhstan, graduated from
> the Department of Choreography of the Grozny College of
> Culture and Enlightenment and the Voronezh State Insti-
> tute of Arts. From 1981 to 1990, actor with the Khanpasha
> Nuradilov Grozny Drama Theatre.
>
> From 1991, Chairman of the Union of Theatre Workers of
> Chechnya and Board Member of the UTW of Russia.
>
> From 1994, Minister of Culture of Chechnya.
>
> From 1995, from the beginning of the First Chechen War,
> Commander of the Urus Martan Front. Subsequently
> Brigadier-General, Aide to the President of Ichkeria for
> National Security, member of the delegation preparing the
> Khasavyurt Agreements [which ended the First Chechen
> War in 1996].
>
> Stood in 1997 for the presidency of Chechnya.
>
> From 1998, Deputy Prime Minister. From the start of the Second
> Chechen War, commander of a special operations brigade.
>
> In March 2000, wounded and evacuated from Chechnya.
>
> From 2001, Special Representative of President Aslan
> Maskhadov.

A request to Interpol for Zakayev's extradition was issued by the Russian
Prosecutor-General's Office. This led to his arrest for the first time on
October 30, 2002 in Copenhagen. On December 3, 2002 he was freed
by the Danish courts, which refused extradition on the grounds of inadequate evidence. On December 5, 2002 Zakayev arrived in London, where
he was again arrested at Heathrow Airport but released on bail three
hours later. After a number of technical sessions, the hearing of the case
began at Bow Street Magistrates Court in London on June 9, 2003.

*   *   *

A short Chechen advances towards the witness box to the right of the judge. His legs are unnaturally straight and he is forcing his recalcitrant feet forward, trying not to look at anybody and doing his best to conceal the difficulty he has in walking. This is Duk-Vakha Dushuyev. Though we are in London, the Second Chechen War has trained me to recognise the problem immediately: Duk-Vakha walks exactly the way many other men in Chechnya do who have survived the "anti-terrorist operation" but been left with limbs first fractured and then badly set.

"What do I have to swear on?" the witness asks the translator, reaching the stand, and his smile doesn't seem real. It is mask-like. "On the Bible or the Quran?"

"As you please."

Having taken the oath, Duk-Vakha explains that he was born in 1968, so he is only 35, although he looks nearer 50.

Barrister Edward Fitzgerald, QC, begins the cross-examination for Zakayev's defence:

"Did you testify against Mr Zakayev on December 2, 2002?"

"Yes."

"Is this the testimony?"

Duk-Vakha is shown the case materials sent to London by the Prosecutor-General's Office and confirms to the court that this is the record of his own questioning in Grozny by Junior Judicial Counsellor Konstantin Krivorotov, Investigator of Particularly Serious Cases of the Chechen Prosecutor's Office. It reads:

"In approximately October 1996 I learned that it would be possible to become a bodyguard in the Ministry of Culture of the Chechen Republic. For approximately four months I took shifts guarding the building of the Ministry of Culture. In approximately February 1997 (name obliterated) invited me to work as Zakayev's bodyguard. I agreed and from February 1997 to February 2000 was beside Zakayev virtually all the time. On one of Zakayev's visits to Urus Martan, I was tasked with accompanying him together with (obliterated). Even before this I had observed a white metal chain worn by (obliterated) on his trousers. I asked him where he got this chain, to which (obliterated) replied that he had taken it from an Orthodox priest who had worn an Orthodox cross on it. (Obliterated) told me that in 1995 two priests had arrived in Urus Martan to negotiate the release of Russian servicemen. Zakayev ordered that the priests should be kidnapped with the aim of obtaining ransom of $500,000 to finance weapons and equipment for the resistance fighters.

"Carrying out Zakayev's orders, (obliterated) recruited five or six members of Zakayev's bodyguard to take part in the kidnapping. In order to implement the plan successfully (obliterated) himself changed clothes and had his subordinates change into militia uniforms. I asked (obliterated) who could pay such a huge amount for freeing the priests, to which I received the reply that the Pope was prepared to pay $1 million, and also $500,000 had been promised by [Russian Orthodox] Patriarch Alexiy II. I understood from his account that Zakayev failed to obtain the ransom. From the beginning of the counter-terrorist operation, that is from 1999, Zakayev was in charge of the so-called Chernorechiye Front which offered armed resistance to the Armed Forces of the Russian Federation on the approaches to Grozny. During that period I was constantly beside Zakayev. We offered armed resistance to Russian troops until February 2000 when there was a mass retreat from Grozny. At that time Zakayev was paralysed. That is where I saw Zakayev for the last time."

"Yes, that is my testimony."

"You said then that Mr Zakayev gave orders to kidnap two priests?"

"Yes, I did."

"Is that the truth?"

"No, it is not true."

"So why did you do that?"

"I was forced to."

"But why? What preceded this?"

"I lived in Grozny. Some time in November 2002 I and a comrade were stopped at a checkpoint. We showed our documents. Two armoured military vehicles were standing nearby. Armed men in masks jumped out of them, pinioned us, not explaining anything, handcuffed us, put bags over our heads, and threw us into the vehicles. One of the soldiers sat on me and they took us off. We drove for 20 to 25 minutes."

"Where did they take you?"

"I don't know exactly, but I think it was Khankala. There I was lifted by the arms and dragged for some 30 metres. They told me to raise my legs, threw me into a pit and sealed it with a metal lid. They kept me there for about six days."

"Were you interrogated during this time?"

"Yes, every day."

"By whom?"

"I do not know exactly – I had a hood on my head the whole time – but they were Russians. Then I discovered they were from the FSB. I was dragged out of the pit and led to some premises. At the first interrogation they warned me that I should not use the words, 'I don't know' or 'No' because if I did they would immediately kill me."

"Did they know you were acquainted with Zakayev?"

"Yes. They told me to tell them how I had fought with Zakayev in Dagestan, and also in the Islamic Jamaat battalion which Zakayev commanded. 'You cut the heads off Russian soldiers!' When I said that had not happened, they said, 'What difference does it make?' and began their torture."

"How were you tortured?"

"With electricity, and they kicked me, and probably used truncheons. I could no longer see what with. At one of the interrogations they asked whether I knew Zakayev's telephone number. I said no. Zakayev was at that time already under arrest in Denmark. They told me that they had telephone equipment and the telephone number. They tied me to the chair, attached something to my feet, one dialled a number saying this was a call to my friend in Copenhagen, and the electricity started. That went on every day. When this procedure ended they threw me back into the pit, and I was there the whole time."

"In November?"

"Yes, it was already winter. It was cold. The pit was too small to stand up in. Your head was pressing against the metal hatch, and you also couldn't sit – there was water on the ground. Eventually I told them I would do anything they wanted. I could no longer stand the torture. You have to understand, I am human. Please understand."

There is a shocked silence in the court. Everybody is motionless. The judge is no longer shuffling papers in front of him and, like everybody else, is looking directly at Duk-Vakha. Does he not believe him?

"They told me to sign a statement that Zakayev had ordered his bodyguards to kidnap priests. I told them, 'I didn't know Zakayev then and I don't know what he did then.' They said, 'That doesn't matter. We know. All you have to do is sign.' They warned me that if I should ever think of withdrawing my testimony, 'We will skin you alive.' Then they drove me to the FSB's Chechen headquarters in the center of Grozny. There, for the first time, they took the handcuffs off and the hood off my head. I signed what they gave me."

"Including the bit about the Pope?"

"Yes."

"While you were signing were you being filmed with a video camera?"

"They told me beforehand to learn by heart the text they gave me to sign. They warned me not to hesitate in front of the camera when they started asking questions. I would be pretending to reply. They led me into a room. There were seven or eight soldiers there and two civilians. One of them introduced himself to me as being from NTV, from the program *Top Secret*."

"All this took place in the FSB building in Grozny?"

"Yes."

"Where were you taken after the recording?"

"To prison in Grozny, but first to the court. They organised documents of some sort. I was in a very bad state, completely beaten up, covered in bruises, but the judge (in the Staropromyslovsky District Court) did not ask me anything, he just placed me under arrest for 10 days, to give time for my injuries to heal. After that they took me to the prison, but they wouldn't accept me because they said I would die there and they would be held responsible. They took me that evening to a different prison which did accept me and I was there for two months."

"Did you know that your evidence against Zakayev had been televised?"

"Yes, the prison guards told me it had been shown on all channels. Two months later I was taken back to court. There was a member of the FSB, a Chechen, there. I know him, we went to school together. He warned me, 'Do you know why they are freeing you now? So they can kill you and blame it on Zakayev. They will say he murders people who give evidence against him. If you want to live, get out of Grozny today.' That's what I did."

The British judge is very good at keeping his thoughts to himself. Judges are not expected to say much, just "Yes" or "No," and possibly, "Mr Zakayev, the next hearing will be on such and such a date. If you are not here at 10 a.m. you will be arrested." But the traditional British reserve was ruffled by this insight into Russian justice. The judge was moved to remark, "This is an extraordinary situation, a dramatic turn of events." He demanded a prompt response to a number of fundamental questions. For example, why had the Russian Prosecutor-General's Office been assuring the court that witness Dushuyev was in danger from Zakayev and that this was why his name had been obliterated in the extradition papers delivered to Britain, when in fact Dushuyev was in prison and hence in the custody of those making these claims? Had the Prosecution deliberately misled the court? The judge was outraged.

Misleading the court constitutes grave professional misconduct in Britain. The system works in a way which means that Zakayev has defence lawyers and the Prosecutor-General's Office has lawyers supporting its demand for extradition. They are appointed by the Crown Prosecution Service, which works with the Prosecutor-General's Office. If it transpires that there has been a deliberate attempt to provoke a miscarriage of justice, which the lawyers of the Crown Prosecution Service failed to detect through being unduly trusting of their Russian colleagues, they [the CPS] will face a disciplinary investigation and penalties. This would be a severe blow to their reputations which the profession would not forgive, a blot on their entire careers. Britain does not tolerate such games.

Accordingly, the lawyers of the Crown Prosecution Service were also thrown into disarray. They found themselves obliged to defend their own reputation, which was in jeopardy. What the court was now discussing was this sample of Kremlin justice, and the fact that even in Stalin-era trials such a thing had been unheard of. The lawyers humbly asked the judge to allow them an adjournment until September 8, repeating, "These are very serious charges. We are not prepared . . . We have no comment to make today . . ." The judge however insisted on a reply "today, without fail," and gave them just two hours to contact Moscow (probably Fridinsky). When Judge Workman heard the replies he would decide how the trial should proceed.

Two hours proved insufficient and Judge Workman relented, agreeing to give the Prosecutor-General's Office until September 1 to provide explanations in writing, and warning that the case would resume on September 8. He added unambiguously that hearings would continue for no more than four or five days, after which he would retire to consider his verdict.

What have we just witnessed? We have tried to spill out into Europe our corrupt legal practice of fabricating cases whenever and however the state authorities decree, and we have fallen flat on our faces.

The Russian state didn't get away with it in Britain. There was no way it could, because the British have no reason to allow this virus of ours to infect them. Who can blame them? But what of us now, the citizens of Russia, with our law enforcement gangsters ranged against us? The British will survive our invasion. They will merely note for the record the kind of people they are dealing with in the Russian legal system, and of course they will not extradite Zakayev.

But what about us? We citizens must make ourselves heard, not just keep our heads down. If you don't feel moved to defend Zakayev, then at least rise to your own defence. The state system poses a deadly threat. Anyone can be tortured. These are terrorist acts perpetrated by the regime against us all.

CHECHNYA–LONDON: ANOTHER COURTROOM
MARVEL IN THE ZAKAYEV CASE

September 11, 2003

In London, in Bow Street Magistrates Court, at the hearings concerning the extradition to Russia of Akhmed Zakayev which resumed on September 8, marvels of getting at the truth about the Chechen War through the law continued. This is something we rarely are treated to in Russia, hence our interest. On this occasion Mr Justice Timothy Workman was presented with information about the stranglehold in which the Russian Prosecution Service and other federal law enforcement institutions have the administration of justice in Chechnya, and why as a result of their stewardship we need recourse to the British legal system.

We remind our readers that the main event of the previous hearings in the Zakayev case on July 24 was the cross-examination of 35-year-old Duk-Vakha Dushuyev, formerly of Grozny, who was listed in documents of the Russian Prosecutor's Office as a witness for the prosecution, but in court in London under oath began giving evidence as a witness for the defence, relating how in November–December 2002 he was tortured in Chechnya by members of the FSB who demanded that he give false evidence against Zakayev, to which he agreed. It was precisely this plotline which on September 8–9 received a sensational new twist.

Investigator Konstantin Krivorotov himself proved to have been "zombified" by the Russian Criminal Procedure Code. Junior Judicial Counsellor Krivorotov, Investigator of Particularly Serious Cases of the Chechen Prosecutor's Office, no matter what he was asked in the Bow Street court, even if a question was entirely specific and required only "Yes" or "No" as an answer, responded with a long lecture on the subject of the Criminal Procedure Code, explaining how wise and benign it was, what blessings it brought to those arrested and under investigation, and what vast opportunities it gave representatives of the investigative agencies for treating suspects humanely.

Only, nothing to the point. It was futile to try to stop Investigator

Krivorotov when he was in full flood on the theory of Russian law. He became irate, demanded that he should not be interrupted, and even wagged his finger threateningly at the courteous British lawyers.

Why was that, you may ask? Quite simply, Investigator Krivorotov had a different task. He had been brought here to flannel, to confuse, and to divert the case from details, because the details of the saga of Duk-Vakha Dushuyev are potentially lethal to the extradition case.

But everything in its place. Krivorotov, the ardent supporter of the Criminal Procedure Code, found himself in London only because of Dushuyev's testimony. At the end of November 2002, when the Prosecutor-General's Office, demanding the extradition of Zakayev from Denmark, sent supporting documentation of very low legal quality and Zakayev was about to be released, Dushuyev was caught at a checkpoint in Grozny and taken, hooded, to Khankala. Under torture, he was offered his life in exchange for bearing false witness against Zakayev. He was taken to the FSB building on Garazhnaya Street in Grozny, next door to the Prosecutor's Office. Investigator Krivorotov wrote several statements which Dushuyev was told to sign. A television crew was summoned to the FSB building to record the "voluntary confessions of Zakayev's bodyguard," which were then shown on NTV. Dushuyev was held in prison for two months on a charge routine in Chechnya – "membership of an illegal armed group" – but this was then dropped on the grounds that he had supposedly confessed, and he was released. Dushuyev left Chechnya that same day and fled through a number of countries before deciding to find Zakayev's lawyers and admit what he had done. Such were the events which brought him, and consequently Krivorotov, before Judge Workman.

"Tell me, Mr Krivorotov, would Mr Dushuyev have been able to reveal any ill-treatment of himself during the course of the investigation? Before this hearing in London?" James Lewis, a lawyer acting on behalf of Investigator Krivorotov, asks a question which seems important to him. Mr Lewis is acting for the British Crown Prosecution Service, which is supporting (such is the way things are done here) the demand of the Russian Prosecutor's Office for extradition of Akhmed Zakayev.

"There is a clear procedure," Krivorotov says, staying firmly in his theoretical realm. "Dushuyev had several opportunities to state that impermissible methods had been used against him. In the first instance at the Preliminary Investigation, to me. The Criminal Procedure Code . . ."

The courtroom is verging on despair. Only Sergey Fridinsky, Deputy Prosecutor-General of the Southern Federal Region, who has publicly vowed to have Zakayev returned to Russia, looks pleased. Today he is present in London and smiles into his moustache with satisfaction when Krivorotov gets on his hobby-horse.

"What was Dushuyev believed to be guilty of when you brought criminal charges against him?" By now it is Zakayev's barrister, Edward Fitzgerald, asking the questions. He approaches in a roundabout way, and why this detail should interest him is unclear. "Was it illegal to be Zakayev's bodyguard? After all, the government of which Zakayev was a member was recognised by President Yeltsin."

"It is news to me that Maskhadov's government was recognised by the President." For the first time Investigator Krivorotov replies honestly. He is genuinely taken aback. Nevertheless he rapidly regains his composure. "Under the Russian Constitution there is no provision for the Minister of a self-proclaimed republic to have an armed bodyguard. Dushuyev was bearing arms at that time illegally. From 1999 Dushuyev was a member of an illegal armed group, the Chernorechiye Front. That is why charges were brought."

"In other words, anybody who resisted the Russian troops in 1999 is considered to have committed a criminal offence?"

"Of course," Krivorotov shrugs, glancing expressionlessly at Fridinsky and barking out the sentences he has memorised. "Anybody who opposes the federal troops is guilty of an act endangering society. In accordance with the Criminal Code."

So the case proceeds, constantly returning inexorably to the central question to which Russia has no answer: what was and is actually going on in Chechnya from a legal point of view? Who is resisting whom there, and why? And how is the situation to be resolved?

This time Mr Fitzgerald is interrupted by Mr Lewis, to whose back the indignant Deputy Prosecutor-General Fridinsky has addressed a remark. Discussing the political aspect of the Prosecutor's Office's work is not permitted.

'Fine. Explain how Dushuyev was provided with a lawyer."

Reader, you should know that Aisa Tatayev from the Staropromyslovsky District Legal Assistance Service was brought to Dushuyev many days after he had been held in a waterlogged pit in Khankala, from which he was periodically dragged for interrogation under torture. She advised him to "tell them everything they want to hear."

"Defence lawyers can be chosen by the accused, or appointed by the court. I knew where I could find Tatayev at that moment, and he was summoned. That is, I personally invited Tatayev."

"How did you write the record of Dushuyev's interrogation? Did you write down everything he said?"

"I have my own method. I first listen to everything a person says, and then note it down, asking supplementary questions. Dushuyev came with an admission of guilt, I listened, and then wrote."

The official version, sent to London over Fridinsky's signature on the eve of today's hearing, is that Khankala was never involved, that there was no torture, that Dushuyev had invented everything. He came to the Prosecutor's Office in Chechnya on December 1, 2002 of his own volition, wishing to confess his guilt in having participated in an illegal armed group, and the topic of Zakayev came up only by chance during his questioning.

"Well why, in that case, in the record which you compiled is there very little about what Dushuyev did, and a whole page about what Zakayev did, based moreover on hearsay? You were supposed to be investigating Dushuyev's crimes, were you not? This seems strange."

Investigator Krivorotov again changes tack and heads for the thickets of the Criminal Procedure Code.

"Fine. But did you know about Zakayev's extradition case?"

"Yes. I realized that the record of Dushuyev's interrogation would be used in the criminal case against Zakayev."

"Then why in that record is there no indication that the witness was himself under investigation?"

"What would have been the point of that?"

"You knew that Dushuyev would be filmed by a television crew? In the FSB building?"

"I supposed so. The relevant request had been received from the FSB Press Department."

"In writing?"

"Verbally."

"Dushuyev had been detained and was in your custody, and you handed him over to members of the FSB, and they took him to their own premises for filming. Is that correct?"

"Yes." Krivorotov is losing patience. He again wags his finger at the court. "It is Dushuyev's right either to talk to the press or not."

"It did not occur to you that this filmed interview, where Dushuyev, on the basis of hearsay, accused Zakayev of serious crimes, of illegal arms trading, might harm Zakayev's case?"

"I don't understand the question."

"Does it not seem strange to you that Dushuyev was your suspect but that the FSB had access to him when it wanted? How did the FSB even know that Dushuyev was with you? Did you report that to the FSB? And if so, why?"

"No. I did not report it." For the first time Krivorotov looks as though he is telling the truth. "When Dushuyev came to the Prosecutor's Office with his admission of guilt, he was accompanied by FSB officers, and accordingly I released him to the FSB for filming."

QED. Thus did Investigator Krivorotov slip on a banana skin. This admission was fraught with consequences: it meant that all the official documents, including those signed by Deputy Prosecutor-General Fridinsky, were untrue. The court could place no reliance on them because they had been found to contain lies. Moreover, it was evident from them that Dushuyev was right when he claimed that the Prosecutor's Office in Chechnya did not work independently, that it knocked together whatever procedural papers were required, and thereby in effect legitimised the torture to which people were subjected by the FSB.

"I do not consider it substantive where Dushuyev came first, to the FSB or to us." Krivorotov has suddenly realized what he has said. He explains that the majority of those arriving with an admission of guilt go first to the FSB, and then the FSB brings them to the Prosecutor's Office to formalise their confession. But the more he goes on, the more obvious is the lawlessness perpetrated in Chechnya with the blessing of the Prosecutor's Office.

"Do you really not know that people are tortured by the FSB in order to obtain the evidence they want?" Although Barrister Fitzgerald is calm, it is evident that he already knows he has won. It had seemed at times, at the hearings on Monday and Tuesday, that this was a dead end. One side said one thing, the other the exact opposite, and how could it all be reconciled? How could one find the highest common factor which alone would make the dead-end submissions comprehensible to the judge, and hence also relevant to the issue of deciding on extradition? Investigator Krivorotov's inadvertent admission that it was precisely the FSB who had dragged Dushuyev in to him had been brilliantly engineered by Fitzgerald. A subtle, virtuoso victory over falsehood.

"I don't know anything about torture."

Krivorotov is invited to familiarise himself with the official conclusions of the European Committee on Torture on precisely this issue. The investigator is forced to claim that he does not see what is going on right next door to him, but only a minute passes, and once again we see the man mesmerised by the Criminal Procedure Code:

"We in the Prosecutor's Office are under an obligation to take legal action where facts such as these come to light."

Of course you are, but the whole point is that for years you have been ignoring it!

Thus it was that Investigator Krivorotov became a witness for the defence, and hence against any possibility of extradition. Why? It had been been proved in court that the law enforcement agencies functioning on the territory of Chechnya are totally arbitrary and lawless. That is why Krivorotov could treat his listeners in a London courtroom only to long explanations about how things are supposed to be. He knew only too well how they are supposed to be, but he also knew that how they are bears no relation to that. Poor wretch. Anything goes, and nothing seems wrong. Barbarity becomes the norm.

At precisely 1300 hours Greenwich Mean Time Judge Workman interrupted Investigator Krivorotov with the magic words, "One hour for lunch." By tradition, nothing on earth takes precedence over the lunch hour. The same inflexible rules, however, require that a witness whose cross-examination has not been completed should not discuss matters relating to what he is being cross-questioned about with anyone. This meant that while everybody else was having lunch, Investigator Krivorotov stood as lonely as a statue at the courtroom door, smoking nervously. Deputy Prosecutor-General Fridinsky walked past him from the Italian restaurant across the road. Others involved in the case made their way back for the afternoon sitting. One couldn't help feeling sorry for Krivorotov, and an exceptionally humane impulse prompted your correspondent to go over and offer him a sandwich. Lord, how he recoiled! "No!" He shook his head as if he had been offered an arsenic sandwich. "But I have two. I have more than I need." "No!" Investigator Krivorotov blushed and turned away, as if we did not know each other. Something wasn't right.

THE PROSECUTOR-GENERAL'S OFFICE LOSES: LEGAL COSTS WILL BE MET BY THE RUSSIAN TAXPAYER

November 17, 2003

People can have entirely different perspectives: love Zakayev or hate him, support the Kremlin's atrocities in Chechnya or fight them, rejoice at world leaders' love of Putin or be horrified by it, but on November 13, 2003, shortly before noon Greenwich Mean Time, the entire Russian nation was given a good and deserved kicking by Europe. The Prosecutor-General's Office had been asking for it for a long time. In Bow Street Magistrates Court, in the case of The Government of the Russian Federation versus Akhmed Zakayev, Mr Justice Timothy Workman delivered an outspoken and uncompromising judgment, beyond anything the most wild-eyed optimists had dared to hope for when they assured us that Zakayev would not be extradited.

The refusal of Judge Timothy Workman to extradite Zakayev

was based firstly on the grounds that Russia lacks an independent judiciary, so there can be no confident expectation of a fair trial; secondly, on the fact that racism flourishes in our country; and thirdly, because what is going on in Chechnya is not a rebellion or an "anti-terrorist operation" but a full-blown civil war instigated by the Russian Government itself in contravention of its obligation to avert wars, to extinguish them, and not to foment them within its borders.

The verdict was announced not in the ordinary magistrates' court-room where the case had been heard but in a lofty ceremonial hall with something resembling a throne set at a considerable height. On this the judge seated himself. The translator promised on oath not to lie, and Mr Justice Workman began:

"The Russian Federation seek the extradition of Akhmed Zakayev in respect of some thirteen allegations of conduct which, had it occurred in the United Kingdom, would have amounted to the offences of soliciting persons to murder, three counts of murder, two counts of wounding with intent to cause grievous bodily harm, one count of false imprisonment and six counts of conspiring with others in a course of conduct which would necessarily involve the commission of offences of murder, wounding and hostage taking.

The judge continued:

"I am quite satisfied that the events in Chechnya in 1995 and 1996 amounted in law to an internal armed conflict. Indeed, many observers would have regarded it as a civil war. In support of that decision I have taken into account the scale of fighting – the intense carpet-bombing of Grozny with in excess of 100,000 casualties, the recognition of the conflict in the terms of a cease fire and a peace treaty. I was unable to accept the view expressed by one witness that the actions of the Russian Government in bombing Grozny were counter-terrorist operations.

"Having satisfied myself that this amounted to an internal armed conflict which would fall within the Geneva Convention, I reach the conclusion that those crimes which allege conspiring to seize specific areas of Chechnya by the use of armed force or resistance are not extraditable crimes because the conduct in those circumstances would not amount to a crime in this country. On that basis I propose to discharge counts 7, 8, 9 and 13."

The next section of the ruling bears the highly eloquent title "Abuse of Process." This is more to do with the professional methods of the Russian Prosecutor-General's Office, whose representatives were conspicuous by their absence. Rumors were circulating yesterday that Sergey Fridinsky, who was in charge of the campaign to extradite Zakayev and who had given the President his word that he would be returned, had been warned by the Crown Prosecution Service that an adverse ruling was likely, as a result of which the whole lot of them had decided to absent themselves from their public humiliation.

One can see their point. The evidence of prosecution witnesses was found not to be reliable. It is worth recalling who was in this group which Fridinsky had assembled: Akhmar Zavgayev, a Senator representing Chechnya, currently preparing to enter the Duma; Yury Kalinin, Deputy Minister of Justice responsible for the prison system; Konstantin Krivorotov, Investigator of the Chechen Prosecutor's Office; Yury Bessarabov, Professor of Law at the Research Institute of the Prosecutor-General's Office; and Stanislav Iliasov, Russian Government Minister for Chechnya. These individuals should not continue to occupy their posts after such public disgrace.

"The alleged offences on which Mr Zakayev is sought occurred in 1995 and in 1996. The offences would have been apparent to the Authorities at the time, and two witnesses assured me that they made statements to the Prosecution shortly after the event. It was not until some six years later that a decision was made to arrest Mr Zakayev, and it was not until October 25, 2002 that the Russian request for his arrest was circulated by Interpol. Throughout 2001 and 2002 Mr Zakayev acted as a peace envoy, travelling extensively, but his whereabouts were apparently known to the Russian Authorities. Indeed, on November 18, 2001 Mr Zakayev travelled to Moscow Airport in an attempt to negotiate disarmament. He met with senior Government officials who had themselves been reassured that there were no proceedings anticipated against Mr Zakayev. The existence of the decision to

arrest Mr Zakayev taken two months earlier appears to have been overlooked. Mr Fridinsky, the Russian prosecutor in this case, has explained
that they had no idea that Mr Zakayev was going to attend a meeting
in Moscow. Whilst I do, of course, accept that Mr Fridinsky may not
have known, I find it surprising that a warrant for such serious crimes
alleged to have been committed by such a well-known person should
not have been noticed by the Russian Immigration Authorities.

"In addition to the delay in arrest, it is apparent that there has been
delay in the investigation and preparation of the Prosecution's case.
Although two witnesses told me that they had made statements soon
after the events, those statements have not been produced or provided
to the Defence. With one exception (an unnamed witness) who made
a statement on March 13, 2000, the other 11 witnesses made their statements after Mr Zakayev was arrested. In respect of four of those
witnesses, their statements were not taken until after the extradition
request to Denmark had failed. Note that in the request to Denmark
it was being alleged that Mr Zakayev was involved in the Moscow
theatre siege and that he had murdered Father Sergius (now known
as Father Philip). Both allegations were later withdrawn, and indeed
Father Philip has given evidence before me.

"I have also noted that the Kremlin denied the existence of any
criminal proceedings against Mr Zakayev when in fact a warrant was
still extant. I have noted that the Russian Government continued to
negotiate with Mr Zakayev despite the existence of the warrant, and
that there was no attempt to extradite Mr Zakayev until the moment
of the World Chechen Conference and the Moscow theatre siege. I
have also noted the statements of the Russian foreign minister likening
Mr Zakayev to Osama Bin Laden.

"When those factors are added together the inevitable conclusion
is that it would now be unjust and oppressive to return Mr Zakayev
to stand his trial in Russia.

"I found that the evidence given by Mr de Waal, Mr Rybakov and
Mr Rybkin was truthful and accurate, and from their evidence I am
satisfied that it is more likely than not that the motivation of the

Government of the Russian Federation was and is to exclude Mr Zakayev from continuing to take part in the peace process and to discredit him as a moderate. I therefore find as a fact that the Russian Government are seeking extradition for purposes of prosecuting Mr Zakayev on account of his nationality and his political opinions. I take the view that Mr Zakayev is entitled to the benefit of the protection provided by Section 6(i)(c) [of the European Convention on Extradition].

"With some reluctance I have to come to the inevitable conclusion that if the Authorities are prepared to resort to torturing witnesses there is a substantial risk that Mr Zakayev would himself be subject to torture. I am satisfied that such punishment and detention would be by reason of his nationality and political opinions. I therefore believe that Mr Zakayev is entitled to the benefit of Section 6(i)(d) and should not be returned to face trial in the Russian Federation . . .

"I am therefore discharging the defendant."

That is an end to it. The judge is silent, the courtroom animated. People are trying to congratulate Zakayev, but the case is not over yet. Edward Fitzgerald, Zakayev's defence lawyer, rises to his feet. His concerns extend beyond the law to the financing of all this. Who is going to pay the legal costs? The judge calmly accepts the bills and invoices as is the way in Britain. This means it is clear who is going to pay. The costs of a court case which has lasted almost a year will be payable by the losing side, that is, by you and me, since it is we who employ the officials of the Prosecutor-General's Office, officials who have failed to learn to work in accordance with the law but excel in carrying out political orders, as the London court has demonstrated.

Each has received his just desserts. Zakayev is free, his passport will be returned to him in the immediate future, and he will again be able to travel at will throughout the world. Representatives of the Crown Prosecution Service of Great Britain who, in accordance with the British judicial system, represented the Russian Prosecutor-General's Office, have strongly advised Mr Fridinsky against thinking of lodging an appeal because it would have no prospect of success and could lead only to an even more shaming outcome; all the charges have been rejected as without a basis in law, meaning that no new evidence would be accepted. The Russian Prosecutor-General's Office has egg all over its face.

These, however, are only details. Three important truths were established in London on November 13. The first is that, for the first time in many years of a monstrous war, the federal authorities and the Chechens have been communicating with each other in legal language rather than the language of armed conflict, security sweeps, ambushes and explosions. The forum for this was a British court which demonstrated that it was concerned only with hard evidence and had no interest in political expediency.

The second is that it has been established in a court of law, not in the newspapers or on television, not in the drawing rooms of the establishment or at conferences, after lengthy examination of the evidence for and against now marshalled in several volumes, that, as most of us already knew but were unable to prove, what is happening in Chechnya is not an "anti-terrorist operation" but a war.

The third is that, after the London court ruling, it is impossible to go on pretending that our country is on the road to democracy. There are no reforms; instead we have authoritarianism, subservient courts, torture in places of detention and racial harassment. The framework of international relations is collapsing because it has been shown in court that the system the Russian regime talks about simply does not exist. Russia is a radically different country from the one which the politicians pretend exists. We have a brutal war, racism and violence as the means of resolving all issues.

That is the end of the story of the London court proceedings in respect of Akhmed Zakayev. The Government wanted to show the world how cool we are and how we stand for truth, but succeeded only in showing our true nature. The Russian Government is the laughing-stock of Europe because it has no substance, only wild pretensions.

The fact that the court ruling was going to go against the Russian Prosecutor-General's Office became clear in Sheremetievo-II, the Moscow airport from which I was flying to London to hear the verdict.

I handed over my passport. The young frontier guard tapped at his computer for a long time and finally said,

"You have problems."

"What kind of problems?"

"You know yourself."

"No I don't."

What had popped up on his screen was that the bearer of this passport was to be detained and subjected to general unpleasantness and all manner of additional and humiliating searches.

"Why?"

"That's a military secret," he replied. One would have liked to think he was joking but there was no hint of a smile.

The woman in charge of the shift arrived, a pretty girl, Yuliya Demina. She took away various things that she had no right to take: my passport, my ticket. She ordered me to stand in a particular place and not to move, and then she went away. She was gone for a very long time and the plane was about to leave. The young guardian of the border came out of his booth and prattled on again about "problems" which "you know yourself."

"Are you going to have problems coming back in?"

"What do you mean?"

"You might not be allowed back in, for instance."

It's the usual approach in this, the era of the Second Chechen War. You can become nobody at any moment, especially if you have witnessed something. No laws are required to do that, as was proven in London, where I was permitted to fly to at the very last moment.

Part III: The Kadyrovs

THE WAR SUPERMARKET. EXTERMINATING CHECHENS IS NOW SELF-SERVICE

June 26, 2000

The Kremlin continues its Michurinist labor of planting and nurturing civil war in Chechnya as assiduously as the late father of Soviet hybridisation. Its most recent contribution was made on June 8, when the President signed an order appointing 49-year-old Akhmat-hadji Kadyrov "Chief of Chechnya" (Director of the Provisional Administration). Kadyrov is associated by most of the population solely with conflict and division. They call him the "middleman Mufti," the link between Chechen bandits and those highly placed citizens in Moscow whose main priority is to prolong the policy of intimidation in the North Caucasus.

The three weeks since June 8 have served only to confirm the worst predictions regarding Mr Kadyrov's appointment. The conflict between Chechen and Chechen has flared up with new vigour. The news images are following the same script as when civil war flared up in Tajikistan.

Within these three weeks, only three heads of district administrations out of 18 have agreed to work under the middleman Mufti. Twelve of them sent an abrupt demand to President Putin, the "Letter of the Twelve," either to change his edict or expect sabotage. When Moscow chose to ignore this, a meeting of administrative heads in Gudermes on June 16 considered a proposal to try to persuade the Center to at least delay Kadyrov's accession to the throne by a couple of months, until the end of the harvest season. The reason is that people need to be able to harvest the 85,000 hectares they have sowed with such difficulty without the fear that Kadyrov's coming to power heralds either a renewal in the near future of combat operations or that the Kadyrov gang, whose existence he no longer bothers to deny, will simply set about brazenly filching the harvest, every hectare of which has been watered with blood and tears.

What is more, Chechnya is being abandoned by members of the Provisional Administration led by the already ex-Acting Head, Yakub Deniev. They too first sent a petition to the Kremlin (the "Letter of the Forty-Four") in which they categorically stated that they would find it morally unacceptable to work under a man who had declared jihad on Moscow only for Moscow to hand him the throne of Chechnya, and who was now also demanding that he should have control of the budget.

Blood has been shed. A well-known Urus Martan imam, Umar Idrisov, has been assassinated, and PR games immediately began in connection with his tragic death. As if in response to orders from above, most of the media declared the Imam to have been a supporter of Kadyrov, which he never was. Indeed, Idrisov was a determined opponent of Kadyrov and refused to recognise him as Mufti or condone his pretensions to being the chosen spiritual leader of Chechnya. People have immediately connected the assassination of the Imam and the lies in the media, and have concluded that Moscow is artificially inflating Kadyrov's standing, not holding back even from murdering the Imam so that they could pretend he had been martyred because he supported Kadyrov.

What, specifically, are the grudges most Chechens hold against the middleman Mufti?

In the first place, money. In 1992 Kadyrov was the treasurer of a mass pilgrimage of Muslims from Chechnya to Mecca. Kadyrov collected between $300 and $500 from each of them, only for the King of Saudi Arabia to pay for all the Chechen pilgrims. Kadyrov did not return the $220,000 he had collected. Outrage ensued, a criminal case was brought, and for six months Kadyrov was held in a pretrial detention facility, after which the case was dropped by the Prosecutor's Office and, on the orders of then President Dudayev, Kadyrov was released.

The next detail of his portrait is more recent. It concerns one of Kadyrov's first acts after his appointment, and also tells us something about his morals. Budruddin Djamalkhanov, by now already the ex-director of the provisional administration's liaison department with the security agencies, relates, "My father-in-law, Nasukha-hadji Akhmadov, built a mosque in 1989 in Kurchaloy, which was later turned into a madrasah. My father-in-law supported it to the best of his ability, but in the spring he asked the provisional administration for support. Koshman [the Russian Government's representative in Chechnya] agreed, seeing that the children were at least being taught something there. At this point came Kadyrov's appointment. Naturally, all the papers with the detailed budgets, staff lists and time-sheets were passed to him. The first thing he did was to write in his own name: 'Kadyrov – 3,000 roubles.' He went on to demand that the staff list should be augmented with his relatives as sham teachers. My father-in-law gave up in disgust."

In the second place, Kadyrov is not a mufti, since there already is a living mufti, Mahomed-Bashir-hadji Arsanukayev, elected in 1992 in accordance with Chechen custom at a council of *ulema* (delegates from all districts). Arsanukayev, one of the Republic's most eminent theologians, fell into disfavor with President Dudayev for cursing his actions in dividing the Chechen people. The history of the rise of Kadyrov as a counterweight to Arsanukayev is that in August 1995 a famous assembly of the major field commanders took place in Vedeno. Here Dudayev proclaimed the founding of a new state, the Islamic Republic of Ichkeria. He next proclaimed Kadyrov Mufti, who until then had been a little-known and unpopular mullah. Kadyrov was, however, agreeable to declaring jihad on Russia. The appointment was contrary to Chechen tradition, and accordingly the population came to regard Kadyrov as no more than a kind of chaplain or mufti for the field commanders. From February 1996 Kadyrov orchestrated the persecution in Chechnya of all members of the Arsanukayev Muftiate. Mullahs have been mercilessly abducted and killed and the elected Muftiate destroyed. Presidents Dudayev, Yandarbiev, and subsequently Maskhadov several times reconfirmed Kadyrov's status without consulting the *ulema*.

Maskhadov rewarded him with several oil tankers and oil wells in the Nozhai-Yurt and Grozny Rural Districts, enabling Kadyrov to become extremely rich and maintain a large detachment of well-armed

mercenaries. In the spring of 1999 one of the periodical redistribu-
tions of influence began between the members of Chechnya's ruling
elite, and Kadyrov fell out with Shamil Basayev who was encroaching
on his oil interests. This was the real reason behind Kadyrov's con-
demnation of Basayev's incursion into Dagestan [which the Russian
Government used to justify beginning the Second Chechen War]. The
split between them deepened, and in August 1999 Maskhadov relieved
Kadyrov of the post of Mufti. Kadyrov refused to acknowledge this
and to this day considers himself the Mufti of Chechnya, having now
switched sides to support the federals, the very people on whom he
had declared jihad.

Yakub Deniev, who until he retired on June 20 was the Acting Head
of the Provisional Administration, having worked as such for eight
months of the war, says, "Kadyrov is the worst possible option for
Chechnya. His appointment is an insult and a humiliation for most
Chechens and a slap in the face for the clergy. There is no getting away
from the fact that he is a brigand. Indeed, the appointment of Kadyrov
is a signal that the military phase of the operation will be continued
and escalated. There is absolutely no desire for peace in Moscow at
present and Kadyrov feels at home in conflict. His policies aim to
deepen the divisions within Chechnya. One does of course come across
confrontational individuals, but Kadyrov breaks every record in that
respect."

What does the Kremlin need all this for? What does it hope to
achieve by these provocations? We appear to be facing a transition to
a new phase of what it calls the "counter-terrorist operation." Since the
guerrilla warfare shows no signs of slackening and the sore tooth which
is Chechnya can't be extracted by military means, the intention seems
to be to destroy Chechnya by the tried and trusted method of sowing
internecine strife.

The West will turn a blind eye, taking the view that "they are just
fighting among themselves," and nobody in Russia will be particularly
bothered by the slaughter, even though it has been instigated from
above.

SKETCHES FOR A PORTRAIT OF AKHMAT-HADJI KADYROV

September 16, 2002

The "Chief of Chechnya," Akhmat-hadji Kadyrov, controls his own illegal armed group which engages in abductions, and which also has a private prison in the village of Tsentoroy.

How come? First of all, the unvarnished testimony of an eyewitness who survived. The necessary explanations can come later.

"Opposite the house in which Kadyrov lives in Tsentoroy, some 20–30 metres away, near the road and the water tap, is a small single-storey building. The Kadyrovites call it their HQ. The Head of the Republic's bodyguards are usually in there. The house has five rooms, one of which is permanently used as a cell for prisoners.

"Behind the HQ a lean-to has been built which has a further three cells, invariably occupied by detainees.

"Who are they? Firstly, people caught planting explosives. Secondly, people associated with the [Islamist] Wahhabi jamaat. Thirdly, miscellaneous other people. Their cases are judged by Ramzan, Kadyrov's younger son. It's like a real court, only with Ramzan presiding.

"People he finds not guilty of anything very serious are left in the cells for various periods; sentences are decided by Ramzan and Ruslan, the head of Kadyrov's 'Security Service.' Those found guilty of something serious are sent off to Youth Soviet Farm No. 15, about 15 or 20 kilometres west of Grozny. What happens to the detainees after that nobody knows.

"Youth Soviet Farm No. 15 has a reputation as a haven for kidnappers. Under Maskhadov's rule, too, there were many kidnappers and their victims in this village. The Zavgayevs' sister was held there for a year and eight months, for example. Today the same outlaws are in the same place, only legitimised by Kadyrov's protection."

Before explaining in detail exactly what this is all about, I should mention that I have chosen this tale as typical of many others. Much the same thing is described by other people who have had the misfortune to come into contact with Kadyrov's "Security Service," but who have succeeded in getting out and even agreed to testify on condition of anonymity.

What is going on in Chechnya today? It is my profound conviction that what is going on is an unambiguous civil war, deliberately provoked by the three-year-long so-called "anti-terrorist operation," which sees brother rise up against brother, one family against another.

The whole area is crammed with armed detachments of every sort. These are mainly Russian Army troops, special operations units, rapid reaction squads, militia special purpose units, alpha groups and so on. These troops are opposed by the so-called resistance forces, illegal armed groups, a thoroughly diverse collection of fighters who, for the most part, answer only to their own consciences.

During the last six months, however, a new punitive force has appeared, a kind of Chechen sandwich filling in the sense that they are not on either side, although they have an ideological affinity with the federals.

These punitive detachments are known as the Kadyrovites, named after their organiser, Akhmat-hadji Kadyrov, who two and a half years ago was appointed Chief of the Republic by President Putin of Russia.

The Kadyrovites are also an illegal armed group. They are commonly referred to as Kadyrov's "Security Service," which would appear to provide them with a vestige of legitimacy, but this is not the case. The Chechen Ministry of Justice has confirmed that Kadyrov's "Security Service" is not registered anywhere, and accordingly has no legal right to exist, any more than Basayev's brigade, or what remains of the detachments of Khattab or Barayev.

Exist it nevertheless does, and it feels right at home in a civil war. The "Security Service" has no desire at all to see Putin's promised "dictatorship of the law" arrive. Quite the reverse.

At first things looked less ugly. Kadyrov's personal security detachment was assembled mainly from the ranks of his relatives, but with the passage of time it has degenerated into a monstrous hybrid in the traditions of the Tsarist secret police and the Soviet NKVD–KGB.

The secret prisons and the torturing are, of course, highly secret; the more so since the Kadyrovites are no fools and try to leave no witnesses. Modern Chechen life has, however, conspired against them.

One of the most terrible tragedies for Chechnya is the mass disappearance of citizens. Today there are almost 3,000 "disappeared," although nobody can give a precise figure. Their relatives go out seeking them, on the earth and under the earth, among those on the Russian side and among those on the other side. When the war ends we can be confident that the best investigators in Russia will be the relatives of the disappeared.

It is these "investigators," recruited by misfortune, who uncovered the Kadyrovites. For some time, the tracks of abductions had been stubbornly leading to the village of Tsentoroy, famously the place where Kadyrov lives. The evidence pointed to buildings adjacent to Kadyrov's house, and more precisely to Kadyrov's very agreeable country estate and the buildings occupied by his bodyguards. Another path led stubbornly to Youth Soviet Farm No. 15, a village on the road to Grozny.

A recurrent pattern emerged: while some did return to freedom from the Tsentoroy torture chambers, all that came from Youth Soviet Farm No. 15 was the coldness of the grave. Sometimes, by chance, the bones of those who had been traced to Youth Soviet Farm No. 15 were found, scattered or half buried by dogs.

With time, one further piece of information emerged: Kadyrov is busily buying up plots of land in Tsentoroy, displacing to other villages families he doesn't want and replacing them with his bodyguards' families. Dracula is building a castle hidden from prying eyes, whose inhabitants are tied to him by the powerful bonds of shared guilt.

Many conversations with relatives of the disappeared, who found that all roads led to Tsentoroy and Youth Soviet Farm No. 15, show that people at first simply didn't believe the Kadyrovites would dare to return to their old ways, to the kidnapping notorious in the time of Maskhadov, before Akhmat-hadji Kadyrov was reborn as a law-abiding and Kremlin-fearing gentleman.

Gradually, however, the facts began to speak for themselves; acts of terrorism ensued, and those of Kadyrov's men considered guilty of the murders were themselves dispatched to the next world in accordance with the tradition of the blood feud. There were numerous reports of Kadyrov's motorcades coming under fire or being blown up. He never suffered personally, but nephews, cousins and second cousins who were members of his security detail were killed.

You may approve of this approach to matters of life and death or categorically reject it, but what you or I think is not going to change anything. Given that most of the law enforcement agencies currently operating in Chechnya are fully aware of the evil-doing of Kadyrov's "security service" but are not raising a finger against it, what can be done to stop this? More broadly, how could the intelligence agencies, with which Chechnya is teeming, have allowed things to come to such a pass?

There are two answers, one logical and the other irrational. To begin with the second: the overall policy of the agencies keeping the area of the anti-terrorist operation under surveillance is simply: "Let them fight it out among themselves. The more bloodshed, the better." Starting from this premise, Kadyrov's reign is just what you want.

The logical answer is that Kadyrov and the intelligence services both want to destroy Maskhadov and his supporters by whatever means they can. For the present, they are allies united by this aim, their interests overlapping so much that each closes his eyes to the criminality of the other. There are two facts to note here. The first is that some of those in Kadyrov's torture chambers did indeed wage war against Russia in the era of the Islamic Republic of Ichkeria, or were prominent members of that government, or at least sympathised with it. Kadyrov has shown on more than one occasion that he cannot tolerate any sort of competition or rivalry. He makes an exception for resistance fighters who have recanted and sworn allegiance to himself, turncoats like Suleyman Yamadayev, the Gudermes kidnapper appointed to the position of goat in charge of the kitchen garden as Chechen Deputy Commissar of War. Yamadayev enjoys lording it over his former comrades-in-arms, many of whom he has put in the Tsentoroy cells.

The other thing to note is that, since the beginning of this year, a recurring theme in the accounts of those who witnessed abductions subsequently traced to Tsentoroy and Youth Soviet Farm No. 15 is that unidentified men in combat fatigues, flak jackets, masks, and helmets with built-in microphones came very quietly into the victim's house, communicating between themselves in a whisper. They have become known as "The Silent Ones" because they work so soundlessly, co-ordinating their actions by radio and moving around in shoes with thick, springy rubber soles. There have been instances when relatives sleeping in neighbouring rooms didn't even wake up until the door closed behind the Silent Ones, and it was only when a mother went into the room where her sons had been sleeping that she realized they had been taken.

This stealth technique is Kadyrov's modus operandi. These abductors are not Kadyrovites at all, but most probably agents from the federal Central Intelligence Directorate, the GRU. This leads to the very unpleasant conclusion that GRU agents are either acting under direct orders of the Kadyrovites, abducting citizens on their instructions, or that, if they find they have abducted the wrong person, are handing him over to the tender mercies of Kadyrov's "security service."

I have talked to officials in the Chechen Prosecutor's Office about the Kadyrov gang often enough to know that they are fully aware of what is going on and have tried to oppose this lawless mayhem. But they have also admitted that Kadyrov's "security service" acts as it does because Kadyrov is now effectively beyond the reach of the law, thanks to his intimate relationship with the Russian authorities.

This state of affairs is not going to last for ever. Interests will diverge, and when they do Kadyrov and the Kadyrovites will be in an unenviable position. It is difficult to imagine anywhere on the planet where they will be able to find refuge.

ABUSE OF ADMINISTRATIVE AND MILITARY RESOURCES, UNBRIDLED AMBITION WITH GANGSTER TENDENCIES, ONLY THIS TIME THE ELECTIONS ARE NOT IN RUSSIA, BUT IN CHECHNYA

September 23, 2002

We continue sketching in our portrait of Akhmat-hadji Kadyrov, the "Chief" of the Chechen Republic appointed by President Putin more than two years ago.

Why is Kadyrov allowed to act without constraint? Why is it all ignored by the intelligence agencies? As usual, when things are complicated there are simple explanations. The answers in this case are crude and cynical. The victims who are traced to Tsentoroy are tortured and disappear purely because of Kadyrov's electoral weakness.

The former Mufti is possessed by a desire to be "democratically elected." Whatever the cost, he wants to feel the equal of Maskhadov, enjoying the same measure of legitimacy. Kadyrov may today be Chief of the Chechen Republic, but only because he was appointed, which is not the real thing. In actual fact his power is derisory, but he wants genuine power, and he craves it so insanely that common sense is banished.

Accordingly, the illegal armed group commonly known as Kadyrov's "security service" is hunting down his enemies, by which he means those who would be obvious rivals if the militarised political process in Chechnya ever finally came to the point of an election.

His primary enemies are the so-called Ichkerians, those who served in and supported the Chechen Republic of Ichkeria and President Maskhadov, the Islamist Wahhabis, members of their jamaat groups, terrorists who sympathise with any of the above, and anybody associated with the separatist ideals of Djohar Dudayev, who supported the idea of Chechnya seceding from Russia.

These are the targets against whom the Kadyrovites direct their main efforts and, naturally, they enjoy the support of the Joint Military Command and FSB who are responsible for conducting the "anti-terrorist operation in the North Caucasus." Since all debate about what methods of combating terrorism are acceptable and all criticism of excessive violence has long ago ceased, Kadyrov's manifest enthusiasm for death squads raises no eyebrows.

The absence of constraint fosters depravity and enables Kadyrov to settle scores with anyone who has offended him in times past. This goes beyond political or ideological enmity. The bodyguards' second target seems at first to be entirely random individuals, but in fact many of these are people who in their youth in some way offended Kadyrov, or were less than supportive of his religious career.

The third, special category of people likely to be murdered by Kadyrov's "security service" are the unofficial leaders of Chechen villages, people who – by dint of the military situation, of villagers' despair at what is happening, and because there is no protection – have become very active in their districts and villages and demonstrated leadership qualities. The Chief of the Republic has discerned a threat to his electoral prospects in their growing grassroots popularity. Not in the sense that they might themselves be elected: Turko Dikayev, for example, had no such ambitions. They have simply shown that they are capable of mobilising their villages, and would be unlikely to mobilise them for Kadyrov.

Turko Dikayev was one of Kadyrov's personal friends. They went back a long way, but this did not save him. In recent months Turko had found himself in this category of popular unofficial leaders. It was not something he sought, and resulted only from the suffocating bureaucracy which left him performing essential tasks everybody else was too scared to do.

The result was that this August, in mysterious circumstances which point to the complicity of Kadyrov's "security service," Turko Dikayev was murdered. By this time, as a responsible and popular individual, he had become the Administrative Head of Tsotsan-Yurt in Kurchaloy District. Tsotsan-Yurt's recent history has been appalling. The New Year of 2002 saw it subjected to one of the most brutal security sweeps Chechnya has known. On January 1, soldiers entered the villagers' houses and wished them, "Miserable New Year!" The then head of the village simply fled. The soldiers were willing to negotiate the return of bodies only with the village head and it was at that point that Turko, as one of the Council of Elders of Tsotsan-Yurt, assumed responsibility.

We met in early March. In Tsotsan-Yurt's central square there was a permanent wake for the victims of the security sweeps. Turko had been unable to sleep for days and was in a terrible state because of high blood pressure. In the spring the Army's incessant raids on the tormented village were replaced by a new horror: almost every day mutilated corpses were being systematically dumped on the outskirts. The villagers were living in a state of constant shock and panic. They appealed to Turko, but he found it impossible to persuade any officials from Grozny to come to the village. He did everything he could to ease the situation of his fellow villagers, attempting to negotiate with the federals, going to Grozny himself, and trying to obtain an audience with his old friend Kadyrov.

Kadyrov refused to see him, not even allowing him into the waiting room. All the while the head of Kadyrov's "security service" was strutting up and down the corridors of the government building telling everybody this brutality was the only way to treat Tsotsan-Yurt because it was a bastion and symbol of lawlessness.

Let us be quite clear: Kadyrov left the village to survive as best it could with no support from him. He abdicated his responsibilities in Tsotsan-Yurt, and all that Turko did was refuse to betray his fellow villagers. He accepted that authority and did all he could for them at the moment of their greatest distress. He earned immense respect for that and, incidentally, made no secret that he had lost faith in the moral qualities of Kadyrov. And so he was killed.

Turko had a presentiment that something of the kind would happen, and told me that he saw Kadyrov as the gravest danger to himself. Like a runaway locomotive, Kadyrov was steaming towards elections of his own devising, and hurling aside anybody who might get in the way or speak out against him.

This answers our main question as to why the Kadyrov regime is as it is. His gang are smoothing the way for their chief to be elected President. His bodyguards abduct and torture people, his obnoxious son, in tandem with the head of the "security service," judges them, and then they simply disappear. All because Kadyrov has this electoral itch, this lust for legitimation. He has been in power for two years now, but sitting on a stool, not a throne. He can talk about nothing other than his imminent ultimate victory over Maskhadov. Whatever you ask him, he always returns to that.

Kadyrov understands that only an election will set the seal on his victory over his former comrade, his one-time spiritual pupil, and his present-day Enemy No. 1. Kadyrov has even concocted a new constitution for Chechnya to further his ends, because elections need to be constitutional. The only one Chechnya has dates from the period of Presidents Dudayev and Maskhadov, and under that Constitution Chechnya already has a President.

Kadyrov has agreed with the Kremlin that November would be the best time for a referendum on the new Constitution. They need to hurry, while Chechnya is still full of Russian troops who can vote the right way once his path to the throne has been cleared.

He has overlooked just one detail. In this squalid tale of murderous passion, the Kremlin – with its stubborn support of Kadyrov, support which frees him of all moral constraint – insists on ignoring the fact that Kadyrov Senior can only win an election in which the security forces, numbering many thousands, distort the "democratic" vote.

The two years during which he has ruled by fiat have been spent not in earning the respect of his electorate but in losing any he ever possessed. If Putin went into his election as an unknown quantity, which allowed for all sorts of manipulation, Kadyrov has no such option. He is poisonous, and the whole of Chechnya knows it. How can you entrust government of the country to the likes of Kadyrov, who has no prospect of ever enjoying any sort of approval rating from the electorate? The result is that he has to resort to extreme measures. Is Putin not guilty of a crime against people who are infinitely weary of waiting to be freed from the imposition of war, disasters, funerals, dead bodies and torture?

If, Mr President, you do not know the names of decent people in Chechnya, ask those who do. It is so elementary, and lives will be saved.

PS An argument broke out in the *Novaya gazeta* office over whether we should write Security Service or "Security Service"? Anti-terrorist operation or "anti-terrorist operation"? Opinion was divided. From a grammatical point of view clearly there should be no inverted commas, but the present-day reality in Chechnya is so phoney as to make it impossible to observe grammatical rules. In Chechnya everything is in inverted commas, because an illegal war is taking place in a zone whose existence is itself illegal. An illegitimate government spawns lawless soldiers. The knot has already been pulled so tight that it is difficult to imagine how it can be undone, even if at some magic moment enlightenment should come to those with power in their hands, and perhaps even a flicker of responsibility in their minds.

A BLOOD FEUD HAS BEEN DECLARED AGAINST THE FAMILY OF THE "ACTING PRESIDENT OF CHECHNYA"

June 16, 2003

In the remote Chechen village of Bachi-Yurt "unidentified masked individuals wearing camouflage fatigues," speaking only in Chechen, executed four members of one family, the Ablayev-Dautkhadzhievs. Three men, aged between 45 and 55, were shot along with a 27-year-old woman, who leaves a two-month-old baby and two sons aged four and five. The executioners came for them in the night and said they were exacting blood retribution for the events of May 14, when female suicide bombers made an attempt on the life of "Acting President of the Chechen Republic" Akhmat-hadji Kadyrov near the village of Ilaskhan-Yurt. In the attack five of his bodyguards died; these the murderers described as their comrades, and said they had accordingly come to "take blood" for them.

Up till now, no monuments have been placed on the graves of those executed and the men of the family of the four who died do not visit the cemetery. This means they have declared a blood feud for the killing, this time on Ramzan Kadyrov, younger son of the "Acting President," who, with his father's full support and occupying the post of Commander of a mythical "Interior Ministry Special Unit" at his court, engages with his brigade in robbery, murder, and general score-settling with those he regards as his enemies.

"Well, Shakhidat and Aimani could not have been guilty," Zinaida Dautkhadzhieva says, shaking her head and no longer wiping her swollen eyes. She is a grandmother and in May six of her family were killed. "Why did my daughter die? They dragged her here, to the cellar where we have a kitchen. I was shouting, 'Take me, she has a baby!'

They replied, 'You are not a blood relative. We don't need you.' Her children were crying. People in masks woke everyone from their beds and asked, 'Who are you?' Or 'Whose are you?' They took those they wanted down to the cellar and just shot them. My Liza first of all. What for? Shakhidat and Aimani were not guilty of causing the explosion. Everybody knows that."

The women around us are crying like kittens, moaning quietly. Liza's old father breaks down. It is unbearable, because everybody can see what the continuation will be.

First, however, a chronology of this latest misfortune to befall Bachi-Yurt, and why these events happened.

On May 14 a terrorist attack took place in Ilaskhan-Yurt, a village in Gudermes District, during an election rally for the ruling United Russia party which coincided with the day of the Prophet's birth. There were many casualties. Chechen television had assiduously invited people to come to the field near Ilaskhan-Yurt, promising a meeting with Kadyrov and gifts in his honor from United Russia. It was only after the bombing that Kadyrov claimed on television that the Ilaskhan-Yurt meeting was a religious celebration; the propaganda put out through the Chechen media before May 14 made it clear that this was pre-electoral campaigning on behalf of United Russia candidates, supported by the administrative resources of the state. The heads of rural administrations were instructed to organise buses to systematically bring their people to Ilaskhan-Yurt in order to swell the numbers.

People arrived in vehicles and on foot. For several days beforehand local television reported that Kadyrov would be speaking and, as a sign of clemency, would talk to mothers whose children had been disappeared during security sweeps. Thousands responded to that inducement. A crucial factor in the turnout of many thousands was this hint that Kadyrov would make an announcement about the fate of some of the disappeared. There have been thousands of them in Chechnya, and most of their relatives comb the Republic daily in the hope of finding traces of their dear ones.

Among the crowd were Shakhidat Baimuradova, her sister Aimani Visayeva, the mother of 11 children and long since an old-age pensioner, and Zulai Abdurzakova. They were there for good reason. A typical part of the modern Chechen scenery, these are mothers fruitlessly seeking their sons, hoping by chance somewhere to come across an honest law enforcement officer. They always carry bundles of documents with them.

On May 13, the day before the gathering, Shakhidat and Aimani went to the home of Kadyrov's father in the village of Tsentoroy to ask him to help them get a meeting with the "Acting President" at which they could hand over their letters and documents. The father told them to go to Ilaskhan-Yurt, saying that it would be more convenient to meet him there. They took his advice. On May 14, what happened happened, and by that evening the Prosecutor's Office had issued the names of these three elderly women as the suicide bombers. On May 16, after inspection by forensic medical specialists in the Dagestan mortuary of Khasavyurt, the bodies of Shakhidat and Aimani were returned to their relatives, and on May 17 they were buried in Bachi-Yurt, their ancestral home.

The bandits who burst in in the night shouted, "Why did you bury them here?"

"Well," I ask, "why did you, when in fact they lived in other villages?"

"So that they would be next to their mother's grave. They no longer had anybody where they lived," the relatives answer. They are convinced that Shakhidat and Aimani were not the bombers.

"How can you be so sure?"

"They both had too many things to take care of, and they just weren't like that."

Towards evening on the day of the funerals two men, Roman Edilov and Arbi Salmaniev, came to the family's house. Although Dautkhadzhiev is the surname of Shakhidat and Aimani's brother, their maiden name is Ablayev because their father had more than one wife and some children took their mother's name. The Ablayevs and Dautkhadzhievs have adjacent houses in Bachi-Yurt. The wake was taking place after the funerals of Shakhidat and Aimani.

Edilov and Salmaniev are well known in Bachi-Yurt. Edilov is the recently appointed Head of the Kurchaloy District Interior Affairs Office.

Before that he was a soldier in Kadyrov's "Security Service" or, as people here put it, "one of Ramzan's gang." Edilov is regarded as someone charged with defending the ruling family's interests in Kurchaloy. Salmaniev, his deputy and another Kadyrov soldier, lives in Bachi-Yurt.

Salmaniev and Edilov declared the families guilty of the terrorist act committed by Shakhidat and Aimani. "Now," they said, "you must pay in blood for the attempt on Kadyrov's life and for the deaths of Ramzan's soldiers."

"Did you know this was coming?" I ask Akhmat Temirsultanov, the Qadi (Islamic judge) of Kurchaloy District and Imam of Bachi-Yurt. The old man – respected, ill, stooped – pretends to be deaf in order not to have to answer the question. I press the point, but to no avail. Even the Qadi and Imam is desperately afraid of falling into disfavor with the Kadyrovs. That fear can today be felt throughout Chechnya, fear of a kind unknown even a year ago. People have learned from the blood-letting, and only the bravest will whisper, "We are afraid of Kadyrov."

"Does anybody else, do the families of other people who died at Ilaskhan-Yurt, bear a similar grudge against you? Have you been warned by them?" I asked Zinaida Dautkhadzhieva. The ritual of declaring a blood feud is strict. It is not something undertaken lightly, and a qadi or imam should be involved in the procedure.

"No, nobody else has a grudge against us because they know Shakhidat and Aimani were not guilty. The Prosecutor's Office admitted it made a mistake."

And so it did. A thorough examination of the bodies of Shakhidat and Aimani, conducted at the insistence of the investigative team at the Prosecutor's Office leading the inquiry into the bombing, showed there was no need even for a forensic medical examination. The nature of their injuries proved it had not been them. A death sentence caused by a slip of the tongue.

Ivan Nikitin is a tall young man who wears trainers and has a rifle casually slung over his shoulder. He is the leader of the team investigating the "act of sabotage and terrorism" within the framework of

Criminal Case No. 32046. Nikitin's team was set up by the Republican Prosecutor's Office and is based in Gudermes, close to Ilaskhan-Yurt, in order to be able to question witnesses conveniently.

"These women, Baimuradova, Visayeva and Abdurzakova, were not wearing the explosive devices," Nikitin confirms. "They were simply standing two metres away from the epicenter. I told Qadi Temirsultanov that when he came to ask whether they were guilty or not. I could see he needed to know that in order to avoid a blood feud."

"Tell me, then, why was the Prosecutor's Office in such a hurry to declare that they were the bombers? Here we are with four completely guiltless people killed, one of whom had a two-month-old baby she was breast-feeding."

Nikitin understands perfectly. He sighs and parries with "It is all the fault of the media." In fact, it was none other Sergey Fridinsky, the Deputy Prosecutor-General of Russia for the Southern Federal Region and Nikitin's immediate boss, who announced the names of the alleged bombers before anything was known for certain. Nikitin declines to comment on this and refers me "upstairs." Needless to say, "upstairs" the officials in the Chechen Prosecutor's Office are in no hurry to comment on their own murderously irresponsible utterances.

Back in Bachi-Yurt. Zina Dautkhadzhieva, the mother of the executed Liza, also has very little to add. She is terribly afraid of saying something she might regret, something which might prove fatal for some of her other children.

"You have to understand, the Kadyrovites are everywhere, and to declare a blood feud on Kadyrov today is . . ." The Bachi-Yurt villagers try to explain the situation but can't.

"Is what?"

"It is to take on too much. It is a death sentence. That's the way life is here."

It seems there is nobody capable of protecting them, neither the Prosecutor's Office, nor President Putin, nor the United Nations.

Edilov and Salmaniev went away, and because their accusations seemed so preposterous, so completely at odds with all the rules and customs, the men remained at home. Nobody went off to hide, as is traditional when somebody declares a blood feud or is preparing to do so. In those circumstances the men at risk do not sleep at home. They all stayed, and on the night of May 17 were executed: two of Aimani's sons, Khanpash and Movsar Visayev; Aimani's brother, Said Mahomed Ablayev; and Shakhidat, their niece.

Why? Because this has now almost become a custom. The Kadyro-vites can do anything they please, even things forbidden by tradition. They live as if there will be no tomorrow, despising the laws, written and unwritten. If Ramzan wants land in Gudermes for his petrol station, he takes it without even bothering to inform the Ministry of Education to whom the teacher training institute standing on that land belongs.

So now instead of the Gudermes teacher training institute there is Ramzan's petrol station. That is how it is with business, where money is involved; but the same thing applies to blood, to the torrents of it shed at the hands of the Kadyrovites. For they are in charge of this blood-letting; everybody in Chechnya knows that if you need to take revenge on someone for spilling blood, you go to work in Ramzan's division. You will be welcomed and given weapons and their blessing to exact retribution. The Kadyrovs are in the business of setting every-body against everybody else. What for? In order to consolidate their own power. Where there is no order, there remains only blood and fear to secure the base of your throne.

BALLOT BOXES OR FUNERAL URNS?

August 25, 2003

Power struggles are never noble or fine, but the power struggle in Chechnya, taking place against the backdrop of a war now in its fifth year, is as nauseating as a reusable traitor.

Ibrahim looks like a pirate. Scars are healing under his hair and his eyes are hidden behind dark glasses. He was hurt very badly. He limps clumsily, his weight falling heavily first on one leg then on the other, a common sign here of someone beaten on the kidneys. Ibrahim Garsiev, the 36-year-old father of a family, is from Tangi Chu. He is a bodyguard of Rustam Saidullayev, the brother of opposition politician Malik Saidulayev.

On August 7 he was driving from home through the Urus Martan District when he was stopped by "unidentified masked individuals wearing combat fatigues," the usual Chechen story. They disarmed him, took him to the district militia station, and started interrogating him.

"They wanted me to confess to blowing up a military water tanker in Tangi Chu and killing Batalov, the Head of the District Office for Combating Organised Crime," Ibrahim relates. "But that was just for show. The Head of the Criminal Investigation Department is a decent man. He said, 'Look, at least admit to having a hand grenade. That will be better for you, you will only go to prison for a year. Otherwise the Kadyrovites will kill you. It is they who are calling for your head.'"

Ibrahim, however, dug his heels in, and shortly afterwards was hooded, pushed into a car, and driven off.

In Chechnya the "Kadyrovites" are units subordinate to Ramzan Kadyrov, the son of the "Chief of Chechnya." Ramzan is the head of "Daddy's 'Security Service,'" and behaves in a manner reminiscent of President Yeltsin's bodyguard Alexander Korzhakov, who interpreted his role so broadly as to behave like the second-in-command in the state hierarchy.

An example of this in action: how funds are collected for Akhmat-hadji Kadyrov's election campaign. As a majority of ministers in the Chechen Government admit, Ramzan names a sum of money which their Ministry is to contribute. We are not talking thousands of roubles here, but thousands of dollars. The Minister draws up a list appor-tioning the levy between officials in accordance with the post they occupy. Deputy ministers have to contribute up to $5,000, while heads of departments or boards are assessed at $1,000–2,000 per head. The officials are warned that if the Ministry fails to deliver the sum demanded by Ramzan, they will be sacked. Civil servants are desper-ately afraid of losing their jobs because wages funded by the state budget are the only more or less stable form of income in Chechnya. As a result, half of Chechnya is today in debt to the other half. Everybody has borrowed and re-borrowed from each other in order not to come to the attention of the Kadyrov family.

After the officials, there are Chechnya's markets. This is the Republic's second most important cash cow. Unfortunate Chechen women – teachers, doctors, housewives, nurses, and journalists – stand in the markets, which is how most families have managed to feed themselves throughout the war. The Chechen men are at home trying to avoid security sweeps and checkpoints, and the Chechen women are trading. Every such market trader also has a tribute levied on behalf of Akhmat-hadji. The approach is the same: Ramzan names a figure to the market's Director, who then allots everybody a contribution.

The officials, naturally enough, did not protest, but the women went on strike. They had each been assessed for $500 (political services in Chechnya are, you will note, quite pricey), and said they would not return to the market until the demand was made more reasonable. The strike collapsed, however, when the Kadyrovites threatened to murder the families of one or two of the ringleaders, and the money was handed over. You can judge for yourself how remarkably fair and democratic the coming elections are going to be.

The word "Kadyrovite" in Chechnya is applied to a large number of decentralised and anarchic detachments, each armed to the teeth with all manner of weaponry, including Israeli rapid-fire rifles and murderous Berettas banned on the territory of the Russian Federation.

Officially there are 61 people in Akhmat-hadji's security detail but if we include units under Ramzan's command, some of the militia firearms teams, and all manner of special operations units with which Chechnya is teeming and into which Kadyrov has succeeded in infiltrating his own people, the official figure rises to 1,200.

In reality, however, throughout Chechnya the Kadyrovites number several thousands. They themselves put the figure sometimes at 3,000, sometimes at 5,000. Where do they all come from? The divisions Ramzan Kadyrov controls today accept anybody who wants to go on fighting, for example ex-resistance fighters who have been amnestied. In effect, the amnesty declared by the Russian Duma obliges those amnestied to be absorbed into the Kadyrov detachments. Amnestied former resistance units now form the backbone of the Kadyrovites. This summer they recruited in every district center and most villages. Fighters and members of the resistance who refused amnesty on these terms testify that those who did surrender were regarded by and large as brutes and criminals in their communities.

Although the Kadyrovites claim to be sweeping Chechnya clear of Islamic extremist Wahhabis, they are in practice clearing the Republic of anybody they want to get rid of. At present that means Akhmat-hadji Kadyrov's political enemies.

Another recent example: Movladi Baisarov's detachment is based in the village of Youth Soviet Farm No. 15, near Grozny. The detachment was previously commanded by Maskhadov's deputy, Vakha Arsanov, and has moved directly from the ranks of the separatists into the Kadyrovite organization.

Baisarov's men recently abducted three FSB officers and attempted to ransom them in exchange for one of their criminal comrades who had been arrested for his involvement in another kidnapping. The Baisarovites got away with it because now they count as Kadyrovites.

In the Urus Martan District Militia Station it was precisely one such turncoat that Ibrahim Garsiev found himself facing, namely a participant in several sensational kidnappings back in Maskhadov's time, a man with a federal warrant out for his arrest but who is now the Deputy Head of the District Militia Station in Urus Martan.

It was this criminal who organised Garsiev's kidnapping, knowing that he worked in Saidulayev's security detail, and called upon the services of "unidentified masked Chechens wearing combat fatigues." Ibrahim was driven off and soon found himself before Ramzan Kadyrov in the courtyard of his fortress home in Tsentoroy.

Were you interrogated by Ramzan personally?
Yes. He asked me what kind of vehicle Saidulayev used and how many bodyguards he had. I didn't reply. I was beaten all over my body with a spade handle; Ramzan beat me himself. They strung me up by the arms from a tree and beat me. Ramzan was not the only person

directing this, there was a second person who later told me he had been Basayev's Chief of Staff but was now Ramzan's Head of Reconnaissance. Ramzan said he would give his gold watch to whoever thought up the cruellest death for me.

How many of them were there?
Sixty or seventy.

Who won?
It was Basayev's ex-Chief of Staff. He said I should be hung up by the arms and have a thousand cuts made on my skin. They went away and conferred. I thought they were deciding how to kill me but when they came back they started beating me again, intermittently. They would beat me and then ask, "Are you going to do it then?" The third time I said I couldn't take any more and would do what they wanted.

So what was it they wanted?
They wanted me to take a landmine into Rustam's house and blow up Malik Saidulayev when he arrived. I agreed. Ramzan shouted, "Do you think I'm going to let you have the presidency? Even if Malik gets elected I will shoot every last one of you."

He was talking about organising the assassination of Malik Saidulayev? Ramzan was commissioning it and you were to carry it out? They were to give you a landmine?
Yes.

What if you had not agreed?
They would have killed me.

After you agreed, what happened?
They stopped beating me and dragged other people from the cells. There are cells for prisoners which open directly into Ramzan's courtyard. I saw three prisoners myself. I don't know what they had done. They shot two of them in the legs in front of me. The third, who had already been

shot in the legs, was put in a car and taken away. Then they gave me tea, as if now I was one of them. They gave me something to eat. They brought some girls who sang and danced. They let me go the next day. I am supposed to tell them when Malik is coming to see his brother, and then they will immediately give me the landmine. I have gone into hiding. I have taken my family away. Ramzan warned that if I did not do what I promised he would massacre me and my family. I sent a statement to the Prosecutor-General. If Kadyrov Senior becomes President, my only option will be to join a group to fight him. What can I do? We just have to survive. I won't let them take me alive a second time.

Hiding behind his black glasses, Ibrahim hobbles off. Everything that happened to him this August is typical of life in Chechnya in the run-up to the election. One could substitute names of other people who have been tortured in the same place and for the same purpose. The real pre-election campaigning by Kadyrov's emissaries is mass intimidation under the slogan, "With Kadyrov, or Death!"

What we see looming is truly an election of despair. The Kremlin has created a monster worse than those which preceded him, and now he is not so easy to get rid of. If Kadyrov wins, it is inevitable that he will settle scores with his opponents, that they will retaliate, that there will be more bloodshed and atrocities, mistrust and radicalisation. That will be a war, whether you call it civil war or the Third Chechen War.

WHY KADYROV TOOK AGAINST OLD BALU: PRESIDENTIAL POWER IN THE ZONE OF THE SO-CALLED "ANTI-TERRORIST OPERATION"

November 20, 2003

Does Kadyrov want to be a real president? Does he want to live up to the election results declared on October 5 and, in accordance with the Constitution, protect the people of Chechnya from war, abductions, starvation and humiliation? What is he doing? What sort of a bargain are the populace getting?

For the past five months Marat Isakov has been searching high and low for his 77-year-old father, Said Mahomed-hadji Isakov, Village Elder of Dyshne-Vedeno, a well-known man respected in this region as authoritative, upright and devout. In fact, as the people of Vedeno say of him, as pure as gold. He has made ten pilgrimages to Mecca, has stood up against the Wahhabis, and you will not find a house here where Old Balu, as he is affectionately known, has not buried the departed, reconciled enemies or counselled the young.

For some time, however, the elder Isakov had been an obstacle, in Kadyrov's opinion. Old Balu failed to support him, spoke out against his methods, and on June 21 this year, during the period between the referendum on March 23 and the election on October 5 when Kadyrov was sweeping away all opposition, Said Mahomed-hadji Isakov was abducted by "unidentified military personnel," from the street next to his own in Dyshne-Vedeno, as he was going to a wake. His family have no doubt that the Kadyrovites were behind it.

Zeinap, Said Mahomed's 75-year-old wife, who has borne him ten children and shared 60 years of her life with him, wrote letters to everyone she could think of, from the Prosecutor of Vedeno District to President Putin and Patriarch Alexiy. She enclosed a copy of his labor record book as a worker at the Vedeno forestry mill and as a blacksmith, his awards, expressions of appreciation for his numerous successes in socialist competition. It was all futile. "Information regarding the circumstances of the detention and present whereabouts of S. Isakov is not in the possession of any of the Ministries of the Russian Federation on the territory of the Chechen Republic." In today's Chechnya, this is a fearsome dismissal which leaves no grounds for hope. It came to Zeinap signed by the Military Prosecutor of Army Unit 20116, Judicial Colonel I. Kholmsky.

Balu appears to have been swallowed up by the earth, a man "who enjoyed unchallengeable authority among all strata of the population," as a collective appeal from the Citizens' Assembly of Vedeno District to President Putin put it when they demanded that the old man be returned.

"It was odd the way even people who agreed to help, people who go into the military bases, to Khankala, suddenly changed their tune one or two days later," says Marat, one of Said Mahomed's seven sons. "One day they would be saying, 'Yes, I've seen him. He will certainly be released,' but the next it was, 'No. I don't know anything.'"

"Why do you think that is?"

"It was if they had discovered something, and suddenly wanted out."

Zeinap continues:

"He is ill, taking medicine. He has high blood pressure and stomach trouble. I sense he is no longer with us. He would not have lasted this long in prison. They might at least return his bones. We went to Kadyrov's father to petition. I tried to go to Kadyrov himself but his bodyguard shouted at me and drove me away. If a resistance fighter gets killed in the fighting, the soldiers return his body to the relatives for 15,000 roubles. But here is someone who was not guilty of anything. None of his sons were involved in anything either, and we can't even have the body. I went to the Army Commandant in Vedeno and said, 'If someone is guilty, he gets put on trial; but if he is not guilty does he simply disappear?' The Commandant had nothing to say."

Old Balu was as uncompromising as he was legendary. He famously never bowed down before anyone. He ignored Kadyrov's demand to all mullahs and religious leaders and did not urge his fellow villagers to vote in favor of the new Constitution in the March 23 referendum. Nearly everyone else grumbled but did as they were told. More than that, Said Mahomed categorically rejected Kadyrov's methods for ruling Chechnya, for example when it was announced that the Islamic fast was not to be observed as required by the Islamic calendar but to be moved by one week. This was his way of finding out which mullahs would defy him. The majority were scared and complied, if without enthusiasm. They wanted to live. Said Mahomed did not comply. He said publicly, "We should fear the Almighty, not Kadyrov." This, of course, was passed on to Kadyrov, and retribution was not long in coming.

"Kadyrov was just establishing which of the mullahs were on side," says a fellow villager. "We were very afraid for Said Mahomed, we begged him to go to his son in Moscow. Kadyrov was removing from his path anybody who enjoyed authority and was not on his side, but Said Mahomed refused. He said, 'I am too old to run away.'"

Shortly before he was disappeared, old Balu went to Ilaskhan-Yurt where a religious festival which is important for Chechens takes place once a year. People pray together. As he was approaching the village, the old man saw that the United Russia party was electioneering in the middle of the religious festival, and of course Kadyrov was there in person. Isakov did not disguise his outrage and left immediately. Again, Kadyrov was informed.

Strong people usually have no difficulty respecting the authority of other strong people. It is the weak people who seek revenge. Very little time passed before they came for the old man, a whole column of armoured vehicles. Some 200 soldiers, all to seize one ill old man.

Said Mahomed went outside the gates. Zeinap tried to dissuade him but he replied that they would not harm an old man like him. He had been checked hundreds of times. He walked through the gates and that was the last anybody saw of him. Zeinap heard the engines of the armoured column roaring as it turned and drove off. She and his sons wrote letters to every conceivable institution. The villagers held a meeting to demand that Kadyrov and the Army immediately return their greatly respected elder. The Prosecutor's Office even opened Criminal Case No. 24049, but the official responses, when they came, were mere stonewalling. "No special measures (security sweeps) were conducted in the village of Dyshne-Vedeno by members of the federal forces between June 20 and 23."

"There was just the pretence of an investigation and of inquiries," Marat Isakov is convinced. "He was taken away by Kadyrovites. Kadyrov forces the mullahs to be corrupt, but my father was completely different. Kadyrov removes all genuinely religious people who separate religion and money. That has always been the way in our family. We kept out of politics and avoided friendship with government officials."

Almost all the mullahs in Chechnya who found Kadyrov un-acceptable, and openly said as much to the people, have by now been eliminated. The same is true of almost all the heads of rural administrations in Chechnya. (The Chechen administrative system is based on enormous "villages" of up to 15–20,000 inhabitants.) But what, meanwhile, of the "President of the Chechen Republic"?

Having been proclaimed President, Akhmat-hadji Kadyrov is today rarely to be found at his desk, and the way he spends his time can hardly be described as "leading the Republic." Kadyrov's life is divided between his fortress-home in Tsentoroy and Moscow, with a great deal more time being spent in the latter. This should be no surprise. Kadyrov cannot free himself from the past and continues to see keeping the Kremlin sweet as the first priority of his presidency, well ahead of working for the people. Truly he would need to move mountains in order to earn their respect. His "work" in Moscow of late has centerd on the long, drawn-out retirement of Alexander Voloshin, the Head of Putin's Presidential Administration. Kadyrov was never away from the Kremlin while this was playing out, because his installation in power had been Voloshin's swan-song project, and without Voloshin he was powerless. He started to become nervous when oligarch Mikhail Khodorkovsky was imprisoned, and frequently travelled to Moscow to try to find a new and equally powerful patron.

Kadyrov in Chechnya is also a pretty gruesome spectacle. When he travels from Tsentoroy to Grozny, "to work," so to speak, the arrangements are becoming even more spectacular than those in place for Putin's journeys around Moscow. All roads and footpaths are closed, and cars and Kadyrov's pedestrian subjects alike find themselves in a state of siege. He is scared that one of his subjects may decide to blow up the champion of their wonderful new life.

Kadyrov's presidential ideal is also gradually becoming clearer. He has lately started hinting that it is the Turkmenbashi, the father of all Turkmen, who has turned Turkmenistan into the most oppressive of oriental despotisms in the post-Soviet territories. The Turkmenbashi is scared stiff of his people and roots out any semblance of dissent; he allows his officials free rein to thieve, and personally controls the corruption. He has an army of brutal mercenaries and influential backers beyond the borders of his land.

Who would deny that all the world's dictators share a family likeness? Kadyrov has Putin and the Kremlin as his backers; his murderous campaign against old Isakov and the mullahs; his regal progresses; and his levelling of society by the simple expedient of cutting off any heads showing above the parapet. As for corruption and officialdom, Kadyrov's Chechnya is one big playground of graft and corruption.

One current example is what has happened to the promised compensation payments, the main plank of Kadyrov's election campaign and something he and Putin were forever seen talking about on television. It is already November, and no compensation is being paid. The way Kadyrov organised it was to set up numerous special Payments Commissions (with a consequent sharp rise in the number of officials). These are headed by a phalanx of dodgy individuals, and a war is being waged between these officials and citizens who have lost their property and the roof over their heads. The purpose of this campaign is to loot the compensation fund. Just as he himself controls the oil pipeline, just as the Turkmenbashi controls the gas pipeline, so Kadyrov has made a gift to the officials of the compensation pipeline.

Senior compensation officials are hard at it, having mastered the well-known "tube of toothpaste" technique of squeezing out a percentage, a kickback. First they made sure that nobody could simply produce the documents proving their entitlement to compensation and get the money. People had to be registered and re-registered, lists had to be weeded and co-ordinated. Those removed from the lists had to make immense efforts to get reinstated, efforts expressed in terms of a percentage deducted from the compensation payment.

By now the population is so conformable it does not complain. In Avtury, the only person in the village to have received any compensation got 175,000 roubles instead of the 350,000 she was due, the remainder being siphoned off. She is happy and grateful to Kadyrov. In Grozny I could not find any such fortunate person who could say, "Oh, yes. I got the compensation and am building my new house."

Either Kadyrov does not know what is going on, or Putin's promises were a lot of hot air. And believe me, where there is money around, Kadyrov knows all about it.

Akhmat-hadji Kadyrov is shown on Russian television side by side with Putin far more frequently than the Russian Prime Minister, Mikhail Kasianov. Kadyrov it is whom President Putin insistently presents to East and West as "the face of the new Chechnya." The new Chechnya is now in the second month of its existence. Nobody knows the whereabouts of Old Balu, and there is nobody to gainsay Kadyrov. Putin's Chechen stalemate, Kadyrov's land of despair. Late 2003, the "peace" after the "election."

USING AN IMPRISONMENT PIT FOR A BALLOT BOX: CHECHNYA IS BACK IN THE MIDDLE AGES

November 17, 2005

In the six or more years of the latest war Chechens have become so used to frequent, dishonest elections that the imminent return of parliamentary elections has generated no discernible excitement. Popular apathy is consolidated by the racketeering which pervades the Republic. Everything depends only on whether you have paid or not; the officials and local security agencies either pay tribute, or levy it. Abductions continue to be a daily occurrence, and in that sense nothing has changed, except that now there are only two reasons for nearly all abductions: either somebody has not paid up (in the case of officials); or someone has not bought himself out (in the case of renegade resistance fighters).

My old friend Mahomet from Gudermes is a notable person in the Republic. A gentle, educated man, in earlier years he wrote a good book about the Chechen artist Pavel Zakharov. The blown-up Kadyrov Senior first made Mahomet, who had many orphans living in his house and was seriously in need of funds at the time, Minister of Labor and Social Development. Later also First Deputy Prime Minister for Social Affairs. But did Mahomet thieve?

Recently, the Kadyrovites kidnapped him and dragged him off to Tsentoroy, where the main Chechen "re-education base" is now located, numerous *zindan* punishment pits having been dug there for the purpose. They beat him up and presented him with a bill for $200,000 if he didn't want to end up on the list of human rights activists disappeared without trace. The $200,000 was apparently part of a debt he hadn't paid, plus interest.

Mahomet gave it to them, cash in hand, on the nail. They brushed down his suit, smoothed it, and returned the official, whose job is to support the socially deprived, to his workplace. In other words, one set of state officials extorted protection money from another civil servant.

A similar instance involved a promising young leader of the Shali District, Akhmed, who was also invited by Kadyrov Senior to work as Head of the Administration out of Togliatti. Akhmed too was recently abducted and taken to Tsentoroy, beaten up, and ordered to pay $100,000 for his release. He handed it over, but lost his job anyway because the Kadyrov extortion controllers concluded he was unreliable and they saw no prospect of coming to a satisfactory arrangement with him. He immediately fled abroad. Now the Head of the Administration of Shali District is absolutely one of their own, a certain Edward Zakayev, a friend of Kadyrov Junior rather than of Kadyrov Senior.

What are these debts we are talking about, on this kind of scale? And how in any case can such debts arise between state officials?

Even a year ago, in the months following the enthronement of Kadyrov Junior, "on side" in Chechnya referred to people who were considered loyal. Admittedly, "loyal" primarily meant "bound by ties of kinship," but nevertheless loyal. Now "on side" means anyone who thieves and is capable of paying tribute. All officials and all security officers in Chechnya pay it to those above them – the Kadyrov gang – and the more highly placed an official is, the more he has to pay. A security official or a social welfare official pays on a regular basis. There is a requirement, for example, for a single local militia station to subscribe $1,000 for every person working there: 150 militiamen equates to $150,000 monthly, remitted to Tsentoroy.

And heaven forbid that anyone should try to conceal anything. The Kadyrovites have an enviably efficient protection racket control service, far more efficient than whatever outfit Putin kids himself is pursuing Basayev. If you don't pay your tribute, or if you try to conceal some-

thing, you get a smack on the head and the sum due from you is
increased as an ongoing fine. If you fail to pay a second time you had
better flee before you are abducted, with fatal consequences.

In other words there is a market, and it is ruled by bosses who do
their rounds and get their cut. The bosses are a gang in private practice, and in Chechnya they enjoy the patronage of Russia's most senior
state authorities. Accordingly, absolutely anything goes in terms of
robbery with violence or depravity, economics or politics, or the appointment of candidates to stand as Deputies. Not even membership of
Putin's United Russia party confers immunity. You need to pay and
promise to keep paying.

One last example: a man who was close to the Kadyrovs, Taus, the
most loyal of the loyal, their guard dog of Chechenisation. Taus lived
with the Kadyrov family for a long time. He respected Akhmat-hadji.
He served him and was inherited by Ramzan, whom he had known
since he was little. Taus aspired to be a major politician. He was the
architect of the agreement on how powers were to be divided between
the Russian and Chechen regimes, and he was someone Surkov talked
to in the Kremlin. He longed to be leader of the Parliament, and for
a while enjoyed the rank of Chairman of the State Council of the
Chechen Republic, a quasi-parliamentary institution which rubber-
stamped political decisions on behalf of Akhmat-hadji and Ramzan.

But then there was an argument. In the end even the most loyal of
the loyal could no longer tolerate the super-insolence of Kadyrov's gang
and the super-exactions they levied. Trading on his position as an old
comrade, he had the audacity to make a remark to the totally berserk
Ramzan, who beat him like a dog, in public, as he was accustomed to
beat anyone he didn't like. He punched him in the face and kicked
him out.

Taus left and, even before the election, Ramzan appointed a different
head of the Parliament, Dukvakha from the Ministry of Agriculture,
to be Deputy Prime Minister. Incidentally, the Ministry of Agriculture
pays even more than the other Ministries to Tsentoroy; Dukvakha had
decided that might help his career along.

What am I getting at? On the eve of this latest round of "European-style" elections, Chechnya has finally been turned into a big Bey's bazaar where the Bey is the sole oligarch, complete with his Hummers and his golden WC pedestals, a completely brutal, repressive apparatus that stops at nothing, and other tell-tale signs of the Turkmenbashi syndrome. Do you know what Parliament does in Turkmenistan? It rubber-stamps the decisions of the Turkmenbashi. Well, in Chechnya a "European" façade is being built by a regime of total Turkmenbashism, a mechanism for rubber-stamping whatever Ramzan's visceral urges dictate.

Of course, you have to feel sorry for the people racing to hand over money for the right to become nonentities, as Alu Alkhanov has in the past year by being "democratically elected" President of the Chechen Republic. But everybody makes his choice, and for those who wish to run and deliver the money there are others out there who were also urged to be election candidates but categorically refused.

One thing, however, is unbearable. What was it that thousands and thousands of people, from the start of the Second Chechen War in 1999, laid down their lives for? For this? And why are those who are still alive suffering so much, eking out an existence without any twenty-first-century amenities in the ruins and wrecked homes of Chechnya?

It is hard to admit, but we must: all the sacrifices that were made have been rendered senseless by the regime which has been installed. As election day 2005 approaches we are effectively back in 1997, the year when Maskhadov was an ineffectual head of state and Basayev's gun law, raised to the status of national policy, was lording it over everybody.

The year 1997 led to the new war in 1999. Today's arrangements cannot last long either. Another war in this land, which has already wept until it has no more tears to shed, is highly probable. Make a note in your diary: the elections take place in ten days' time.

A VIDEO PREMIERE IN CHECHNYA

March 20, 2006

Last week that section of the Russian public which takes an interest in such matters was intrigued when a couple of photographs appeared on the Internet featuring Someone Resembling Ramzan Kadyrov (hereafter, in the interests of brevity, referred to as "SRRK"). The photographs were stills from a video made using a mobile phone. This was said to be in the possession of a Canadian Chechen website. In the image SRRK is embracing an attractive young brunette in a crimson bra, and making no secret of how humanly happy he is.

A scandal erupted. The guardians of morality railed, the Chechen Prosecutor's Office managed a turn of speed not seen for a long time by announcing that very evening that it was opening a criminal case against the perpetrators of this impertinence. Not, needless to say, in order to establish the identity of SRRK.

Those two photos, however, were mere child's play. The "Bathhouse Video', as it was titled, is nothing compared with other videos featuring that same SRRK and his henchmen, also made with the aid of mobile telephones, which have come into the possession of *Novaya gazeta*.

Right, then: Scene 1. Chronologically the first video, this was also the first to arrive at our office. A typical Grozny street, evidently in late autumn 2005, probably November. A trivial local incident: a road accident involving a federal armoured personnel carrier (there are no non-federal APCs in Chechnya) and a car belonging to somebody from the so-called Chechen security forces. Numerous people in the uniform of the Kadyrov "Security Service" run in from off-camera. Among the crowd there are also members of the Highway Patrol Militia. The crowd is rushing over to where Russian soldiers are lying on the ground, evidently from the APC involved in the accident.

One federal who is still on his feet is pushed by men in Kadyrovite uniforms to where the others are lying. The mob crowds round. Flailing arms, fists, rifle butts. The one-eyed mobile phone follows what is happening.

A member of the Highway Patrol shouts in Chechen, "Stop beating them! Disperse! Aslanbek!" Those filming with the mobile phone say in Chechen, "They haven't had enough yet" and in Russian add, "The bastards." And again in Chechen, "We'll show them not to disrespect Ramzan!"

Eventually the crowd parts. The bodies of the soldiers, sprawled on the wet, muddy shoulder of a Chechen road, are left lying motionless, face down in the mud. One of them gets his head stamped on. He does not react. Either they are dead or completely unconscious. One thing is clear, they have been thoroughly beaten up.

Scene 2. Possibly January this year, or maybe December last year. A dense crowd of men wearing a variety of combat fatigues in a market, either in Grozny or Gudermes. From the loudspeakers of a market booth pour the lyrics of a Russian pop song: "There is harmony in the world . . ." In the middle of the crowd SRRK is visible.

The filming is being done from a car window. The two people involved in the filming are speaking quietly in Chechen. "What's he doing, shoving him in the boot?" "Yes." "They're shoving another one in." "Yes, two of them." "Do you see? It's a Lada 10." "Is Ramzan getting into the 10?" "I can't hear what they're saying because of you!"

The crowd of men in combat fatigues is churning about in Brownian motion. SRRK is directing the process from the middle of the mêlée. The paramilitaries are manhandling someone, who is not resisting, into the boot of a white Lada 10. Then they start shoving in a second man who is less willing. One paramilitary sets about him. Finally they slam down the boot lid and the vehicles prepare to leave.

SRRK has already climbed up on to the car's running board. In the heat of directing the abduction he throws his arm forward, like Lenin on the armoured car at the Finland Station in 1917. "What is he doing on that 10?" those taking the video exclaim. Quite so, bigwigs in Chechnya drive around fast in armour-plated jeeps.

Scene 3 is in effect the "Bathhouse Video," two stills from which were made public last week. The significant thing about this clip is what was not shown. After SRRK embraces the lady in the crimson bra, there is some incomprehensible action. SRRK several times releases the lady in red then draws her back to himself, laughing. The lady tries to dance as he talks to her in bad Russian, but then he shouts in Chechen to somebody off-camera, "Go on, take your trousers off!"

Again, "Give him some shampoo [sic] so he takes his trousers off!" All this with much chortling. SRRK is enjoying himself, relaxed, unself-conscious.

Finally the scene becomes more comprehensible. SRRK wants his young lady to feast her eyes on someone off-camera who is lowering his trousers on SRRK's orders. After that we see a harassed young man in a black baseball cap pulling down his trousers. He has either been beaten up or is mentally disturbed, or in a state of narcotic intoxication. He moves slowly, but obeys the orders.

SRRK on the other hand is clearly on a high. With joyful yelps he tears himself from the young lady and skips over to the other man in the baseball cap, by now with his mobile phone in hand, and starts photographing the lower part of the unfortunate man's body. The young lady no longer figures, as the "cameraman" concentrates on SRRK squealing and enthusiastically continuing to video the personal attrib-utes of the man in the baseball cap. SRRK is really enjoying himself. How? By photographing the extreme humiliation of someone who took his trousers down on his orders and is not even averting his face. Sex would have been preferable. This is sick.

The significant question, however, is who has decided to disseminate this material and why? Why right now? Who is the target audience?

Without the slightest doubt, those responsible were right by SRRK's side, trusted bodyguards and soldiers, "brothers," because nobody else could have done it. Or rather, they could, but they would have been killed as soon as it became evident that the videos had strayed beyond their own circle.

The Kadyrovites all own cutting-edge mobile phones, especially those in the upper reaches of the hierarchy, closest to the Big Man. They have plenty of easy money and this is how they amuse themselves. They video everything and everyone, but mainly themselves and their amours. I have seen it myself, and they have boasted to me about how cool their mobiles are, and how much better than mine.

Videoing criminal acts like the armoured car and the boot episodes is not, however, an occupation for anyone with ambitions to remain alive and stay close to the Boss in the future. It is time to speculate: who has allowed themselves this liberty?

Not long ago in Vedeno District several dozen Kadyrovites transferred their allegiance to the resistance fighters. This went almost completely unreported, but the fact of their defection is not denied even by Khankala, the generals at Regional Operational HQ who direct all the continuing monstrousness in the North Caucasus.

We may suppose that it is these renegade Kadyrovites who have been distributing compromising material they had been storing up. Did it help them to be accepted back into the ranks of the resistance fighters, which is where most Kadyrovites originate? Unlikely. The recordings are an incidental detail, and for now it is an open question why they were not killed when they attempted to return to their former colleagues.

Who is the video's target audience? This is really the important question. Who is the intended "consumer" of the mobile phone recordings of SRRK? The Russian public? Nobody out there has had any illusions about Ramzan for a long time. Even in Kremlin circles, most realize that Putin made a bad mistake in choosing the Kadyrov family to be his team in Chechnya.

Chechnya's voters? The influence of the Chechen electorate is no longer of interest to anybody. A Parliament has been elected which, when the times comes, will appoint Ramzan Kadyrov President. The Deputies there are no threat to anyone. They worship their Prime Minister with their knees knocking, and this video is of no concern to them.

I have no doubt at all that this mobile video has been released for the benefit of just one person in Russia: Putin. It is for showing in an auditorium where the only spectator obstinately refuses even to pretend he is concerned about the vileness of what he cobbled together from the material most readily available.

PS. We formally request that the Prosecutor-General's Office should treat this as a witness statement. We are prepared unhesitatingly to forward the recordings in *Novaya gazeta*'s possession.

[The response was that on April 24, 2006 the Chechen Prosecutor's Office opened a criminal case into the incident of the attack on federal soldiers, which occurred on October 7, 2005 in Grozny. The other videos were to be examined in the context of an existing criminal case.]

A HEAD ON THE GAS PIPELINE. KADYROV'S MEDIAEVAL BARBARISM – IN JULY 2006

August 3, 2006

According to a report by the Memorial Human Rights Center, on July 28 in the district center of Kurchaloy armed Kadyrovites exhibited a severed human head on a gas pipeline in the middle of the village. This was the outcome of events there the previous night. At about midnight two resistance fighters had been ambushed on the western outskirts. There was a firefight, one of the fighters, a Kurchaloy man, Khozh-Akhmed Dushayev, was killed and a second, Adam Badayev, was captured.

At dawn some 20 cars with armed men congregated in the village by the Interior Ministry District Office and placed Dushayev's severed head on the gas pipe. Beneath the head they hung bloodstained trousers. Dushayev was identified by residents living near the Interior Ministry building.

This was all directed by an aide of Prime Minister Kadyrov, Idris Gaibov, a former Head of the Administration of Kurchaloy District. Onlookers heard Gaibov phoning Prime Minister Kadyrov and reporting that they had killed "Devil No. 1 from Kurchaloy and hung up his head." ("Devils" is how the Kadyrovites refer to Wahhabis.) After that, the Kadyrovites spent the next two hours photographing the head with their video cameras and mobile phones.

On the morning of July 29 militiamen from the Kurchaloy Interior Ministry District Office removed the head, but the bloodstained trousers were left hanging there. At the same time, officers from the Interior Ministry and members of the Prosecutor's Office began work at the site of the conflict. Local people heard one of the Interior Ministry officers asking his subordinate, "Have they finished sewing that head back on yet?" Soon Dushayev's body was brought to the scene of the ambush with his head sewn back on.

The Memorial Human Rights Center believes the desecration of Dushayev's body by Gaibov was personal revenge. The villagers say that on June 10 Dushayev had killed Idris Gaibov's nephew, Adam Gaibov, a soldier of the Yug (South) Battalion, and also beheaded him.

Let's be clear about what happened here. One civilian government official, an aide to the Prime Minister of a government which is a constituent part of the Russian Federation, gave orders to soldiers who were not under his command to cut off a human head. The Prime Minister of that territory was aware of what was happening, or was at least informed about it while it was happening, and made no attempt to intervene. The Kadyrovites, who are now officially recognised as employees of the Russian Interior Ministry, carried out the order. Officials from the Prosecutor's Office, the institution charged with supervising proper administration of the law, being fully aware of what had happened, merely told those responsible to hurry up sewing the head back on. Finally, all these misdeeds took place in full view of the children and adults living in Kurchaloy.

The question we have to ask is whether this is a component part of our new "sovereign democracy" or merely a side effect?

We look forward to hearing from the Military Prosecutor's Office, the province of Sergey Fridinsky, whose duty it is to supervise the actions of members of the Russian Interior Ministry; from Yury Chaika, the Prosecutor-General, whose duty it is to supervise the behaviour of top-flight state servants, and also less exalted members of the Prosecutor's Office.

The Chechen Prosecutor's Office has confirmed the above report both in respect of the severing of the head and its being sewn back on, on July 28–29 in Kurchaloy. It has not yet indicated that it has opened a criminal case in this connection.

Vasiliy Panchenko, the Head of the Press Service of Russian Interior Ministry Troops, told *Novaya gazeta*, "As of August 2 no applications or requests have been received at the Headquarters of the Interior Troops from the Prosecutor's Office, or by the Commanding Officer of the Joint Military Command in the North Caucasus Region. Accordingly it is not possible to make any comment, but we are prepared to respond to any inquiry from the Prosecutor's Office in respect of Interior Troops."

The Press Service of President Alu Alkhanov of the Chechen Republic declined to comment.

LAYING DOWN ARMS, GETTING RID OF KADYROV

August 14, 2006

An amnesty is a good thing. Hope is always better than no hope, but how is the "2006 Amnesty" for resistance fighters proceeding in the North Caucasus? Why have those who have surrendered (officially there are about 80 of them) behaved as they have? Who are they? What needs to be included in the law on amnesty which will begin its passage through the Duma in September to encourage others to follow their example? What conditions and whose guarantees are needed by those who wish to surrender?

In search of answers to these questions I have travelled through Ingushetia, Dagestan and, of course, Chechnya. I have found the situation very different from how it is presented in reports by the intelligence services.

Discovery No. 1, and the most important one: those who have laid down their arms as claimed in the official propaganda simply do not exist. Nobody who was hiding in the forests and mountains or cellars has gone to the Prosecutor's Office or has given an undertaking to stay at their registered address. Why not? What is the real situation?

First, Dagestan and Ingushetia. The situation in Chechnya is radically different from that in these other republics. Dagestan is currently home to the greatest number of active "jamaats" in the North Caucasus. In the anti-terrorist terminology of our intelligence services, jamaats are considered to be illegal armed groups. There are plenty of people in jamaats who could surrender if they chose to.

Surrendering Dagestan-style has, however, uniquely commercial characteristics. There is already a going rate. You have to pay the Prosecutor 60,000 roubles to get him to formalise your surrendering with an admission of guilt. If you haven't got 60,000 roubles you face the consequences, which Putin has described as "active measures against those who fail to lay down their arms." In Dagestan they say wryly that the statistics about those seeking to take advantage of the amnesty tell us only how well the mainly district and city prosecutors involved are prospering.

On August 8 it was reported that, in another act of terrorism, Bitar Bitarov, the Buinaksk District Prosecutor, was killed by a bomb. During all the years of the Second Chechen War, this district has been the bloodiest in Dagestan in terms of terrorist acts, secret operations and skirmishes. Bitarov has been killed, but it is unlikely that this act of sabotage bore any relation to the new amnesty and its money-making opportunities. The resistance fighters know full well, and they have told me as much, that this 60,000 rouble pay-off will have to be paid, given the totally corrupt state of Dagestan, irrespective of personalities, to whoever is appointed to replace the assassinated Prosecutor.

My next stop was in Ingushetia, where the boldest and most militant jamaats operate. Only three people are claimed to have surrendered there. Their statements were shown on Republican television, but all three had been abducted several months ago. The procedure was what is by now entirely customary in Ingushetia: they were kidnapped by members of "unidentified security agencies" and later turned up in the pre-trial detention facility in Vladikavkaz, accused of participation in an illegal armed formation.

A detail common to all of them is that they are currently imprisoned. They are now in exactly the same situation as they were before they stated that they wished to be amnestied. None of them has been allowed to return home. The investigation against all of them is being conducted by a team at the Prosecutor-General's Office led by Konstantin Krivorotov. His efforts to eradicate the causes which led to Beslan were supposed to decrease the enthusiasm for terrorist activity in the North Caucasus but have, unfortunately, had precisely the opposite effect. For almost two years his investigative activity has consisted of designating people as terrorists while the real bandits roam freely through the forests and mountains, and plant bombs when and where they will.

Of the three Ingushes who surrendered (and that they had done so was announced by their relatives and lawyers long before Patrushev made his amnesty proposals), we know that they were tortured during the investigation and signed "voluntary confessions." Lawyers defending different accused under investigation by Krivorotov's team say no offers to include them in the amnesty were made by the investigators. They comment that the statements made by the three are merely part of a deal struck by their relatives to get their sentences reduced.

In other words, the amnesty in Ingushetia too is closer to plea bargaining than conciliation. It in no wise indicates an increase in the number of resistance fighters who have seen the light and want to return to civilian life. Those who have been "amnestied" have in any case been returned to "civilian life" in strict-regime labor camps.

"Do people who wish to avail themselves of the amnesty appeal to you or to the Parliament to mediate?" I ask Mahomet Sali Aushev, a Deputy of the People's Assembly of Ingushetia and member of the recently created Parliamentary Commission on Violation of Civil Rights.

"No. That doesn't happen."

"In your view, is this amnesty going to bring about an improvement in the situation in Ingushetia, in terms of bombings, shelling and armed clashes?"

"This is not a true amnesty, it is simply an appeal for people to lay down arms. A number of people have taken to the forests. Some of them will never turn back from that path. There are, of course, those whom we might call romantics. For any of those who are vacillating this proposal is of course very important, but for the majority, some 90 per cent, the amnesty is an irrelevance. Somebody close to them has been killed, and they are seeking retribution. There is nothing for them to repent of. It is they who are waiting for those who have wronged them to repent. Actually, it seems to me that this 'amnesty' was not devised with us in mind. It is intended to have an impact mainly in Chechnya."

And so to Chechnya, which has a defining role in the region. It is asserted that almost 70 individuals have asked to take advantage of the amnesty, only none of them are fighters. There are a great variety of people who, for a great variety of reasons, have said that they would like to take advantage of Patrushev's proposal. One baked bread for Dudayev, another once said he sympathised with Maskhadov, a third took food to the forests. The nearest we come to a resistance fighter, whom they are showing on television, used to be in Doku Umarov's detachment, but on closer inspection even he turns out to have been trading in the Urus Martan market for several years now, not hiding from anybody. He has been given a hint that it might be in his interests to help inflate the statistics, and that is what he has done.

What is needed for the amnesty to be real and genuine? That is a question I put to everybody. To resistance fighters who have not the slightest intention of "going legal," as well as to those who are asking their relatives to help them make contact with the law enforcement agencies while the opportunity is there. Also to commanders of pro-Moscow Chechen security agencies, many of whom are themselves former resistance fighters amnestied under guarantees from Kadyrov Senior. These are precisely the men who for a long time were considered to be the bulwark of Kadyrov Junior's power.

Their answers are extraordinarily consistent. "It is unlikely anybody will surrender to Kadyrov."

There you have it, and this in a republic which is claimed to be infatuated with Ramzan, which is inundated with outward signs of deference. There are posters everywhere: Ramzan with Daddy, Ramzan with Putin, Ramzan on his own with a furrowed brow, and "You Are Our Hero," and "We Are Proud Of You." They are plastered along all the roads, at the entrance to even the smallest villages, in all schools and state institutions, on fences, doors and lamp posts, on the concrete blocks of disused checkpoints ... Everyone in Chechnya just loves him so.

So why would people not be prepared to lay down their arms to him? This is where we can no longer name names. All my conversations on this subject took place on condition of complete anonymity.

"Why do you believe Ramzan has to be removed before people will come out of the forests?" I ask an influential commander of the pro-Moscow Chechen security forces whom I have known for a long time. He trusts me and I trust him. We have had good reason for that in worse times.

"They will not come out to be slaves, and for us Ramzan is a continuation of the enslavement. They will come out when the rule of law is established, and not before. A second condition is that they should be guaranteed a job which doesn't involve a rifle, not armed detachments they will be drafted into in place of the forest."

"What do you mean? They want jobs waiting for them? That's impossible. Unemployment here is the same problem for everyone."

"No, I mean something else. Nobody in Chechnya today, including those who never fought anywhere and have nothing to be amnestied for, can be sure they will have a job tomorrow if Ramzan for any reason takes a dislike to them. They can't even be sure that they will be alive if Ramzan takes a dislike to them."

After that we talk about Eshiev. My informant has not the slightest sympathy for him, but what happened has to be discussed. Maierbek Eshiev, a well-known field commander from the mountainous Vedeno District whose radio code name was Mullah, surrendered along with his detachment under Ramzan's guarantees after Maskhadov was killed. Let us have no illusions, Eshiev is a religious fanatic.

Kadyrov promptly appointed him Commander of the Anti-Terrorist Center for Vedeno District. Each anti-terrorist center has divisions in the towns and villages of Chechnya and its officers are drawn from the old A. Kadyrov Regiment in which former fighters could enlist. They were all directly subordinate to Ramzan Kadyrov. For a long time the ATC was his power base, but in spring this year it was disbanded. This was seen as a first move by Moscow to cool Ramzan's ardour. Most members of the Anti-Terrorist Center were drafted into the North and South Battalions under the umbrella of the Interior Ministry Troops of the Russian Federation. On June 1 they swore the oath of allegiance to Russia.

Incidentally, this federal plan for taming Kadyrov Junior did enjoy some success. Many ex-resistance fighters who had become Kadyrovites took this opportunity to distance themselves from him. Kadyrov reacted by becoming hyperactive and tried to ensure the next batch of amnestied fighters came his way. The idea for the present amnesty, which Patrushev announced after Basayev's death, came partly from Kadyrov's determination to restore his power base.

But to return to Eshiev. On November 10 last year, on Militia Day, Kadyrov put Eshiev forward for a medal, which he was duly awarded in a solemn ceremony by generals of the Interior Ministry. Many Chechen militiamen refused to enter the hall on that occasion. In the winter, however, a section of Eshiev's detachment rejected Kadyrov and again took to the hills. There was fraternisation between Eshiev's people and resistance fighters, and Ramzan accused Eshiev of treachery. It was claimed he had surrendered on instructions from Basayev solely in order to inveigle his way into Kadyrov's confidence and kill him.

The upshot was that all the members of Eshiev's family to be found in the Vedeno and Gudermes Districts were first abducted and then disappeared off the face of the earth. There were 24 of them, including women and a three-year-old child. Only one very ancient member of the family was left alive, on the grounds that he was too old to have children.

The fate of the Eshiev family became widely known in Chechnya and, naturally, among the resistance fighters. Nobody is going to be in a hurry to surrender to Ramzan now.

"Was Eshiev really going to betray Ramzan?" I asked people in the know.

"Yes," they replied.

As the commanders of the pro-Moscow Chechen security forces point out, "loyalty" meant accepting total subservience to Kadyrov, not an attractive proposition, but those days are rapidly coming to an end. The situation now is that demonstrative loyalty to Ramzan, which helped many here to flourish, is being replaced by firm confrontation of him by the security forces. That was not the case before this summer.

On July 25 German Gref and Alexey Kudrin, respectively Russia's

Ministers of Economic Development and Finance, flew into Grozny. There was a Party pow-wow on how to finance the rebuilding of Chechnya. Kadyrov, in his usual loutish manner, baldly demanded almost two billion roubles for projects which had already been completed, to which Gref and Kudrin responded in an unprecedented manner by demanding that he should provide them with full documentation, including invoices, on the projects.

The documentation is in a state of complete chaos. Building takes place, but there is no paperwork in respect of some four billion roubles. Gref was succinct in his reply: "Nice try ..." The intonation, those present claim, was suggestive of "Up yours, Sunshine!" Kudrin said outright he had no intention of ending up in prison because of Ramzan: the money would be released only when full, receipted documentation for the projects was received. Kadyrov was indignant: "We'll send you documentation by the suitcase tomorrow!" Kudrin was having none of it: thanks, but he would send his own valuation commission from Moscow to estimate how much the projects should have cost. Kadyrov went ballistic, but swallowed it.

There were a great many people present at that meeting, and none failed to register the change in the tone the federal ministers adopted with Ramzan. They also reminded him about the funds allocated for "flood damage," which needed to be accounted for. Ramzan had no comeback. Dukvakha Abdurakhmanov, the Speaker of the Chechen Parliament, was about to start singing his favorite song of recent months – to the effect that Moscow hadn't given Chechnya a copeck in aid – but was cut off in mid-sentence.

There had been nothing quite like this before. In the past, those same federal ministers addressed the "Kadyrov team" only in the tone of indulgent fathers. Witnesses also noticed that the ministers declined to be transported from the airfield to the meeting in Kadyrov's black Land Cruisers with their Moscow number plates, preferring Alkhanov's presidential fleet.

Behind the scenes at that same meeting, the federal ministers were advised that if Kadyrov became President, half the Chechen Republic would leave Chechnya. They were also told that nobody was likely to sign up to amnesties underwritten by Ramzan.

Word spread like wildfire around Chechnya to the effect that Moscow was dumping Ramzan. After this meeting, which felt as if a starter's pistol had been fired, there came the first stirrings of mutiny.

Unrest was first evident in the so-called "Oil Regiment," the Inter-departmental Security Service. The oil security guards refused to pay their tribute to the so-called Kadyrov Fund, and warned Kadyrov not to try to get them to attack their own people. They told him they would not shoot, and would take no further part in settling his gangland scores. They would hand in their weapons and leave. Next, the officers of the Ministry for Emergency Situations revolted and also refused to pay tribute – 3–4,000 roubles deducted from their salaries – submitting official complaints to the Prosecutor's Office about those gathering the levies. The detachment commanded by Movladi Baisarov joined the rebellion and, although there are not that many of them left, they continue to be influential. The West Battalion, now formally subordinate to the Central Intelligence Directorate, were drawn in immediately after them.

It finally came to open war. Muslim Iliasov, commander of one of the battalions transferred to the Russian Interior Ministry troops and himself a former resistance fighter who had surrendered to Kadyrov Senior, was a close friend of Ramzan. He nevertheless ambushed him. Other detachments were drawn in: the West, East, OMON, North, and South Battalions. These split internally, with some siding with Ramzan and others opposing him. The balance of forces was not in Ramzan's favor, and Iliasov, who had instigated the rebellion, declared Ramzan his enemy. He explained why: for the humiliations, insults and derision, for the slavery. Ramzan raged but retreated because of lack of support.

"This will not last long," said one of the commanders who took part in the events. "I would give it two months before it's all over." Another of his colleagues who will also be unable to avoid taking part in the showdown said "three months." Everyone with detachments subordi-nate to them in the pro-Moscow Chechen security agencies agrees that

Ramzan's removal from the scene is only a matter of time. "Although," they add, "anything might happen."

"What do you mean by that?"

"If Moscow decides to keep him, they will keep him."

"But who is Moscow, in your opinion?"

"Putin personally. Ramzan has been requesting an urgent meeting through Surkov."

A meeting did indeed take place in the Kremlin on August , but Ramzan got relatively little out of it: his face on television, but no money.

Let us return to what happened after the revolt. What happened was August 3, the Day of the Oath, of swearing allegiance to Ramzan Kadyrov on the Quran. Poor Quran.

"We were all summoned to Khosi-Yurt (another name for Tsentoroy) to a sacrifice," one of the participants relates. "It was some anniversary of Akhmat-hadji Kadyrov (fifty-five years since his birth). They took us to the gym and said we were to swear allegiance to Ramzan on the Quran. All the battalion commanders were there. The Mullah read and everybody was supposed to repeat it. The cameras were on. For several days after that they were showing our lips moving on television. I personally swore loyalty to my father." Another commander laughs: "I swore to be faithful to my wife."

For the participants this oath was by no means the first. My interviewees smile; "We saw people there who have sworn allegiance on the Quran to different leaders five times before, and broken the vow. They will break this one at the first opportunity."

That is no more than the truth. The enforced oath only irritated more of those who are now opposed to Ramzan.

"This oath-taking was a panicky affair," one of the commanders says with conviction. He, incidentally, did not go to Tsentoroy on August 3. "Ramzan was trying to show Moscow that he has everything under control, that he is in charge, but what he showed Chechnya was that he is in a blue funk."

"How many people do you think Ramzan will have when it comes
to the showdown?"

"Between 50 and 100."

"His very closest circle?"

"No, only those who see that deserting him will leave them facing
prison. Not one of them will be accepted back in the forests now. His
closest circle will be the first to betray him. That's the kind of people
he has lured to his side."

So, what change has there been in the situation in Chechnya at the
end of this summer? The declaration of the amnesty and the killing
of Maskhadov's successor as President of Ichkeria, Abdul Khalim
Sadulayev, and of Basayev which preceded it suddenly dispelled the
inertia. These events prompted people to think about where they were,
about the wider picture in Chechnya, what it might lead to, and who
was who. That is undoubtedly a step in the right direction.

There is change also in the fact that, where previously almost everyone
in Chechnya believed that in time Ramzan would be removed by those
who had raised him up – "the Russians" – those in the security forces,
and I emphasise that these are the pro-Moscow Chechen forces, now
say that they will have to free Chechnya from him themselves. They see
Chechnya's major problem today as being not the jamaats, but Ramzan,
the Kadyrovites, and the widening conflict associated with them.

Why? "Because the Kadyrovites are the best machine yet invented
for exterminating Chechens. This is something a majority of people
now recognise."

That is the explanation I was given about the present-day Russo-
Chechen political situation by a certain wise person, a Grozny resident
I know, who under Maskhadov lived in Moscow because he found the
Wahhabis unacceptable, who returned when power was transferred to
the Russian Government's representative, Nikolai Koshman, and now
finds it almost impossible to live under Ramzan.

"The problem is that they can't make up their minds in Moscow
whether to force Chechnya to obey the law or not. Until Moscow decides,
Ramzan will continue. Ramzan is a symbol of lawlessness. Those

who want to come out of the forests are waiting for the law to be re-established. People want legality."

"But it is not simply a matter of Moscow failing to make its mind up," I reply. "The problem surely is that you Chechens periodically demonstrate that you don't want to live under the law. How is Moscow to make its mind up if at every turn people here say 'Khyo nokhchi vats?' ('Are you not a Chechen?'). What is the way out? How are Chechens to be compelled to live within the law? Even if they want to surrender to the law, and not to Ramzan's lawlessness, will they be able subsequently to obey it? That is the snag. Incidentally, Maskhadov faced the same problems in the late 1990s. In 1998 he told me in an interview, in the presence of a group of journalists, that the only way to force Chechens to observe the law was to impose Islam."

"Maskhadov was wrong. What is needed is not Islam but the Adats, the ancient Chechen rules of life. They are full of wisdom. Paradoxical as it may seem, the Chechens can be compelled to live in accordance with Russian laws through the Adats."

"If we return to the amnesty, whose word can be accepted as a guarantee? Putin's?" I ask.

"Remember Khambiev's mission to Azerbaijan, when Maskhadov's ex-Minister of Defence went to Baku on Ramzan's orders to persuade former fighters to return and accept an amnesty? Nobody came back with him except for two of his relatives, and they were arrested at the border. I have no answer to your question. I think the guarantees need to come not from Ramzan, not from Putin, not from Alkhanov, but only from the law."

Aslan is 31. He finished school as the USSR was collapsing and Chechnya was vacillating over which legal system to accept. He has been bearing arms for many years, like most men in Chechnya. He lives under a false name, like many in Chechnya. He would like to surrender, but cannot, also like many in Chechnya. Aslan is no longer the future – he is too weary and disillusioned for that – but the future of Chechnya may well depend on how he is treated. What follows is an interview, almost unedited. Draw your own conclusions: we were talking 24 hours before he surrendered to the Prosecutor's Office.

"I fought from 2000 to 2002, not from the very beginning of the war. I went to fight because my brother was unjustly imprisoned and my younger brother was seriously injured by a bomb. People were always coming into our house from a variety of agencies and terrorising us. I was no longer prepared to put up with it. It was impossible to stay at home and just wait to be humiliated. I fought in a detachment of 12 men who were loyal to Maskhadov."

"Why did you give up on Maskhadov?"

"It was hard fighting in the long term, the conditions were hard. Some lads I knew talked to me, and we agreed to go together to take advantage of Akhmat-hadji Kadyrov's amnesty. I became a Kadyrovite. I was told, 'You have nothing to worry about. There is nothing against you.'"

"What kind of work did you have with Kadyrov?"

"More fighting."

"Was it more difficult fighting for Kadyrov or for Maskhadov?"

"It was the same. Later they started disbanding the Anti-Terrorist Center to create the North and South Battalions. I realized I was tired of it all. I didn't want to run around with a rifle any more. I turned over my weapon and vehicle, but soon I discovered that the previous amnesty had not had legal force and prosecutions had begun under Article 205, Part 3 (Acts of Terrorism)."

"Did you have a different attitude towards Akhmat-hadji and Ramzan?"

"Yes. Akhmat-hadji had a better head on his shoulders. He knew what needed doing."

'Are you afraid of Ramzan?"

"No, I am not afraid of him, but I don't like him."

"There was a lot of talk after the death of Akhmat-hadji Kadyrov that if you, all the Kadyrovites and former fighters, were not handed over to Ramzan, who ought to replace his father, you would all go off again to the forests."

"That was not true. Nobody was planning to return to the forests.

People weren't even thinking about it as a final resort."

"How many are there like you, from the disbanded Kadyrovites, who would like to seek an amnesty?"

"I know some 20 people. They want to, but there are no guarantees. Everybody who left Ramzan has discovered that the federal warrant against us has not been lifted."

"Are you prepared to go back into a different detachment under the amnesty?"

"No. What difference is there whether you go into another detachment or to prison?"

"What hopes do you and those 20 former Kadyrovites have, what are you hoping for?"

"The rule of law. We are waiting for the law to be re-established. But those coming directly from the mountains have no chance at all now, and they know it."

"What significance did the death of Basayev have for you?"

"None."

"Who do you feel yourself to be?"

"I am a resistance fighter."

"What distinguishes a resistance fighter from everybody else? The wish to fight?"

"The inner desire for retribution is what you must have. Just wanting to fight is not enough."

"Who do you believe now? Who do you trust?"

"Nobody. Alkhanov a little, because he has not promised anything. I don't believe in people who promise a lot."

"Patrushev? Putin?"

"I don't know them. I would need to talk to them face to face before I could trust them."

"Nevertheless, you are intending to go to the Prosecutor's Office. What percentage risk do you think you face that they will put you in prison?"

"Eighty per cent."

"But you are going nevertheless?"

"I'm fed up with fighting."

RAMZAN KADYROV, THE PRIDE OF CHECHNYA: THE NEW PRIME MINISTER'S FIRST 100 DAYS IN OFFICE

June 5, 2006

In a few days Russia, and indeed the whole world, will be celebrating the First Hundred Days of the premiership of Ramzan Kadyrov, or so, at least, the Prime Minister of the Chechen Republic believes. He is making suitable preparations.

Hands up anyone who still doesn't know that Ramzan Kadyrov is Ramzan the Builder? He is restoring battered Chechnya to its pre-war appearance, doing away with every trace of the battles which, with brief interruptions, have been taking place here since 1994.

Actually, everybody knows. They know that, without rest, for almost 100 days already, no matter where Kadyrov's motorcade appears, orders will ring out to increase the speed at which everything he catches sight of is being built. Markets have sprung up, and petrol stations, and holes in the roads have been filled. The fences along them have been painted, temporary refugee camps have been demolished, soup is being made in the hospitals for the patients, and the ground is being marked out for branches of future gas pipelines. The children sing, "God save Ramzan!" No, seriously. Almost every day anthems about today's living mediator between the Almighty and the people of Chechnya are to be heard on the Republic's television.

Only one question is rather worrying: whose money is actually paying for this restoration? It seems reasonable to ask. The official answer, being drummed into the heads of the Chechen population, is that it is all being done with Ramzan's money. OK, he is admittedly very good at extracting money from people, but he isn't doing this for himself: he's doing it for the People.

Is that good? Why, it's absolutely marvellous! Chechnya is, however, awash with rumors about the mechanism of this pumping operation. By word of mouth one hears how much, exactly, each worker is shelling out to the ruling family. For example, the latest of a series of preparatory measures for the Hundred Days celebration concerns the personnel of the Interior Ministry's Interdepartmental Security Service. (Alkhanov, the Interior Minister, is a relative of the Kadyrovs and former body-guard of Kadyrov Senior.) The commanding officers announced at morning parade that the new rates for contributions to the Restoration of Chechnya Fund would be $1,000 each for officers, and 10,000 roubles each for the rank and file (which is quite a whack: these are some rank and file!). Anybody who can't or doesn't want to pay up is to be dismissed.

There have no been no reports of dismissals: the Interdepartmental Security Service went to persuade those it protects, the overwhelming majority of whom were only too happy to comply: it was, after all, for the People. All for the sake of the People.

It has to be admitted that Kadyrov Junior is an outstandingly fast-learning pupil of his senior Moscow comrades, including the President of the Russian Federation. What matters is not to actually do things, but to say it was you who did them. This is the main lesson he has learned. Let us dip into the text of Chechen Government Instruction No. 184–r of April 25, 2006, signed by R. Kadyrov. It lists projects financed by capital investment in 2006.

What do we see? Of 27 planned projects, only six are due to be partially financed from "supplementary revenues," where we may at least surmise the personal participation of Ramzan the Builder with a contribution from the so-called Kadyrov Regional Fund, the chest into which the voluntary contributions of citizens pour. Eighteen projects were fully financed from the Federal Budget by us, the taxpayers of Russia. That covers all repairs to school and boarding-school buildings, the promised gas pipelines to villages, construction of outpatient clinics, even the restoration of the "Akhmat-hadji Kadyrov State Museum." Two other projects are financed jointly by the federal budget and the Federal Regional Development Fund. In other words, in 19 projects out of 27 Kadyrov Junior has played no part whatsoever. He has only had to keep an eye on things to stop the funds from being trousered. Or . . . ?

An "or" has to be conceded. Ramzan is allowed to do anything he likes. As the sole inheritor of the noble mission of Kadyrov Senior, he knows better than the Chechens how to spend money on the People.

The basis of this claim is the belief that Kadyrov Senior was the middle-man between the Almighty and the People, the Best of the Best, as he was called, and that he has bestowed this vicarious mission upon his son.

The legend of the Best of the Best, of course, requires constant cosmetic attention. Leaving it to develop spontaneously would be the utmost folly, and that is why Kadyrov Junior's Hundred Days has fused naturally with the "Republic's preparations to mark the 55th anniversary of the birth of the first President of the Chechen Republic, Hero of Russia, Akhmed Kadyrov," as Government Order No. 241 of May 24, 2006, signed by R. Kadyrov, puts it. The odd idea of marking this anniversary is in fact a convenient way of bypassing such undesirable distractions as Victory Day, because it would clearly be inappropriate to have Chechens celebrating May 9 when that is also the day Kadyrov Senior was blown up. That consideration must clearly take priority over any rejoicing at the victory over fascism.

No creative initiatives are invited as to how to mark Akhmet-hadji Kadyrov's 55th birthday. The Son of the Best of the Best has already made all the "preparations." These the document lists as:

1. Quotations from A. Kadyrov to be used in television broadcasts:
   "My aim is not to stop the war, but to end war once and for all"; "My weapon is the Truth, in the face of which any army is powerless."
2. A list of those to be interviewed about Kadyrov Senior. Who are they?
   First and foremost, the son: "Interview with R. Kadyrov, 'My Father Taught Me How To Live'"; followed by "Reminiscences by Khozh-Akhmed Kadyrov" (an uncle), "He Grew even as I Watched"; and "Speech by the Chairman of the People's Assembly of the Chechen Republic, D.B. Abdurakhmanov, 'A.A. Kadyrov – Architect of Peaceful Construction in Chechnya'"
3. Titles of publications and their contents:
   1. Publication in the newspaper *Vesti*, "A.A. Kadyrov –

A Leader for his Times." The historical inevitability of A. Kadyrov's appearance on the political stage of Chechnya and Russia.

3. Publication in the newspaper *Molodezhnaya smena*, "A. Kadyrov, the Peacemaker."

... 17. Broadcasts on Vainakh and Grozny TV: "V.V. Putin and A.A. Kadyrov, Architects of New Russo-Chechen Relations"; "A. Kadyrov, the Diplomat."

18. Broadcasts on Radio Vainakh and Radio Grozny: "He United All the Muslims of Chechnya."

... 34. Television series, "A. Kadyrov: the Highway of Life"(weekly).

35. Humorous program, "Smiling Kadyrov" (The "Chechen Fingerprints" team).

... 38. Congratulatory telegrams and messages. Appreciations of the merits of A. Kadyrov.

... 42. Billboards, street banners, wall hangings, "R. Kadyrov: 'I Will Carry my Father's Cause Forward to a Victorious Conclusion'" ...

This plan, egregious even by present-day standards, includes a list of publications which must without fail be published in June as Ramzan's Hundred Days near the finishing line:

... 5. Publication in the magazine *Nana*, "A.A. Kadyrov Remembered by his Comrades-in-Arms, Family and Friends."

6. Publication in the magazine *Orga* (a writers' magazine), "A Portrait of A.A. Kadyrov, the Artist."

7. Publication in the magazine *Vainakh*: poetry by various authors and dedicated to A.A. Kadyrov.

... 10. Broadcast on State TV and Radio. Chat-show "'I Am a Citizen.' A. Kadyrov, the Man who Restored the Good Name of Chechens."

4. Events:

... 23. Scholarly symposium, "The Role and Significance of A. Kadyrov in Modern History."

24. Competition to find the best reader. Poetry dedicated

to A.A. Kadyrov.

25. Exhibition of children's drawings, "Akhmat-hadji Kadyrov, the Man who Brought Peace to our Home."

To be arranged by R. Alkhanov, Interior Minister: oath of loyalty to the cause of A.A. Kadyrov and presentation to the best militia division of a standard bearing the portrait of A. Kadyrov.

*   *   *

Ramzan Kadyrov is still a very young man and hasn't read much history, but what about those who grew up long ago, and remember when plans exactly like these were drawn up by central committees, municipal committees, district committees, and all the rest of them on the 100th Anniversary of the Birth of Lenin, the 70th Anniversary of the Birth of Brezhnev, and so on ad nauseam?

To be fair, we should mention that the 55th anniversary celebrations are being financed by the A. Kadyrov Foundation with funds extorted by official racketeers from the Chechen people.

One striking example of the Foundation's financial practices is provided by the recent inaugural Chechen beauty contest, organised within the framework of the Hundred Days. As we know, Kadyrov Junior undertook to make the people around him as happy as possible during this period.

Both Kadyrov Junior and his "team," as it is now customary to call them, went out of their way to emphasise that the beauty contest was the brainchild of Ramzan. He is richer today than his father ever was, effectively an oligarch, wallowing in money and enjoying throwing it about, as the contest was to show.

After the jury had announced the name of the winner and many girls had been awarded cars, a celebratory dinner was held in a Gudermes restaurant. Kadyrov Junior and several dozen bodyguards arrived. The winners were commanded to dance for him and his entourage and, as the dancing continued, Kadyrov Junior ordered his bodyguards to throw banknotes at the young ladies, $100 and 1,000-rouble banknotes.

A reporter for *Chechenskoye obshchestvo* calculated that some US$30,000, including the rouble equivalents, ended up on the Olympus

Restaurant's marble floor. The young ladies duly picked up the money. When one of the competitors suddenly burst into tears, Ramzan arranged for her to be given a diamond-studded Chopard Swiss watch. The watch with all its diamonds materialised instantly in Gudermes, the tears were dried, and a watch bought with money extracted from the citizens of Chechnya was publicly thrown at the feet of another of their number.

The years will pass, all things will pass, and nobody will have any desire to recall any detail of these Hundred Days with their oaths of loyalty to the Kadyrov cause. But what of the girls who in May 2006 crawled around on that restaurant floor? What of the young journalists who put their signatures to a publication titled *Kadyrov, the Peacemaker*, at a time when hundreds had been tortured to death in Tsentoroy? How will they live with themselves? I cannot imagine.

PS. On the morning of May 31, Kadyrovites (who no longer officially exist, as they have been reassigned to the Interior Ministry) caught resistance fighters in the hill village of Nesterovskaya in Ingushetia. As reported by the Russian Interior Ministry Troops Press Office, "Brigands, pursued by members of the militia, crossed the border of Chechnya and Ingushetia and hid in house No. 91, taking hostage the people living there."

In the house surrounded by the Kadyrovites live the Khaikharoyevs, the family of Field Commander Ruslan Khaikharoyev, a kidnapper killed in 1999. With the family was Ruslan's 19-year-old son, Rizvan, who, as their neighbours testify, was not a resistance fighter. When the fighters wounded a militiaman, the Kadyrovites retreated, taking with them Rizvan Khaikharoyev. He was pushed into the boot of one of the vehicles, which they positioned opposite the house. They used it for cover and began a two-hour gun battle. When everything fell quiet, Rizvan was hauled out of the boot and one of the Kadyrovites fired a pistol at the back of his head; another finished him off with his assault rifle. The murder was committed in full view of the people of Nesterovskaya, an extra-judicial execution committed by men who are now officially counted as members of the Interior Ministry Troops of the Russian Federation.

THE KADYROVITES WILL BE BEATEN: FOR NOW, ONLY IN INGUSHETIA

September 11, 2006

On September 7, a huge fight broke out at a checkpoint on the outskirts of Alkhasty on the Chechnya–Ingushetia border. Men in military fatigues approaching from the Chechen side and claiming to be the security detail of Prime Minister Ramzan Kadyrov became impatient at the "cheek" of the checkpoint guards. These were Ingush Interior Ministry troops of the regiment guarding the administrative border, and they demanded to see the documents, military orders, and other forms required for taking firearms across the border. The Kadyrovites started waving their arms about and firing in the air.

Three militiamen were injured as a result, two of whom are in hospital. The Kadyrovites proceeded to cross the border without authorisation. Officers of the Ingush Interior Ministry issued warrants for their arrest, vowing to give them a good beating if they were found in Ingushetia. Ramzan Kadyrov's entourage issued a statement claiming it was all lies, because their people do not take armoured personnel carriers across the border.

Whoever it was who turned up in APCs on September 7 – current Kadyrovites, former Kadyrovites now reclassified as officers belonging to battalions of the Russian Interior Ministry, or some other kind of thugs – what happened is a manifestation of the long-established Kadyrov syndrome whose principal distinguishing features are insolence, loutishness, and brutality masquerading as courage. In Chechnya the Kadyrovites beat men and women at will, in exactly the way the Wahhabis beat people in the days of Maskhadov's Ichkeria. They behead their enemies just as the Wahhabis did, and the institutions of law and order turn a blind eye or even officially refer to this behaviour as the result of a heightened national awareness following the Chechen people's irrevocable choice in favor of Russia.

In Chechnya itself there has been no attempt to halt the spread of this infection. Rather, it has been encouraged. "Come on, guys, we're something else. We'll show them who's boss. We have every right!"

The Kadyrov syndrome is catching on among Chechen teenagers who are known as the New Wahhabis, or the R. Kadyrov Fan Club. They "graduate" from the Fan Club and take their place in adult life and the world of work.

For a couple of years all this was festering only in Chechnya, with occasional outbreaks in Dagestan, mainly in the bordering Khasavyurt District. Now, however, the Kadyrov syndrome is spreading. Today many Chechens living outside Chechnya and even outside Russia are being infected with the virus.

Those around them have also moved on, though. By no means everybody is taken in by the televised fairy tales depicting Ramzan Kadyrov as a Hero of Russia. Many are getting very tired of the Kadyrov syndrome and it has produced a countervailing tendency in the form of a movement called "We Will Beat You." Not everybody is willing, like many Chechens, to let the Kadyrovites walk all over them. This is what led to the anti-Chechen disturbances in Kondopoga, Karelia, and now also this incident in Alkhasty.

3. The Cadet

The failure of Russia's rulers, despite their public pronouncements, to support the rule of law has allowed war criminals to flourish in Chechnya. The courage and tenacity required to stand up to forces bent on perverting the course of justice is illustrated by several cases which Anna Politkovskaya reported; as a result she successfully had evil men brought to book.

THE CADET AFFAIR: THE DISAPPEARED

September 10, 2001

Imagine that a group of unidentified men in Army uniform burst into your house, drag off a member of your family, and . . .

And nothing. Someone existed but now they don't. It is as if they have been rubbed out, like a matchstick man from a school blackboard. You can rush around, go out of your mind, beg for at least some modicum of information, but the official who should be searching for them quite straightforwardly advises you, "Forget it." And that is the end of that.

The most appalling tragedy in Chechnya today is the disappeared, those who vanish without trace. Officially they currently number about 1,000; unofficially, almost 2,000. They have been disappearing throughout the war, right up to the present, from different towns and villages and in different circumstances, but all such stories have two common characteristics. The first is that those who disappeared were last seen being taken away by soldiers; the second is that the numerous ramified law enforcement agencies of Chechnya are incapable of finding anyone.

Once a month a special meeting on abductions is held in the new government offices in Grozny. Another job ticked off the list. It is usually chaired by Vladimir Kalamanov, the President's Special Representative for the Observance of Human Rights and Freedoms in Chechnya.

The Chechen Prosecutor, Vsevolod Chernov, does most of the talking, because it is primarily his responsibility to find the disappeared. Also present, of course, are representatives of the main Army base at Khankala, who attend with ineradicable scepticism written all over their faces. Those present from the National Military Prosecutor's Office sit as silent as the grave. The meeting stretches out interminably, the various gentlemen discussing matters wearily and finding it difficult to conceal quite how boring, and indeed objectionable, they find all this.

Losing patience, Taisa Musayeva jumps up. Her voice quavers. "What are you talking about here? I have just one wish for the lot of you: that you should find yourselves in my place. Nobody is looking for my husband, or has any intention of doing so." Taisa is 25, and does not know whether she is a wife or already a widow.

On July 2, during the now notorious brutal mass security sweeps in the hill villages of Assinovskaya and Sernovodsk, Taisa's husband, Zelimkhan Umkhanov, was taken in front of his entire family from his home on Kutalov Street in Sernovodsk and driven away to an unknown destination. The whole world duly came to hear about these security sweeps, the President had his say, and for the first time in the long months of this war he waxed indignant about the senselessness of the "special measures" employed. The Prosecutor-General publicly assured us all that a meticulous inquiry was in hand.

"That was a lie. There is no inquiry," Taisa hammers home her truth. For two months, the families of 28-year-old Zelimkhan and 22-year-old Apti Isigov, also abducted by the military from Sernovodsk, have been unable to persuade the Chechen Prosecutor's Office even to take a statement from them about what they witnessed. The relatives have been scurrying round the Republic after Prosecutor Chernov, begging him to accept their evidence. To no avail.

What is it that the Prosecutors in Chechnya are keen not to know? Perhaps this might at least be of interest to their superiors in the Russian Prosecutor-General's Office? Well, they do not want to know, for example, the identification number of the armoured personnel carrier in which masked individuals abducted Umkhanov and Isigov without even glancing at their passports. It was "4025." Neither do they want to know the radio call sign of the vehicle, "88"; or of the commanding officer in charge of the abduction, "12." The number of the military Urals truck which accompanied the abduction was "O 1003 KSh." On July 3 both Umkhanov and Isigov were sighted in the back of this truck. It was parked in Assinovskaya and the abducted men were lying covered by a tarpaulin. They were alive and asked for water when they heard voices nearby. There are witnesses to whom the unfortunate men managed to say that they had not been allowed out from under the canvas for more than 24 hours.

"The search for the disappeared could be completed, we believe, in a matter of hours," write the mothers of the Sernovodsk men in a letter to President Putin. On August 28, having lost hope of finding any help in Chechnya, they wrote to Moscow: "All that is needed," the mothers advise the President, "is to assemble those in charge of that special operation (who are all known), to question a number of soldiers and officers (who are also known), and, if necessary, to conduct an identification parade. There are witnesses living in Sernovodsk."

The mothers are simple women, untrained in detective work, but simply stating the obvious. They do not know that hundreds of Chechen families have already been down this road. Nearly all of them wrote to the President with information in their possession which made it possible to find the disappeared in a matter of days. Given the will, of course. And that is the snag.

On January 2 this year Zelimkhan Murdalov, a 26-year-old man from Grozny, was walking down the street when he was suddenly assaulted by six men in combat fatigues, stripped, and bundled into a car in full view of the passengers on a bus which had stopped nearby. Later, two women on the bus, a mother and daughter aged 73 and 40, came forward as official witnesses of the abduction. They tried to help Zelimkhan, and suffered for their pains. The 73-year-old had her false teeth broken when she was punched on the jaw by "soldiers."

Both were knocked to the ground and had shots fired over their heads. Undeterred, they later had the courage to identify their attackers, members of the October District Interior Affairs Temporary Office from the Khanty-Mansiysk Combined Militia Unit.

Murdalov was very unlucky. The Khanty-Mansiysk detachment have an atrocious reputation in Grozny. In the Militia Unit's headquarters Zelimkhan was handed over to Major Alexander Prilepin, Head of the Criminal Militia and better known by his code name of "Alex." Also to Investigator Zhuravlyov and officer Sergey Lapin, alias "The Cadet." The latter had this name shaved on the back of his head. A later inquiry established that it was they who personally presided over and took part in the torturing of Zelimkhan.

In the early hours of January 3, The Cadet dragged Murdalov to a cell in the temporary holding block, where he was seen by other prisoners.

His fellow cell-mates saw the results of the militiamen's sadistic orgy. The bone was sticking out of Zelimkhan's right forearm. His right ear had been cut off. His ribs had been broken. He was unconscious. The prisoners began saying a prayer over him, in the belief that he was dying. They demanded a doctor who, after inspecting the victim, pronounced that urgent surgical intervention was essential. The officers refused, declaring that the man had shown himself to be a real Chechen, tough, unwilling to surrender, and therefore perfectly able to survive without medical treatment.

On the morning of January 3, the prisoners heard someone warn over a radio link, "The Prosecutor is at the frontier . . ." The response to this unannounced inspection was, "Let him wait." ("The frontier" is how they referred to the Unit's security checkpoint.) A doctor came, injected Zelimkhan for a long time, and he was dragged away by the arms. In the evening the prisoners were informed that Murdalov had been taken to hospital but had escaped. Nobody believed this, and they assumed that as Zelimkhan was plainly in no state to move, let alone run, he must have died that morning. In order to avoid repercussions, his killers had evidently hidden the body. The October District Office is surrounded by ruined houses from which explosions are constantly being heard. Nobody knows who causes them or why but, as the whole of Grozny knows, the area is suffused with the stench of corpses.

Once Murdalov had been dragged away, the Prosecutor was allowed into the cell and registered that there was nobody there by the name of Murdalov. He apparently did not think to enquire why he had been denied access for such a long time.

The Prosecutor appeared in the October District Interior Affairs Office only because he had been forced to go there by Zelimkhan's parents, Rukiyat and Astemir Murdalov, who had pulled all the strings at their disposal. They are well known in Grozny. From then on until now, it was the parents, not any lawyers or investigators, who have conducted the real inquiry into the circumstances of their son's abduction, and who have effectively compelled the Grozny Prosecutor's Office to do its job of opening Criminal Case No. 15004 into his abduction, torture, and subsequent disappearance.

A telling detail: the Khanty-Mansiysk Militia Unit terrorised not only the citizens of Grozny but also the Grozny Prosecutor's Office. When one of the militiamen involved in the Murdalov case was summoned by the Prosecutors, a militia brigade armed to the teeth surrounded the building for the duration of his questioning. They smashed furniture in the corridors, and kept grenade launchers targeted on the building, promising to burn it to a cinder if their comrade was not released. There was no reaction to this from General Headquarters in Khankala, as if this is just how soldiers of the Joint Military Command in the North Caucasus are expected to behave.

On January 7, the criminal investigators decided to arrest Investigator Zhuravlyov of the October Office, having established that he had tortured Zelimkhan. However, the Head of the Department, Colonel Valeriy Kondakov, hastily issued an order backdated to January 5, sending him home to Nizhnevartovsk. According to witnesses, Kondakov himself was implicated in what befell Zelimkhan, and had no wish for anyone to start talking to the Prosecutor's Office. On January 18, the trick was repeated. An attempt to detain Lapin, "The Cadet," was foiled when Kondakov hurriedly had him sent home; and on February 7, the entire Khanty-Mansiysk contingent, celebrating the end of their 90-day tour of duty – the usual period for which Russian troops are sent to Chechnya – returned to Nizhnevartovsk.

There they became virtually inaccessible, either for questioning or for arrest, as if Nizhnevartovsk were not a Siberian city with a quarter of a million inhabitants but a far-off place in Latin America where war criminals could hide. On March 12, for example, the Grozny Prosecutor's Office sent two of its officers to Nizhnevartovsk to detain The Cadet and return him under guard to Chechnya, where the alleged crime had been committed. On April 2 they returned with only a signed under-taking from him not to leave Nizhnevartovsk. On April 20 the inves-tigation was informed that the Nizhnevartovsk Municipal Court had released him even from this undertaking. They also learned of state-ments by the Deputy Prosecutor of Nizhnevartovsk to the effect that he would not be handing over anybody from his city to face charges relating to the disappearance of a Chechen and that the case should be closed. Neither did he. The case faced stalemate. For the past eight months the collective might of Russia's law enforcement agencies has proved insufficient to resolve the matter.

Murdalov's crime, it transpired, had been only to be in the wrong place at the wrong time. On January 2, the militiamen had urgently needed a Chechen informer to falsely accuse a suspect so they could report a success to their superiors. The Khanty-Mansiysk detachment seized the first person they came across and tried to force him to collaborate, using their usual methods. It was as simple as that.

"Why?" That is the only question his mother Rukiyat wants answered, having lost her only son. Zelimkhan's father, Astemir, has shed more than 20 kilograms in weight and admits he will never be able to forgive this crime.

Abdulkasim Zaurbekov from Novosadovaya Street in Grozny had just started work at the October District Office as a temporary crane operator. At 9:00 a.m. on October 17 last year he went into the building to collect his wages, signed a receipt for 2,400 roubles, and was never seen again. His 18-year-old son, Aindi, waited for his father at the security checkpoint until evening, but he never emerged from the office and to this day there has been no sign of him.

On August 27 last year, Mahomed Umarov was abducted at dawn from his home on Klyuchevaya Street in Staropromyslovsky District, Grozny, by men in combat fatigues. By 9:00 a.m. his parents, Ruslan and Leila, were able to identify several of his abductors as working in the District Commandant's Office. They succeeded in having a criminal case opened by the Prosecutor's Office, but at this point that particular contingent of soldiers returned home from Chechnya and there the matter ended.

Even the risk-averse Eva Khubalkova, an official working in the Council of Europe Mission in Znamenskoye, eventually provided a statistic showing that, of applications relating to the "disappeared" sent by the office of Vladimir Kalamanov, the President's Special Representative, to the Prosecutor's Office and other law enforcement agencies of Chechnya, 55 per cent receive no reply at all. For the 45 per cent that do, the overwhelming majority of responses are callous and casually dismissive. A blatant refusal by the law enforcement agencies to take action in abduction cases involving the Army is only too apparent.

One minute someone is there, and the next they are gone. In Chechnya any encounter with a militiaman can prove fatal. He might be The Cadet. This is a time of shameful depravity in the Army and militia, when everything that should be stamped on is allowed. For the present that applies only in Chechnya, but this state of affairs has the tacit consent of our most senior state leaders. What next?

FROM THE EDITORS

September 24, 2001

We are fairly used to threats of various kinds, from officious fists banged on the table to fussy whispers over the telephone or online, warning us anonymously that it would be "inadvisable" to run a particular piece. We take these in our stride because we have found an antidote. We put any little plots or obscure hints into print, because we want no part in them. Ours is a different profession, and that is the rule we are following now.

In *Novaya gazeta*, No. 65 we published Anna Politkovskaya's report "The Disappeared," a journalistic investigation based on materials from the Prosecutor's Office and witness statements. It included lines referring to specific officers of the Khanty-Mansiysk Combined Militia Unit, including Sergey Lapin who uses the alias of "The Cadet." We quote: "A later inquiry established that it was they [that is, The Cadet and a number of other officers] who personally presided over and took part in the torturing of Zelimkhan." The criminal case against The Cadet has come to a standstill. The local municipal court even released him from his undertaking not to leave Nizhnevartovsk and it is apparently this circumstance that he has decided to take advantage of.

Last week a letter arrived in the electronic mailbox of *Novaya gazeta*'s investigations department:

There is reliable information that an officer of the Criminal Investigation Department who has served in the Chechen Republic and uses the personal code name (not alias) of "The Cadet," has received special training from the Federal Security Bureau in sabotage, sniper fire, and also has skills for survival in extreme conditions while conducting combat operations. His current whereabouts are unknown, but there are indications that he is in possession of firearms and has the intention of visiting Moscow. Can you shed any light on why this disgraced member of the Interior Ministry Office might be coming to Moscow?

The e-mail's subject heading is "The Disappeared," and the sender is Cadet@email.ru.

We do not intend to check whether this is a malicious joke, a hoax, a serious warning or a threat. That is not the function of journalists. Our duty is simply to inform our readers and the authorities of what we have learned and trust that the law enforcement agencies will take effective action. It is their professional obligation to trace the author of this message and establish his motives for writing to our newspaper.

Meanwhile, we continue to fulfil our obligations by publishing another report from Grozny by Anna Politkovskaya.

[After the appearance of the article of September 10, 2001, threatening letters addressed to Anna Politkovskaya began arriving at the newspaper's offices.]

THERE WILL BE NO RETRACTION

Novaya gazeta, October 15, 2001

This is the second e-mail message we have received:

> Forgive my troubling you, but you have just 10 days to publish a retraction of your article "The Disappeared," otherwise the militia officer you have hired will be unable to protect you. Yours sincerely, The Cadet.

We immediately sent an inquiry to the Interior Ministry Directorate in Khanty-Mansiysk, where the putative source of these threats works, in order to find out whether the special operations agent code-named "The Cadet" had any connection with them. We still do not exclude the possibility that this whole business is a hoax. At the time of going to press we have received no reply.

Let no one be in any doubt that we will take all necessary measures to protect our colleague.

And incidentally, *Novaya gazeta* does not respond to ultimatums.

To the Interior Minister of the Russian Federation, B.V. Gryzlov

Dear Boris Vyacheslavovich,
In *Novaya gazeta*, No. 65 we published Anna Politkovskaya's article "The Disappeared," which describes atrocities committed by certain members of the militia in Chechnya. Following publication, threats, signed in the name of one of those featured in the article, began arriving at *Novaya gazeta* by e-mail.

Journalists working for *Novaya gazeta* are increasingly being subjected to criminal violence: in May 2000, Igor

Domnikov was murdered; and in December 2000, Oleg
Luriye was brutally attacked. The perpetrators remain at large.
This persuades me that these threats should be taken
seriously and might be carried out. In my view, the life and
well-being of Anna Politkovskaya are seriously at risk.

I request that you take all the measures required by law to
identify and detain the guilty parties and to prevent the
committing of a crime against a journalist.

Yours sincerely,
Yu.P. Shchekochikhin
Deputy Chairman,
Security Committee of the State Duma
[Deputy Editor of *Novaya gazeta*]
October 15, 2001
Enclosures: 5 pages

SILENCING THE WITNESSES: WHY THE KHANTY-MANSIYSK COMBINED MILITIA UNIT IS RETURNING TO CHECHNYA

March 11, 2002

In this issue of *Novaya gazeta* we should have been publishing an
entirely different report from Chechnya, continuing the chronicle of
one of the most appalling security sweeps of 2002 in Starye Atagi. We
are obliged to postpone it until next Monday, in order today to describe
events which, if we were to delay reporting them, might lead to fatalities.

As time passes one has the ever more insistent impression that
there are several parallel states functioning simultaneously within
Russia, and that they are at loggerheads. Moreover, even within the
bounds of a single security ministry we find different state systems
coexisting which not only have different tasks and aims, but completely
dissimilar constitutions. The result is one tragedy after another when one
system protects a person, while another, in retaliation, sets about him.

You will recall that more than a year ago the Khanties were on the
rampage in Grozny. That is how the soldiers of the Khanty-Mansiysk

Combined Militia Unit were known, many of whom served in the
October District Temporary Interior Ministry Office in Grozny.
Today these temporary district offices are a real thorn in the flesh of
Chechnya. The permanent district offices are staffed by local militia-
men, but those in the Temporary Office have been seconded to
Chechnya from all parts of the country, usually for a 90-day tour of
duty in accordance with a plan drawn up in Moscow.

For a long time the October Temporary Office was one of the most
feared places in Grozny, and it has featured in *Novaya gazeta* on more
than one occasion. Were there any men in charge of the Interior
Ministry groups in Chechnya with the courage to try to stop the criminal brutality of the Khanties? Some fatherly commander sitting in
Khankala with responsibility for restoring the system of law enforcement in the Republic, part of which, according to the plan, was the
October District Office?

No. Not one. There were plenty of generals, but no courageous men
of that kind. Even the Prosecutors were reluctant to investigate the
goings-on at the October District Office, fearing the Khanties just as
much as anyone else living in Chechnya.

March 6, 2002, Grozny. The spring is unseasonably warm. Even the
lilac buds have opened and smile out at the people of Grozny who have
shivered through the winter. Yet Rukiyat Murdalova weeps quietly in
despair. We are driving through Minutka, the square in the center of
this ruined city where, on January 2, 2001, the Khanties seized
Zelimkhan, Rukiyat's 26-year-old son, bundled him into a car, in the
process brutally beating up two women (one of them a 73-year-old
grandmother), who tried to protect a boy who was simply walking down
the street. Both women are today witnesses against the Khanties, and
this is an important detail in our story.

Zelimkhan was taken to the October Temporary Office. As has now
been proven by the investigation team, his torture was directed and
participated in by Major Prilepin (alias "Alex"), Major Lapin (alias "The
Cadet"), and Investigator Zhuravlyov. The torture was truly inquisitorial,
so brutal and pathological that I will not describe it, although

I know all about the monstrous, feral acts perpetrated that night of January 2, 2001 by these Interior Ministry officers.

Were there witnesses? There were, and it is they who are today the issue. There were witnesses who survived and have given evidence about the state in which The Cadet dragged Zelimkhan into the October Office's temporary holding cell. They have told how and by whom, on the morning of January 3, the dying man was dragged out of that cell, after which he vanished without trace.

Rukiyat weeps, "Where is Zelim? Where is my son? Has Lapin said anything? Tell me . . ." It is already a year and two months later. We are standing by the fence of the offices on Garazhnaya Street of the Prosecutor of the Chechen Republic. We are not being allowed in and the security guards laugh at us and deride us. They make no secret of the fact that they are acting on instructions. We stand directly opposite the windows of Vsevolod Chernov, Prosecutor of Chechnya, and from time to time the cream venetian blinds are moved slightly to one side. The Prosecutor is peeping, wondering what this is all about.

Criminal Case No. 15004 has been opened by the Grozny Prosecutor's Office only because Zelimkhan's parents, Rukiyat and Astemir Murdalov, have achieved something seemingly impossible in current Chechen circumstances, in which the law and the law enforcement agencies, including the Prosecutor's Office, have virtually ceased to function where war crimes are concerned for fear of incurring the wrath of soldiers who have run amok. Rukiyat and Astemir are neither lawyers nor investigators, but they have stood in for the Republic's entire law enforcement system, selling all their possessions in order to conduct their own investigation and visit all the prisons and pre-trial detention centers of the North Caucasus. Their first priority was to look for their son, alive or dead, but they are also determined that those who took him from them on January 2, 2001 should answer in accordance with the law. In their place, would you want any less?

Alas, it has been precisely with the law enforcement agencies that they have had the greatest difficulty. The Khanties' immediate superior, Colonel Valeriy Kondakov, the Commanding Officer of the

Combined Militia Unit, did his utmost to ensure that his "colleagues" under investigation should be able quietly to slip away from Chechnya back to Siberia. And then what? Then nothing. Although the investigators of the Prosecutor's Office went to Nizhnevartovsk to arrest the suspects, the Khanties spat in their faces, and the Prosecutor's Office of Nizhnevartovsk and the senior officials of the provincial militia leaped to the defence of The Cadet and his accomplices. The investigators wiped their faces and left. People who had committed the most heinous crimes continued not merely to enjoy their freedom but even to be employed as officers of the Interior Ministry, as "guardians of the law" on behalf of the state. This continued for one month, a second, a third, six months. One had to wonder whether Russia has a functioning Interior Ministry or some virtual surrogate. A Prosecutor General's Office? A President? Or were they good only for appearing on television to talk hard-line nonsense?

On September 10, 2001 *Novaya gazeta* published an article, "The Disappeared," about the main issue in Chechnya today, the thousands who, having been taken away by the federals, disappear without trace. We told, among others, the story of Zelimkhan Murdalov, and received a prompt reply. It was very much in keeping with a state in which where there are many states. It came not from the Interior Ministry, the Prosecutor-General's Office or the President, but from The Cadet himself, who clearly considered himself a lord of life. The Cadet was so indignant that he sent threats to the newspaper: a first, then another, giving us 10 days to retract our accusation, otherwise the author of the article, who is the author also of this article, would be killed. There followed a succession of official requests from the editors to the Interior Minister of Russia, Boris Gryzlov, for protection, and also dozens of publications in the mass media of the whole world about what is going on in Russia with officers who have served in Chechnya. The result was that in late January this year The Cadet was arrested and sent under guard to Grozny, in accordance with the law, to the place where the crime was committed.

Finally something had happened which is still exceptionally rare in

Chechnya, where most soldiers, with the connivance of their superiors, have created total mayhem, and where the Prosecutor, timidly slinking past them, is a figure of fun.

With The Cadet now in a cell, it seemed to us that, largely thanks to the persistence of *Novaya gazeta*, the law would take its course. The case was being taken care of at the highest level.

We were wrong. On February 28 the author of these lines was summoned to Grozny, to the Office of the Prosecutor of the Chechen Republic, to "assist investigations related to Case No. 15004," to be questioned as someone who had been wronged. *Novaya gazeta* naturally felt duty bound to comply, firmly believing that it had helped the Prosecutor's Office to restore law and order and should continue to do so.

Things began to go wrong the moment I arrived in Chechnya. Vladimir Ignatenko, the Investigating Officer, behaved so inappropriately that from time to time one had the uneasy feeling that his main objective was not to keep all the witnesses in this case on board but rather to demoralise them, to coerce them into refusing to testify and thereby to torpedo the case. At one point Ignatenko ordered the security guards to take me outside the confines of the Prosecutor's Office late at night, having deliberately dragged out the questioning until it was pitch dark and the curfew was in force. In Grozny that is tantamount to – well, obviously it is tantamount to what The Cadet had promised in September. On another occasion he forced me to stand under guard for several hours by "the kiosks," a patch of ground not far from the Prosecutor's Office, visible from it but not on its territory or under its control. Cold and hungry, I was refused permission to use the toilet, or the telephone to tell the newspaper what was going on. I was given water only infrequently, again under guard. Members of the Prosecutor's Office staff joked sympathetically, "Consider yourself under administrative arrest." Thank you very much.

I will omit details of the campaign of humiliation which went on for many days. It was so discourteous as to leave me without a shred of respect for those wearing combat fatigues and styled "Civil Prosecutors" in Chechnya. All attempts to get through to Chernov, the Prosecutor of Chechnya, to find out what was going on, failed. He was too busy. On one occasion he was in the bathhouse, another time having lunch, another time having dinner. Or so, at least, his security people said.

All this, however, is not what really matters. What matters is the witnesses, without whom the case will fall apart in court and The Cadet will walk off into history as if nothing had happened, and even, in the eyes of his ilk, wearing the halo of a martyr.

Ignatenko assured me that representatives of the Memorial Human Rights Center, who are well acquainted with the witnesses from Grozny, had supposedly refused to assist the investigation unless they were paid. This was a ludicrous assertion. I have known these people very well throughout the course of the Second Chechen War, risking their lives to get accurate information about what is going on, selflessly doing work which, incidentally, is the responsibility of the Prosecutor's Office. I did not believe Ignatenko and, of course, set out to check his claims.

Here is what I learned. The witnesses really are terrified of giving evidence. They are moving round the city, trying to stay alive and to protect their families. Their chances of doing so have just been markedly reduced because the Khanties are coming back: the Khanty-Mansiysk Combined Militia Unit is returning for another tour of duty in Grozny in accordance with a decision taken by the central administration of the Interior Ministry.

So it seems that the right hand of the Interior Ministry, controlled by Minister Boris Gryzlov, is doing all it can to bring this unit's crimes to court, while the left hand is simultaneously doing everything to ensure the opposite: to make it easy for those who have dared to raise their voices against a war criminal to be dealt with by their oppressors.

And what about the Grozny Prosecutor's Office, what about Ignatenko? They are shaking with fear.

A crucial detail: nobody, neither the witnesses, nor those in the Prosecutor's Office building the case against The Cadet, doubts for a moment that the reason the Khanties are so keen to get back to Grozny is to take revenge and to help The Cadet. The one way they can do that is by silencing the witnesses and by shooting it out with the investigators. Such things have happened in Chechnya before, and it is well known that the Russian law enforcement system has consistently failed to protect the witnesses of war crimes in Chechnya, or even to see through to its conclusion a case involving the murder of their own colleagues, members of the Prosecutor's Office.

When the witnesses appealed to Ignatenko for protection, to ask where they should send their children and where they could find safety themselves, he just tried to laugh it off because, of course, he is himself terrified of the consequences. In Chechnya they call this "the Chechen fear," and everybody understands that what is meant is fear of the Army. It prevents Ignatenko from raising a finger to help himself or to help people who, through no fault of their own, have had been grievously wronged but have had the courage to fight back.

As if the news of the Khanty-Mansiysk Unit's imminent arrival was not enough, the Chechen Prosecutor's Office came under intense pressure from the Prosecutor-General's Office in Moscow. I do not believe in coincidences or chance. Investigator Ignatenko was subjected to extraordinary pressure, as in the end he himself admitted to me. He buckled. He was frightened and gave in, transferring that pressure to the already completely defenceless witnesses, and also, of course, to me, amongst others.

Is Ignatenko capable of fighting, even though he wears the medal For Courage from the First Chechen War, even though he is a lieutenant-colonel? No, he isn't, and that is a great pity. Regrettably this conclusion is supported by the way he has conducted other cases since he came to work in the Chechen Prosecutor's Office. There was the case when doctors of the Ministry for Emergency Situations were murdered, which collapsed when Ignatenko chose not to dig deeper. As a result, a man who had an alibi is now in jail while the killers have walked free. Why did Ignatenko let that happen? Because he wanted to hold on to his job. He wanted to avoid "personal problems." He was pressured by superiors who wanted the case closed and he lived up to their expectations. Chechen human rights activists characterise Ignatenko as an expert in shooting down cases brought against the Army.

Will so demonstrably tractable an investigator prove capable of conducting such a difficult case as that against the Khanties, a case which calls for great personal courage? Can we assume everything will go smoothly now The Cadet has finally been arrested, and hope that this time at least justice is going to be done? Let's not kid ourselves.

We insist that the Khanty-Mansiysk Unit be sent back home without delay. We consider that this should have been the first priority of Investigator Ignatenko and the Chechen Prosecutor, Chernov. Always assuming, of course, they do still aspire to see the law triumph over the right of the strong to mete out their private version of justice.

We firmly believe that the Khanties have no business showing their faces in Chechnya again. They are *personae non gratae* for the rest of time. We are in no doubt that the witnesses in The Cadet case need to be protected by the institutions of the state. Otherwise it will be clear that the state is not doing its job and intervenes only in order to encourage criminal behaviour by the Army.

We insist that there should at the very least be an internal inquiry focusing on the conduct of the generals at the Interior Ministry head-quarters who decided to send the Khanties back to Chechnya. These generals are facilitating the ongoing committing of war crimes in Chechnya and their decision is tantamount to obstructing the course of justice. If this was simply the result of incompetence, we trust that an explanation to that effect will be forthcoming from the agencies whose job it is to plan deployments in Chechnya, together with an apology for their carelessness and for failing to appreciate the situation. Let it, nevertheless, be clear that this carelessness is criminal. Whoever was guilty of it, whether deliberately or not, is impeding investigation of the crimes of the Khanty-Mansiysk Combined Militia Unit.

MATERIAL EVIDENCE IS IN THE TRUSTWORTHY HANDS OF THE SUSPECTS

April 8, 2002

On March 11 we published a report, "Silencing the Witnesses," about the ambiguous situation developing around Criminal Case No. 15004 in which one of the Khanties, Major Lapin, alias The Cadet, is charged with the torture and murder in January 2001 of a 26-year-old Grozny man, Zelimkhan Murdalov.

On March 11 we called upon the Interior Ministry immediately to withdraw the Khanty-Mansiysk Combined Militia Unit from Grozny and demanded that the witnesses in the case should be afforded protection by the state. Finally, we called for an inquiry into the conduct of those highly placed officials at Interior Ministry Headquarters who plan tours of duty in Chechnya.

On March 19, without unduly high hopes that the relevant issues of *Novaya gazeta* would have been read at Interior Ministry headquarters, the editors forwarded by hand a formal request to Boris Gryzlov, Interior Minister of Russia. The Memorial Human Rights Center also addressed the same demands to the country's political leaders.

Unfortunately, Moscow is a long way from Grozny and that same week, between March 11 and 19, part of the Khanty-Mansiysk Militia was deployed without a hitch to Grozny. They moved faster than we did. While we were writing heartfelt appeals, trying to track down ministers and hand them indignant letters, and waiting anxiously for them to make some response at least, hoping that the next phone call would be from the office of Boris Gryzlov, on March 15 the Khanties paid a visit to the makeshift accommodation in Grozny where Zelimkhan Murdalov's parents were living.

Only his mother, Rukiyat, was at home. Masked individuals drove up in a vehicle without registration markings (a trivial matter in Chechnya, no matter how often General Moltenskoy, the Commanding Officer of the Joint Military Command, pronounces on this issue), and warned Rukiyat to be more careful because the Khanties were back in town. They then left. What state is Rukiyat in? One is reluctant even to talk about it. You can imagine for yourself how it is living in the midst of ruins, in a lawless place where, if someone decides to kill you, no one will hear your cries for help.

There were reasons for the visit from the Khanties. Newly returned to the October District Interior Affairs Temporary Office, they observed their colleague The Cadet, now in custody in Grozny, starting to grass on his pals.

Firstly, he demanded the arrest of the officer who had inspired him to perform these feats, "Alex," to use his Chechen code name, but known to the outside world as Major Alexander Prilepin.

Secondly, when taken to the crime scene, the grounds of the October Temporary Office, he at last pointed out the location of the pit where the Khanties threw the bodies of those they had tortured and killed.

Yet the anomalies get worse. The Chechen Prosecutor's Office made no attempt to excavate the pit, on the grounds that the rains had arrived. As a rule, it is the relatives of the disappeared who voluntarily carry out such exhumations in Chechnya. Here that was impossible because the grave was in a high security zone. As a result, the pit, whose contents might have become major evidence of the crimes committed by the Khanties, was handed over into the safe keeping of the Khanties themselves. What do you think? Have they had enough time by now to destroy the material evidence, namely the bones of their victims?

The wailing of the mothers, sisters and wives of the victims of the Khanty-Mansiysk Unit is constantly to be heard in Grozny, and accordingly:

> We demand to be told by the Interior Ministry of Russia how much longer the Khanties will be allowed to remain in Grozny;
> We insist that Interior Minister Boris Gryzlov should immediately intervene in this ongoing travesty;
> We request that the families should have the bones of their dearest returned to them;
> We beg Russia's most senior officials to start behaving like human beings.

Hello, Prosecutor-General's Office – is anybody there? What is going on with Criminal Case No. 15004 which, according to *Novaya gazeta*'s information, has been hastily removed from Chechnya? Where is it? Are pages being torn out of it? Are replacement pages being inserted? What guarantee is there that the file will ever be placed before the courts?

Give these undertakings to society. Finally!

PUT THE WITNESSES IN JAIL? ONE OF THE MOST BRUTAL WAR CRIMINALS OF THE SECOND CHECHEN WAR HAS BEEN RELEASED FROM PRISON

July 8, 2002

Sergey Lapin has been set free from the pre-trial detention facility in Pyatigorsk. Such is the ruling of the Pyatigorsk Municipal Court, acting at the behest of Lapin's self-appointed defenders from the Regional Board of the Prosecutor-General's Office in the North Caucasus. The grounds for releasing him were simple: The Cadet is no danger to society and can roam free while awaiting trial.

Lapin was arrested in February 2002 and was taken under guard to the investigative detention center in Grozny, where the crimes had been committed. The investigation progressed for a time, but then the atmosphere surrounding Case No. 15004 began to change and The Cadet was transferred to Pyatigorsk Prison. The investigators working on the case were switched around like pieces of glass in a kaleidoscope, and eventually they were all in Essentuki and not in Chechnya at all. As a result nobody treated the excavation of mass graves at the October District Interior Ministry Temporary Office as a matter of any urgency.

In the end what we were beginning to suspect was found to be true: the materials of the investigation had been blatantly "weeded," and incidents dropped from the indictment which were central to bringing criminal charges against others, together with whom, and often with the direct authorisation of whom, Lapin had committed his crimes. In places the tampering was laughable: the Prosecutors started referring to the officers who were so carefully being exculpated as an "unidentified group of individuals"; this at the end of an investigation where there were not only witnesses but also documents which made it unambiguously clear who was on duty at the Office on which days and at which hour.

It was no laughing matter, however, when the Khanty-Mansiysk Unit was returned to Grozny (on the instructions of President Putin, as we were officially informed by Ivan Golubev, Deputy Interior Minister of the Russian Federation), and the witnesses in the case, until then left to their own devices in Grozny, could no longer risk sleeping two nights in the same bed.

And now we hear that Lapin has been set free until the trial.

There is something fundamentally wrong in Russia. Life has been turned upside-down and the law has no substance. The entire range of public services is put to work on behalf of the criminal: the lawyers, Prosecutors, courts, – and even, sad to relate, public opinion. There is precious little help for the victims, especially if they happen to be Chechens. Today the party which has suffered, Murdalov's family, do not even have a lawyer, paid or unpaid, despite the fact that this is required by law. They have no protection from the Prosecutor's Office because they have no money, having long ago spent all their resources in searching for Zelimkhan.

All this, however, is being extended to Lapin. He enjoys the sympathy of the Prosecutor's Office, the understanding of the court, he has a lawyer, appreciative colleagues, and as a result of their efforts he is at large.

We await a prompt reply from Prosecutor-General Vladimir Ustinov: are these actions by members of the Prosecutor's Office in accordance with the law? Why does the reply need to be prompt? Because at any moment it may become too late. There is a major problem in Russia with officers who have served in Chechnya. The most modest estimates suggest that The Cadet has almost half a million comrades-in-arms in Russia, a large city's worth of Cadets.

From the Editors:
It was The Cadet who, on more than one occasion, threatened to kill our columnist Anna Politkovskaya, after which she was first placed under the protection of the Interior Ministry, and subsequently obliged to move abroad. The Cadet acknowledged these facts without showing any remorse. We demand that [. . .] Citizen Lapin should be re-arrested as we are certain that the life of the witnesses and of our columnist are again threatened.

HOLES IN THE PROSECUTORS' SAFES: IMPORTANT DOCUMENTS FROM THE CADET CASE GO MISSING

August 8, 2002

A major problem relating to Criminal Case No. 15004 [. . .] has been discovered. Documents of fundamental importance have disappeared. Although they were attached to the criminal case and had been numbered and indexed in the requisite manner, placed in the safe of Investigator Ivanteyev of the Board of the Prosecutor-General's Office in the North Caucasus, a safe located in Essentuki and kept locked, with a key in the custody only of Investigator Ivanteyev, nevertheless . . .

To tell the truth, the latest disappearance of documents is not unexpected. The way the case has been conducted for several months now suggested it would arrive at court laundered and "optimised" for the benefit of Lapin. That seemed to be the opinion of the members of the Prosecutor's Office in Essentuki too.

But surprise, surprise! Copies of the missing documents are secure in the possession of *Novaya gazeta* whose safes, unlike those of the Prosecutor's Office in Essentuki, have no holes through which papers can slip for which certain criminals, as the unforgettable film sleuth Gleb Zheglov used to say, "will give anything." We kept copies in case of just such an untoward accident. Not everybody in the Nizhnevartovsk Militia is on Lapin's side. Don't ask how we came by these copies. For the time being, until the court hearings, we can only reply that they came from the bowels of the earth.

And so, dear reader, we invite you to view photographs of members of the Khanty-Mansiysk Militia Unit rampaging through Grozny, and as they appear in the photographs attached to Case No. 15004, identifying The Cadet's accomplices.

Look closely at these faces. There is nothing unusual about them. They look like anybody else. They are the people around us. They are like us. Yet these faces belong to people who tortured, or killed, or who were jacks of all trades both torturing and murdering and blowing to bits the bodies of those they had murdered.

Why did they do it? Don't look for special reasons: they just did.

They hated their victims. Hatred is the mantra of the Khanties, sanctioned from the very pinnacle of the state. For the greater glory of their mantra, these people were pulverised (not just figuratively, but literally), dozens of them just like themselves. We would probably never have printed these mug shots of the Khanties, not least because they are part of a criminal case and should not be made public. The Prosecutor's Office, however, has left us no alternative.

In addition to the photographs, records of the interrogation of witness Dalayev have also disappeared. Lapin, trying to force him to incriminate himself, ground Dalayev's teeth down with a file. Dalayev's testimony is also important in respect of the disappearance of Zelimkhan Murdalov because he was the last person to see him when Murdalov was dragged by Lapin personally, a Russian militiaman with his nickname "Cadet" shaved on the back of his head, into the cell of the holding facility in the October District Office after being tortured. We will not deny that we too are looking for those records, in order that the Russian Constitution should win in its battle with those who are supposedly there to protect it, and so that the court should be in possession of all the available information.

Finally, a few words about the way the Board of the Prosecutor-General's Office of the Russian Federation in the North Caucasus works nowadays. It is the main center to which prosecutions for war crimes in Chechnya are sent. How can this sort of thing be possible? Why should the Prosecutor's Office be so dogged in its whitewashing of war criminals? How has this institution been reduced to Essentuki plc, a state enterprise with extraordinarily limited liability?

From the very beginning of the Second Chechen War, the Prosecutor's Office gained the reputation of being subservient to the will of the Kremlin, behaving like a baggage wagon trundling along in the distant rearguard of the Army in all matters relating to war crimes. We are now reaping the bitter fruits of its failures. In order even to have a criminal charge brought against a serviceman observed looting, robbing, abducting people, trading in corpses, torturing and murdering (to list only the most routine war crimes in Chechnya), it is essential to make the case "resonate," as everybody from the District Prosecutor to the Prosecutor-General himself will explain. A case resonates when the prosecutors get a kick up the backside from the public, from the pages of newspapers, from television screens. The mere fact that murders, abductions, looting and the like have taken place is not sufficient to get the Prosecutors to act.

This has been the state of affairs for three years now, since the beginning of the war itself. During this time dozens of people working for the Prosecutor's Office have received government awards, titles and ranks for profaning their profession, while the few honorable activists who try to fulfil their obligations are relentlessly purged from these serried ranks, and the very best have actually been killed in Chechnya in mysterious circumstances. Like, for example, the fearless Alexander Leushin, the first investigator who took up the Cadet affair and was trying to have an arrest warrant issued when he was shot dead by "unidentified assailants."

Naturally, "keep your nose out" has become a Pavlovian conditioned reflex for Prosecutors working in Chechnya and Essentuki. They salivate when they hear the bell. Because of this, we once again have a region in our country where the laws of the Russian Federation do not operate. It is called Chechnya. Where soldiers can do whatever their appetites dictate, and criminal cases brought against them, even when they have been opened, are subject to "laundering" in Essentuki, with a kindly nod towards the murderers, and quite extraordinary heartlessness towards their victims.

THE CADET AFFAIR: A CRIMINAL CASE IS OPENED INTO DEATH THREATS TO *NOVAYA GAZETA'S* COLUMNIST, ANNA POLITKOVSKAYA

September 5, 2002

"Forgive my troubling you, but you have just 10 days to publish a retraction of your article 'The Disappeared,' otherwise the militia officer you have hired will be unable to protect you. Yours sincerely, The Cadet."

This was the second message bearing this signature to arrive in *Novaya gazeta*'s electronic mailbox. We were obliged to take additional security measures, and Anna Politkovskaya left Russia under the Program for the Protection of Journalists.

Almost a year has passed. Criminal cases were opened against The Cadet and a number of other officers, charging them with abductions, diabolical murders, desecration of bodies and other extremely serious crimes.

Then something odd happened. Documents began disappearing from the case file, witnesses were afraid to give evidence, and the ruling that Anna Politkovskaya should be classed as a victim (she had after all received a death threat) was effectively overturned. To crown all this absurdity, the suspect Lapin was released upon signing an undertaking not to leave Nizhnevartovsk.

Novaya gazeta has written on more than one occasion about this scandalous affair, in which, with variable success, a struggle is being waged against lawlessness. Here is the latest document we have received:

Notification
I hereby inform you that your application of October 26, 2001, addressed to the Head of the Directorate of Interior Affairs of the Khanty-Mansiysk Autonomous Region regarding receipt by the offices of *Novaya gazeta* on September 15, 2001 by electronic mail of a message regarding the departure for Moscow of an armed agent of the Criminal Investigation Department of the Interior Affairs Department (personal code name, "The Cadet"), who had undergone sniper and sabotage training, was examined and on December 14, 2001 instigation of a criminal case was refused.

On July 29, 2002, the Prosecutor of the Khanty-Mansiysk Autonomous Region withdrew the directive refusing to instigate a criminal case and a criminal case has now been instigated in view of an apparent crime as defined under Article 119 of the

Criminal Code of the Russian Federation (threat of murder or causing serious bodily harm).
Investigator of the Prosecutor's Office, Nizhnevartovsk
V.A. Churikov

This is one more serious crime linked with The Cadet which is being investigated, and we can only welcome this victory for the law. The question remains, however, whether The Cadet, who supposedly "does not pose any threat to society" and is currently at large, represents a threat to Anna Politkovskaya, whom he has threatened to kill. And what about the other witnesses and victims?

We believe the answer can only be "Yes, unquestionably." We would like to know the view of the Prosecutor's Office.
Novaya gazeta

"STOP WORRYING . . .": THE CADET ADMITS HIS GUILT AND TRIES TO APOLOGIZE

December 5, 2002

You can't take a mentally ill person to court. You have to pity a sick person and get treatment for him. Some people may disagree, but that is what I believe.

Sergey Lapin, whom readers of our newspaper are more familiar with by his Chechen nickname of The Cadet, has written to our editorial office. He reads *Novaya gazeta*, and accordingly we are publishing this Reader's Letter.

Moscow
To A. Politkovskaya
Dear Anna,
I read a piece about myself in the last issue of *Novaya gazeta*, No. 36, the one addressed to the Prosecutor. "The lives of *Novaya gazeta* journalists are again threatened" and that was because of my letters from the pre-trial detention facility in

Pyatigorsk and I have altered my decision now. That is, I have
changed my mind about shooting you with a sniper's rifle.
Specially because I haven't got one and it would be silly for
me to pay for one just because of you. Stop worrying I don't
need you. Which is what I told the court and so they let me
out as not a danger to society. I wrote because I had nothing
to do and it was a joke. I am not such a complete fool to write
letters with death threats to you and report my exact location.
I was joking so I can just write you another letter and you can
even print it in your "column" so everyone can read it and see
my literary talent. It can be part 2 of my letters to you. I think
it reminds me of somebody but perhaps it only seems that
way to me because this is all my own literary work, and not
anybody else's. Anyway The Cadet writes

REPENTANCE
I am writing you this letter
Because I want you now to see
That I don't care if I'm your debtor
Or if you look down on me
At first I thought I'd just keep mum
And you'd have never known of that
You'd have thought I had gone dumb
But then I thought that was just sad
And so this poem now I write
It's difficult to make it suit
And make it all come out all right.
To torture you and maybe shoot
and cut your throat and strangle you when I am drunk . . .
The Cadet

The letter needs no commentary. This former militia officer is just very
sick, a common condition given the way the Second Chechen War has
developed under our supreme Commander-in-Chief, Vladimir Putin.
The majority of soldiers who have served in Chechnya need serious

rehabilitation but are not getting it, and the state machine which propelled them into the tragedy now spits on them from the great height of its Kremlin bell-tower. As it does on the rest of us.

We will not take out proceedings against a sick man: I forgive him and accept his "repentance."

Let it be clear, however, that in our opinion Sergey Lapin should be condemned for the crimes he committed in Grozny, and this newspaper will do everything a newspaper can to report fully the trial of Criminal Case No. 15004. We will do our utmost to prevent his being represented as some perverse new "Hero of Russia" in the mould of ex-Colonel Budanov, rather than showing him to have been a fiendish torturer and killer.

THE SERGEY LAPIN CADET CORPS: HOW MANY PROSECUTORS' OFFICES ARE THERE IN RUSSIA?

August 7, 2003

Strange things are going on. The Prosecutors' Offices in different parts of Russia are declaring unilateral independence. There seems to be no controlling hierarchy and they seem to have no nationally established goals and obligations. In short, there is no "dictatorship of the law," each of them within their own region making up the law as they go along. The struggle for independence from each other of the city, district, regional and national Prosecutor-General's Offices is demonstrated in the quite extraordinary way they are pulling in different directions in the case of The Cadet, No. 200201389/46.

Novaya gazeta has written about this saga more than once. Our indignation that, after all that had happened, The Cadet was still employed as a militia officer in Nizhnevartovsk led to his being charged and sent to prison in Pyatigorsk. Not, however, before he had had time to contact our offices to express his great displeasure and threaten to kill us. Afterwards, when he was surprisingly released from prison as posing no danger to society, he went on to withdraw his previous threats in writing, mentioning that he could no longer afford to buy a sniper's rifle.

At the present time The Cadet nevertheless faces court proceedings, while simultaneously contributing, to the best of his ability, to the internecine strife between the Prosecutors' Offices of Russia. No sooner had the Basmanny District Prosecutor's Office in Moscow summoned me for further questioning (the last time was on July 30) than Investigator G. Rodionov wrote to demand that the original of Lapin's letter withdrawing his death threat should be produced, this having long since been delivered to the Nizhnevartovsk Prosecutor's Office. On August 2 an official letter, Notification No. 104402 of July 24, 2003 from the Nizhnevartovsk Prosecutor's Office, was brought to my front door.

I hereby notify you that pursuant upon the results of the preliminary investigation of Criminal Case No. 200201389/46 I have issued a ruling that the criminal case (prosecution) should be closed on account of S. Lapin not having committed any offence provided for under Article 109 of the Criminal Code of the Russian Federation. Senior Investigator of the Prosecutor's Office of the City of Nizhnevartovsk, E.N. Shchinov.

The date, we note, is one week before my questioning in the Moscow Prosecutor's Office, where I was officially assured that the case was continuing and hence further investigation, for example analysis of the handwriting of the letter, was required. Now, no less officially, Senior Investigator Shchinov appears to have closed the same case.

Which of our territorially sovereign Prosecutors' Offices is to be believed? On whose breast should I lay my weary head and crave protection? It is a serious question. And that is not all. There is in addition to the City and the District also the Prosecutor's Office for the Southern Federal Region under the direction of Sergey Fridinsky, from which come even more rulings on the Cadet affair. And then there is the Prosecutor-General's Office, directly subordinate to Prosecutor-General Vladimir Ustinov. They have their own, fourth, version of how events may unfold.

Almost a year has passed, during which time the case has been closed and reopened four or five times by different Prosecutors' Offices.

The Prosecutor-General's Office opens it and issues demands, the Nizhnevartovsk one closes it and does not want to receive anything. The Southern Federal Region reopens it, and the Basmanny loses it and forgets all about it.

One could simply resign oneself to all this and put it down to Russia's age-old inability to get its act together. The telephone isn't working, the fax has been switched off, there's been a downpour, a snowstorm is expected, there's been a blizzard of bureaucratic paper. But what if someone really does need the state to protect them from some weirdo with a grudge? The feuding of the Prosecutors' Offices rules out any possibility that such protection will be forthcoming.

There is one further possible explanation for what is happening, summed up by the expression, "they are reeling us in." Officialdom is doing everything in its power to ensure that The Cadet, who stands accused of war crimes committed during the Second Chechen War, should have the best possible chance of eluding justice.

Look out for yourselves, readers! If by chance your hitmen have failed to do their job, beware of Prosecutors' Offices. That is the real Corps of Cadets. The National Association of Prosecutors for Aid to the Accused. If your hitman has not yet proved himself, he can be sure of a sympathetic ear in a Prosecutor's Office. If not in one, then in another, because they all work entirely independently.

SHOULD THE CADET BE ARRESTED FOR ABSCONDING?

October 23, 2003

Today The Cadet, Sergey Lapin, until recently a militiaman in Nizhnevartovsk, is one of more than a million federal military personnel who have served in Chechnya. He came away with an evil reputation as a torturer and abductor. Now, in addition, The Cadet/Lapin has shown himself to be a coward. On October 14 neither he nor his lawyer showed up at the court hearing.

Let us recall the background. In January 2001 there was no more dreaded place in Grozny than Pavel Musorov Street where the Khanties – the Khanty-Mansiysk Combined Militia Unit – were stationed. On January 2, a group which included Lapin abducted 26-year-old Zelimkhan Murdalov in the street. He was dragged into the Khanties' compound, brutally tortured and then disappeared without trace. It was a typical atrocity for Chechnya but had an untypical aftermath, because in this instance it proved possible not only to get a criminal case opened against Lapin, but actually to have it brought to court.

What is more, it came to court in Grozny, despite several attempts by the Chechen Supreme Court to torpedo the first such trial of a federal serviceman. It was only thanks to the resolve of the Russian Supreme Court that Lapin's trial opened in the October District Court of Grozny. The presiding judge was Maierbek Mezhidov, a professional who had practised for many years under all manner of regimes. As he intoned the customary, "Hearing of the case of . . ." the voice of the grey-haired judge was shaking, as if he were a schoolboy taking an exam. "He is so frightened," people who have come to the courtroom whisper understandingly. Fear, of course, is something everyone in Grozny lives with; fear of suffering the fate of Zelimkhan Murdalov underlies the words and deeds of people who have lived many years in the embrace of war and death. Judges are no exception, despite supposedly enjoying the protection of the President himself. But the President is far away in the Kremlin, and the Khanties, who in the build-up to their colleague's trial have threatened everybody associated with this case, are very near. There is no escaping them in Grozny.

"The accused, Lapin, has failed to appear at this hearing," Mezhidov quavers. "No explanations have been received. Your submission?"

In his nervousness, the judge forgets the correct judicial procedure and calls upon the plaintiffs' lawyer rather than the Prosecuting Official. Stanislav Markelov is the first Moscow lawyer in the course of this war to have risked coming to Chechnya to protect the interests of a Grozny family seeking a disappeared son. He is laconic but precise, and demands that Lapin should be arrested and brought under guard before Judge Mezhidov.

"In the past the accused has regularly disrupted the investigative process without providing reasons," Markelov says. "This is a flagrant contempt of Russian law. The court should take appropriate measures."

The judge looks horrified. This Moscow lawyer is outspoken in a way unheard of in Grozny. There is, however, no escaping the fact that Lapin's behaviour is the height of insolence. It was a condition of his bail – granted more than a year ago when the Pyatigorsk Municipal Court ruled that this torturer and abductor "did not pose a threat to society" and promptly released him from prison – that he would immediately surrender himself to the court when summoned.

"And you, Murdalov?" the judge asks.

"I don't just support the lawyer, I insist on this," Astemir Murdalov, the father of the disappeared, replies abruptly. He is a hero. By his own titanic efforts he has done most of the investigative work in this case which should have been done by the Prosecutor's Office.

"I invite the representative of the Prosecutor's Office to speak," the judge quavers.

The role of Prosecuting Official has devolved upon Prosecutor Antonina Zhuravlyova:

"I would be inclined to agree with this view, but having familiarised myself with the documents . . ."

Zhuravlyova has noticed that, surprisingly (or perhaps deliberately), the court itself has been quietly playing into The Cadet's hands. Judge Mezhidov has simply failed to take the requisite procedural steps to ensure attendance of the accused. Is that credible in such an important case, the outcome of which is awaited by tens of thousands of people whose relatives have been disappeared by the federals in Chechnya? When an opportunity has finally arisen to use the law to establish what happened to one of them at least?

Prosecutor Zhuravlyova insists that the court should follow the letter of the law:

"The court should issue a summons through the court bailiffs. It should issue a warning to lawyer Derda [Lapin's defence lawyer] through the Stavropol Regional College of Lawyers and raise the matter of disciplining him with the College."

"The bench will retire to consider," Judge Mezhidov murmurs and hastily leaves.

We don't have long to wait. We talk quietly to other people in the courtroom. Shamkhan Khaisumov's eyes are haunted. He has come here because for three years he has been searching in vain for his brother, Sharip, who was also abducted by the Khanties, from his own home opposite their compound.

"We call their base Buchenwald because we can hear the groaning all round the neighbourhood. I know exactly which Khanties were involved in my brother's disappearance. Their names are Rauf Baibekov, Andrey Karpenko and Rashid Yagofarov. Several investigators have been replaced in the course of the case. The present one is Konstantin Krivorotov from the Chechen Prosecutor's Office. I asked him to question a witness who could show him a place where the Khanties bricked in people they had abducted while they were still alive. Perhaps we might find my brother's bones in there. I asked Krivorotov to inspect that brickwork, but he said they had been forbidden to travel to the scene of the crime because it was too dangerous. How about that? I have written to Putin, Gryzlov, Patrushev . . ."

Alaudin Sadykov, a 53-year-old former physical education teacher, is also in the courtroom. The Khanties picked him off the street on March 25, 2000, tortured him, and cut off his left ear. Afterwards, one of them, Igor Vanin, who is in charge of the holding cells at the October District Office, paraded around flaunting Alaudin's dried ear on his chest like an amulet. Alaudin miraculously survived and now his case is being conducted by Investigator Krivorotov.

"I asked Krivorotov to find them, but he said, 'They just cut off some flesh you don't really need. My rank doesn't allow me to question the person who cut your ear off. You need to appreciate my situation.' Now I can't hear. I am half-deaf."

Judge Mezhidov bustles back into court and rattles off his ruling: ". . . be compelled to appear." Not a word about the measures Prosecutor Zhuravlyova was demanding, no response to the behaviour of Lapin's lawyer. From Mezhidov's tone you would think he was dealing with a naughty schoolboy.

Grozny is in the grip of a fear which paralyses civic action and breeds apathy. The next hearing of the Lapin case is set for October 24. Perhaps at least Chechnya's journalists, of whom only one was in court at this precedent-setting case, will overcome their fear. After them, who knows, perhaps the judicial authorities will square their shoulders and give hope to those living in Chechnya that all is not lost and that it is still possible to get at the truth.

TOTAL CADETOPHILIA ON THE PART OF THE PROSECUTOR'S OFFICE

November 3, 2003

On October 30 the trial of The Cadet in Grozny was postponed indefinitely at the insistence of the Prosecutor's Office.

The trial was scheduled to start at 10:00 a.m. but Judge Mezhidov conspicuously failed to appear. By midday the public were becoming restless. Had he been taken ill? The security guards told me in confidence that the judge had left the court building.

What was going on? Those in the know explained that early that morning the telephone had been disconnected in the court on Popovich Street. This left the judge isolated, without any telephone down which he could be given instructions. At this point the Prosecutor's Office got up to another of its tricks: at 10.10 Antonina Zhuravlyova appeared in Mezhidov's office. She is an imposing, elegantly dressed blonde from Stavropol who is both the Prosecutor and Prosecuting Official in The Cadet's trial. She informed Mezhidov that the Prosecutor's Office was outraged by his actions and had lodged a supervisory appeal against him with the Chechen Supreme Court for his misconduct at the previous hearing when Mezhidov had dared to reject The Cadet's demand that the trial be moved far away from Chechnya, to somewhere in Russia where he would feel less at risk. Zhuravlyova continued to berate the judge, warning him not even to think of ruling today that The Cadet should be arrested. One has to admire her foresight, since this was precisely the ruling everyone was expecting.

Mezhidov went to pieces. He couldn't even use the telephone. He hastily absented himself and went to consult his superiors in the Chechen Supreme Court. What was he to do now about The Cadet, with the Prosecutor's Office on the warpath?

At 12.13 word spread that he was back, and a few minutes later Mezhidov began the hearing. Stanislav Markelov, representing the plaintiffs, immediately demanded the arrest of the insolent accused. He presented the court with the opinion of Yury Savenko, President of the Independent Psychiatric Association of Russia, a consultant with the highest professional qualifications and 42 years of service. This related to whether The Cadet was unfit to attend the court because of "problems of adaptation," which he had given as the reason for his absence.

"According to current understanding, as registered in the international classification of illnesses, adaptational dysfunction is a state of protracted discomfort caused by local or prolonged stress. It is accompanied by reduced productivity in normal activity and is regarded as being on the borderline between normal reaction to stress or grief, and minor mental disorder. In the spectrum of mental disorders this is one of the least serious diagnoses, and is not dangerous. It cannot be used to justify non-appearance at a court hearing. Neither is it usually regarded as sufficient basis for issuing a medical certificate of inability to work. Indeed, one of the commonest causes of adaptational dysfunction is an indefinite situation or the expectation of unpleasant events, like an imminent court hearing. From the point of view of psychotherapeutic practice in such cases, precipitation of such events is indicated, rather than avoidance of them."

The judge attaches this opinion to the case file, and the floor is given to Mme Zhuravlyova. Her speech is halting and illogical – she is not much of an orator – but her drift is unmistakable. It is a typical lawyer's speech. She is looking for any conceivable excuse not to upset The Cadet by arresting him, thereby deliberately ignoring his unforgivable flouting of the laws of Russia.

"Yes, of course, the accused is not here. But was the doctor who issued Lapin's certificate warned of his liability for giving false evidence?" (Well who was supposed to warn him? The Cadet? Was that not the job of the Prosecutor's Office?) "I have another request. You rejected Lapin's request for a collegiate hearing." (On October 24 The Cadet demanded that the case should not be heard by a single judge.) "However, you gave a contradictory ruling in July. The Prosecutor's Office has lodged an appeal and the trial must be postponed until this issue has been examined."

But the issue to be examined is not why The Cadet has so blatantly shown his contempt for the court. On the contrary, it is the acts of Judge Mezhidov which must be scrutinised in daring to demand that "S.V. Lapin should without fail appear in court on October 30." It is an example of the topsy-turvy world of distorting mirrors of the Russian Prosecutor's Office. We live in times when the Prosecutor's Office is truly independent: independent of the law, of logic, of decency and of conscience. At the same time what the Prosecutors are totally dependent on is instructions from above, the Party and government line as formulated on Kremlin Hill. The institution making such efforts to ease conditions for a killer and abductor is the Prosecutor's Office of the Southern Federal Region, headed by Sergey Fridinsky, the Deputy Prosecutor General of Russia. According to the law it should be doing the exact opposite, namely ensuring compliance with the law and respect for the interests of the victims.

Judge Mezhidov rushes out of the court. It is painful to look at Astemir Murdalov, the father of The Cadet's victim. He clasps his hands round his bowed head as if it will explode. Mme Zhuravlyova ostentatiously opens a detective novel by Marinina. The judge is soon back: "The hearing is postponed indefinitely . . ." Mezhidov has been steamrollered: the Chechen Supreme Court has evidently advised him just to put up with it. Satisfied with her tour de force, Zhuravlyova immediately leaves the court with a spring in her step. The Cadet has once again been let off the hook. Astemir Murdalov exclaims loudly in despair. The public stand silently, looking as if they have been spat on, or punished. And indeed, how in Chechnya today are you to get the law to act, and an end to be put to the abductions and extra-judicial executions if even the court and the Prosecutor's Office, the main legal forces in this territory ravaged by unidentifiable gangs, are against it?

The shrapnel-scarred building of the October District Court is adorned with fresh graffiti proclaiming, "Wolves of Jihad!" How eloquent. What the Prosecutor's Office and court in Chechnya are doing is playing directly into the hands of those who painted that slogan. The Prosecutors, like the whole rotten apparatus of the so-called "war on terror in the North Caucasus," are the real support group of terrorism.

THE COURT IS CORDONED OFF, BY THE ACCUSED'S BODYGUARDS
November 29, 2004

In Grozny the first court proceedings in the history of the "anti-terrorist operation" to be brought against a federal officer, militiaman Sergey Lapin, continue.

In the October District Court, with Maierbek Mezhidov presiding, the legal investigation has been under way for one and a half years, but only now, during a number of hearings in late November 2004, has it proved possible to move the trial forward. Consideration has begun of charges against The Cadet under Article 286 of the Criminal Code, Part 3, "Exceeding official powers"; Article 111, "Intentionally causing grievous bodily harm"; and Article 292, "Forgery by an official."

Until now this "warrior against terrorism" has openly defied the court and got on with his life. Despite the gravity of the crimes of which The Cadet stands accused, our own dear Interior Ministry quietly, without attracting unwelcome publicity, reinstated the accused as a militia officer, and now, while under bail conditions not to leave Nizhnevartovsk, he is once again working in the Criminal Investigation Department of the Nizhnevartovsk City Interior Affairs Office.

Despite this, at the November hearings The Cadet behaved like a seasoned old lag, insolently changing his story for the sixth time, utterly refusing to admit his guilt, and trying to blame everything on colleagues in the "anti-terrorist operation" who have since been killed. Very manly behaviour, don't you think?

Maierbek Mezhidov is the Chairman of the October District Court in Grozny, and presides in the half-ruined building of the former Department of State Security of Ichkeria on Popovich Street. From the front this box-like building looks like an apartment block, but from the back you see it is little more than a façade. Less than half, on the ground floor, has been crudely repaired for the exercise of justice. Inside it is as cold as a refrigerator, and the sparse Soviet-era lightbulbs provide such meagre light that the reading Judge Mezhidov – already well on in years – has to do of reports, interrogation records and the like is a truly heroic feat in the cause of justice.

Another heroic feat is dispensing justice at all in a building which has been surrounded. Where else would you find anything like this? This morning, individuals in combat fatigues, with shaven heads and festooned with rifles, drove up to the court building in armoured personnel carriers and military trucks, and pointed their weapons at anybody entering or leaving the court. Some of us also got shouted at in colorful language.

These are bodyguards escorting the accused. The Cadet arrives with them and he departs with them. Even when he goes out for a smoke during the breaks, members of the brigade shield him with their bodies. The Commanding Officer of this Interior Ministry unit introduced himself as Oleg. He looks totally villainous, and cradles a huge rifle or grenade launcher in his arms. He explains that he is acting under verbal orders from the commander of the Interior Ministry troops in Chechnya to protect Lapin.

"Who from?"

"You know yourself," Oleg spits out.

From Chechens, presumably.

From Aleta, the aunt of Zelimkhan Murdalov whom The Cadet tortured to death, who became ill when the court started reading out how and what the Khanties did to her nephew on January 2–3, 2001; from Astemir Murdalov, Zelimkhan's father, who clutches the grey hair on his lowered head; from those victims of the Khanties who survived by a miracle and emerged from the torture chambers of the Interior Ministry's Temporary Office in the October District of Grozny; from the wives and mothers of those the Khanties abducted, who are listening now to every word the judge or The Cadet say in the hope that some clue will slip out about the fate of their husband, son or brother.

All these Chechen men and women are huddled over to one side of the courtroom. Lapin's personal brigade smirk in blatant self-satisfaction; it is a monstrous tableau of a state which encourages criminals in uniform.

The hearing finally begins. Only the breath of those present in the cold courtroom will gradually take the chill from it. It becomes warmer, but people are still shivering from the damp atmosphere when The Cadet demands to be allowed to speak. He sounds a complete gangster, and now denies all his previous testimony.

Judge: Then why did you say it?
The Cadet: I was afraid. I was tortured. I was tortured for a month in the Chechen Directorate for Combating Organised Crime.
Judge: Who tortured you?
The Cadet: Investigator Baitayev. I would have admitted assassinating President Kennedy. I had no choice. I had to say something.

The Cadet adopts a tearful tone. His claim that he was tortured during the preliminary investigation will be repeated many more times. The following picture emerges: whenever Baitayev, or Moroz (the Acting Prosecutor of Grozny at the time), or Ignatenko (an investigator in the Chechen Prosecutor's Office) questioned The Cadet, he was being subjected to intolerable psychological or physical pressure. "Confess your guilt," they said, "or we'll send you to jail."

"I didn't want to go to the holding cells, so I confessed," The Cadet says.

"But this was all taking place in the presence of a lawyer," the judge reminds him.

"What lawyer? Abalayeva said people like me should have their throats slit."

Vladimir Rozetov (Prosecutor of the October District and the

Prosecuting Officer at this trial): Did you sustain any physical
injuries while you were in custody in the holding cells of the
Directorate for Combating Organised Crime?
The Cadet: "Yes, and I was detained without a toothbrush and
toothpaste. Can you imagine?"
Attorney Stanislav Markelov (a Moscow lawyer for the plaintiff,
Astemir Murdalov): "Why is there no statement from you in the file
about your having been subjected to duress?"

Attorney Grigoriy Degtyarev (a lawyer from Nizhnevartovsk
defending The Cadet) immediately raises his voice almost to a scream.
He has a very odd manner which even infects the judge: "My defendant
has been mentally traumatised. He has symptoms of post-traumatic
stress disorder! You have no right . . . !"
This is a bluff. In the preceding hearings it has already been
established that The Cadet has nothing of the sort.

Judge: But previously you said you took Murdalov away from the
compound of the Temporary Office, after which he disappeared.
Why are you denying that now?
The Cadet: I said it because Moroz put psychological pressure on me
when he was questioning me.
Prosecutor Rozetov (quietly and bitterly): Moroz has since been
murdered.
Judge Mezhidov: Did you complain about Moroz's actions?
The Cadet: I decided it was better not to.

The tale of Moroz's "psychological pressure" is just more nonsense,
and here we need a brief digression. In 2001, when The Cadet was
summoned by Moroz to his first questionings at the Grozny Prosecutor's Office, the Khanties turned up in force and surrounded the
building, pointing their rifles and grenade launchers at it throughout
the time The Cadet was with Moroz. While he was being questioned,
they rampaged through the building threatening to take revenge on
everybody who worked there. There certainly was psychological pres-

sure, but it was not coming from the Prosecutors – instead it was being brought to bear on them.

Judge Mezhidov: Who was putting pressure on you in Nizhnevartovsk? When you were there you were no longer in Chechnya.
The Cadet: Prosecutors Din and Leushin, who came to question me from the Chechen Republic. (Leushin has also been murdered.)

The Cadet swaps his nauseating lachrymosity for a loutish tone, and periodically jabs his finger threateningly at the judge. He announces, "I think Murdalov was beaten by Taimaskhanov [Salim Taimaskhanov, an officer at the October Office]. It was Taimaskhanov took him off somewhere out of the holding cell."

Judge: You gave no testimony against either Moroz or Taimaskhanov while they were alive, and immediately changed your testimony when you learned they had been killed. How is that to be explained?
The Cadet: If you are being tortured for days on end you will sign anything. I had no choice.

From his seat Astemir Murdalov asks pointedly, "And did our people have any choice?"

Finally the lawyers begin to run out of patience. Prosecutor Rozetov asks the judge to read out Lapin's previous testimony so as to remind him of what he said, since there are major discrepancies. Judge Mezhidov begins reading out the records of previous questioning of The Cadet, conducted in Nizhnevartovsk, his place of residence; in Pyatigorsk; in Grozny; in different places and with different investigators: "I refuse the services of a lawyer. I can conduct my own defence." "I plead not guilty to the charges." "I have given this evidence voluntarily." "I am prepared to repeat this testimony in the presence of those it refers to."

The Cadet pushes the Penal Code and the Criminal Procedure Code about on the table. He is annoyed and makes no attempt to conceal it, but the judge continues.

"*Question from the Investigator:* 'Who is influencing you? Why do you keep changing your testimony?'
Reply: 'Nobody is influencing me. I am changing my testimony now for the first time because I didn't take the proceedings seriously before.'"

That last revealing remark really is the truth. The vast majority of federals in Chechnya never for a moment imagine that the criminal law might be applied to them for abducting and murdering the civilian population. Among them, anyone who has killed a Chechen is a hero; a coward is anyone afraid to kill one. This has been going on for five years and The Cadet, who is suddenly facing justice, is the sole exception to this impunity. Several times during the November court hearings The Cadet repeated, "I never thought this would be taken seriously," so he lied through his teeth again and again.

The next hearing of the case will be on December 15, when witnesses for the prosecution are to be questioned.

THE CADET GETS LONGER THAN BUDANOV: THE FIRST TRIAL OF A WAR CRIMINAL HAS ENDED

March 31, 2005

On March 29 the Chairman of the October District Court in Grozny, Maierbek Mezhidov, finally passed sentence in the case of Sergey Lapin. The trial lasted one and a half years, and at times had looked like collapsing.

The charge against Lapin, the sentence, and the circumstances in which a war criminal has eventually been found guilty in Grozny, are without precedent. This is the first time in the entire history of the Second Chechen War that a criminal case for something very common – the abduction and torture of a civilian – has been brought against a federal officer in Chechnya.

The conviction was extremely difficult to achieve, and only the principled position of the Supreme Court of Russia made it possible to withstand immense pressure from the Interior Ministry. The militia's Ministry at first did everything it could to ensure that Lapin was tried anywhere other than in Chechnya. Later, when the Supreme Court refused to back down, it blatantly tried to intimidate those taking part in the Grozny trial.

However, both Judge Mezhidov and Prosecutor Vladimir Rozetov stood their ground. The result is that Lapin will serve 11 years in a strict-regime labor colony, with a further three-year ban on working in the law enforcement agencies. An interlocutory ruling was addressed to those in charge of the Khanty-Mansiysk Interior Affairs Directorate, who did their utmost to obstruct the course of justice and conceal brutal crimes.

Details will follow in our next issue.

LAPIN, A BRUTAL TORTURER, FOUND GUILTY BUT REFUSES TO IMPLICATE HIS ACCOMPLICES

April 4, 2005

As already reported, on March 29 in Grozny sentence was passed in the case of Sergey Lapin (alias "The Cadet"). The torturer was sentenced to 11 years in a strict-regime labor camp. Let us first present some quotations from the verdict:

"Lapin, receiving Murdalov into his custody from Investigator Zhuravlyov, took the former into his office where, for several hours, together with other colleagues unidentified by the investigation, he beat Murdalov, inflicting numerous blows with his hands, feet, and also a rubber PR 73 truncheon on different parts of his body, causing him injury in the form of cranio-cerebral trauma accompanied by pathological life-threatening states, namely, a prolonged loss of consciousness, convulsions and respiratory failure. When the officers at the holding cell, having observed Murdalov's physical injuries, refused to accommodate him, Lapin wrote an explanatory report in Murdalov's name maintaining that the injuries had been sustained by Murdalov when he fell from the equivalent of his own height."

"Witness N.G. Malyukin (the then medical officer at the Interior Affairs Temporary Office) testified that on January 2, 2001 at about 9:00 p.m. he examined Murdalov in the holding cell. He was present in the cell with Murdalov until midnight. During this time Murdalov had several fits. All the muscles of his body contracted violently, he clenched his teeth, and rolled his eyes. He ceased breathing and was unconscious. Malyukin gave Murdalov four injections. At about midnight he left the cell."

"Witness K.D. Khadayev (a cellmate) explained to the court that on the evening of January 2 Lapin, with three or four others, brought Murdalov to the holding cell. Murdalov could not stand. His right ear had been ripped and was hanging off by the skin. His arm had been broken and his clothing was soiled. A doctor examined Murdalov, and he heard the doctor telling the senior officer, Prilepin, that Murdalov had a compound fracture of the arm, cranio-cerebral trauma, crushed testicles, and was in need of urgent surgical intervention because he would not survive with such injuries. The doctor left. Half an hour later the individuals detained with him in the cell began shouting for the duty officer and informed him that Murdalov was dying. The officer advised them to pray for him, in accordance with Muslim ritual. Murdalov remained in this moribund state until the morning of January 3, when Lapin, Prilepin and several other officers dragged him away. He was incapable of standing. The witness was certain that with such injuries Murdalov must have died and that the militia officers hid his body. Lapin was exceptionally brutal in his torture of detainees. Detainees Dalayev and Gazhayev told him they had been tortured with electricity, clubs and hammers by him. Dalayev had flesh torn from his chest with pliers, had dogs set on him, and was beaten as a nail was hammered into his collar bone. While being tortured he was asked where resistance fighters could be found."

"Witness S.K. Batalov testified that in the course of checking the statement by plaintiff Astemir Murdalov, members of the Prosecutor's Office discovered on territory adjacent to the October Interior Affairs

Temporary Office the bodies of three boys who had been seen riding bicycles in the vicinity. The bodies were mutilated, with their eyes gouged out and their scalps removed. A separate criminal case has been opened in respect of the unidentified individuals who conspired with Lapin to commit these crimes."

"On the morning of January 3, Lapin, fearing that the physical injuries he had inflicted on Murdalov would become known, conspiring with officers not identified by the investigation, signed Murdalov's name on an order for his release from the holding cell in the box for the detainee's signature; and also on the record of the personal search of Murdalov in the box confirming items returned and received. Then officers of the October Interior Affairs Temporary Office not identified by the investigation, acting with the knowledge and consent of Lapin, took Murdalov from the holding cell and drove him away to an unknown destination."

It is clear what happened. The witnesses' testimony, accepted by the court, leaves no possibility of doubt, but where is the victim? That is the overriding question. Zelimkhan Murdalov remains one of the disappeared, and the trial has done nothing to clarify that issue. For over four years, many people did everything they could to bring about this verdict. They tracked Lapin down when he was on the run. They discredited medical certificates when he tried to pretend he was too ill to appear in court. They endured the thuggish behaviour of Lapin and his colleagues from the Khanty-Mansiysk Interior Affairs Directorate at the hearings. What was it all for? A sentence of 11 years in a strict-regime labor camp?

Of course not. The Murdalov family began this almost hopeless campaign against the system – something which before them none of the thousands of families in the same situation in Chechnya had had the courage to do (and still haven't) – because they wanted to find Zelimkhan. The Murdalovs expected the state to provide the answer to that question because Lapin is a government employee.

They have had no reply. From time to time during the trial Lapin, addressing Astemir, Zelimkhan's father, only repeated, "I didn't kill him. I didn't kill him." Or again, "I am only here to prove to the father that I did not kill his son." Judge Mezhidov did ask, "Was he killed? If so, who killed him? And if not, where is he now?" He got no answer, and could do no more. Under our present Criminal Procedure Code, a judge has no right to enquire into anything beyond the charges brought by the Prosecutor's Office, and the Prosecutors' Offices of the Chechen Republic and of the Southern Federal Region not only brought no further charges, but even conducted the case in a way that enabled Lapin's fellow sadists to remain "unidentified." Even though the testimony of witnesses named Lapin's direct superiors, Prilepin and Kondakov, who were both present while Lapin's crimes were being committed, the Prosecutor's Office directed that neither of them should figure in the trial. They were not cited as co-defendants. The court could do nothing about it: the law was on the side of the torturers.

This means that the sentence passed is a compromise between justice and those federal security officers' legal immunity. It is less than just, only half a result. It will be satisfactory only when Zelimkhan Murdalov or his body is found, and that will happen only when Prilepin and Kondakov, and perhaps somebody higher up the chain of command who was giving instructions, are put in the dock.

The trial has highlighted once more the disgraceful fact that in Russia the abduction of people by state employees, and extra-judicial penalties meted out by them (our Abu Ghraib), continue because the state, in the guise of the Prosecutor's Office, covers up for those who have enough stars on their epaulettes. The state does not search for the disappeared, and families are thrown back entirely on their own resources.

Who paid for this case? How was it possible to achieve this verdict? The Murdalovs had a good lawyer. The trial itself lasted a year and a half and was preceded by a long, hard investigation. A good lawyer needs to be paid, the more so because a major part of the work on the case had to be done in the Supreme Court in Moscow, which necessitated a Moscow lawyer. For the first time in a trial taking place in the zone of the "anti-terrorist operation," a Muscovite and, importantly, a Russian lawyer, Stanislav Markelov, was representing the interests of a Chechen family. Markelov was a pioneer. Everyone who saw how he conducted himself in Grozny admired his courage, self-possession and professionalism in some extremely uncomfortable situations.*

So who paid Markelov, who had to fly constantly, sometimes every week, to the North Caucasus? Let it be recorded in the history of the Second Chechen War that the entire financial burden of Lapin's trial was borne by the London Office of Amnesty International, the famous international human rights organization. Amnesty took on that burden because nobody else would, not a single Russian civil rights or voluntary organization. Chechen businessmen, without exception, also spectacularly ignored the opportunity of supporting such a crucial, precedent-setting trial, one vitally important for thousands of Chechen families in the Republic who find themselves in the Murdalovs' situation. Alas, rather than do anything so constructive, rich Chechens cheerfully dig deep when the federals demand ransom for someone they have abducted. They pay the ransom, providing financial support for the federals' lawlessness and the hierarchy of state terrorism. It is a shame.

Apart from providing the finance, Amnesty International also organised a world-wide petition demanding a fair trial. Thousands of letters came in addressed to Putin and were subsequently included among the case materials. Judge Mezhidov simply could not ignore them and himself referred to them in court. The letters also strengthened his position and, to be fair, he too behaved heroically. For the duration of the trial he was treading a knife edge, because he was walking around Grozny.

Will the efforts of so many prove fruitless, or will the federals finally be forced to recognise that they cannot abduct and kill in Chechnya

---

*Stanislav Markelov was gunned down in central Moscow on January 19, 2009, together with Anastasia Baburova, a freelance journalist working for *Novaya gazeta*. He was leaving a press conference protesting at the early release of rapist and murderer ex-Colonel Yuriy Budanov. Anna Politkovskaya had been instrumental in securing the conviction of Budanov. Neither President Medvedev nor Prime Minister Putin commented on these murders.

with impunity? And will people in Chechnya recognise that they too must not allow themselves to be intimidated, but must stand up to the war criminals, as the Murdalov family managed to? God give them strength. As of now, there is no other way of reducing the number of extra-judicial executions and massacres in Chechnya.

WARRANTS FOR THE ARREST OF TWO MORE "KHANTIES": THE CADET'S ACCOMPLICES ARE ON THE RUN

February 9, 2006

Information has now come to light about the exact role played by The Cadet's superiors in the crime he committed. On November 18 last year the Chechen Prosecutor's Office instigated a new criminal case against Alexander Prilepin (alias Alex) and V. Minin under Articles 286 and 111 of the Russian Criminal Code.

Initial attempts to question The Cadet's superiors, who may be able to explain what happened to The Cadet's victim, Zelimkhan Murdalov, ran into strong opposition from their colleagues in the Khanty-Mansiysk and Nizhnevartovsk Interior Affairs Directorates. Prilepin and Minin categorically refused to meet the investigators.

Both have now had federal warrants issued for their arrest by the Chechen Prosecutor's Office.*

*In autumn 2006, Investigators of the Prosecutor-General's Office who went to Khanty-Mansiysk to examine one line of inquiry into the murder of Anna Politkovskaya discovered that Prilepin and Minin had been living at their home addresses all this time, going to work, and nobody had been looking for them.

4. Nord-Ost

On October 23, 2002 the hostage-taking in Moscow by Chechen terrorists of the audience of a musical, Nord-Ost, made worldwide headlines. Anna, who attempted to negotiate inside the theatre with the terrorists, was ultimately able to show with a high degree of certainty, with information provided by the FSB whistle-blower Alexander Litvinenko, since murdered, that this event and its disastrous outcome had been another production of the Russian regime.

ANNA POLITKOVSKAYA FACES DIFFICULTIES RETURNING TO MOSCOW TO ASSIST IN NEGOTIATING WITH THE TERRORISTS

October 24, 2002*

From the Editors of *Novaya gazeta*:

12:30 p.m.

Novaya gazeta's columnist Anna Politkovskaya is prepared to enter negotiations with those who have seized hostages in Moscow. She is sympathetic to their demands for an end to the Chechen War, but disapproves of their methods. Civilians should not suffer because of mistakes made by the state authorities.

Anna Politkovskaya is currently in Washington, DC where she was engaged in discussions with senior State Department and White House officials about finding a peaceful solution to the Chechen issue. Others taking part in these discussions included Ilias Akhmadov, a politician respected by the Chechens; Dr Zbigniew Brzezinski, former US Secretary of State for Foreign Affairs; and Lord Judd, who has several times visited Chechnya on behalf of the Council of Europe. Thus Anna Politkovskaya, although far from Russia, was

*Date of posting on the *Novaya gazeta* website.

effectively engaged in fulfilling the demands of the hostage-takers in Moscow.

As soon as she returns to Moscow, which can be no sooner than 13 hours from now since the first plane to Moscow leaves Washington in four and a half hours' time, she will immediately go to the scene of the events and contact the hostage-takers. Unfortunately, representatives of the US Embassy are asking us to wait until 9:00 a.m. local time (it is currently 5:00 a.m. in Washington, DC) to seek official assistance. It seems to us that we are asking for a very small favor of getting someone on the first flight from Washington to Moscow. Lives – including those of American citizens among the hostages – depend on this favor. Anna Politkovskaya is the only person in whom the hostage-takers have expressed confidence and whom they have requested as a mediator in the negotiations.

We urge the Americans to help Anna Politkovskaya return to Moscow as soon as possible.

1:30 p.m.

As of now the issue of facilitating an emergency flight from Washington, DC to Moscow for *Novaya gazeta*'s columnist, Anna Politkovskaya, remains unresolved. The hostage-takers in Moscow have expressed a wish to negotiate with her.

As Anna is presently in America, we appealed to the US Embassy for help and received a reply from Mr Paul Carter of the Embassy's Legal Department. He said they were prepared to assist, but required confirmation from the Russian Foreign Ministry that this was a government initiative, and that the state was prepared to negotiate rather than to resolve the problem by force.

We rang the North American Department of the Russian Foreign Ministry, who confirmed that Paul Carter had phoned them but said that, "since this matter was not within their jurisdiction," they could not take any decision and would not involve themselves in facilitating Anna Politkovskaya's urgent return to Russia. They advised us to phone the operational information section of the Foreign

Ministry, whose Director, Vladimir Oshurkov, said he had "no information for the mass media." We asked whether they would in fact ask the Americans to help, to which Mr Oshurkov replied, "What has the Ministry of Foreign Affairs got to do with this anyway? Why should the Ministry bother itself with getting Anna Politkovskaya to Russia? That's what the security ministries have staff for. If they consider it necessary for Anna Politkovskaya to return to negotiate with the terrorists, she will fly. It is nothing to do with the Foreign Ministry."

In order to re-register her ticket, Anna Politkovskaya requires more than 1,000 US dollars. If our Foreign Ministry (which represents the Russian Government) does not wish to address the problem, jeopardising negotiations with the hostage-takers and thereby putting at risk the lives of the hostages, we shall find the money ourselves.

2:30 p.m.

The latest information is that Anna Politkovskaya is returning to Russia on the first available flight.

NORD-OST: THE PRICE OF TALKS

October 28, 2002

My personal involvement in this crisis began at about 2:00 p.m. on October 25. At 11:30 a.m. I had spoken on my mobile phone to the hostage-takers for the first time and they agreed to a meeting. At 1:30 p.m. I arrived at the headquarters of the security operation. Another half-hour was spent getting everything co-ordinated: some unknown person was resolving matters behind doors which kept slamming.

Finally, I was led up to a protective cordon of trucks, someone said, "Give it a go. Perhaps you can do it," and Dr Leonid Roshal [Head of the Disaster Medical Center] and I made our way to the entrance. It was very frightening.

We went into the building. We shouted, "Hello! Anybody there?"

There was no response. It felt as if the building was completely deserted.

I shouted, "It's me, Politkovskaya! It's Politkovskaya!" I slowly started climbing up the right-hand staircase. The doctor said he knew the way. In the first-floor foyer there was again silence, darkness, and it was cold. Not a soul. I shouted again, "It's Politkovskaya!"Finally, a man appeared from behind what had been the counter of the bar.

His black mask wasn't on properly and I could see his features clearly. He was not aggressive towards me, but 'hostile towards the doctor. Why? I don't know, but I did my best to calm a situation which was becoming heated. "What are you up to, doctor, helping your career along?" the man in the mask taunted. Dr Roshal is 70 years old, an Academic, and has already achieved so much that he really doesn't need to worry about his career.

I said as much, a bit of an argument started, and it was time to lower the temperature again since otherwise . . . Otherwise it was obvious what could happen.

The man with the ill-fitting mask went off into the depths of the darkened foyer, still muttering, "Why do you say you treat Chechen children too, doctor?" There was some further fairly incoherent nastiness which amounted to suggesting that mentioning that he also treated Chechen children showed he didn't think they were the equal of other children, perhaps even that Chechens are not human beings.

It was a familiar tune and I interrupted it, not because that was a particularly clever thing to do but simply because I had had enough. I said, "All people are the same. They have the same skin, the same bones, the same blood." This less than original thought unexpectedly had a conciliatory effect. I asked permission to sit on the only chair in the middle of the foyer, 5 metres or so from the bar, because my legs had turned to jelly.

Permission was immediately granted. My shoes slipped on some disgusting red mess trampled into the carpet. I looked down cautiously at this ghastliness, anxious not to seem to be taking too much of an interest, but even more anxious not to put my feet in congealed blood. Thank God, it was only some kind of dead dessert, possibly fruit and ice-cream. I trembled a little less.

We waited 20 minutes or so while the leader was sent for. While we waited there, heads in masks appeared over the balcony occasionally. Some of the masks covered their faces properly, others only did half the job.

"Was it you who helped the people in Khotuni against the paratroop regiment?" the heads ask.

"Yes."

The heads are satisfied. Khotuni, a village in the Vedeno District, turns out to be my safe-conduct pass. If I have been there I am worth talking to.

"Where are you from?" I ask the man from the bar counter.

"Tovzeni," he replies. "Many of us are from Tovzeni, and from Vedeno District generally."

There follows a lot of confused coming and going by men in masks, the sign of a tragedy in the making. Time just passing by, disappearing into nowhere, fills me with idiotic foreboding. The leader still hasn't appeared. Perhaps they are going to shoot us here and now.

Finally, a person in combat fatigues comes out, his face completely covered. He is stocky, and with exactly the deportment of Russian special operations officers who give serious attention to their physical fitness. He says, "Follow me." My legs again turn to jelly, but I wobble after him. This is The Leader.

We end up in a dirty service room by a ransacked buffet, behind which is a water tap. Somebody walks behind me and I turn. I realize this looks nervous, but what can I do? I haven't had much experience of talking to terrorists under conditions as tense as these. The leader brings me back to cold logic.

"Don't look behind you! You are talking to me, so look at me."

"Who are you? What should I call you?" I ask, not really expecting a reply.

"Bakar. Abubakar."

By now he has pushed the mask up to his forehead. He has an

open face with high cheekbones, also very typical of our military. He has a rifle on his knees which he puts behind him only at the very end of our talk, when he even apologizes. "I've got so used to it I no longer feel it there. I sleep with it, eat with it. It is always with me." Even without this explanation I already understand everything.

"How old are you?"

"Twenty-nine."

"Have you been fighting in both wars?"

"Yes."

"Did you sit it out in Georgia?"

"No. I never left Chechnya."

Bakar belongs to a new generation of Chechens who for the past 10 years have known nothing but a rifle and the forests. He left school, and life in the forests became his only option. A destiny devoid of choice.

"Shall we get down to business?" I suggest.

"OK."

"First, the older children still in there. You need to let them go. They are only children." Sergey Yastrzhembsky, Aide to the President of the Russian Federation, had asked me to raise this with them as my main priority.

"Children? There are no children in there. In security sweeps you take ours from 12 years old. We will hold on to yours."

"In retaliation?"

"So that you know how it feels."

I return to the subject of the children many times, asking for them to be allowed at least some relief, for me to bring food, for instance, but the answer is a categorical no.

"Do you let ours eat in the security sweeps? Yours can do without too."

I have four other requests on my list: food for the hostages, items of personal hygiene for the women, water, blankets. To anticipate, I get agreement only to bring water and juice. I will be allowed to bring them, shout from downstairs, and then I will be let in.

"Can I come several times? I can't carry much in one go. There are

Anna, starting out

Raisa and Stepan Mazepa with
daughters Anna and Elena,
New York, 1962

At Moscow School No. 33, 1971

The three schoolfriends:
Masha, Anna, and Elena

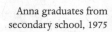

Anna graduates from
secondary school, 1975

Marriage, April 1978

A family: Alexander, Ilya,
Anna and Vera, summer 1980

The children. Anna's
favourite photograph

At a party with her husband
Alexander, early 1990s

With Alexander
and Martyn the
Doberman, late
1990s

With her sister Elena,
London, 2002

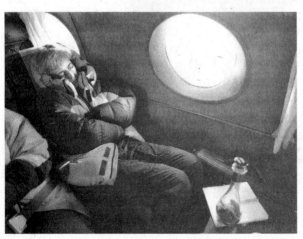

On the flight to Tura,
where a small delegation
from *Novaya gazeta*
unveiled a monument at
the geographical centre of
Russia, December 2000

Vnukovo Airport, Moscow, February 2001, returning after her detention by Russian troops

The *Nord-Ost* siege. Anna and others take water and juice to the hostages, Moscow, 25 October 2002

Presentation of the Global Award for Human Rights Journalism by Amnesty International, London, July 2001

Olof Palme Prize 'For Courage and Composure While Working in Difficult and Dangerous Conditions', Stockholm, January 2005

2006-10-07 14:22:21

The last image of Anna Politkovskaya, captured by a super-market CCTV camera, 7 October 2006

March 2002

so many hostages. Perhaps you will allow me to bring one of the men."

"OK."

"Do you mind if that's another of our journalists?"

"No. And also somebody from the Red Cross."

"Thank you."

I start asking what it is that they want, but politically Bakar is all at sea. He's a simple soldier and no more. He explains what this is all about, at considerable length but not at all clearly, and from what he says I identify four points. The first is that Putin must "give the word" – declare an end to the war. The second is that within 24 hours he must demonstrate that these are not empty words, for example by withdrawing troops from one of the districts.

"From which district? From yours? Vedeno?"

"What are you, a GRU agent? You're interrogating me like a GRU agent. That's all I've got to say, go away!"

It is impossible for me to go away at this point, although I very much want to. I hear myself almost pleading, which is completely the wrong tone, of course:

"Please understand, I need to know what it is you want. And I need to know exactly. Otherwise . . ."

From time to time I trip over myself. I am racking my brains over an intractable problem: how can I ease the plight of the hostages as much as possible, since the hostage-takers have at least agreed to talk to me, but not lose my credibility in their eyes? And I am making a mess of it. Quite often I can't think what to say next, and blurt out a lot of nonsense, just hoping not to hear Bakar say "That's it!", whereupon I would have to leave empty-handed, having failed to negotiate anything at all for the hostages. As we approach the third point of "their" plan, Boris Nemtsov [chairman of the Union of Right Forces political coalition] phones Bakar on his mobile. The resistance fighters took it from one of the hostages, a *Nord-Ost* musician, and now they are using it for all their conversations.

While he is talking to Nemtsov, Bakar becomes very agitated. Afterwards he tells me Nemtsov is trying to trick him. Nemtsov said yesterday that the war in Chechnya could be ended, but today, October 25, the security sweeps have been renewed. Then I ask, "Who will you believe? Who would you trust if they told you that troops were being withdrawn?"

Only Lord Judd, it transpires, the Council of Europe's rapporteur on Chechnya.

We get to "their" third point, which is simple: if the first two demands are met, they will release the hostages.

"And yourselves?"

"We will stay behind to fight. We will behave like soldiers and die in battle."

"But who in fact are you?" I ask, scaring myself with my audacity.

"The Reconnaissance and Sabotage Battalion."

"Are you all here?"

"No. Only some of us. We had a selection process for this operation and chose the best. If we die, there will still be others to continue our struggle."

"Do you accept Maskhadov's authority?"

He is thrown by this, and again becomes extremely irritated. His rambling explanation is best summarised as, "Yes, Maskhadov is our President, but we are fighting on our own."

This is confirmation of my worst fears: the group is one of those acting independently in Chechnya. They are waging their own very radical war autonomously. By and large they have no time for Maskhadov, considering him insufficiently hard-line. I continue:

"But you do know that peace negotiations are being conducted by Ilias Akhmadov in America, and Akhmed Zakayev in Europe, who both represent Maskhadov. Perhaps you would like to contact them now? Or let me dial them. Yours is the same cause."

"What for? We don't acknowledge them. While we are dying in the forests they are slowly conducting their negotiations because it is not their heads the rain is falling on. We are fed up with them."

There is no real fourth point to their plan, other than some strongly felt remarks of Bakar's own: "People have been asking to come here

as suicide bombers for a year and a half," and "We have come to die."
I have no doubt of that. These are doomed men and women prepared
to die, and to take with them as many lives as they see fit.

The mobile phone rings again. Bakar listens. It is a phone call from
home, from the Vedeno District of Chechnya. He starts shouting and
raging: "Don't ring here any more. Ever. This is the office. You are
interfering with my business."

"May I talk to the hostages?"

"No."

But five minutes later, he says to a "brother," sitting almost behind
my back, "OK, bring one."

He goes and brings from the auditorium a terrified, pretty girl called
Masha. The hostages have had nothing to eat and she is so frightened
and weak that she can't speak.

Bakar is irritated by her mumbling and orders her to be taken
away. "Bring another one, older." In the interim, Bakar tells me how
noble they all are. They have so many pretty girls in their power – and
Masha really is very pretty – but they have no desire. All their strength
is being kept for the struggle for the liberation of their land. I understand him to mean that I should be grateful for their not having raped
Masha.

We speak briefly about morality and ethics, if these are the right
words.

"You won't believe it, but morally we feel better here than at any
time in the past three years of the war. We are finally doing something.
We feel entirely at home. We feel better than ever. We will be glad to
die. The fact that we will go down in history is a great honor. Don't
you believe me? I can see you don't believe me."

Actually, I very much do believe him. This kind of talk has been
heard among Chechen fighters for a year already. Resentful of the
virtual Maskhadov's inaction, many resistance units have sat through
an entire winter in the forests and have now had enough. They can't
come out of the forests, they can't fight. They need something to do,
but there are no orders from their Commander-in-Chief. As this mood

has grown, units have either fallen apart or become radicalized, in effect embarking on parallel wars over which Maskhadov has no authority.

The "brother" brings another pretty girl in a state of extreme nervous exhaustion.

"I am Anna Andriyanovna, a correspondent of *Moskovskaya Pravda*. Everyone outside must please understand, we are already expecting to die. We realize that Russia has abandoned us. We are a second *Kursk* [a submarine which sank with the loss of all hands shortly after Putin became President]. If you want to save us, come out to demonstrate in the streets. If half of Moscow begs Putin, we will survive. We can see clearly that if we die here today, a new slaughter will start in Chechnya which will rebound on Russia and cause new carnage."

Anya talks incessantly. Bakar is getting edgy but she doesn't notice. I am again very much afraid that he will decide to be masterful. Finally she is taken away and we agree that I shall organise things at once and bring some water into the building. Bakar unexpectedly adds, "And you can bring some juice."

"For you?"

"No, we are preparing to die; we are not eating or drinking anything. For them."

"And perhaps some food? If only for the children."

"No. Ours are starving, so let yours starve too."

I go outside. I find that Dr Roshal has already left. It begins to pour, damn it, just at the wrong moment. "I haven't even got an umbrella," I think. "I look like a wet hen." Well, you have to think something.

We have a whip round among everybody standing nearby. The journalists are the first to dig deep, and the firemen. Somebody runs to the nearest shop to get juice. We find that the representatives of the state have no change available at this moment. That seems odd, but there is no time to think about it, only the realisation that we must move as quickly as possible before the hostage-takers change their minds.

The juice is brought back. Roman Shleinov (a colleague at *Novaya gazeta*) and I take two packs each in our arms and try to walk. On our right is an Interior Ministry officer, on our left an FSB officer. They are arguing. The one from the Interior Ministry has orders to allow us in since this is aid for the hostages and represents an opportunity to prolong contact with the outlaws as long as possible. The one from the FSB has orders not to let us through.

They quarrel. The rain pours down and we stand there like idiots in full view of all the snipers, just waiting, it seems to me, for someone to start shooting. Finally the FSB agent agrees: "Go on, then."

We take one batch and then another. Darkness falls; the gunmen had told us to bring it before dark but a criminal amount of time passes before the state manages to come up with juice for the next batch.

The third time, they allow a group of male hostages out to meet us. I'm afraid to say anything to them in case the hostage-takers start shooting. I just say "Hello," and they reply. They are allowed out in single file. A young man in evening dress and a white shirt passes me. Presumably he plays in the orchestra. He whispers tersely, "They have told us they will start killing us at ten this evening. Pass it on."

The next time I just nod silently to him, making eye contact, to let him know I have told the relevant authorities. They are leading the hostages down the steps to meet us, perhaps intending to make a point of showing how well they are treating them. Picking up his crate of juice, my musician whispers on the way back, "Understood."

The gunmen suddenly start becoming very nervous. They shout and pace up and down. A hostage calls from above, "Bring some disinfectant. We really need it. We did ask for it." He is driven back. I ask permission to bring the disinfectant, but am met with a complete refusal.

"At least some food? Just a little? For the children? Please . . ."

"We are dying of hunger, let them die of hunger too. Go away."

This day in history comes to an end, to be followed by the assault. Now I keep asking myself whether we did everything possible to help avoid those deaths. Was it a great victory to have 67 hostages killed (excluding those who died after they got to hospital)? Was I any help

to anyone with my juice and my last-ditch efforts? I believe I was, but
that we could have done more.

Too much is now behind us, and a great deal still lies ahead. The
tragedy of *Nord-Ost*, for which there were of course reasons, will not
be the end. From now on we will have to live in constant fear when
our children or old people go out of the house. Will we ever see them
again? It will be just the way people in Chechnya have been living
these last years.

There are only two alternatives. The first is finally to recognise that
the more excessive force we use there – the more blood, killings,
abductions and humiliations – the more people there will be in
Chechnya who want revenge at any price; the more recruits there will
be to the ranks of those wishing to die in retaliation.

And since this war will be fought not on a battlefield but amongst
us, involving completely innocent people – you and me, and all of us
– we can be sure that there will be another *Nord-Ost*, and that nobody
anywhere can feel safe, whether going out or staying in their own
flat. A cornered fighter will devise ever more ingenious means of
retribution.

The second option is fraught with difficulties, but is at least a move
in the right direction. We need to start talking to Maskhadov, a man
clinging to what little remains of his power. Otherwise we are doomed
to conduct negotiations like those over *Nord-Ost* within a framework
of hopelessness, with innocent lives at stake.

57 HOURS

November 4, 2002

The last few days have passed in a feverish delirium. Moscow is burying
the hostages. Today, just like yesterday, just like tomorrow. It is unbearable. The faces of the dead are calm, not contorted, as if they had simply
fallen asleep. And actually that is just what they did, because Russia
failed to administer the gas [used prior to the assault] in the correct
concentration.

I make it a rule not to write reports from funerals but this will be an exception. Lena, my old, dear friend, is burying her son Andryusha and her husband Sergey. On October 23 the three of them went to the theatre together. They were seated together, waited together for help to come, but only Lena survived.

The coffins of Andryusha and Sergey are side by side in the church, with a narrow passage between them. There are so many people you couldn't push your way through. Nobody makes any speeches, there is no politics, only Lena walking up and down this passage, murmuring from time to time. When she stops walking she rests a hand on each coffin and tries not to collapse. She lowers her head between the coffins and so resembles a bird with outspread wings, or somebody wounded struggling to get to their feet.

I too am terribly, irredeemably guilty for what has befallen Lena, and only I know why. It is too late to do anything about it.

After the funerals I fly to Paris for a few hours and very soon regret having done so. The television station France 2 has invited me to take part in the country's most popular Saturday evening program. I agreed only because people were telling me how little the West understood what is happening in "the East."

On the show, compered by French television celebrity Thiérry Ardisson, a well-known French singer was to perform immediately before me. I didn't write his name down and can't remember it now. There was also the Minister of Health from the Chechen Government when Maskhadov was in power, Umar somebody. Torrents of words poured forth about the Chechens, and how long and tirelessly they have been fighting for their freedom. The singer thought it was terrific, as did the presenter. It only left a very short time for me to say . . . Well, to say what, now that I had this prime-time opportunity?

I spoke badly, briefly, and not at all to the point. It was a disgrace, of course, because if you are given an opportunity to state your viewpoint, you should be ready to do so. No matter how hard I tried, though, I felt completely alien in this environment. We were on different wavelengths. Nobody in the audience wanted to hear about what, having just come from all these funerals, mattered most to me – the victims, the dreadful consequences. The Ichkerian Minister of Health (who really had nothing to do with anything, and who seemed rather at sea) found himself the focus of a whirl of emotional exclamations from admiring, ecstatic Frenchwomen of the same, far from young, age as me. Their superficial, romantic nonsense left me feeling nauseated, because they were as blind to the reality as . . . well, as we are. Only for them, Chechens are all good, and for Russians they are all bad.

I flew back to Moscow. The World Chechen Congress took place in Copenhagen immediately after the assault, and was subjected to an unprecedented barrage of protest from the Kremlin, which cancelled visits and summit meetings. (Moscow had to make do with the arrest of Akhmed Zakayev as a booby prize from the Danish Government.) On November 1 the Moscow participants of the Congress, in accordance with its concluding resolution, laid a wreath where the *Nord-Ost* victims had died.

They invited me to join them, but I didn't. The first reason was simply that, on principle, I avoid marching in columns and have never laid anything anywhere as a member of a crowd. The second reason was even simpler; I was still on the plane. There was, however, a third and most important reason, which I am sad about and unsure how to express, but which I think I need to explain.

Something wasn't quite right about this wreath-laying ceremony. It wasn't because, as so many people now believe, "the Chechens are to blame for everything." Even less was it because I personally have anything against Chechens. Of course I haven't.

But I really didn't like the way most of the Chechens I know behaved during those 57 hours when everything was on a knife edge, when at any moment the *Nord-Ost* audience might have been blown sky high, when a message from influential Chechens addressed to those under Barayev Junior's command would have carried far more weight than anything anybody else could say. That, at least, is how I felt. They said nothing. No statement came, and now their silence is a historical fact. That is the other reason I was so upset by those nauseating Frenchwomen.

Only Aslambek Aslakhanov, a Chechen and a Deputy of the Russian Duma, went in to talk to the terrorists, despite the fact that his act could have had extremely unpleasant consequences for him: he is, after all, an Interior Ministry general, and unambiguously a "federal" in the minds of those who took the *Nord-Ost* audience hostage. But Aslakhanov went in, despite his own young children at home. He went in, and that too is a matter of record.

But where were all the others? Where was businessman and politician Malik Saidulayev? Where were the Umars? (I've forgotten their surnames too, and really can't be bothered trying to rediscover them.) I mean that rich Umar somebody who owns a hotel near Kievsky Station in Moscow. And what about Bislan Gantamirov, sometime Mayor of Grozny? And Salambek Khadzhiev? And so on and so forth, ad infinitum?

None of them spoke out; not even Kadyrov, whom most of the Moscow Chechens are so busy buzzing around when he comes from Grozny that you start having dark suspicions about vested interests on both sides. In his old age, Kadyrov has covered himself with ineradicable shame by valuing his own life higher than the lives of 50 completely innocent spectators of the *Nord-Ost* musical. The terrorists invited him, as the Chief of Chechnya appointed by Putin, to visit them in exchange for 50 hostages but he didn't go, subsequently claiming he "hadn't heard about it."

During these 57 hours, the Moscow Chechens were whispering in corners. That was completely inadequate. They didn't even decry Kadyrov, or attempt to persuade him to go down in history as a man who saved the lives of 50 women and children. For 57 hours the so-called Chechen diaspora, almost to a man, went underground, some of them turning up only in Copenhagen.

My own feeling is that this leaves a bad taste. It just wasn't the way these people ought to have behaved. Perhaps I am completely wrong and I will be told later that the Chechens were terrified of the consequences, and that their main priority is to survive in a society now bristling against them even more than before, and so on and so forth.

No doubt that is all true, but can you really rank fears? The diaspora seemed heedless of the fact that the hostages were even more terrified of what seemed like their imminent inevitable death; and that for more than 100 of them (and we still don't know how many more) those 57 hours facing death were the last hours of their lives. That is why today we are attending funeral after funeral where the priests lose their voices because even their highly trained vocal cords cannot cope with so many services.

So, should we sympathise with the fears of the Chechen diaspora? Absolutely not. You will have to excuse me, but I totally reject their fear. Everybody involved was scared, including those who mounted the assault and those on the receiving end of it. So let us come back to our initial question: why did the Chechens behave as they did during these 57 hours?

Because they are cowards. Faced with their own younger generation who have turned into uncompromising radicals the whole lot of them bottled out. They slunk away. And perhaps, too, they considered it all beneath them. They think they are so elevated, but now we can see how low they are.

That too is a fact of history. The myth of the incomparable fearlessness of the Chechen nation has been relegated to history, to the period before October 23, 2002.

In Chechnya security sweeps are proceeding incessantly. People are being tortured, suffering just as much as before. Villages have been blockaded. The zone behind the Chechnya barrier has once again been turned into a training ground for the Army. On this side of the barrier things are better, but not much.

ONE MEMBER OF THE *NORD-OST* TERRORIST GROUP SURVIVED: WE HAVE FOUND HIM

April 28, 2003

Six months ago there was a terrorist act at the *Nord-Ost* musical. Since then we have puzzled many times over how such a thing could have happened. How did they get into Moscow? Did someone allow it? Why? Now we find there is a witness, who was also a member of the terrorist group.

At first there was only the bare information that one of the group of terrorists who took the audience hostage was still alive.

We checked the information out, repeatedly analysed the list of Barayev's group published in the press, made enquiries, and tracked him down: a man whose name is indeed officially listed with those of the other terrorists.

Were you a member of the Barayev group who took the Nord-Ost audience hostage?
Yes, I was.

Did you go into the theatre with them?
Yes.

I read an ID document with "PRESS" on its cover in capital letters on a dark background: "Khanpash Nurdyevich Terkibayev. *Rossiyskaya gazeta*. Special Correspondent. Pass No. 1165." Signed Gorbenko. Sure enough, *Rossiyskaya gazeta* does have a director of that name.

What topics do you write about? Chechnya?
No reply.

Do you go in to work at the newspaper? What department do you work in? Who is your editor?

Again, no reply. He pretends not to understand Russian very well, but how can you be a special correspondent of the country's main government newspaper if you don't speak Russian? Khanpash's narrow, mongoloid eyes, not much like those of a Chechen, register incomprehension. He is not putting it on, he genuinely does not understand what I'm talking about. He is no Russian journalist.

Was this pass given to you by someone as cover?
He smiles slyly.

I would not mind writing. I just haven't had time yet to think about it. I only received this pass on April 7. See the date? I don't need to go into the office, I work in the President's Information Service.

Under Porshnev? What job do you do?

(Igor Porshnev heads the Information Service of Putin's Presidential Administration, which should make him Khanpash's immediate superior.) Even Porshnev's name produces incomprehension in *Rossiyskaya Gazeta*'s "special correspondent." Khanpash has no idea who Porshnev is.

When necessary I meet [Presidential Aide] Yastrzhembsky. I work for him. Here is a photograph of me with him.

Sure enough, here is Khanpash photographed with Sergey Yastrzhembsky. Sergey is looking past the camera and appears displeased. Khanpash, on the other hand, now sitting in front of me in the Sputnik Hotel on Lenin Prospect in Moscow, is looking straight into the lens, as if to say, "There! That's us." You can tell from the photograph how palpably unwelcome it was to Yastrzhembsky, and deduce that it was insisted upon by the man now telling me his complicated life story, punctuating the narrative with numerous photographs which he pulls from his briefcase. "That's me and Maskhadov, me and Yastreb, me and Maskhadov again, me and Arsanov, me in the Kremlin, me and Saidullayev, me and Gil-Robles (the Council of Europe's Human Rights Commissioner)."

I look more closely, and quite a few seem to be rather inexpert photomontage. (They were subsequently checked by specialists and this was found to be the case.) "What's the game?" I ask. Khanpash again looks uncomprehending, rummages in the briefcase and pulls out "me with Margaret Thatcher and Maskhadov," to show how familiar he is with the London scene. It is 1998, Maskhadov is wearing a tall astrakhan hat, Thatcher is in the middle, and Khanpash is on the other side. Intriguingly, Maskhadov looks as he did before the war, while Khanpash looks as he does today. Odd. But he is already showing me another photograph of himself with Maskhadov during the present war. Maskhadov is wearing combat fatigues, his beard is very grey, and he looks terrible. Khanpash doesn't look too chipper either. This one is genuine.

Aren't you afraid of walking around Moscow with photographs like these? In Chechnya they would shoot you on the spot for the one with Maskhadov. Here they will plant firearms on you and put you in prison for years.
He replies, "I am in with Surkov." Khanpash begins to sound boastful. "After *Nord-Ost* I visited Surkov. Twice." (Vladislav Surkov is the influential Deputy Head of the Presidential Administration of Russia.)

Why?
I was helping him to work out a Chechen policy for Putin. After *Nord-Ost*.

And were you able to help?
Peace is needed.

That's an original thought.
I am currently working on peace negotiations for Yastrzhembsky and Surkov. The idea is to negotiate with the fighters hiding in the mountains.

Is that your idea or the Kremlin's?
Mine, supported by the Kremlin.

Negotiations with Maskhadov?
No. The Kremlin will not agree to negotiate with him.

With whom, then?
With Vakha Arsanov [former Vice-President of Ichkeria, repudiated by Maskhadov]. I have just had a meeting with him.

Where?
There.
But what are you going to do about Maskhadov?
He needs to be persuaded to give up his powers until there is another presidential election in Chechnya.

Are you involved in that too?
Yes, but I haven't been asked to do that, I'm just doing it on my own.
Actually, there may not be an election.

But if we do, nevertheless, live to see an election, who would you put your own money on?
Khasbulatov or Saidullayev. They are a third force. Not on Maskhadov, not on Kadyrov. That's what I think. After *Nord-Ost* it was me who organised negotiations between the Deputies of the Chechen Parliament and the Presidential Administration, with Yastrzhembsky.

Yes, that surprised a lot of people, when Isa Temirov together with other Chechen Deputies turned up openly in Moscow, spoke at the famous press conference in the Interfax news agency, and called on people to vote in the referendum. That was a blow against Maskhadov, although previously they had been for him. So you were behind that?
"I was," he replies proudly.

And did you vote afterwards in the referendum yourself?
"Me? No." He laughs. "I am from the Charto family *teip*. They call us Jews in Chechnya."

Would it be accurate to say that the Nord-Ost *tragedy was intended to have the role the Budyonnovsk hospital hostage-taking played* [in 1995, a turning point which eventually led to the ending of the First Chechen War], *only this time to end the Second Chechen War?*

This is not an idle question. It is crucial. Khanpash has a finger in every pie of Russian politics. He knows everybody, he's accepted everywhere. He's capable of engineering all kind of twists and turns in the North Caucasus. If you need to bring Maskhadov into play, he will lead you to Maskhadov. You want to exclude Maskhadov? He can fix that too. So, at least, he tells me. But his profession, he says, is acting. He graduated from the Drama Faculty of Grozny University. Never mind that there never was any such faculty, and that he can't remember the name of his acting teacher, this enables him to claim he is friends with Akhmed Zakayev. "We worked together in the theatre." In the First War he acquired a video camera and started working in television. He accompanied Basayev on the Budyonnovsk raid, but was not imprisoned for taking part in it. On the contrary, he was amnestied in April 2000.

Where did you get the papers for the amnesty?
In the Argun Office of the Chechen FSB.

This is an important detail. The Argun FSB section has been one of the most dreaded throughout this war. At precisely the time Khanpash was receiving an amnesty from them, almost everybody else who fell into their hands was being dispatched into another world. Khanpash is the first person I have met who survived being in their hands, and he was even given a certificate of amnesty for his Budyonnovsk involvement.

Between the two wars Khanpash, as a "hero of Budyonnovsk," became a leading consultant to President Maskhadov's Press Service. He had his own television program on Maskhadov's channel, *The President's Heart*, later renamed, *The President's Path*. That said, he was obliged to leave Maskhadov's entourage even before the Second War, but when military operations resumed he was back, and again became a furious jihadist. It is astonishing, but right under the noses of the federal troops and every imaginable Russian intelligence agency, in the midst of heavy fighting when everybody else was running for cover, Khanpash managed to make a television program whose title can be roughly translated from the Chechen as, "My Homeland Is Where Jihad Is."

Admittedly, neither then nor now did I believe that.

What do you mean? Your homeland is not where jihad is?
That was just the name of the program.
I heard Maskhadov has turned you away again recently?
Not Maskhadov, his representatives abroad, but I don't trust them.

Rakhman Dushuyev in Turkey told me that he had received a cassette from Maskhadov saying the President no longer wanted me to call myself his representative, but I did not hear the cassette myself, or talk directly to Maskhadov. I recently had no trouble meeting Kusama and Anzor (Maskhadov's wife and son) in Dubai. They accepted me. I ate and slept at their house.

Dubai, Turkey, Jordan, Strasbourg. You seem to be travelling all the time. How do you get visas?
I know all the Chechens. I travel to all countries and call on everyone to make peace and unite.

You travelled to Dubai from Baku?
Yes.

You turned up there after the terrorist act in Moscow in October and asked Chechens living there to help you? You told them you were one of the participants in the Nord-Ost hostage-taking who had survived, and now urgently needed contacts in the Arab world in order to escape pursuit?
How do you know that?

Chechens in Baku told me, and I read it in the newspapers. Your name is on the list of terrorists who were in Nord-Ost. Incidentally, are you suing over that?
No. Why should I? I just asked Yastrzhembsky, "How did that happen?"

What did he say?
"Just ignore it."

The most recent upward spiral of Khanpash Terkibayev's vertiginous political career in politics is indeed associated with the disastrous events of October 23–26, 2002, when the hostage-taking at the *Nord-Ost* musical caused the loss of many lives.

Had you known Barayev Junior for long?

Yes. I know everybody in Chechnya.

So did they have any explosives in there?
No, of course not.

After *Nord-Ost*, Khanpash really did become a confidant of Putin's Presidential Administration. He held every authorisation he needed to enable him to move unobstructed from Maskhadov to Yastrzhembsky. He negotiated on behalf of Putin's Administration with Deputies of the Chechen Parliament to get them to support a referendum. He obtained guarantees of immunity for the Deputies so they could come to Moscow. It was none other than Khanpash who, as leader of their group, took them to Strasbourg, to meet senior officials of the Council of Europe and the Parliamentary Assembly, where the Deputies did everything required of them at the behest of Dmitriy Rogozin, Chairman of the Duma Foreign Affairs Committee.

Naturally, the question arises, why did they choose Khanpash? What services had he rendered? How had he demonstrated his loyalty? Because without such proof he could not possibly have become involved in all this. We come now to a retelling of the most important part of our long conversation.

Khanpash appears to be the man for whom everybody involved with the *Nord-Ost* tragedy has been looking so diligently. He is the insider who made the terrorist act possible. Information in the possession of *Novaya gazeta* (which he doesn't deny: he is vain), indicates that Khanpash was an agent sent in by the intelligence services.

He entered the building with the terrorists as a member of their unit. He claims he secretly enabled them to travel through Moscow and to the *Nord-Ost* venue itself. It was he who assured the terrorists that everything was under control, that there were plenty of corrupt people, that the Russians had again accepted bribes, as they did when high-ranking resistance fighters were able to break out of the encirclement of Grozny and Komsomolskaya. They needed only to make a lot of noise, he told them, and there would be a second Budyonnovsk, enabling peace to be secured. Then, when they had fulfilled their mission, they would be allowed to escape. Not all of them, but many. "Many" turned out to be only Khanpash himself.

He left the building before the assault began. He had a map of the Dubrovka Theatre Complex, something possessed by neither Barayev, who was in command of the terrorists, nor even, initially, by the special operations unit preparing the assault.

How come? Because Khanpash belongs to forces far higher in the militia and security hierarchy than the Vityaz and Alpha special operations troops who were risking their lives to storm the building.

Whether he was telling the truth about the map is not, actually, all that important. Khanpash would lie for a copeck, as his faked photographs demonstrate. Those who could confirm or deny certain details of his story, like where his firing position was, have, to all appearances, been eliminated or are less garrulous. Do I believe there was more than one agent sent in? I think it is entirely possible.

What matters is that if there was an insider operating in *Nord-Ost*, the authorities knew about and were involved in preparing a terrorist act. It doesn't matter why. The main thing is that they (which section of them?) knew what was going on long before the rest of us did. They set up their own people for a terrible ordeal, knowing what was going to happen, fully aware that thousands would be permanently affected and hundreds killed or injured. The regime stage-managed another *Kursk* disaster. (Remember the messages sent by the unfortunate hostages from the occupied auditorium? "We are like a second *Kursk*. Russia has forgotten us. Russia does not need us. Russia wants us to die." Many outside the hall were indignant and thought this completely hysterical, but in fact they were accurately describing the situation.)

The question remains, then, why was this done? Why were all those people killed six months ago?

The first step is to work out who was responsible. Who, within the regime, was in the know? The Kremlin? Putin? The FSB? – the classical triad of modern Russia?

The state authorities are not a monolith and neither are the intelligence services. It is definitely not the case that most of the officers working in the operational headquarters beside the Dubrovka Complex were only pretending to be trying to avert the tragedy, in the full knowledge that the whole thing was a put-up job. Most of them were entirely committed, like the Vityaz and Alpha Units, like the rest of us.

But if Khanpash was in there, there is no escaping the fact that some dark nook of the state authorities did know and was only going through the motions of sympathising during those three days of insanity. This completely alters the complexion of those events.

So who were the intelligence agencies who knew? Certainly not the special operations soldiers who carried out the assault. If they had known the depths of the duplicity, there might simply have been a repeat of 1993 when the units refused to mount an assault [on Yeltsin's White House at the behest of the leaders of the anti-Gorbachev putsch], and the ending might have been completely different.

Neither was it the officers of the FSB and Interior Ministry, who planned the operation to rescue the hostages in all good faith. It was not they who infiltrated Khanpash into the terrorist group and subsequently fixed him up with a job.

Khanpash was not going to tell me who it was, but clearly the FSB and Interior Ministry were only acting out somebody else's script.

In the Second Chechen War methods such as these have been used extensively by military intelligence. In the so-called death squads it is officers of the GRU, the Central Intelligence Directorate, who make the running. The extra-judicial killing of their fellow citizens there is their stock in trade. Against these blood-soaked leaders neither the FSB, nor the Interior Ministry, nor the Prosecutor's Office, nor the courts can lift a finger. It is the practice of GRU units to exploit Chechen criminals and also their own victims, like those widowed by the death squads, as convenient fodder for achieving their aim of intimidating the whole of Russian society.

So was it the GRU, or someone as yet unknown? I have no answer, but it is vital that we should find out.

Why did those people die? Why such an unbelievable death toll of 129 lives?

That is what we get when we lift a corner of the curtain, when we hear the story of a double agent, a provocateur of our days so uncannily like Yevno Azef.*

People died, but the provocateur is alive and well. He is the political insider. He has his snout in the trough, looks good, and, most importantly, is still in business. In a few days' time he will be going back to Chechnya. What will he be cooking up this time?

"I need 24 hours to meet up with Maskhadov," he boasts.

"Just 24 hours?"

"Well, OK, two days."

Khanpash is forbearing towards naive people like us.

A SCHEME FOR PROTECTION AGAINST WITNESSES: MANAGED TERRORISM IN THE LAND OF MANAGED DEMOCRACY?

December 22, 2003

The information agencies tapped it out: "Khanpash Nurdyevich Terkibayev has been killed in a car crash in Chechnya." In the course of what we now know to have been his short life, the 31-year-old from Mesker-Yurt was to play many roles, of which the most important was unquestionably his complicity in the *Nord-Ost* hostage-taking in October 2002.

Who was Terkibayev? At first appearance, he was the last surviving witness from among the hostage-takers at the Dubrovka Theatre Complex. Officially listed as one of the terrorists, he claimed to have entered the building on October 23 last year as a member of Barayev's unit. In reality, as Terkibayev himself told me, and as is indirectly confirmed, he was a turncoat, an informer who once inside first fed information to the secret services, then left the building shortly before the assault.

Khanpash Terkibayev had previously been a journalist for Maskhadov, presenting the President's television program between the two wars. After *Nord-Ost* he was a member of President Putin's Admin-

*A Tsarist police spy who organised deadly terrorist acts, even assassinating the Tsar's uncle to entrap his colleagues in the Socialist Revolutionary Party.

istration, on whose behalf he led a delegation of Chechen Deputies to the European Parliament in Strasbourg in April 2003. He would also show to anyone interested to see it his press pass as a special correspondent of the official newspaper *Rossiyskaya gazeta*. He was, in short, the servant of many masters.

The pinnacle of Terkibayev's career was undoubtedly *Nord-Ost*. His was a horrifying tale which proved that Khanpash genuinely did move in the circles he described and that, accordingly, the atrocity was stage-managed by at least one of the Russian secret services. Simultaneously, another Russian secret service and several special operations divisions were combating it, culminating in the use of a secret chemical weapon against Russian citizens.

In May this year our newspaper published an interview with Terkibayev who at that time was still firmly in the saddle. From his revelations it was clear that the *Nord-Ost* tragedy was advantageous to the highly original regime known as "Russian managed democracy."

What happened after our interview? We called on the team investigating *Nord-Ost* to question both Terkibayev and the author of these lines on the subject of Terkibayev. On one occasion the investigator actually did come to *Novaya gazeta*'s offices. In his record of the visit he wrote whatever he fancied, as is now common practice, a so-called free paraphrase. His interest in Terkibayev did not extend beyond the fact that, after our report, Basayev was threatening him for his treachery.

Terkibayev lived for much of this year in Baku, where things got so bad for him that he had no option but to move. Sooner or later Basayev's people would have eliminated him, so he moved to Chechnya. This was a step born of desperation, putting his head in the tiger's mouth. The federal forces now had no time for him, and he had no other source of support. The car accident followed.

What is the most important aspect of this? Historically, as everybody knows, double and triple agents end up getting murdered. For us, however, this only makes things worse. Terkibayev never was questioned, and accordingly one further fragile link in the chain leading to the truth about *Nord-Ost* has been broken. He took with him information which ought to be known to everyone in Russia, the

answers to fundamental questions about *Nord-Ost* to which we, thanks
to the efforts of those at the top of the political pyramid, have no
answers. Who supported Barayev's unit in Moscow? (We are not talking
here about corrupt officials issuing visas, although, ironically, some are
facing trial this very week.)

How did Barayev's people get into Moscow at all? How were preparations for a terrorist attack in Moscow made? Who was Terkibayev's
controller in the secret services, and in which one? Why was there an
assault? Why were negotiations which had some prospect of success
in getting the hostages released terminated? Who was involved in taking
such criminal decisions?

If we reduce these questions to their lowest common denominator,
they indicate something we all suspect but cannot prove: that this was
a managed act of terrorism in which Barayev was manipulated, and in
which the female suicide bombers in black who accompanied him were
dupes.

One important detail for anyone interested in receiving accurate
information is that not only was Terkibayev not questioned by the
members of the official *Nord-Ost* inquiry, he was even ignored by
the members of the Public Commission of Inquiry, which does exist,
although it is so inactive that it might as well not.

The timing of the car accident is also revealing: Terkibayev might
have been about to open his mouth. The CIA was taking an interest
in him. CIA agents were (quite properly) conducting their own inquiry
into the death of an American citizen who had been among the
audience, and had been signalling that Terkibayev was of interest to
them as a source of evidence. (This may also have been a reason for
Terkibayev's move from Baku; in Baku he was accessible to the CIA,
while in Chechnya he was probably not.)

Where does that leave us? "The agent must not be allowed to talk,"
and Terkibayev has been duly silenced.

That is the main surmise about the causes of the car accident.
Nobody will ever be able to prove that it was a genuine accident. Even
if it was, nobody would believe it.

More generally, in the now eternal absence of Terkibayev the unquestioned and liquidated, I personally will never believe that the secret services are not involved in organising terrorist acts. They have done everything they could to torment me with the belief that they are. If there is another hostage-taking, the first question that will spring to mind will be, who is behind it? Which of those supposed to protect us are actually orchestrating the terrorists?

ONE MONTH BEFORE THE NORD-OST INQUIRY ENDS, THE STATE AUTHORITIES BURY ANSWERS TO THE MAIN QUESTIONS, AND THROW TRUTH TO THE WINDS

January 19, 2004

At the end of a two-hour meeting [between the head of the official investigation into the Nord-Ost hostage-taking and victims and relatives], I had to intervene and remind Mr Vladimir Kalchuk about the truth of the Terkibayev affair.

His reaction was bizarre. He told me to get lost and to stop writing to him, otherwise he would "hint" to the Nord-Ost victims that my son's mobile telephone number had been discovered in the memory of the phone the terrorists were using, "and then we will see what they will do to you. They may well be interested to know exactly what kind of personal links you have with the terrorists, you and your son . . ."

In view of this, I will have to persist with my reminders to Mr Kalchuk. Firstly, negotiations needed to be conducted during the siege, which I did. Secondly, the person I chose to help me was indeed my son, Ilya Politkovsky, and help me he did, courageously, conscientiously and openly trying to save, among others, the life of his close friend, Ilya Lysak, a musician in the Nord-Ost orchestra. Lysak was inside the occupied auditorium and used his personal connection with my family in order – equally courageously and heedless of the possible consequences – to facilitate negotiations. It was he, who today is still extremely ill, who handed his mobile telephone to the terrorists, and they used it to talk to me and my son, to agree the exact time I would enter the occupied building. They also used it to talk to Sergey Yastrzhembsky, the President's Aide.

I am sure the overwhelming majority of people would have done the same in the circumstances. Apparently the individual entrusted with leading the inquiry into the *Nord-Ost* tragedy would not.

5. Beslan

One of the most appalling atrocities in the course of the Second Chechen War was the taking hostage in Beslan, North Ossetia, on September 1, 2004 of up to 1,200 people, including 770 children, on the first day of the school year. Russian government troops stormed the school on September 3: 331 hostages died, including 186 children. Here too it seemed that the regime's primary concern was to manipulate the situation for its own political advantage. A Russian Diary contains more of Anna Politkovskaya's writing on this tragedy.

WHAT HAS HAPPENED TO POLITKOVSKAYA?

September 6, 2004

By Dmitriy Muratov and Sergey Sokolov (*Novaya gazeta*'s special correspondents in Rostov-on-Don and Moscow)

As the Beslan tragedy has unfolded, hundreds of our journalist colleagues, state officials and readers have been asking what has happened to *Novaya gazeta*'s columnist, Anna Politkovskaya. They believe that her presence in Beslan might have been of value, but Politkovskaya never reached Beslan.

On the evening of September 1, Politkovskaya was sent in *Novaya gazeta*'s car to Vnukovo Airport. Before that she had contacted a number of Russian politicians and Maskhadov's representative in London, Akhmed Zakayev. The basis of her proposals was that everybody who could get in touch with the terrorists should do so promptly, without considering the consequences, in order to save the children. "Let Maskhadov go and reach agreement with them," she urged. Zakayev reported that Maskhadov was prepared to do that without conditions or guarantees.

At Vnukovo, flights to Vladikavkaz had been cancelled. Those to nearby towns had also been cancelled. Three times Politkovskaya checked in and three times she was unable to fly. The newspaper ordered her to go to Rostov, and from there to travel onwards by car. The Karat airline allowed her to board.

Politkovskaya had had no time to eat all day. In the plane – and she is an experienced person – she refused food, having taken an oat biscuit with her. She felt fine and asked only for tea from the stewardess. Ten minutes after drinking it, she lost consciousness, having just had time to summon the stewardess back.

Thereafter she remembers only fragments. Valiant efforts were made by the doctors at the Rostov Airport Medical Center to get her out of a coma. They succeeded. The work of the doctors from the Fifth Infectious Diseases Department of Rostov City Hospital No. 1 was irreproachable. In underfunded conditions they revived her by all the means at their disposal, even surrounding her with plastic bottles full of hot water, administering a drip feed, giving injections. By morning she had recovered consciousness.

Grigoriy Yavlinsky, our colleagues from *Izvestiya*, and friends in the Army made every effort to help the medics in what, in the doctors' opinion, was an almost hopeless task. Many thanks to them.

On the evening of September 3, with the assistance of other friends (thank you, bankers!), Anna was transferred by private plane to one of the Moscow clinics. The Rostov laboratory analysis has not yet been completed. For some incomprehensible reason the first analyses, taken at the airport, were destroyed. The Moscow doctors said openly that they could not yet identify the toxin, but that a poison had entered her body.

Until these circumstances have been clarified, we do not want to engage in conspiracy theories. However, both the situation with Andrey Babitsky, a journalist with Radio Liberty, removed from a flight to the North Caucasus at Vnukovo Airport on suspicion of having explosives in his baggage (!) – needless to say, they found nothing – and the incident with Politkovskaya oblige us to think that attempts were being made to keep a number of authoritative journalists respected in Chechnya from reporting on the tragedy in Beslan.

Politkovskaya is now at home under medical supervision. Her kidneys, liver and endocrinal system have been seriously affected by an unidentified toxin. It is not known how long she will need to convalesce.

Why on earth don't those officials so exercised by Politkovskaya's activity just get on with doing their jobs? Averting terrorist acts, for example.

THE HUTS NEED PEACE, THE PALACES NEED WAR

September 13, 2004

The first three days of September 2004 have demonstrated once again that the moral and intellectual level of the Kremlin's current occupants gives no grounds to hope there will never be another Beslan. The days since the tragedy have demonstrated, moreover, that they have no intention of learning any lessons from the school massacre. They persist with their lies and evasions, and insist that black is white. This leaves our children and grandchildren in danger.

Our state authorities operate out of sight and, during times of national tragedy, they hide. We need people who at the very least will not hide themselves away. The crucial question in the light of recent events is, how have the state authorities responded to the Beslan tragedy? What have they done to improve their citizens' security?

There has been only one visible response: an administrative "anti-terrorist" reorganization in the South of Russia. In each region a senior "anti-terrorist" officer has been appointed from the ranks of the Interior Ministry's troops. They rank as second in command to those with overall responsibility for the region. In the current bureaucratic structure, which existed before Beslan, each region has an Anti-Terrorist Commission headed by Presidents Zyazikov, Alkhanov, Dzasokhov, Kokoyev, et al., and they bear full responsibility for terrorist acts on their territories. In addition, the new senior anti-terrorist officers will each command a further 70 special operations troops. The post-Beslan reinforcement of security in the South Russian regions,

254 IS JOURNALISM WORTH DYING FOR?

accordingly, amounts to 71 extra anti-terrorist agents apiece. Is
that it? Yes. It is a typical bureaucratic manoeuvre to avert bad
publicity.

What do we actually know about the heads of the Anti-Terrorist
Commissions in the South of Russia? Let us cast an eye over the files
of some of these gentlemen whose duty was to prevent Beslan from
happening and who, after it erupted, were personally responsible for
conducting the operation to free the hostages.

Every age has its own characteristics. The Brezhnev era was typified
by cynical dementia. Under Yeltsin it was think big, take big. Under
Putin, we live in an era of cowardice. Take a look at those who surround
him.

First, Mr Murat Zyazikov, the President of Ingushetia. Zyazikov has
been in power for a little over two years, before which his career was
spent entirely in the KGB and FSB. He is one of Putin's professional
cronies. Nobody is in any doubt that Zyazikov was strong-armed into
the office of President of Ingushetia by Putin and his team. His presidency has seen the secret services run riot in Ingushetia, flouting the
Constitution. Citizens have been abducted by the FSB and death squads,
and as a direct consequence young people have been heading to the
mountains to join the fighters and there has been a wave of terrorist
acts. What did Zyazikov do, this abysmal Head of Ingushetia's Anti-
Terrorist Commission? He has just sat there in his presidential seat,
a typical FSB goon.

An FSB goon is, after all, somebody who sees the world from behind
other people's backs. That's their profession. They are invisible fighters
against an invisible threat. The problems begin when the threat becomes
visible and real, and the President needs to come out and organise
effective resistance to outlaws like those who took over Ingushetia on
June 21, 2004.*

That night dozens of people died while Zyazikov sat it out in his

---

*On the night of June 21, 2004, some 300 resistance fighters occupied the city of
Nazran; 98 people were killed and more than 100 injured. The resistance fighters seized
1,056 weapons and burned down several administrative buildings, including the offices
of the Nazran Interior Affairs District Office.

cellar, waiting to see what would happen and keeping his own highly important skin safe. No doubt the President's life is very precious and important, so perhaps he really ought to be hiding in his cellar. But it is no more precious than the lives of everyone else.

The result of that night was the loss of many lives in Ingushetia, attributable to a total lack of organised resistance to the invaders. Another important result was that the fighters were encouraged to think about undertaking something similar in the future.

Let us look, then, at August 21, 2004 and the seizure of Grozny by resistance fighters in an exact replay of the Ingushetian scenario. Where were Putin's favorites that night, Alu Alkhanov and Ramzan Kadyrov, who so often tell us on television that they have all but caught the last of the outlaws? They too were down in their cellars, rather than leading resistance to the fighters. They too were saving their precious skins for future battles against international terrorism. The result that time was the loss of more than 50 lives, and a further boost for the resistance fighters' self-confidence.

Finally we come to Beslan, where brutes planted explosives around small children and demanded an end to the accursed war in Chechnya. What should Zyazikov, Alkhanov, and the redoubtable Ramzan Kadyrov – responsible for dealing with terrorism in their territories, who had given Putin every assurance that the enemy would never pass – have done on that first morning of September 1? They, along with Maskhadov, whose name was being bandied about by the brutes, should have been standing there in the school and, with all the means at their disposal, without attempting to haggle over guarantees of their personal safety, should have tried to talk these brutes, whom they themselves had created, into releasing the children. Only after that should they have wrangled over who was right and who was wrong.

What happened? Neither Zyazikov, nor Alkhanov, nor Ramzan Kadyrov, nor Maskhadov went anywhere near the school. They bottled out, valuing their own lives above those of hundreds of children. To my mind, in the light of what resulted from the actions of both sets of citizens, the cowards are no better than the criminals.

Clever people say now that it would have been foolish for them to have rushed to negotiate in Beslan, foolish because it would have meant certain death. Quite possibly. What of it? Those who are guilty have to take responsibility. What actually happened was that innocent children bore the consequences of the cowardice and stupidity of those who, you may remember, chorused at election time, "We take full responsibility on ourselves."

You will remember too that, before this, the only person in our recent history who decided to save his own skin rather than the lives of women and children was Kadyrov Senior (who was in any case assassinated on May 9 this year). In October 2002, when the terrorists who had occupied the *Nord-Ost* musical announced they were prepared to release 50 women if Akhmat-hadji Kadyrov came to them, he refused. Shortly afterwards, Putin signalled that Akhmat-hadji was his favorite in Chechnya.

Zyazikov, Kadyrov Junior and Alkhanov are all three of them Putin's current favorites, and they have done exactly the same. The one person who did dare to go in, ex-President of Ingushetia Ruslan Aushev, got the brush-off from the Kremlin. Now the new anti-terrorist initiative consists of allotting each of these cowards a senior officer and 70 special operations troops. That is who will be averting future acts of terrorism.

Except that cowards are incapable of averting acts of terrorism: cowardice is powerless in the face of terrorism. Obviously. Those senior Interior Ministry officers can only serve to preserve the lives of the Big Three the next time the balloon goes up. They will do nothing for the rest of us.

The conclusion is simple: neither Zyazikov nor Alkhanov, nor Ramzan Kadyrov can be allowed to remain in their jobs. It is a death sentence, not for them, but for us. And that is only in the first place. In the second place, what can we oppose to terrorism? How are we to stem the tide of terrorist acts and gradually put an end to them? What we need most is courageous authorities with a transparent plan to counteract terrorism. Then what? What needs to be changed in the North Caucasus to minimise the probability of future terrorist acts?

Here is my proposal. It is the plan of a journalist very critical of much that has been going on in our country during the first term of

Putin's presidency, and that is still going on now. These are ideas about how it may be possible gradually to regulate the Chechen crisis; and that this crisis is at the root of all that happened in Beslan and immediately before Beslan nobody apart from Putin seems to be in any doubt.

Here is what we should do now about suicide attacks in the North Caucasus; about Maskhadov; about the fact that the ranks of the resistance have been swelling this year more than in any of the previous years of the Second Chechen War; about the detachments of mercenaries active there and in adjacent territories; about the growing numbers of those seeking vengeance for the murder or disappearance of their nearest and dearest; about the unprecedented depravity of the troops; about the federal death squads operating outside the Constitution, persecuting civilians and carrying out extra-judicial executions; about federals who "wage war" only for the statistics, for combat premiums, for rank, decorations, and not in order to seek out and take out outlaws; about the absolute corruption of the Kadyrov regime, supported by the Kremlin and hated by the population; and as a result, about the level of distrust of the federal authorities among all sections of Chechen society, which today is completely off the scale.

What gives me the right to pronounce on this and to propose a plan? Only my experience of working in Chechnya over many years. This is, of course, a journalist's experience, which consists mainly of constant meetings with people at every level of Chechen society: with those who are pro-federal, and those who are anti-federal; with those active in the resistance, and their opponents; with children and young people, old people, and women; with Kadyrovites, and militiamen; with special operations troops, and Kadyrov's bureaucrats; with mullahs and muftis, and with everybody else.

My job has been to go from one village to another, from one town to another, and to ask, and ask, and ask; to try to understand what moral code people live by, what they will settle for, and what they hold unacceptable.

In other words, this journalist's work has been conducting social surveys, month after month, since the summer of 1999, in all the

towns and villages of Chechnya about the crucial topic of what needs
to be done to bring peace there. What part in the process do individuals see themselves playing? What is the future for Chechnya – with
Russia or without? If with, then how are we to be reconciled? How are
we to be reconciled when Maskhadov has been effectively removed
from the equation as a potential negotiator, and it is in any case practically impossible to conduct negotiations with those who squeezed
him out?

Proposals for Settling the Chechen Crisis

1.   Set up a Federal Council for Settling the Chechen Crisis (a collegiate, advisory institution). The main prerequisite is that it should
contain no representatives of the security ministries or the bureaucracy,
because nobody trusts them. There should be only representatives of
civil society, chosen from those who have worked in Chechnya as
human rights observers throughout the years of the war. It is they
who have earned the trust of the population, not those hiding behind
the high fences of the government compound in Grozny. It should
include public figures in Russia who have consistently opposed the
war, whichever way the wind was blowing, have spoken out for a
peaceful settlement and a genuine political process (and not the ridicu-
lous elections twice conducted in Chechnya and almost totally ignored
by the population).

2.   From the moment this Council is established, no political or financial decision relating to Chechnya must be taken without being approved
by the Council.

3.   The Council should draw up a plan for clear and specific actions
– "1, 2, 3, 4," – and announce it publicly. The aim is for all the points
of the plan to be completely transparent to everybody in Chechnya:
what will be done and when, with deadlines, in order to settle the
conflict.

4.   Political negotiations with Maskhadov are essential, even though
a majority of the population no longer respects him. It is, nevertheless, necessary to proceed through such negotiations, the aim of which

would be to give Maskhadov an opportunity to apologize to his people and either to depart or answer in accordance with the law for what has happened. This is important not only for him, but also for those who at one time elected him. This is regarded by a majority as the starting point for a credible political process of settlement.

5.   A public apology, without fail, by the Federal Center for the civilian victims of the war.

6.   A demilitarisation, without fail, of the territory of Chechnya as the first condition of a political settlement. This is impossible without a troop withdrawal. Troops can remain only in their places of permanent deployment for a strictly defined transitional period, with a publicly announced deadline for withdrawal. How the troops are to be withdrawn also needs to be made public, with sanctions for infringement of the conditions.

7.   The only way of effecting demilitarisation, given the total distrust between the federal troops and intelligence services, the civilian population and the Kadyrovites is for it to be implemented in the presence of international observers of sufficient status for the population to have confidence in them (the United Nations, OSCE, PACE, etc.). International observers are seen as the only possible guarantors of an even-handed demilitarisation. It would be possible to conduct an enforced disarmament of all who hold firearms illegally, but the population will accept this only if it takes place in the presence of international observers, and without the involvement of federal military personnel.

8.   The presence of international observers is essential throughout the transitional period while passions are cooling. A request from the Federal Center to the international community for observers should be seen not as a sign of weakness but of strength.

9.   Political leadership during the transitional period should be in the hands of a Russian Governor (the terminology favored by the majority) with the rank of Plenipotentiary Representative of the Russian President for Settling the Chechen Conflict. This could be a Deputy Prime Minister with special powers. The continued presidency of Alu Alkhanov is likely for a time, but retaining Ramzan Kadyrov in any capacity is out of the question. He is reviled.

10.   The main criterion for the Russian representative is that they should be a civilian. He or she should be well known and respected by Chechen society, and should have a record as a consistent opponent of the war in Chechnya who has not wavered in response to the "Party line."

11.   It is essential that there should be a Chechen Office of the Russian Representative in Grozny, with Russian and Chechen representatives of civil society well acquainted with the situation and with people's needs throughout the years of the war. These should be individuals who have worked in the thick of the war as human rights observers, and accordingly have earned popular respect. No bureaucrats.

12.   The economic institutions for governing the Republic should be subordinate to the Office of the Russian Representative. Revenues should be under the control of civil society and members of the Federal Council who have an unblemished reputation.

13.   A public discussion on the future of Chechnya should be organised gradually. Should it be a parliamentary or a presidential republic? This cannot be decided by Moscow. Decisions from Moscow will not be accepted, and national harmony will be undermined.

14.   Organization of a public discussion on the type of constitution people should live by. It is essential to do away openly, through discussion, with the present constitutional "dual power," where one section of the population does not accept the 1992 Constitution, while another section does not accept the 2003 Constitution. Such a discussion can bring about a normalisation, and genuinely fair and free elections in accordance with a single constitution in which everybody will feel able to participate.

15.   Finally, after a few years of this process of peace and demilitarisation, free elections should be held in accordance with the pattern of a presidential or parliamentary republic adopted by a majority of the population.

Other people may have other plans and different arguments to mine. This is all to the good. We had a Constitutional Convention in Russia: let there be a Chechen convention to discuss and debate the options.

There is no time left. We need high-powered brainstorming and soon, without personal ambition, without bragging about who was invited first and who second, and without the usual swinish misconduct from our political elite.

We need to think now in order to survive, for all our sakes. In memory of the children of Beslan.

The cowards can help only by quitting. They have already done quite enough.

GROWING DOUBTS

December 1, 2005

It is finished. The conclusions of one of the parliamentary commissions into the Beslan slaughter have been published at a session of the North Ossetian Parliament. The inertia has been overcome, which can only be to the good.

Some of the report's conclusions, however, create a strange impression. For example, Mr Kesayev, the Head of the Commission, assures us that the first telephone contact with the separatists occurred 28 hours after the start of the terrorist act, that is, towards noon on September 2. That is incorrect. Contact had been established two hours after the start of the terrorist attack, on the morning of September 1, as anybody who took an interest in the matter has known for a long time. Who initiated these contacts? Well actually, as it happens, I did, which is why I know. Indeed this fact of when contact was made with Maskhadov's side was later recorded in the evidence of Alexander Torshin's "Parliamentary Grand Commission." Again, I gave that evidence in the Soviet of the Federation and Mr Torshin subsequently made use of it when discussing the Beslan tragedy in a television documentary on its first anniversary. The documentary was televised, and I can only suppose that somebody from Kesayev's Commission must have seen it.

According to the Commission, the North Ossetian leaders (Dzasokhov and Mamsurov) attempted to contact Maskhadov but were unsuccessful. That too is incorrect. On September 3 Mr Dzasokhov spoke to Mr Zakayev, at that time Maskhadov's Special Envoy in Europe, and Mr Zakayev asked only for a corridor for Maskhadov to travel through. Mr Dzasokhov promised to make the arrangements, but didn't lift his mobile phone again, and the assault began.

One other conclusion of the report: it is asserted that these contacts were in any case pointless, because Maskhadov and Zakayev were complicit in organising the terrorism. This leads to a claim that the North Ossetian leaders were right to rule out negotiating with these guilty parties.

The Beslan inquiries fail to consider the most important point: that all these questions (whether tanks fired on the school and when, whether there were Bumblebee helicopters overhead) would never have been necessary if the leaders had only negotiated. Higher-ups in Moscow, however, gave the signal to attack, and the small fry in Vladikavkaz did as they were told. Taking that hard-line path, they turned the tragedy into a full-scale military operation, with catastrophic consequences.

It seems legitimate to ask what, actually, was the point of this inquiry? Was it for the victims, firstly, so that they should be clear who was responsible for the deaths of their dearest? Was it for society, to avoid anything of the sort being repeated?

To avoid a repetition does not mean making sure that during the next terrorist attack the next FSB general thinks twice before bringing in tanks, and instead decides to use a top secret weapon which is silent, colorless, has no smell and can never be detected.

That is not what is meant at all. To avoid a repetition it is essential that next time the state authorities should immediately, without losing a minute, enter into negotiations, should know how far they are prepared to negotiate, and have negotiators to hand. And that that plan should be carried out fully, so that it never again comes to gunfire and explosions.

"THE PRESIDENT SIMPLY DISAPPEARED FROM THE LIST OF WITNESSES"

January 23, 2006

The first meeting in the New Year of the Federal Parliamentary Commission on Beslan, chaired by Alexander Torshin, will be held on January

26, 2006. As already reported, there has been a split. On December 28, just before the New Year holiday, an account of the work the Commission has done in the past 16 months was delivered, rather than the long-promised report. The account was manifestly superficial and derived from the assertions of the official investigation. Most of the Commission's members kept entirely silent, true to their signed undertaking not to talk about material matters or how the Commission's work was proceeding. One member with a different view is Yury Ivanov, a Communist Deputy in the State Duma, who replied to our newspaper's questions.

Yury Pavlovich Ivanov has been a Communist Party Deputy of the State Duma since 1994 and is currently Deputy Chairman of the Duma Committee on Development of the Constitution. He is no longer a signed-up member of the Communist Party, is aged 61, and is a well-known barrister. He defended Vladimir Kryuchkov, Director of the KGB, during the case against the 1991 putsch conspirators; Alexander Rutskoy after the shelling of Parliament in October 1993; and the Communist Party in the Constitutional Court.

Why were the members of the Commission pledged to secrecy? What fearsome secret is it that you all have to keep?
I have no idea. I firmly believe that all the officials who passed before the Commission should have been questioned openly and publicly, in the presence of the press. That is a fundamental principle. The Commission was working to procedures approved by Sergey Mironov (Head of the Soviet of the Federation) but the rules were not even discussed in the Duma. I was informed that all the members of the Commission had signed a secrecy agreement and accepted legal liability if they breached the undertaking. I should mention that the recently passed law on parliamentary inquiries contains no such requirement. Our procedure specified that all the Beslan meetings were to be held behind closed doors, despite the fact that the law on parliamentary inquiries requires quite the opposite: that all sessions should be held in public except in exceptional circumstances, where matters involving state secrets are being investigated.

What part of the evidence heard by the Commission bore any relation to state secrets?

There were no classified matters, no state secrets. After we had been working for a year and a half Alexander Torshin, Chairman of the Commission, declared that only 1 per cent of what we were discussing was secret. What I could see as necessarily secret was only some diagrams showing the position of snipers and revealing their names, and also those of members of the tank corps who fired on the building. That was all. Even if nobody had signed anything, we would never have dreamed of talking publicly about that.

Then why was it necessary to shroud the Commission's work in this ambience of high secrecy?

Boris Gryzlov, the Chairman of the Duma, came to one of our sessions. It was one of the sessions, incidentally, where every one of my proposals was turned down. I recommended that you and Andrey Babitsky from Radio Liberty should be questioned by the Commission to establish why you were unable to reach Beslan at that time, and what was behind the scuffle at Vnukovo Airport on September 2 for which Babitsky was detained just before he was to fly to Beslan, and so on [see above, p.252]. I also wanted us to seek information about the Alexander Pumane affair. You may remember, several dozen FSB and Interior Ministry generals met at a district militia station in the middle of Moscow, after which Pumane wasn't just killed there but so badly beaten that neither his mother nor his wife were able to identify him. They had made mincemeat of him and DNA tests were required. It was claimed at the time that Pumane had been planning to blow up the President's motorcade on Kutuzovsky Prospect, and that it was all closely related to terrorism.

Gryzlov, however, declared all that to be irrelevant, nothing to do with the Commission. They didn't even vote on my proposal. The paradox is that the procedure made clear that Torshin was the Commission Chairman in charge of all sessions while Gryzlov, as Chairman of the Duma, could only attend as an observer, not take the chair or issue rulings about my proposals.

To Mironov's credit, he was more tactful. He attended the sessions fairly frequently, sat, listened, asked permission to speak, and had to be granted it. Mironov, however, also made it very clear what the Commission's job should be: "You need to channel, channel, and again channel." Then everything became clear to me.

Channel what?
The public mood. Our job was to reassure the public.

But the only way you could do that would be by establishing the truth.
I doubt whether even the truth would salve the suffering of the mothers of Beslan, but I emphasise that the Head of the Soviet of the Federation from the outset saw the Commission's main task as being to channel public concern. He regarded the members of the Commission as public relations ditch-diggers. I believed instead that the Commission should be reporting the truth to society. I had been entrusted with establishing the causes and circumstances of the terrorist attack, and I should set them out clearly. The campaign of reassurance led to completely perverse interaction between the public and state authorities, for example when the investigators were obliged to appear before the victims in a Beslan community center and give a joint report at the very beginning of their inquiry. In my view, it was Putin and his administration who should have been explaining themselves to the victims at that time.

What are the main facts about Beslan which were excised when the account of December 28 was being written and which might have been fundamental to an assessment of the tragedy?
I divide all the inquiries into Beslan into criminal and parliamentary categories. The Commission did not, and still doesn't, have the tools required to fully establish the actual circumstances. We have no right to caution people about giving false evidence; to oblige witnesses to confront those they are testifying about; or to carry out tests ourselves. That means that any conclusions we draw in this area will be based 75 per cent on information from the official investigation, which may have been economical with the truth or distorted. We were supposed

to concentrate instead on the actions of federal officials. The national aspects were to be covered by a Commission of the North Ossetian Parliament under the chairmanship of Stanislav Kesayev which, in my opinion, did a good job. Their report is frank and honest, and that's what really matters.

We should have started by evaluating the actions of the President and Patrushev, the Director of the FSB. Unfortunately, in all these 16 months the Commission did not consider the matter of the President's responsibility for Beslan. We initially expected to question him; Putin was listed as a witness for a whole year, but suddenly disappeared.

The Commission passed no resolution to take Putin off the list?
No, and neither did it discuss why his name disappeared from the list of witnesses.

One other extremely important question, which I raised many times, was the matter of calling representatives of the Caucasian clergy. Nobody in the Commission seemed to object to hearing from the Wahhabis. I wanted to contact them all the time, to talk to them and understand them. Wahhabism is not banned. I began trying to find them. When we were hearing from the heads of the FSB and Foreign Intelligence Service, I asked them who the emissaries of Wahhabism were in the Caucasus. Either they do not know or they did not want to answer, but I remain convinced we should sit down together and talk. I remember I went to the Duma Committee on Religious Affairs and asked if they could give me the names of the leaders of Wahhabism, because I wanted to meet them. One of the vice-chairmen said, "Here is the telephone number of the main Wahhabi. He will tell you all you need to know." I rang, and it turned out to be the number of Geidar Djemal, a well-known Moscow philosopher and political commentator. That's our level of understanding of these problems.

If Putin had not been removed from the list of witnesses, what would you have asked him?
The Kesayev Commission confirmed that Zakayev had said Maskhadov was prepared to take part in negotiations. It is clear that Maskhadov's

going into the Beslan school might well have resulted in the children being released. I am certain the resistance fighters would have deferred to his authority. They had stated that they were under Basayev's command, but that Maskhadov was their President and that negotiations should be conducted with him. Putin, however, did not want Maskhadov turning up in Beslan because any raising of Maskhadov's profile would immediately have deflated the authority of the Kadyrov gang.

When Kesayev's report was published, the pro-presidential press claimed it emphasised that Aushev and Dzasokhov had phoned Zakayev and asked for Maskhadov to come, but that he had not made contact. That was wilful misrepresentation of the situation.

In my view, everything should have been handled differently: all television broadcasts should have been interrupted, the President should have appeared on all channels and announced that he was providing Maskhadov with a corridor of safe conduct and guaranteeing his immunity. Urgently, no matter where he might be, Maskhadov should appear in Beslan and order the resistance fighters to cease their action. Then he would be free to depart.

Putin chose not to do that. He had already announced that Maskhadov was a criminal and the only way to treat Maskhadovs was to pulverise them in in the shithouse. The chickens had come home to roost: in that dreadful situation in Beslan the President was a hostage to his own big mouth. His vanity did not allow him to go back on his words, and the lives of thousands of people took second place to his vanity. That is why Putin delegated the problem from a federal to a regional level, and as President of North Ossetia Dzasokhov had no authority to organise a corridor or guarantee safe conduct.

That was followed by the assassination of Maskhadov. He could have been questioned about many things afterwards. Instead, somebody gave the order not to take him alive but to throw grenades at him. Putin talks a lot about international terrorism, but if they had taken Maskhadov prisoner, who would have been better placed to say who is financing the terrorists, whether the resistance fighters have their own network of agents and bribe-takers in the Kremlin, and where the weapons came from that were used in Beslan? Quite clearly, Putin did not want Maskhadov taken alive.

You have stated on several occasions that there was no sign of international terrorist involvement in Beslan. On what basis?
The Commission has no evidence of the involvement of international terrorism in Beslan. The munitions were Russian, and nothing is known about who financed the group. Lebedev, the Director of the Foreign Intelligence Service, speaking at the Commission, talked a lot about how they had "terminated" things both abroad and in Russia, but what does terminate mean? Did they kill people? Did they bring them to court? Let's see the reports of the investigative agencies and the court verdicts. There is nothing. The Commission has only a vague report. If I am given specific information I will change my view, but for the time being it is all just talk.

What percentage of those testifying to the Commission caused you to have doubts of this kind, that the quality of their information was dubious?
I didn't count. I have given you the example of Lebedev. I asked him to name the emissaries of Wahhabism in Russia, and he replied that was not a matter for him. As regards Arab mercenaries, we were told some had been present in Beslan, but I appealed repeatedly to the representative of the Prosecutor's Office to speak to the Saudi Arabian Embassy and find out if there were Saudis involved. Without that confirmation we really cannot make that categorical assertion. But actually, how much difference would it make even if Saudi Arabia did confirm some were present? From my point of view, none. Individual terrorists might go for a shoot-out, either for money or motivated by their religious fanaticism. There are plenty of people like that around in some parts of the world, but that does not mean they are members of an international terrorist network called al-Qaeda.

As for that mysterious tape which Torshin played during his public account, it was not discovered by the official investigators but supposedly by children, who handed it to an American journalist. On this tape a supposed Arab, Abu Dzeit, rattles away in Russian so fluent you couldn't better it! Where is the file on him? Again, all the information comes from abroad. The Commission has nothing.

I state publicly as a member of the Commission that I heard nothing specific from the appropriate intelligence agencies. I saw no evidence from which I could conclude who Abu Dzeit was. If I look at the report of the American Congress's 9/11 Commission I find extremely detailed information about each of the terrorists: where he was born, where he studied, where he took his flying lessons, what resources he lived on. In our Commission there is just a list of names from the Prosecutor's Office. Do they correspond to reality? Why did these individuals become resistance fighters? Why did they carry out such a dreadful act? The public will not be getting any answers.

What conclusions have you come to as to why the group which seized the Beslan school was formed?
For that you would need to study the composition of the group. The identity of eight of the terrorists has not even been established; on the others we possess only such general information as their names, their nationality, the fact that some had previous convictions, and that some were taking drugs. But how did those who were on drugs manage to resist so desperately for several hours? There is one extraordinary episode: Khuchbarov shot three of the terrorists, two women and a man, for refusing to obey his orders. When the children started drinking urine and were suffering terribly, these people started shouting at Khuchbarov that he couldn't do this and must release the children. In other words, they took part in the hostage-taking but in the course of it repudiated their previous aims, and for that they were killed. Who were those three? Should not their bodies have been returned to their relatives? Are they resistance fighters or victims? There is a concept in law of voluntarily refusing to go through with a crime. That does not completely exonerate you, but it is taken into account when the sentence is being decided. Unfortunately, the Commission did not look into the terrorists' personalities. I may propose that we should.

Beslan is part and parcel of the Chechen slaughter, one episode in an ongoing drama. If the Commission is supposed to be establishing the causes of the school seizure, then quite plainly they are not to be found in Ossetia. I am alarmed that nobody is intending – and here I fundamentally disagree with Torshin's report – to investigate the causes. In the report being prepared there is no consideration of why the resistance fighters appeared in the first place. Why do they enjoy support in their society? What role in all this is played by the massive violation of human rights in Chechnya?

Did the Commission at least study the history of the attack on Ingushetia on June 21–22, 2004, immediately prior to Beslan?
No. What are my disagreements with the Commission? The first point is that Putin, by refusing to provide Maskhadov with safe passage, made it certain that the assault would take place. Secondly, Patrushev and Putin's advisers [Anisimov and Pronichev, Deputy Directors of the Russian FSB] had major involvement but are bearing no responsibility at all. Thirdly, the violation of human rights in the Caucasus is a major cause of the Beslan tragedy, engendering more and more new resistance fighters. Fourthly, we failed to investigate the causes. The seizure of Ingushetia and other terrorist acts were not examined by the Commission at all, as if they were completely unrelated to Beslan.

There is a serious problem. Given all the confusion that arose, and after the assassination of Maskhadov, there is speculation about an appalling alternative explanation. You hear this whenever Duma Deputies are talking among themselves. Perhaps, in order to stop Maskhadov getting to Beslan, somebody organised the explosion inside the school which triggered the assault and all the rest of it. According to the report of the Kesayev Commission, Advisers Anisimov and Pronichev had their own separate office in the operational headquarters. What was going on in there? What decisions were being taken? Who is going to believe now that the explosions were accidental, especially when they didn't occur on the ground floor, where there is not even a crater, but somewhere above the ceiling?

The President himself sowed the seeds for this explanation of events. It is an explanation which people are trying not to discuss and are pretending does not exist, but which would totally discredit the state. That is why I want answers from Putin.

The Commission has officially questioned Anisimov and Pronichev. What did they have to say?
They said they were sent to Beslan by Patrushev to offer advice and that was all. Beyond that, we are in the realm of speculation as to what they did or did not do there. In my view, the President and Patrushev confused the situation unbelievably. Under the law on the struggle against terrorism there should have been no advisers there, just an operational headquarters bearing full responsibility. In Beslan we had uncalled-for advisers functioning unlawfully in parallel with those in command. If Andreyev [Valeriy Andreyev, the Head of the North Ossetian FSB Directorate at the time the school was seized], who was in charge of the counter-terrorist operation, had two of his bosses advising him, how was he to take responsible decisions?

Can you give an assessment of the conduct of senior state officials? Patrushev, for example? Did he do everything he could?
He told us he was in Moscow and not at the scene, but we have a different complaint against him: why to this day have no effective informants been infiltrated into the terrorists' ranks? Why was the FSB unprepared, not only in Beslan but also in Ingushetia, when resistance fighters rampaged unchecked for several hours and killed people who supported the federal authorities? That too was a disgrace.

The same goes for Minister Nurgaliev. The most serious complaint against the Interior Ministry is that it failed to organise an effective cordon round the school. They said that people in the Caucasus are hotheaded and just ignored it. Minister Nurgaliev sent his deputy, Pankov, there. There was a crowd right round the school which joined in the assault and the fire engines could not get through because of a huge number of private cars obstructing them. What was the militia doing in the meantime? I would not say that Nurgaliev should take personal responsibility for this, but Pankov certainly should. Instead, the explanation was: "It was splendid that the local townsfolk assisted.

Without them far more people would have died, and they pulled many of the injured free." Does that mean that next time the hostages' relatives should just grab whatever comes to hand and mount an assault?

How do you rate Dzasokhov's actions?
Do you mean, do I think he should have gone into the school? I have no answer to that. Should Dzasokhov have gone to his death? Your question is too difficult. It is absolutely clear that Aushev, who did go in, was much less at risk than Dzasokhov. Given their past records, Aushev was much less at risk than Zyazikov or Dzasokhov who, I am quite sure, would not have come out alive. For me it is obvious that in situations like that the Republican presidents need to be protected. They should not bear the burden for everything that happens in the course of a counter-terrorist operation. Did Dzasokhov do everything he could? Well, what could he do? He initiated the process of negotiating with Zakayev. He was at the scene, among the people, not hiding. I imagine he did what he could.

What about Zyazikov?
If he had gone in they would have killed him. For them he was a traitor.

Did Dr Roshal do enough?
Roshal was questioned by the Commission. He is a decent man. My impression was that he should not have been asked to go to talk to the fighters. The only conversation he had with them ended with them calling him a kike – a foul, churlish insult. On the other hand, it was he they called for initially, and he came.

How do you assess Aushev's actions?
Aushev is a figure from the Caucasian elite of the Yeltsin era. At the beginning they were all presidents and ministers: Aushev, Maskhadov, Dudayev, Basayev were quite often seated at the same table. The Caucasus is a brotherhood. Then the Chechens went off the rails and started killing people. The war with Russia started and Aushev sided with Russia. In Beslan Aushev did everything right.

The so-called advisers, Anisimov and Pronichev?
The decision to send advisers was taken by Patrushev and Putin. Before
the Commission Anisimov and Pronichev took the line that they had
been given orders, went to Beslan, and gave advice.

What did you learn from your work in the Commission that was new?
The most unexpected discovery was the activity of the human rights
organizations. My attitude towards them was that they were "little shits,"
to use the expression of Pavel Grachev [the Russian Minister of Defence
during the First Chechen War]. My view of the little shits dated from
1993–5 when I was meeting refugees from Chechnya and realized that
what was happening there was a genocide of the Russians, and that
the human rights activists were not speaking up for them but only
for the Chechens. That infuriated me. Today, though, I have to admit
that the human rights organizations have overcome that bias. They are
fighting for the rights of people in the Caucasus irrespective of nationality, protecting the rights of ordinary people, not of the nouveaux
riches. They take risks. They don't spare themselves. At any moment
they could be knifed or shot.

*One final question: Gryzlov, as you describe it, on one occasion effectively
took over the chair of the Commission, but the Commission was also visited
by Lyubov Sliska, the Deputy Speaker of the Duma. What justification did
she offer for interfering?*
In November Sliska and Mironov came to the Commission and told
us we should have our conclusion out before the New Year. She said
the public were very stirred up and we needed to work as quickly as
possible. They got support. Lyubov Sliska is an extremely glamorous
woman who gets featured in the glossy magazines. How could you
refuse her? Of course, Gryzlov had no business delegating Sliska to
come and tell us what to do, but I would not call it interference. Let
us just say it was less a meeting of the Commission than a meeting
with a glamorous woman. She asked the Commission to bring its
work to a conclusion. We agreed and passed a resolution, but then
changed our minds. Instead of the final report, what Torshin presented

on December 28 was an account of the work we have done. Incidentally, neither Gryzlov, Mironov nor Sliska turned up to hear it.

I asked Torshin to state publicly that I was opposed to the account
both in form and in substance. He did not do so, and has effectively
obliged me to go to the press. That is why I am giving this interview,
addressing the Russian public myself.

BASAYEV BLOWN TO BITS: CHECHNYA WITHOUT TERRORIST NO. 1

July 13, 2006

A long-awaited event occurred this week: according to official sources,
Terrorist No. 1, Shamil Basayev, has been killed, a man responsible for
dozens of terrorist acts and the taking of hundreds of lives. If this was,
as claimed, a successful operation by the intelligence services, they are
to be congratulated, as are we all.

There remain not a few questions in respect of the fatal explosion
in the village of Ekazhevo. Distrust of the official version is entirely
understandable: Basayev has been "killed" several times before, only
for it to be found that the claims were premature. Even more often he
has managed to slip out of what appeared to be totally inescapable situations, as during the raid on Dagestan in 1999 [suspected to have been
orchestrated by the FSB, and used as a pretext to start the Second
Chechen War] when his rabble marched out unscathed, in formation,
under the puzzled gaze of special operations soldiers watching the
procession through their telescopic sights.

Be that as it may, whether Basayev was liquidated or liquidated
himself, the bastard is no longer a player in either politics or terrorism.
We can breathe more easily, but can we really relax?

The Career of Terrorist Basayev

1991, October 5: Took part in occupation of the KGB building
in Grozny. Still a secondary figure, under Labazanov and
Gantamirov.

1991, November 9: Took part in hijacking a TU-154 passenger aircraft from Mineralnye Vody Airport. The hijackers were led by Said Ali Satuyev, a professional civil aviation pilot.

1991: Following a decision of the Confederation of Mountain Peoples of the Caucasus, supported by the Russian security agencies and, in particular, by the Central Intelligence Directorate (GRU) of the Russian Armed Forces GHQ, armed detachments of volunteers took part in combat operations in support of Abkhazia against Georgia. The detachment commanded by Shamil Basayev gained a reputation for being particularly brutal towards the civilian population.

After Abkhazia, Basayev and his rabble turned up as mercenaries on the Azerbaijan–Armenian front.

1995, June: Seizure of more than 1,600 hostages in Budyonnovsk, including 150 children. One hundred and thirty people died at the hands of Basayev and his thugs.

Autumn 1999: Apartment blocks in Moscow, Buinaksk and Volgodonsk blown up. Russian intelligence services claim the terrorists were trained through the joint efforts of Khattab and Basayev.

2002, October: Audience of the musical *Nord-Ost* and others taken hostage in Moscow.

2004, June 22: Raid on Ingushetia in which approximately 100 people died. Organised by Basayev and the current President of the unrecognised [sic] Republic of Ichkeria, Doku Umarov.

2004, August 25: Two passenger aircraft blown up with the loss of 90 lives.

And finally, the most dreadful terrorist atrocity of all, the hostage-taking at the school in Beslan on September 1, 2004.

On the night of June 9, 2006 Basayev, Russia's bin Laden, was "blown to bits," according to a press release from the FSB Directorate in

Ingushetia, in a powerful explosion in Ekazhevo. He reappeared, piecemeal, on Tuesday, July 11 when his head was sent to Nazran for one type of identification, and his artificial leg to Vladikavkaz for another.

Such are the official announcements, and if we were not talking about the iconic death of a terrorist we have been trying unsuccessfully to catch for the past 10 years, they might raise a smile. By Wednesday, July 12, however, the intelligence services were putting out completely contradictory accounts of the death of Terrorist No. 1. Basayev was an idiot dynamiter travelling in convoy from abroad in a truck full of explosives and primed detonators; alternatively, Basayev had been betrayed by someone on his own side who had taken the bait of half a million US dollars.

In tripping over themselves, they laid the foundations for future myth-making, like that which for so many years now has surrounded the death of President Djohar Dudayev. Since only those with a "need to know" have any idea where Dudayev's grave is, and because nobody else has seen him dead, many in Chechnya will tell you to this day that Djohar is alive and will return when the time is right; alternatively, that he is alive and has gone into exile with the connivance of the intelligence services; or, then again, that it was not in fact a missile that killed him but . . .

In other words, where reliable information is not provided, look out for myths. Many Chechens are saying today that this is not the end of Basayev. He too will become a legend, and tales will circulate that he has been sighted on a remote island in the Indian Ocean, or . . .

No matter what the circumstances of Basayev's death, whether he was blown up or blew himself up, the important thing is that he is dead. This baneful factor has been removed from the equation. So, what is going to happen in Chechnya now? Which resistance fighters will follow which flag? The explosion in Ekazhevo was probably welcomed by some of them who were plainly opposed to Basayev, and saw him as a black sheep who disgraced everyone. Let us not forget that the detachment of Gelayev, who was subsequently killed in Dagestan, removed itself to Georgia precisely because it didn't want to fight Basayev's way. It was a moment of truth: should the strategy of outrages like *Nord-Ost* and Beslan be continued, or should it be rejected and a policy adopted that in no circumstances should atrocities be committed against entirely innocent victims? Mid-2002 was a watershed moment when our intelligence services should have shown some intelligence, but the opportunity was missed.

Now we are in 2006, almost four years after *Nord-Ost*, and soon it will be two years since Beslan. There is a new group in Chechen society, mainly young people, who are vacillating and uncertain. They refuse categorically to wait passively for Kadyrov's brutes to come for them in the night, but were reluctant to join the fighters if that meant ending up with Basayev, when Basayev meant Beslan.

In the immediate future, the likelihood is that Basayev's followers will fall in with Doku Umarov, who has the same ideas about the terrorist character of the war from now on. The remnants of other detachments are unlikely to follow, so a flood of new recruits, who were deterred by the bloodthirsty presence of Basayev, is more than likely. What the final configuration of the separatists will be is the big question.

Time will tell. One thing, however, is already clear: until relations between Moscow and Chechnya are finally sorted out in a manner acceptable not merely to Kadyrov but to a majority of the population, the situation is unlikely to settle down. Basayev's having been blown to bits is not the decisive factor, merely part of the process.

6. Russia: A Country at Peace

As the following pieces illustrate, a recurrent theme in Anna Politkovskaya's articles is the regime's application of state resources to bolster its stranglehold on power rather than to deal with the huge and pressing problems of the population it rules.

THE TUNGUSKA METEORITE LANDED RIGHT IN THE MIDDLE OF RUSSIA, AND SO DID WE

December 25, 2000

Yielding to the desire to find a contrarian way to start the new century, our newspaper decided to leave its mark somewhere nobody has left a mark before. Apart from the Tunguska Meteorite.

On December 22, the day of the winter solstice, we arrived at the very spot which, since the demise of the USSR, has been the geographical center of the Russian Federation, the Evenki Autonomous Region. There, in the main square of the township of Tura, the capital of Evenkia, we erected a suitable monument designed by the Moscow artist, Dmitriy Krymov.

Admittedly, the square in Tura doesn't yet have a name, so if you do decide to visit it you will have to ask a passer-by where the monument to the center of Russia is. Anybody will be able to point it out, though, because everybody in Tura, apart from infants and the very ill, came to the opening ceremony. Oh, and also those who went instead to the local Palace of Culture for a concert by Dmitriy Kharatian and Alexey Buldakov. At *Novaya gazeta*'s invitation they made the more than seven-hour indirect flight from Moscow to provide a top quality celebration of the unveiling of the monument.

Ivan Bakhtin, the Deputy Governor of Evenkia, told us that even half a day before the celebrations in Tura nobody really believed the monument would be erected, or that the visitors from Moscow would arrive, or that there would be a fireworks display, and a concert, and presents.

"Why was that?"

"Because today's temperature is 48 degrees below zero, which for us is considered warm."

But now, what our readers really want to know is what the center of Russia is like. There is no escaping the fact that it is highly symbolic. What gives meaning to life here, in all its variety, is the struggle for survival. If you want to live, you need to be focused. Relax, and you die. If you want to eat, make sure you shoot plenty of game in season. If you want felt boots and a fur coat so as not to freeze, barter the pelts of bears, reindeer and sable you have killed for clothing. And never be on your own. If you are alone and you have a fall, you are dead. The world is ordered in a primitive but strict and logical manner, as befits a symbol.

We learned that it is a stone's throw from the center of Russia to the pole of cold. The snow was not just very abundant, it was all you could see. Fir and pine trees do not survive, and even birch trees eke out a dismal dwarf existence. The local taiga is exclusively larch so the larch tree should be the symbol of this symbol of Russia, ginger-red and recalcitrant, not the blond, languid birch.

There does seem to be a vast supply of land rich in diamonds, oil and gas. The trouble is that first you have to get here.

There are no cities at the center of Russia, only townships, villages and factories. There is no gas in the houses, although there is plenty underground; no water, no drains, no avenues or embankments, neither along the Podkamennaya River nor over the Nizhnyaya Tunguskaya. Both rivers flow this way and that the length and breadth of Evenkia. Nobody has thought of trying to build anything we would recognise as a respectable road. There are no railways, no metalled roads, only an all-season dirt road 14 kilometres long which links Gorny Airport and Tura. All the other "highways" are passable only in the winter. Hence the work routine of the local administration consists of just three things: firstly, keeping the winter roads in good order;

secondly, monitoring the forces of Mother Nature as she constantly destroys them; and thirdly, starting all over again. If you let your mind wander and stop monitoring the infrastructure every day, you will soon be unable to move at all. Your world will contract to the size of your own inner world and you will exist in a snowbound cell.

Who, you might ask, is capable of enduring such hardship? The answer is, only 20,000 citizens of Russia. Here, in the very heart of Russia, a meteorite fell in the early years of the departed century. It became known as the Tunguska Meteorite. And now we are here too.

HOMELESS OLD LADIES

November 11, 2004

They sit ranged along an institutional wall, old ladies who abandoned Grozny in various years and in various wars. Their coats date from the 1980s, their boots from Soviet times. Everything is worn and looks like somebody's cast-offs. Hopelessness is in their faces and there is a sense such as you find in wards for people who have been abandoned and attempted suicide. This is a meeting of "Our Home," a voluntarily run circle of 53 families which refugees of the "Russian language persuasion" from Chechnya organised for themselves. All are now of pensionable age, and what brought them together was a determination to fight the state for their legal rights, to obtain registration, official status, accommodation and pensions. We are in Moscow and it is now October 2004. For many, it is 10 years since their exodus and the start of their struggle. What success have they had?

Taisiya Tolstova is 81. She listens, sees, moves, and is altogether very active. Taisiya was wounded in the Second World War. She worked for 58 years, 34 of them as a teacher and 30 of those in Norilsk. She returned from the Far North to the capital of Chechnya where she was born, a fourth-generation Russian Groznyan. Now, three times a week, Taisiya cleans all 16 floors of an apartment block in the center of Moscow, all the stairwells and the landings in front of the lifts. She has no choice.

Her remuneration is exactly what she needs, a place to sleep, a little room for the concierges. The women are paid to be there for 24 hours, but instead go home at night, leaving the room free for Taisiya. It is a small, cramped space, into which only a narrow divan can be fitted, but you can sleep there, even if you have to take turns with your mentally disturbed son, Volodya.

Taisiya prays for the people who live in this block. They are her only hope of not sinking into living in filthy cellars. Under the rules of our amazing country, she has lost the legal right to work. She has no status, and without registration you can't have a job or any other rights. In the 10 years which have passed since she fled Grozny, having lost everything she possessed, she has received nothing from the state which might even partially compensate her losses, enable her to get her life back on the rails, and provide a future for her son.

Taisiya has a daughter who is herself a pensioner. She lives in Norilsk, but the city authorities refuse to allow old women to move there. Taisiya couldn't go there directly when she left Grozny. Apart from her daughter the old lady has two brothers of her long-dead husband living in Moscow and the Moscow Region. At their invitation she went to stay with them 10 years ago, and one did everything he could for the widow. He went to great lengths to have her registered to stay in his accommodation, but he too is far from young. His family finally questioned why they had to go to such trouble. It was the state's responsibility to look after the old lady. Of course it was, and here the old lady is now, cleaning 16 floors three times a week, with all her possessions in a mop cupboard.

"Wherever we go people scold us. 'Why have you all come back to Moscow?' they ask. But where else could I go? This is where my family were."

"Where do you eat? You don't have a hob here, or running water."

"I also look after the people who sleep in the entrance to the block. This is a big building, there are always people lying there. That is where I cook."

"Where do you wash?"

"The same place."

"And the toilet?"

"I have to ask somebody to let me in."

Ask yourself how long you would last under such conditions.

"Am I going to die under a roof of my own?" Taisiya wonders. She says to passing residents of the block where she is allowed to live, "Look, a journalist has come to see me. Tell her, does anyone have a bad word to say about me? Am I a bad person? Or quarrelsome?"

Most of the residents don't understand what she's talking about. At 81 you shouldn't really need to prove that you are not the worst member of society. At that age all you want is to be able to rest at the end of your life, on a state pension.

At the meeting of "Our Home" Wanda Voitsekhovskaya has been sitting motionless for several hours. Everybody has been talking except her. She holds her head proudly and her beautiful eyes have a firm gaze. She looks indomitable. But one to one, Wanda is nervous and much less self-possessed.

"I am homeless, an outcast and a beggar. I have no sleep, no life, no rest." Wanda has great difficulty speaking because of high blood pressure. "I had everything then: a house, a dacha, a garage, a car. In Grozny. I lived there from 1950. I was sent there when I graduated from the Kiev Engineering Institute. I worked for 38 years in the same place as a planner. My husband was crippled in the Second World War. In 1992 my daughter married a very good man and came here to Moscow. He has a room in the Komsomol Automobile Factory hostel and that's where all of us live now. My husband died in 1996. I was in a terrible state when my neighbours in Grozny saw me to the train and sent me back to my daughter. I thought it was just for a short while. I thought I would qualify for a pension."

Wanda sleeps on a divan now with her 12-year-old grandson. On the neighbouring divan is her younger grandson. It is a tiny room where you can either sleep or get up and go somewhere else. There's nowhere to sit. For someone old and ill it is intolerable. Because her age means she gets very tired, Wanda has become convinced she is just a burden on her children.

"I am very ill, facing complete immobility. I want to stay on my feet as long as I can so as not to be a trouble to anyone. I collect empty bottles to pay for medicine. Why has the state shifted its problems on to our children's shoulders? I can't understand. Why can't I be allocated my own little corner? It wasn't me who destroyed everything I had in Grozny."

Valentina Kuznetsova is frail and beautiful. She does not take off her headscarf or her coat. Her hands are clenched and her lips pursed. Valentina holds herself in so as not to burst into tears. A feverish flush blotches her cheeks but she is constantly shivering and shifting, even when sweat is pouring off the others because of the stuffiness. Chronic malnutrition is the companion of refugees. It strikes everybody regardless of their merits and Valentina, who was an engineer in Grozny, had many of those in her former life. She is 78 now. In January 1995 she and her elder sister Alexandra were dragged half alive from their cellar in Grozny by soldiers of the Ministry for Emergency Situations and sent to Moscow when it was discovered that they had relatives there. It was a perfectly reasonable course of action.

Almost ten years have passed, and throughout that time Valentina has lived in Moscow with her bedridden 80-year-old sister in the utility room of School No. 1142.

"Of course the conditions are a nightmare," says Headmaster Iosif Protas. "Valentina at first worked as the school caretaker, but then we were ordered to employ private security firms. We couldn't just throw them out on to the street. My conscience wouldn't allow that. The old ladies have been taken in by their nephew now. He is off travelling somewhere and his apartment will be free for a time. They have left us, but their accommodation problem is no nearer a solution. The authorities won't allocate them anything. I don't understand how they can behave like that."

They can behave like that very easily. The legal situation of elderly Russian refugees from Chechnya is as follows: under the law they are "internally displaced persons." That status is awarded for only five years and some of the old ladies gained it. They fought to get it from the Migration Service, which in the last decade has been reorganised several times. Refugees with that status at least had the right to move unhindered around Moscow and to receive free medical care. Others were less fortunate: the migration officials firmly refused it to these guiltless victims.

When the five years came to an end, those with the status found themselves no better off than those without. In the eyes of the Migration Service they had no rights whatsoever. So, five years is as long as the state is prepared to take any responsibility for fulfilling its obligations towards citizens who have lost everything through the state's own actions. For five years the state is obliged to look after internally displaced persons, to provide accommodation, a welfare payment and health insurance. This supposedly gives them time to build a new life, to start afresh after they have irretrievably lost what they had.

Our state has simply cheated the "internally displaced persons" from Chechnya. It has strung them along for five years and provided them with nothing. The Migration Service announced that its assistance was time-limited and when that expired it would divest itself of all responsibility for them.

Who would dispute that the five-year rule is reasonable for young and middle-aged people who can be expected to find work and look after themselves? But what about those in their seventies and eighties? The disabled? How are they supposed to make a fresh start?

You may wonder why this report is confined only to Russian refugees from Grozny rather than including everybody who was forced to leave the zone of this never-ending "anti-terrorist operation" engulfing their beloved city.

It is because Chechen families, even if they themselves are living in poverty, will never fail to support their relatives. Such is the way they behave, and you simply will not find an 81-year-old Chechen lady scrubbing floors on 16 storeys. But Russian old ladies do. What is to be done? How is this situation to be resolved, quickly and effectively? The old ladies cannot wait.

In "Our Home" there are 53 families. These are the very poorest of all the homeless, people with no prospects. It is senseless to hope that resources from Russia's super-abundant "proficit" budget are going to come their way. The officials would rather die than do without their kickbacks.

They must pin their hopes on the world of "socially aware business," in favor of which [pro-Putin oligarch] Vladimir Potanin recently
spoke so feelingly on television. The President bears personal responsibility for what is happening in Chechnya and for all its consequences,
so let the Presidential Commission on Human Rights intercede for
them with business. The Commission's members include illustrious
representatives of civil society like Svetlana Gannushkina, the Head of
Citizen's Aid, the most active voluntary committee in Russia defending
refugees; and also Ludmila Alexeyeva, head of the Moscow Helsinki
Group. The President himself must be persuaded to support their
petition by its Chairwoman, Ella Pamfilova. Fifty-three Moscow busi-
nesses should each buy an apartment, one for each family. They
shouldn't find that too difficult.

The meeting of "Our Home" dispersed. "The state wants to wait for
us all to die so as not to have to spend money on us. I'm quite sure
of that," Zoya Markaryants remarks in parting. A former education-
alist, her house in the center of Grozny suffered a direct hit. With the
destruction of her home she lost everything she had, and now she is
just another refugee from the war.

A HOSTAGE OF THE RUSSIAN FEDERATION

September 8, 2005

Anybody who watches the national Russian television channels saw
the item. It was claimed that Adam Chitayev, a former resistance fighter
with a federal warrant out for his arrest, had been detained in Ust-
Ilimsk, Irkutsk Province. He was supposedly guilty of abducting both
Russian servicemen and members of international missions, and was
said to have been masquerading as a schoolteacher of English.

Russia has long been trained to believe this sort of thing. If a Chechen
has been arrested, that's as it should be, or if it's not quite as it should
be, then it's better to be safe than sorry. Nobody gave a damn about
Chitayev. Hundreds of criminal cases relating to so-called international

terrorism are cooked up like Siberian pelmeni dumplings the length and breadth of the country, on the principle of the more the merrier, and anyway you can't tell the innocent from the guilty. Naturally, the arrest of some Chitayev or other was regarded as only proper, as what the law enforcement agencies are there for. But only by anybody who doesn't know who Adam Chitayev is and, more broadly, who the Chitayev brothers are. In Strasbourg an increasing number of people do know. That, in fact, is where the answer is to be found as to why a man who was not hiding from anybody was suddenly arrested in faraway Ust-Ilimsk, only for it to be announced to the whole of Russia that he had been hiding.

The Chitayevs are appellants in *Strasbourg* v. *the Russian Federation*. What is more, they have almost won. This summer the procedure of having a case considered by the European Court of Human Rights, which takes many years, ended in an interim victory, a so-called "Decision on the Admissibility of Appeal No. 59334/00."

The story of the Chitayev family is one to which *Novaya gazeta* has returned several times. Their fate was not unusual by Chechen standards in 2000. It befell many people, but very few decided to seek redress through the courts.

Arbi, born in 1964, was an engineer who had always lived in Grozny. Adam, born in 1967, was a schoolteacher. Like many Chechens he lived in Kazakhstan for a long time before returning to Chechnya in 1999, immediately before the war. Together with his wife and two small children he moved in with his brother in Grozny. "In autumn 1999 armed clashes began in Chechnya between Russian troops and Chechen rebels," the European Court ruling reads, and, in accordance with the rules of Strasbourg, it is is based on documentation which confirms every word. "Grozny and its suburbs were the target of large-scale attacks by Russian soldiers."

Arbi's flat in Grozny was destroyed (as is confirmed by a certificate, attached to the case files in Strasbourg, from one of the apartment management boards in Grozny). "The plaintiffs, together with their families and possessions, moved to their father's house in Achkhoy Martan. On January 15, 2000, members of the Interior Affairs Temporary Office (temporarily occupied by militiamen from Voronezh Province) conducted a search of the plaintiffs' house. They took with them a new cordless telephone in its packaging."

On January 18, one of the Chitayevs went to complain to the Interior Affairs Office and to demand the return of the telephone. It actually was returned, but on April 12 retribution followed. There was another search and more looting, but also an arrest, followed by yet more looting. Things went from bad to worse, despite the fact that everything of any interest had already been stolen: a video, a printer, televisions, a computer, a heater, and "two files of documents." Interestingly enough, a list of the stolen goods was provided to Strasbourg over the signature of one Vlasenko, an officer of the Achkhoy Martan Interior Affairs Temporary Office.

Arbi and Adam were arrested. On April 14 their father, Salaudi, went to find out what had happened to his sons and was himself arrested, officially for violation of the curfew. He was released five days later. The brothers were held in the Interior Affairs Office for 17 days.

They were fettered to a chair by their handcuffs and beaten. Various parts of the body, including their fingertips and ears, were subjected to electric shocks; their arms were twisted; they were beaten with rubber truncheons and plastic bottles full of water; they were suffocated using adhesive tape, polythene bags and gas masks; dogs were set upon them; and pieces of skin were torn from them using pliers. Plaintiff No. 1 (Arbi Chitayev) had a gas mask put on his head which was pumped full of cigarette smoke. Plaintiff No. 2 (Adam Chitayev) was brought into a room and told he must confess to being a resistance fighter and taking part in kidnappings. When Plaintiff No. 2 refused to sign the confession, he was gagged with tape and beaten on the back and sexual organs. Simultaneously, another person pointed a rifle at him and threatened to shoot him if he moved.

On April 28 the Chitayevs, along with others detained in the Office, were taken away blindfolded and told that they were going to be shot.

In fact they were dropped off at the Chernokozovo pre-trial detention facility where

> They were forced to run to an interrogation room, bending down and with their hands on their heads while the guards beat them on the back. In the interrogation room were an iron table and chair and there was a hook on the wall. They were kicked, and beaten with rifle butts and hammers on various parts of the body, concentrating on their kneecaps; straitjackets were put on them which were attached to the hook so that they were hanging from it, and beaten. Their fingers and toes were crushed using hammers and door jambs; their hands and feet were tied together behind their backs (the "sparrow" position) ... The detainees were not allowed to pray under threat of further beatings.

The Chitayevs were lucky. They emerged from Chernokozovo in October 2000, having passed through all the circles of hell which are customary there but at least they were alive. They were outraged by their illegal arrest and torture, which made them rare among survivors of Chernokozovo, and this in itself testifies to their firm belief that the Russian regime had no grounds whatsoever for impugning them. The Chitayevs were not and never had been members of the Chechen resistance. It also mattered that they are educated, serious, socially active and progressive. Their indignation took them first to the Russian legal institutions – the Prosecutor's Office and the courts – and then, when they were unable to raise any interest in their sufferings there, on to Strasbourg. Arbi and Adam Chitayev lodged official complaints, and Arbi took the difficult decision to emigrate from Russia, seeing no possibility of continuing to live in a country where such humiliations were possible. We met him abroad, where he was not enjoying exile and finding it difficult to make a living, but at least feeling safe. Four years on, remembering the details of his months of detention as he looked out of the window at life in Europe, he was shaking as if he had

Parkinson's disease. Adam, however, decided to stay, moved to Siberia, and got a teaching job. In Strasbourg, meanwhile, the case, with the slowness which seems to be essential, edged up the queue of many thousands of appeals of his suffering compatriots, towards examination.

The Chitayev brothers knew that Chechen appellants to Strasbourg were in a uniquely dangerous situation. Before hearing any verdict, very many of them would be murdered by "masked members of un-identified security agencies wearing combat fatigues," as they are routinely described.

The Chitayevs did not, however, withdraw their appeal. On the contrary, they responded conscientiously to every inquiry from the European Court of Human Rights, wrote supplementary explana-tions, and were very active. Neither did the Russian state authorities leave them in peace. They were threatened with criminal cases, arrests and retaliation. The more vigorously the Chitayevs defended them-selves, the greater the pressure which was brought to bear on them.

On June 30, 2005 their case was finally considered in Strasbourg. You read the court record with a sense that something is missing. Everything the Chitayevs allege has documentary confirmation: all our government's replies to inquiries from the Court of Human Rights about the degrading treatment of the Chitayevs are bald, unsubstantiated assertions, mere fantasy along the following lines: "On April 12 when the plaintiffs' house was inspected eight military greatcoats and four military jackets were found ... video recordings of interviews with Shamil Basayev, a videotape of the documentary film *Nokhcho Chechnya: Day of Freedom*, photographs of Arbi Chitayev with a rifle."

The suggestion is that here was a hotbed of resistance fighters and abductors of soldiers, never mind that the greatcoats belonged to the Chitayev brothers themselves, of whom there are four; or indeed that these are Soviet-era military greatcoats dating back to the days when the brothers were serving in the Soviet Army.

The result of this approach does not reflect well on Russia: a "decision on admissibility" is effectively a ruling in favor of someone whose appeal has been accepted for consideration. The basis and approach of the future verdict is already evident in the decision on admissibility, as is obvious in the Chitayevs' case. The Chitayevs will win their case against the Russian Federation because it has failed to provide any justification either for their arrest or for the looting of their home.

Every stage of the deliberations in Strasbourg has been followed by the Russian authorities, indeed an official government representative has been present at every hearing, including the last one on June 30. While they still had time, before the final verdict, the regime resuscitated their criminal case against Adam, Arbi being beyond their reach. Here we again find the eight military greatcoats and tape of an interview with Shamil Basayev. A warrant was issued for Adam's arrest and locating him was not difficult as he was not hiding, indeed living at his officially registered address. Not merely a law-abiding citizen, but one tenaciously determined to have the law respected, Adam was arrested and sent under convoy to Chechnya.

This is barefaced retaliation for his appeal to Strasbourg, the state's attempt to get even with someone who is not prepared to behave like a sheep.

KHODORKOVSKY AND THE PRISONERS AND STAFF OF PENAL COLONY 14/10 MAY BE IN DANGER

April 3, 2006

People divide into those who believe in conspiracies and those who don't. I belong to the latter category. Conspiracy stories strike me as dull, whether they are about the violent seizure of power, or the Count of Monte Cristo. The weird tangles produced by real life are a thousand times more dramatic.

I have before me a document which, however, has not come *Novaya gazeta*'s way by chance. It was brought here by its author, a self-assured individual with a military bearing. He produced his identification documents, his passport, certificate of graduation from a military college, and certificate of release from a place of detention.

"In February this year," the document reads, "I agreed to take part in a certain operation. The location was Krasnokamensk in Chita Province. Its nature was as follows:

"During the night a group of six persons in two armoured vehicles, having rammed through the fencing surrounding Institution 14/10, were to break into the compound of the labor camp. Having broken through to the sector indicated by the group's Commanding Officer, they were to adopt a defensive position and retain it for five minutes. After this they were to leave by the same route, abandoning the vehicles after a few kilometres and disappearing.

"The rendezvous was to be on April 20 in Khudzhand, Tajikistan. There all the participants would receive genuine passports as citizens of Tajikistan and, in the guise of seasonal workers, would be transported overland to the place of the planned events. They would be registered and prepared for the operation approximately 100–150 kilometres from Krasnokamensk. All equipment essential for conducting the operation would be prepared by another group functioning independently. The group would move out at the very last moment. The precise destination was known only to two of six men, myself and the group's Commanding Officer. The others were operating blind and would receive material recompense. Now, concerning the reasons why I am appealing to you. My principled belief is that MBK has the basic right to take decisions concerning his own destiny. In reaching my decision on February 10 to participate I was certain that he was behind this operation. Now I am no longer 100 per cent certain of that."

Obviously MBK is the imprisoned ex-oligarch Mikhail Khodorkovsky, and Krasnokamensk is a town on the outskirts of which Penal Colony 14/10 is located, where he is imprisoned.

If I understand correctly, the document describes a plan to organise an enforced "escape." There could be only one outcome of any such attempted departure from the colony for Khodorkovsky (and not only for him): a bullet. "Shot while attempting to escape during a break-out planned by members of the Yukos oil company organised crime group." And that would be the end of the "Decembrist Exile" soap opera with its endless court cases on every pretext, its indefatigable lawyers, its Open Russia Foundation, its chemicals and destinies, its discussion of the right to scholarly activity in prison camps, the visits widely reported in the press, and so forth. The soap opera would have a stop put to it, and no doubt Khodorkovsky's colleague, Leonid Nevzlin, would finally be extradited from Israel. Is all this credible? Entirely.

Then again, perhaps it is all complete nonsense, the lunacy of an individual citizen. Such things happen. But what if it isn't? There could be yet another possible outcome: a prison uprising might appear to have happened, and who would be the ringleader of a riot in 14/10? Naturally, a person who aspired, or so the Kremlin claims, to great power. They would have been quite right to detain him in punishment cells, and indeed to have liquidated the rioter.

There are stories, as every journalist knows, which it is better to publish than keep to yourself. It is not beyond the bounds of possibility that this may save somebody's life. If we are to give credence to the plan outlined above and our informant's explanations, then the lives of prisoners in Corrective Labor Camp 14/10, of Khodorkovsky, and also of officers staffing the colony are presently under threat.

Should a newspaper report the probability of a deadly threat to somebody? Undoubtedly, in order to avert a possible tragedy. The enforced "escape," no matter who was preparing it or for what purpose, is hardly in Khodorkovsky's interests. The attempt to implement the escape might lead to the death of other prisoners and officers of the camp, the more so because the "seasonal workers" for the "breakthrough group" proved on closer inspection to be former military men, some of them ex-KGB officers, with a less than unblemished reputation. Some, indeed, had served prison sentences.

And what if it is a complete hoax, and *Novaya gazeta* is merely being implicated in an imaginary plot? We will sigh with relief, and thank God it was nothing more serious. And will ponder a fact which is in any case obvious: that in the expanses of the former USSR the spinners of government PR have a place for retired officers with a prison record. Good old USSR.

AN ALLEGED PARTICIPANT IN A PLANNED ATTACK ON KHODORKOVSKY'S PENAL COLONY HAS BEEN FOUND GUILTY

In the Basmanny Court in Moscow sentence has been passed in the case of Vladimir Zelensky. Zelensky informed *Novaya gazeta*'s columnist, Anna Politkovskaya, of a supposedly imminent attack on the penal colony in which Mikhail Khodorkovsky, the former head of the Yukos oil company, is imprisoned. Zelensky was sentenced to three years in a strict-regime corrective labor colony for "knowingly communicating false information about an act of terrorism."

This bizarre episode has amazed Zelensky's lawyer and other participants in the trial, and left numerous questions unanswered. Zelensky himself refused to give evidence, readily pleaded guilty, and asked only that the trial should be over and done with as quickly as possible.

What Zelensky actually said before his arrest is described in Anna Politkovskaya's article. Zelensky phoned Anna Politkovskaya in spring this year, saying he trusted only her and had important information relating to Khodorkovsky. He gave her a note about the alleged plot to force Khodorkovsky to "escape."

Zelensky named a certain Babakov as the organiser of the plot, a former agent of the Tajikistan KGB, and insistently asked for a meeting to be arranged between him (Zelensky) and Khodorkovsky's relatives or some of his former colleagues, like Leonid Nevzlin.

The tale had the air of a hoax or complete nonsense, but a subsequent psychiatric examination of Zelensky revealed no mental problems. When arrested in Chita he was found indeed to have a fake passport in the name of a citizen of Tajikistan which he had been using to cross the border and also a plan detailing the attack on the colony.

A native of Sochi, Krasnodar District, Vladimir Zelensky is a former soldier who graduated from the Saratov Higher Military Command

Academy of Chemical Warfare Defence. He had been sentenced to six years in jail by a Novosibirsk court for causing grievous bodily harm but was released on parole in August 2004 with almost three years of his sentence suspended, which the Basmanny Court has now re-imposed. He confessed unconditionally to the charge of knowingly communicating false information about an act of terrorism.

Zelensky refused to choose a defence lawyer and the court appointed Anatoliy Avilov, Chairman of the Basmanny Court in 1992–5, to act for him. Avilov finds the case puzzling. He suggests that Zelensky's story was so implausible from the outset that no crime was committed. Neither can he understand why Zelensky should have admitted the charge before he had even been formally identified, hence before it was clear whether the man who came to *Novaya gazeta*'s offices was in fact him or a different person with a passport in his name.

"It is all very strange," Avilov says. "Anyone making a knowingly false statement will usually try to stay out of sight, but Zelensky came forward. Why he should have done that is something only he knows, but I believe it is entirely possible that somebody imperson-ated him."

A number of curious coincidences invite us to think this has been a deliberate dirty trick. After Zelensky came to the newspaper with his story, two public statements were made: the first by a Deputy of Zhirinovsky's far-right Liberal-Democratic Party, who informed the press that *Novaya gazeta* was in possession of important information which it was withholding from the law enforcement agencies. The second, by a prominent political commentator, also accused the editors of with-holding information about an imminent crime.

These speakers made their declarations very categorically and with great aplomb, unaware that by then we had passed all the information to the relevant agencies.

Following Vladimir Zelensky's sentencing on the basis of these very strange happenings, we have a number of questions:

1. Why would a man who had not been identified and who could have pleaded not guilty completely accept the charge, decline a

lawyer, and wish to return to a strict-regime labor colony from which he had only recently been released?

2. Where would a former soldier, unemployed and only recently released from prison, have found the money to travel around the country; and how did he come by a false passport in the name of a citizen of Tajikistan of such high quality as to enable him to pass freely through border controls?

3. Is not the conclusion of this case against Zelensky a ploy designed to preclude a deeper investigation and to conceal the identity of those behind this failed dirty trick?

[On October 11, 2006 Anna Politkovskaya was to have given evidence in court in relation to the Zelensky case, either confirming or not confirming the identity of the man in the dock.]

7. Planet Earth: The World Beyond Russia

Anna Politkovskaya did not only criticize the Putin regime and Russia's "security forces"; she was not uncritical of the West. Nevertheless, she admired civilised and enlightened attitudes when she encountered them there, and hoped they might be transplanted.

THE PRINCIPLE OF DENMARK: A PRISON WHERE THEY DON'T BEAT BUT RESPECT THEIR PRISONERS

February 1, 2001

It is generally accepted that we Russians do not like ourselves much. Clear proof of this is the appalling state of our 195 pre-trial detention facilities in prisons. For the second year in succession the inspectors of the Council of Europe have described conditions in these as tantamount to torture. Out of a total of over one million people in detention, almost 300,000 are awaiting verdicts in pre-trial detention facilities and prisons. According to Oleg Mironov, the Human Rights Ombudsman of the Russian Federation, 85,000 of these have no place to sleep (the facilities and prisons are 226.3 per cent over capacity), more than 90,000 are suffering from an active form of tuberculosis, and more than 5,000 are HIV-positive. Nor are prisoners given an easy time by their warders: in 1999, 3,583 officers in the penal system were punished for violations of the law and 106 were charged with crimes committed in the course of their duties. Their activities directly affect almost two million people, since that is the number of prisoners who each year pass through Russia's pre-trial detention facilities, almost twice the number of people serving a sentence imposed by a court. The main reason for this is unjustified arrest, which remains the usual means of fighting crime; as a result every fifth man in Russia has experienced prison. In 1999, 263,645 complaints were received by the Prosecutor's Office about the methods of investigation and questioning used by members of the Interior Ministry, and one in four was upheld. Seventy per cent of complaints about court verdicts received in 1999 by the Human Rights Ombudsman contain claims that violence was used to obtain testimony during interrogation or preliminary investigation, and that this led to the imposition of an unjust sentence.

Novaya gazeta has discovered, however, that there are prisons in this world where Russians are liked, which is not the case in our homeland; where the warders look forward to seeing us, and will do their utmost to help us with any problems. These prisons are in Denmark, an entirely democratic, modern kingdom, and the inspectors of the Council of Europe deem them satisfactory.

"Personally I like Russians very much." Warder Ani, a large Danish lady with a stylish shock of fair Baltic hair, happily tells me about herself and her world. Admittedly, she paces to and fro out of habit with the military deportment of someone accustomed to discipline, her hands clasped behind her back. "We don't have to tell your people anything twice. They immediately carry out all instructions. They don't go on about their rights. They aren't picky about their food. They are happy to work."

Ani is in charge of the first floor of the pre-trial facility, here known by the old-fashioned name of "The Bridewell," in the coastal town of Esbjerg. She energetically demonstrates her work to me, and I can see that this is also the way she does it. She explains that the matter of gender equality is not left to resolve itself in Danish prisons, and that there is a strict quota established by the Ministry of Justice. In closed prisons and pre-trial facilities not less than 45 per cent of the staff should be female. This is believed to foster gentler attitudes and to create a favorable atmosphere. In open prisons the quota is 30 per cent. The Bridewell in Esbjerg is a closed prison, which means that the inmates are awaiting a court sentence or serving brief periods of less than six months' detention. The entrance doors are firmly locked and you can't go out for a stroll in the town. We will come to Danish open prisons shortly. Meanwhile, Ani continues:

"As soon as we are brought a Russian who has been detained on a court order, we give him a book in Russian to keep. The book's title is *A Guide to Serving Custodial Sentences*. It describes all the minor details of life, the law, and the prisoner's responsibilities."

While we are talking somebody leans against the wall outside cell No. 6, and immediately an indignant-looking prisoner emerges. They had accidentally leaned against the light switch for his cell. No. 6 puts it back on and silently goes in again.

"I expect we stopped him reading," Ani comments. "Many of our inmates are highly strung, which is understandable. Here is our billiards room to help them relax. Here is the gym. Unfortunately the prisoner currently using it has asked not to be disturbed, so we can't view it. We shall have to wait until he finishes. Here is the exercise yard. Here is a special room for drug addicts suffering withdrawal symptoms, and also for violent alcoholics or mentally ill people undergoing a crisis. It has a bed with restraining straps. There are no spyholes in the doors of the cells, and surveillance is forbidden. There is clean linen on all the beds. Each has its own washbasin. They have to ask to go to the toilet. A fridge? Of course, but you have to bring your own television. There are aerial sockets all over the place. Any more questions?"

Ani, for all her evident good-heartedness, has the cold eyes typical of a screw. She is strict and direct and is, ultimately, a warder, but in the course of our conversation I start having doubts. Whose side is she on? Whose rights is she defending? Is it not the rights of her own prisoners? The first, obvious comment which occurs to anybody used to living not in Denmark but in, say, Moscow, is, "But for heaven's sake, this is a holiday home, not a prison!"

"I don't agree. We have strict rules. We are not an open prison. Everybody here is obliged to work daily in the workshops. If you are in prison you have to work all right." Ani has an iron Danish logic, and a similar manner of social interaction. Nuances, such as her implication that people do not have to work in the world outside prison, completely escape her. "The staff are required to find work for the prisoners. We talk to companies and point out the benefits. The prison workforce is, after all, cheaper."

Together, Ani and I leaf through the *Guide to Serving* . . . She is clearly proud of it, and indeed of the entire Danish penitentiary system. The chapters are headed, "Free Time," "Dental Treatment," "Letters." Finally we come to the icing on the cake: "If you have difficulty reading, please report this to the staff who will help you to record your letter on a tape recorder." And in the chapter on "Religion": "If your religion forbids you to work at a particular time, you will be excused from working at this time." Or in "Visitors": "If you have no family members or friends to visit you, you can ask the staff to arrange for you to meet members of the Society of Prisoners' Friends. You may meet representatives of the press."

Well, that's enough, indeed too much. I give up! It is only too obvious why Russians are so well behaved here, like children from a good family, and why nobody tries to escape. The Esbjerg Bridewell not only looks from the outside like the better sort of Russian school, but inside its cheery navy and light blue colors, its dinners, billiards and facilities would be the envy of many a Russian kindergarten. And to top it all, they understand that the most important thing to show a prisoner is that, no matter what happened in the past, they are still a human being and should never forget it. What Russian would be unmoved if someone told him, "We know that you are not shit"?

Ani's boss comes to help her out, as she is increasingly nonplussed as to why we are so amazed by what she is showing us of life in a Danish prison. The senior official in the Bridewell is the District Chief of Police, Jørgen Ilum, a man who looks like a highly paid and very established lawyer and not in the slightest like a provincial militia chief. Jørgen, we are pleased to find, is not fazed by anything. He is a professional and ponders long and deeply, listening attentively to our uniquely Russian questions.

"Do investigators in Denmark torture the accused to extract testimony?"

This admittedly causes some consternation, followed by a lengthy discussion we can't understand between Mr Ilum and the Deputy Chief of Police, Sten Bolund. Sten is wearing a modish, grey, regally elegant suit with a sparkle in the cloth, set off with a bright super-modern tie. They seem genuinely unable to understand how such a question can arise if the investigators' salaries are paid by taxpayers. They finally reply, "No."

"When was a policeman last found guilty of brutality in Denmark?"

Again consternation, and another long discussion in Danish, this time bringing in Nils Hedegger, Head of the Esbjerg Police Association, their trade union. Trade union representatives are required to be present in every police station. The three of them reply that in 1993 there was a complaint against two policemen in the neighbouring district. A man in a bar (the plaintiff) had been behaving aggressively, others in the bar asked for him to be removed and the owner called the police. The aggressive man considered that he had been removed too effectively. The district court found against the policemen but the appeal court acquitted them on the grounds that the force used was justified in order to protect the interests of the other patrons of the bar.

"But we really can't remember any claims of brutal behaviour during an investigation," all three confirmed. As both Jørgen and Sten are pushing 50 and Nils is about 40, their collective professional memory must go back at least a couple of decades.

"What are the criteria for assessing your work?"

The policemen smile with relief and start telling us about things which are as clear to them as the sea and the sun. Every three years there is a public opinion poll in Denmark and citizens are invited to say whether they feel safe in their homes, secure in the streets, and whether they find the police courteous, neatly dressed and well trained.

The survey is their performance assessment. If the results are bad the Chief of Police will be replaced and some officers sent for additional training, while others might be fired. There are no targets for solving a set percentage of crimes, statistics which in Russia have to be inflated by fair means or foul and result in such painfully familiar dialogue as, "Confess, you bastard, that you murdered . . . , stole . . . , fenced . . . , or else . . ."

In another, less direct survey the population are asked which of the public sector employees, paid from their taxes, they rate most highly: doctors, teachers, municipal bus drivers or policemen?

"In recent years," Mr Ilum informs us proudly, "policemen have come first."

The police are subject to sanctions if they work too slowly. At the present time, for example, Danish society is making a concerted effort to eradicate violence on the principle that, while stealing is of course bad, physical violence is wholly unacceptable. The Danish Parliament has decided that the police must give priority to investigating violent crime, and such cases must be brought to court within 30 days. If the police fail to meet the deadline, the suspect will receive a reduced sentence even if subsequently found guilty.

"You're kidding?"

"The public require us to work very quickly," Chief of Police Ilum adds.

"And do you often have to release criminals on these grounds? For failure to produce the evidence in time?"

"Occasionally." Sten Bolund, the Deputy Chief of Police, spreads his hands. "But that is our problem. We are held responsible, and the democratically approved laws are not tampered with."

Travelling on from Esbjerg, you reach the village of Skærbæk. You can enter the village just like any other, although it also hosts the Renbæk Regional Open Prison with 110 inmates and 62 staff. It comprises a group of cottages (cells of a sort), a small shop (the prison store), workshops, a byre, a football field, a golf course and a bus stop. Anybody at all can come here. A wife? A girlfriend? Yes – every day if they like, if you have finished your work. There are no fences or bars here. The only restriction on your freedom is that the houses – ordinary, cosy Scandinavian caravans – are locked at 2200 hours, and unlocked at 0700 by a supervisor who stays overnight with the prisoners. If you are not back by 2200 hours, that counts as an escape attempt. Nobody, however, will go running to look for you. This is considered to be an area of your personal responsibility, and nobody else's. If you run away, when you are caught you will be transferred to a closed prison, where you will not be free again for a long time and will be allowed visits only once a week. And your sentence will be extended. You will lose the football, the golf, the privilege of personal responsibility and your subsistence allowance. In the open prison you have to feed yourself; each prisoner is allotted 40 kroner a day [£5] and has to buy food, prepare it, clear up and wash up in the kitchen of his little house. The logic behind Danish open prisons is that everything has to be worked for. Is that sensible? Yes. After all, you are not being sent on holiday for committing a robbery.

But here is the Governor of Renbæk, a pink-cheeked giant called Eric Pedersen. It is difficult to distinguish him from the prisoners walking through the village as none of them wear a uniform. The Governor invites us into the conference room, lights candles on the table, and, offering tea and coffee, tells us about his prisoners so that we should be under no illusions: the people walking these streets, playing football and tennis, are genuine criminals.

"The man who was happily playing table tennis when we went past murdered his wife. Fifteen per cent of the prisoners here are in prison for sexual crimes, 25 per cent for violence, and only 25 per cent for robbery."

"Then isn't this rather too soft? Perhaps they really are a danger to society and should be isolated?"

"What would be the sense of that? And what should be done with them afterwards, after they had served their time? Work is an obligatory part of being here. Or study, if you don't already have secondary education. Studying in the classrooms is considered equivalent to working in the prison workshops. We regard this as an attempt at re-education."

So much for Hamlet and "Denmark's a prison." Under the pressure of total democracy, prison, let alone the entire kingdom, resembles anything on earth before it resembles a prison.

Finally, we Russians are constantly hankering after being admitted to Europe. Not in a geographical sense, but as a fully valid European state in the Strasbourg sense. We talk and write a lot about this admirable ambition, and occasionally even fantasise that we are already there. However, it is time now to seek not just the forms but also the content, and that means we need to address our total lack of due legal process, and raise our game to the level of Denmark! To the level of Renbæk, of the gentlemanly Chief of Police, and of the Esbjerg Bridewell where they wholeheartedly like Russians.

PS. This article was prepared with the support of the International Helsinki Federation for Human Rights.

THE SECRET OF CLARIDGE'S. WHAT DID THE PRIME MINISTER OF GREAT BRITAIN AND *NOVAYA GAZETA*'S COLUMNIST TALK ABOUT OVER LUNCH?

May 14, 2001

London, April 30, 2001. The city was unwelcoming. People waiting for spring were still faced with driving rain, a cold, bitter wind, a never-ending twilight, an autumn that couldn't be shaken off despite the May tulips lining the avenues in the park.

The weather was a fitting background to the task I had set myself: having flown to the British capital, how was I to get the answer to a question I wanted to ask Tony Blair, Prime Minister of this influential island kingdom? Why, for some time now, has he been on such good terms with President Putin? What are the qualities in Putin he finds so appealing?

Any Russian journalist knows that to get an interview with a head of government you need the patience of a saint. In Moscow, miracles do not happen – such is the nature of the Kremlin – but in London on the morning of April 30 I received a personal invitation to the traditional annual lunch of the London Press Club, founded in 1882, with the Prime Minister of Great Britain. Remarkably, I had not made a huge effort to get this invitation. I was just handed it. For 12.30 at Claridge's, a grand old London hotel. So why not go?

The miracles did not end there, at least in the view of this citizen of the Russian Federation. At 12:20 there was nobody at the entrance to Claridge's other than an elderly commissionaire wearing a heavy grey wool uniform and a high Dickensian hat. It is customary for the commissionaires of very expensive London hotels to be grey-haired elderly gentleman who would have been retired long ago in Russia.

The commissionaire opened the door of my taxi and suggested that, if I was coming for the lunch with the Prime Minister, I would find it more convenient to use a different nearby door. I knew what he was up to. He was surreptitiously directing me to a queue where the British security services would filter would-be guests. They have their own, Irish, terrorists to worry about, after all.

So I marched through the main entrance, and soon realized I had got it wrong. All the aged commissionaire had wanted was to show me a shorter and more convenient route to the Prime Minister. I returned specially to my starting point to check and, while I was at it, looked around to see which rooftops the snipers were on.

There were none. Neither were there any lantern-jawed, shaven-headed security guards with searching scowls, or the bleeping metal-detector frames through which anyone in Russia is obliged to pass if they are likely to be within a kilometre of anywhere the President might show up.

At 12:45 Tony Blair arrived. At 12:50 the gong sounded for lunch. At 2:00 p.m. promptly we took our seats. My table was next to the Prime Minister's. We tucked in to the starter, duck in aspic with milk sauce. Not bad but, to be honest, not that special either. Mr Blair was chasing it across his large plate, just like me.

The diners got on with their duck, and the gentlemen, all of them what in Russia we would call "directors of the media," made no attempt to disturb the Prime Minister's meal. Nobody ran up to him to ask questions while he was pretending to enjoy the starter.

At 13:19 Dennis Griffiths, the Chairman of the London Press Club, introduced Tony Blair to the guests and invited him to speak. What he had to say was intriguing, but for the most part consisted of declaring his love for the press and joking about the fact that he was wearing spectacles for the first time in his life.

A ripple of laughter ran over the tables and people clapped.

At 13.35, while Blair was still speaking from an improvised podium, orderly rows of waiters glided into the room bearing enormous plates. This was the main dish. Everybody got the same: a small piece of extremely tender braised or boiled pink salmon, with three tiny potatoes, a couple of sprigs of sweet basil, and a modest pile of kidney beans.

Blair, who as everybody knows recently had a fourth child, sat down and set about his salmon in exactly the way the hard-up father of four children would in Russia. The Prime Minister got through his diminutive piece of pink fish rapidly and with obvious relish.

He was now free, and I mounted my attack. The path to him was straight and clear, obstructed only by the remains of the first course and Blair's press secretary, Alistair Campbell, a former popular columnist of one of the London newspapers. Alistair, however, was eating his fish, and everything was in place.

The response of the Prime Minister of Great Britain to my inquiry regarding the nature of his affection for Putin was brief but comprehensive. He replied, "It's my job as Prime Minister to like Mr Putin." And that was that. What more was to be said? The chef's job is to cook the fish; the doctor's job is to remove an appendix; the job of one head of state is to demonstrate how much he likes another head of state. It's as simple as that.

At 14.10 speeches by members of the Press Club began and continued until 14.45. Blair listened politely. At 14.50 he quietly left, as had been previously announced in the program. There were no standing ovations or elaborate farewells. It was all very understated and British.

At this point dessert was brought in: tea or coffee and a piece of chocolate praline gâteau with coffee-flavoured custard. The Prime Minister was leaving but turned to the tables one last time. He glanced sadly at the unattainable plates of gâteau which the waiters, seemingly oblivious to the head of their government, were carrying past.

Everybody has a job to do, and nobody should try to stop them.

That really is the British attitude. If a waiter is bringing diners their gâteau you get out of his way, even if you are the Prime Minister.

WHO IN EUROPE WILL TAKE RESPONSIBILITY FOR A WAR IN EUROPE?

August 16, 2001

Here we are, almost at the furthest end of the Old World. A very high bank over a brooding black Norwegian fjord, and a small township climbing up this fjord cliff. It is small, self-contained, wonderful, and feels rather carefree. It is called Molde. Molde does not trifle with lakes or seas; what dominates here is the mighty Atlantic Ocean itself. You could get in a boat and sail to America – the whole world is on your doorstep. Within the borders of Russia few people are aware of the existence of Molde.

Molde, however, is not entirely what it seems. There are people in this town whose whole lives were turned upside down by all that has been going on in Russia.

High above the fjord is the town cemetery, a neat, quiet, sorrowful place, and as unnerving as any cemetery where life meets death irrevocably, leaving only a gravestone in place of a once living, rebellious human soul. I heap red roses on the earth around a severe, grey Scandinavian stone which, at the cemetery's very highest point, looks out towards the ocean. Facing the infinity of the Atlantic, the words chiselled into the stone read, "Død Tsjetsjenia. 17.12.1996."

That means, "Died in Chechnya." Ingeborg Foss, a 42-year-old Norwegian nurse who lived in Molde and left this quiet Atlantic coastal town on December 4, 1996, died together with five nurses and doctors, three of whom were Norwegian, in the Chechen village of Starye Atagi on December 17. She was ten days into her Red Cross mission, working in a hospital which had been set up there.

"Ingeborg rang me twice from Chechnya," Sigrid Foss, Ingeborg's 82-year-old mother tells me. "She said it was very frightening."

"Did you ask her to come home? Did you try to persuade her? Did you insist, as a mother?"

"No," Sigrid replies. "It was her destiny."

Brief, to the point, betraying no sense of hurt, but what a scree of emotion there is in the heart of this woman, her face incised with wrinkles. Love of her daughter, grief at her passing, but also pride that Ingeborg proved so reckless for the sake of people she did not know but who were nevertheless ill. And, of course, the pain of irredeemable loss.

Long before Chechnya, Ingeborg had dedicated herself to working for the Red Cross. She had worked in Nicaragua and Pakistan but when the Red Cross offered her a contract in Bosnia, she suddenly refused, saying, "I have an aged mother. I can't." Nevertheless, she made up her mind to go to Chechnya. The Red Cross assured her that conditions were not as bad as people were saying, and that everything would be fine.

Sigrid catches constantly at her grey braids of hair, blown about by a strong wind which has sprung up here in the cemetery, high above the fjord. She is barely able to hold back the tears. Her eyes redden and her eyelids droop, and then she squats down and lays a hand on the dark brown fjord soil by Ingeborg's gravestone. She steadies herself for a few moments before catching her grey hair again. She pushes it up, away from her eyes in defiance of the wind, and the gesture seems to help her gather what remains of her strength. They say here that the older women of Norway do not cry. It is not their way. They are strong, indomitable, familiar with suffering, and do not usually give way to tears. They lived through the Second World War, when Norway endured a brutal occupation, with partisans, a resistance, fighting, and many dead. Most later lived through great poverty and hunger, and it was only when they were very old that Norway became rich and was able to provide them with decent old people's homes and good pensions.

Sigrid is one such Norwegian woman. You can tell that she is by nature very tough, like anyone who lives with the wind and the sea and who is used to seeing their family sail out, never to return. She is fully aware of what someone standing beside her in the cemetery may be thinking.

"Yes, losing my daughter has put ten years on my age," she nods,

swallowing a lump in her throat in order to continue the simple story
of her family. All her life Sigrid taught Norwegian and English, and of
course brought up her own children, but her husband was a doctor.
Sigrid lost first him, and then the daughter who had decided to follow
in his footsteps.

Sigrid proudly shows me a certificate, Order No. 589, dated
December 11, 1997, issued by President Aslan Maskhadov, awarding
Ingeborg the highest decoration of the Chechen Republic. That award
and a grave are all that Sigrid has left after the death of her daughter.

"Do you feel Russia has wronged you?"

"No. My grudge is against the Red Cross."

Sigrid Foss says that she believes the organization in whose cause
her daughter died was over-ambitious.

"At that time, between the two Chechen wars, the Red Cross wanted
to establish a hospital against all the odds, as if to say, 'Look at us!
We can do something nobody else can do! The Russians are too
frightened, and the Chechens don't have the means.' Their ambitions
led them to assure Ingeborg there was no great danger, when in fact
it was deadly." Sigrid was told this by the Norwegian doctor who by
a miracle survived, and who accompanied the stretcher bearing
Ingeborg's body back to Molde.

"A stretcher? Not a coffin?"

"That's right."

For Sigrid, 1997 and 1998 passed under the initial shock of bereave-
ment, but then she wanted to establish the truth. Gradually, however,
things took a bizarre, heartless turn. As if it was not enough that
Ingeborg's life had been cut short, Sigrid found she had no way, because
of everything going on in Chechnya and Russia, to find out who
exactly was responsible for her daughter's untimely death.

What is left for someone whose child has predeceased them? Given
that it is impossible to right the terrible wrong that has happened, they
do at least want to know what that was. Alas, to this day Sigrid Foss
does not even know whether there is an inquiry into the murder of
her daughter in Starye Atagi, let alone whether it is making progress.

Everybody has forgotten her: Russia, because her daughter was helping the Chechen population to survive, and at present that is unfashionable in Russia; Chechnya, because Chechnya has no time for anything other than trying to survive.

"Two years ago we had a phone call from the Norwegian Foreign Ministry. I was told they had no information. They did not even know whether an investigation was being conducted in Russia. I couldn't make out who our Foreign Ministry was in touch with in Moscow about the murders in Starye Atagi. The Red Cross was no better. They sent me a letter a year ago saying there was no news. In five years you are the first person from Russia to remember Ingeborg and come to visit her grave."

"But what about Norwegians?"

"No Norwegians have come either."

"Død Tsjetsjenia." Norway, Molde, Russia. I say goodbye to Sigrid Foss. Do you still think the world is vast? That if there is a conflagration in one place it does not have a bearing on another, and that you can sit it out in peace on your veranda admiring your absurd petunias?

Our greatest problem today is that this most basic and long-established truth has to be reiterated as if it had just come into existence. Neither that modest grave in Molde, nor the thousands of graves all over Chechnya, have acted as a wake-up call for Europe, which continues to slumber as if the war being fought within its bounds was not already in its twenty-third successive month; as if Chechnya were as far from Norway as it is from the Antarctic.

For all that, Chechnya is no less a part of the Old World than any of its other territories. Mr Kruse, a correspondent for Norwegian state television who has worked in Russia for many years, exclaimed in some surprise during our conversation to the effect that, "Oh, but Russia is a different part of Europe. You can't apply the usual criteria. Even war criminals in Russia are not really war criminals. You can hardly blame the present fate of Milošević on Russia's leaders, given its great spiritual heritage and sheer geographical scale."

Alas, this is an all too typical European attitude. Russia has today been categorised as a maverick territory where, with the tacit agreement of the heads of the European states, the European Parliament, the Council of Europe and the OSCE all lumped together, it is apparently acceptable for citizens to live under laws quite different from those which apply to the rest of the European continent, laws which the rest of Europe couldn't imagine living under in its worst nightmare.

That is why I gave Mr Kruse a hard time. I asked him why he thought it was all right for a Chechen woman to be killed for no reason, just because passing soldiers were in a bad mood, but not for the same fate to befall a Norwegian, or Swedish or Belgian woman. How was a French woman any different from a Chechen woman, or a Russian woman who happened to belong to a "great power"?

It isn't all right, of course, but many people in Norway are taken aback by questions like that. It is obvious that Chechen women are no different, but that does not square with Europe's self-contradictory desire not to fall out with Putin while retaining a semblance of civilised values.

All my conversations, meetings and interviews – in the Norwegian Foreign Ministry, with reporters, at the Nobel Institute in Oslo, with the future Prime Minister Kjell Magne Bondevik, even in the Norwegian Human Rights Center (there really is such an office block in Oslo, where most of the human rights organizations operating in Norway are accommodated under one roof) – only served to further persuade me of something I already knew: Europe has no stomach for opposing the war in Chechnya. Europe is mired in double standards when it comes to human rights. One standard applies to most of Europe; it is distilled, splendid, civilised and tidy. For Russia, where democracy was born only a decade ago, there is another, naturally less distilled and pure. For the rebellious enclave of Chechnya, however, there is no standard at all, a void. Europe effectively condones the existence of a territory where atrocities go unpunished, and pretends that the war being waged there does not concern Europeans. There are few protests, no sanctions are imposed on Russian officials, and crimes that would never be tolerated in the rest of Europe – killings, extra-judicial persecution and executions – are seen as unproblematical in Russia and Chechnya. Indeed, there is even tacit acceptance of the monstrous notion that one particular nation should bear collective responsibility for the actions of a few of its members.

Applying double standards is a dangerous game. Europe has been here before, with infamous consequences. In 1933 the Führer of a new Germany was also "democratically elected." Europe was frightened by his speeches but, until they could no longer be ignored, paid them no attention, preferring to look to its own prosperity and pleasant morning coffee. With Europe turning a blind eye, two nationalities – the Jews and the Gypsies – were held collectively responsible for the deeds of particular individuals. What was the consequence? The consequence was 1945, with millions dead, millions burned in crematoria, and Europe in ruins.

It all started so simply. A particular gentleman with psychological problems took it into his head that one nation was great and the rest were less great, and that some, indeed, should be annihilated. Are we really to say that things are different now? That the Kremlin sometimes gives Chechens honors and medals and even promotes them to top positions and is doing something for them? Hitler did all that too, as a smokescreen for Europe's benefit. There were "good" Jews, "honest" Gypsies were paraded now and again, and sometimes there were even "civilised" Slavs to be discovered, so that Europe wouldn't be upset, would not become alarmed too soon. Europe pretended to swallow all this, but that did not save countless men, women and children from dying subsequently at the hands of the people of that "great" nation.

To return to the present. The double standards Europe applies to Chechnya are gradually infiltrating Europe. What did Ingeborg Foss give her life for? Why does nobody in Europe, not even in Norway, not in the OSCE or the European Parliament think it matters that an aged Norwegian mother knows nothing about how or why her daughter died, or that the investigation of the deaths of six doctors and nurses in Starye Atagi has ground to a halt? (That nothing is being done has been confirmed by the Prosecutor-General's Office of the Russian Federation.)

So what is modern Europe's moral code? A pretence? Self-delusion for some and a convenient fiction for others who don't want it to get in the way of pan-European fraternisation between the major powers to crush those who are weaker?

Russia is in the grip of war fever, Europe reacts sluggishly, and here is the result: Ingeborg Foss, a young Norwegian woman, died in Chechnya and now her old mother, Sigrid Foss, is alone in the world. Just like Aishat Djabrailova from Gudermes, who lost her husband and her sons in the Second Chechen Slaughter. Like Ludmila Sysuyeva from Tyumen Province who received an official form advising her of the death of her only son, followed shortly afterwards by a sealed zinc coffin, and who now doesn't know whom to turn to. We are in close proximity to each other: from Oslo to Moscow is just two hours by air, and another two hours will take you from Moscow to Chechnya. Europe is tiny.

This generation of politicians, to whom we gave the right to rule, have failed us. They act in their own interests, not in the interests of Europe.

As we said our farewells, Sigrid told me, "The fact that you remembered Ingrid has given me a few more years of life." Behind us the Atlantic roared and the seagulls cried out. "People need answers to the questions which most concern them while they are still alive," she added. "That may be the most important thing those in authority can do."

JOSPIN LITE: *NOVAYA GAZETA*'S SPECIAL CORRESPONDENT SPENDS A DAY IN THE COMPANY OF THE PRIME MINISTER OF FRANCE

April 15, 2002

Seventeen candidates are registered in the 2002 French presidential election, a record. Among the hopefuls are: Lionel Jospin, present Prime Minister and Head of the Socialist Party ("moderate left"); Jacques Chirac, present President of the Republic ("right," liberal); Arlette Laguiller ("extreme left"); Jean-Marie Le Pen ("extreme right," archnationalist and friend of our own far-right Vladimir Zhirinovsky); Alain Madelin (leader of the Liberal Democracy Party); and Noël Mamère (Leader of the Green Party.

Our readers may legitimately be wondering what *Novaya gazeta* was doing in France when there is more than enough to report on in Russia. Our intention was simple: it has not been at all clear what President Putin's ideas are for ending the Second Chechen War so we decided to try to find out by asking some of the European leaders with whom Putin, by virtue of his office, has close working relationships. In favor of France was the fact that the intellectuals and politicians here, including Prime Minister Lionel Jospin, have traditionally been more radical on the Chechen issue than the elite of other countries. They have emphatically opposed the war, and helped large numbers of Chechen refugees to settle in France.

After negotiations with his Press Office, *Novaya gazeta* was granted a day when, in the course of a visit to Lorient, a provincial fishing village on the Atlantic coast, M. Lionel Jospin, Prime Minister of France, would reply to questions we had submitted in advance. The quid pro quo was that we would publish an article about his election campaigning in Lorient. We thought that was fair enough.

All election campaigns are as alike as die-cast nuts coming off a conveyor belt. As in Russia, so in France there is The Candidate, his gaze wandering above the heads of The People. He is weary and, of course, preoccupied with affairs of state. He pretends to understand everything he is told. On the other side, The People, wearing new work clothes and clean helmets specially issued by their superiors in honor of this visit from the metropolis. There is also the clicking and flashing of the press, and a full turnout from the Mayor's Office.

Everything proceeded according to plan in the port of Lorient, which M. Jospin visited first. He was shown a new fishing boat in dry dock, nodded silently in time with the explanations, shook the hand of a young engineer in the front row of The People, and in a practised manner took up his position for a commemorative photograph with the Mayor. Then it was our turn. The Press Office whispered in our ear, "Keep strictly to the questions!"

"Prime Minister, what do you think about the anti-terrorist operation in Russia, the war in Chechnya? About the massive violation of human rights? Have you talked to President Putin about ending it? About deadlines?"

The Prime Minister of France was clearly taken aback. A puzzled silence hung in the air until the emotionless gaze from behind his spectacles became tetchy. What was all this about?

"Oh no, not that. Lord, that's all we need," Jospin said, looking at the crowds surrounding him.

"But why haven't you?"

"Why are you asking me about these things in Lorient?"

"I am a journalist from Russia, and I was invited here by your Press Office specifically to ask you about these things."

Jospin is aghast. His press attaché comes out in blotches.

"No, no, and again no. It's all so complicated."

"But Prime Minister, please tell us how relations between Jospin and Putin will differ from relations between Chirac and Putin if you do in fact become President. What could Russia expect from France in that event?"

"Oh these questions. Putin . . . Lord. Oh no, not that. Today I shall only be talking about the sea. Ask me something about the sea!"

"Why is he being so evasive?" I ask those witnessing this strange scene in some perplexity. "Is he afraid of Putin?"

They explain as best they can, journalists from the Prime Minister's press pool, port engineers and workers. It has nothing to do with fear of Putin. It is just that one of the customs of contemporary French politicians is never to let themselves be pinned down. They express themselves in an opaque manner so that they cannot subsequently be held to account for what they have said. Lite politicians with easy European policies which commit them to nothing. General-purpose politics, nothing too specific.

Evidently this is particularly typical of the Socialists, the party currently led by Jospin. The Socialists in France are in a league of their own. Among France's moderate Socialist supporters are many people with a non-traditional approach, but this is not by any means seen as a political minus for the party. On the contrary, in France it is seen as a plus, giving them, including Jospin Lite, a good chance of winning elections.

Let me give an example, which, moreover, illustrates the old adage about knowing a man by the company he keeps. Another major left-wing figure, and ideological comrade of Jospin, is Bertrand Delanoë, the current Mayor of Paris. He is famously an "out" gay politician, which recently enabled him to win the mayoral contest, with the result that Paris now has an entire gay quarter. During the election Delanoë trod warily, but now he is in power his policies are quite aggressive, in accordance with his own radical ideas. Because he regards himself as green, the traffic in Paris is being reorganised, very much to the inconvenience of drivers, to encourage them, in Delanoë's words, to "get on their bikes." I am not joking. To speak in generalities, but then to reform and micro-regulate is very much the way of today's French Left.

I was warned not to take too literally Jospin's airy answer, "Oh no, not that. Lord, that's all we need." In the rather twisted political idiom of modern France, I was told, this actually means that Jospin currently favors Putin's root-and-branch approach in Chechnya but prefers not to say so, because that is not done.

Jospin's political background is extreme Trotskyism. For almost 20 years of his mature life, between the ages of 30 and 50, he belonged to an illegal, underground Trotskyite cell whose main ideas were permanent revolution, total egalitarianism, and taking everything from the rich and sharing it out among the poor, a little for everyone. In the present election race, Jospin is eager to disown this sectarianism. When questioned about his Trotskyite past he lies, claiming that he was never a member of the cell, that it was his brother in the list of members, and that it is their shared surname which has caused the confusion.

Is this a ploy, or might it actually be true? I discussed this with André Glucksmann, a major contemporary French philosopher. For many years Glucksmann was one of France's most brilliant leftists, and you will search in vain for anyone better informed about this section of the French political spectrum.

"Of course it is Lionel Jospin," he told me, "and not his brother. The organization we are talking about existed secretly, it was very conspiratorial, like a sect. Incidentally, nobody is entirely sure whether it has disbanded or not. It is perfectly possible that it exists illegally to this day, and that Jospin is a fully paid up member who is simply carrying out its program."

"So it's something like the Freemasons?"

"Yes. The organization in which Jospin's political personality was formed is essentially a Trotskyite version of Freemasonry. Their aim is to penetrate the institutions and management of the state in accordance with Trotsky's principles. Nobody knows for certain whether Jospin is still a member or not. Perhaps his presidential ambitions are just a project of this Trotskyite sect."

It is time to return to the port in Lorient. The Prime Minister of France makes his escape from questions he does not want to answer and heads for the safe haven of his limousine. Shortly afterwards The Candidate arrives at the local Palace of Nations in the town center, where he is due to divulge his thoughts about the sea.

Jospin's progress to the platform is barred by a crowd of his former fellow thinkers, Communists and representatives of the most powerful Communist trade union in France, the CGT. Red flags, uniforms, slogans through loud-hailers, chanting of "Hands off the Alcatel factory." Jospin again looks irritated. Alighting from his limousine he casts a hostile glance at this left-wing crowd and, showing a fair turn of speed, runs wordlessly into the Palace of Nations, where there is alas no sound insulation. In the hall you can hear everything going on outside: the shouting and yelling of the demonstrators, the Communist songs. Jospin pretends none of it is happening. The moment arrives for his thoughts about the sea.

"The sea unites and brings together. It bears within itself the values of solidarity . . . The sea plays a great part in that freedom which Socialists bring to the world in the name of the all-round development of man . . . The sea is unbounded. It is open to all the winds of firm liberalism, from the rubbish tips on the shoreline to sailors left to fend for themselves . . . To conduct a policy imbued with the spirit of the sea means to reject liberal deviations . . . We want to avoid the submerged rocks of excessive liberalisation."

And finally, "Let us save the sea from the ebbing and flowing tides of liberalism." This soundbite summarises Jospin's thoughts about the sea. It is the core of his politics, and if there was a special *Guinness Book of Records* for political demagogy, would undoubtedly be in it.

We need to translate all this from the idiom of French politics into something more comprehensible. What on earth was he talking about? What did he mean by the references to "firm liberalism," 'rejecting liberal deviations"? This was a uniquely French way of throwing a brick into the political garden of Jacques Chirac, the liberal President and Jospin's main rival. By criticising him in this metaphorical manner, Jospin managed to avoid all mention of his name. By the local rules, this was considered very cool. And we thought he would talk about Chechnya!

The finale was simple, and followed the script of all election campaign finales. The last ebbings and flowings from the platform were greeted with an ovation. "Jospin – Président! Jospin – Président!" the front rows chanted to the rhythm of "Spartak – Champ-i-on!" A minute later The Candidate, in order to avoid any unpleasant contact with The People outside, was led off through the back door.

Returning to Paris very late that evening on Jospin's plane, put at his disposal by the private air charter company Darta, the mood was positive as if after a good day's work. Entirely acceptable wine was passed round, and Jospin's PR team started singing their favorite songs with gusto. First, many times, "Comandante Che Guevara." Secondly, a song of the Italian partisans. Thirdly, "Motivé," a song of the French Communists, conveying the concept that "I am a person with motivation.: The lead singer was a young man who was Jospin's Press Secretary. For the entire hour until we reached Le Bourget private airport near Paris, he kept the team alternating "Che Guevara," "Bella Ciao," "Motivé," "Che Guevara," "Bella Ciao". . .

[In the 2002 presidential elections, Lionel Jospin made it through to the second round, before losing to Jacques Chirac and the leader of the Nationalists, Jean-Marie Le Pen.]

THE "WAVES" OF POLITICAL EMIGRATION FROM RUSSIA

After the rigours of Moscow, the orderly life of London quickly turns you back into a normal human being, someone with the ways of a free citizen.

I imagine many of our compatriots who, for the time being and against their will, find themselves in Great Britain must experience similar feelings. Here they at last settle back into an ordinary way of life denied them in Russia. They cease to jump at any sound resembling a gunshot, and even take the London Underground without a bodyguard.

The air of London is revivifying. The proof was not long in coming; I went to the theatre – just for the joy of it, not to be seen in society – to a local musical which has had an unbroken run of many years and where, accordingly, no self-respecting New Russian would be seen dead in Russia. London is different. As I was sitting down next to Akhmed Zakayev, the Special Envoy of President Aslan Maskhadov of Chechnya, who is awaiting the verdict of a British court in respect of the Russian Federation's entirely political demand for his extradition, somebody turned round from the row in front and said breezily, "Hi, guys." This was none other than Yuliy Dubov, author of the sensational novel *Oligarch*, and no mean oligarch himself. He too has a warrant out for his arrest from the Russian Prosecutor-General's Office, for embezzlement involving Zhiguli cars but principally because of his friendship with another oligarch in exile, Boris Berezovsky, who also now lives in London. In a London theatre Yuliy Dubov was charming, while in Moscow you couldn't have broken through his oligarchic security cordon for love or money. He proved to have a delightful wife, and in the interval ran off to the bar without ceremony to get drinks. He even told us how many stops on the Underground it was from here to his house.

My heart warmed to see how amazingly London's ordinariness heals people spiritually, but I was to make an even more amazing discovery. Boris Berezovsky himself, I found, is also recuperating morally here.

Like anyone else, he attends parents' meetings at school. You have to admit, that speaks volumes for Britain's ability to bring a Russian citizen back to normality, and serves to confirm that today Britain is the most attractive country in Europe for those forced to emigrate from Russia. Apart from Berezovsky, Dubov and Zakayev, London is home to Alexander Litvinenko [assassinated in London by the FSB in November 2006], the ex-FSB officer who came into irreconcilable conflict with his Ministry for refusing to kill Berezovsky without written instructions from his superiors, and then fled to Britain with a false passport by way of Ukraine.

All of them are people to be reckoned with and grandees in their own circles, despite all having warrants for their arrest as criminals issued by the Prosecutor-General's Office. They are, of course, very different people, but have some things in common. They are all friends here, not only with each other but also with Vladimir Bukovsky, who is respected as the patriarch of Russian dissidents and political émigrés in Great Britain, who acknowledge him as the leader of their unplanned assembly of new political exiles.

THE PATRIARCH

When someone no longer refers to the British Prime Minister with a clipped "Bler," but enunciates a long, drawling, diphthongised "Blaier" as the British do, he is quite clearly no longer embedded in Russian society. Berezovsky, Zakayev and Litvinenko still come out with a curt "Bler," but Bukovsky now says "Blai-er." His alien pronunciation in no wise diminishes the immense attractiveness of this unique man with his palpable inner freedom. Political émigrés of every persuasion are drawn to him.

Bukovsky's home is a rather dank, rather small, very English house in the university town of Cambridge. Its owner has been through the mill in a way the rest of us can only guess at. Ten years of labor camps and specialist psychiatric hospitals in his former homeland, followed by decades in exile. He lives here incredibly modestly, but very precisely, as becomes a dissident, without evident luxury and with just a single

fireplace to warm the room. This is fuelled by a mountain of wine corks
piled to the left of it. These indicate frequent, forgivable departures
from its owner's asceticism. Bored by the adults' conversation,Tolya,
Alexander Litvinenko's eight-year-old son, who already mixes Russian
words with English and writes poetry in English, busies himself with
setting fire to the corks.

Bukovsky is not young. When he says "we" he means "the British."
That said, he greets his guests as he always has, wearing his traditional
Soviet blue tracksuit with its baggy knees and incongruously offering
us Courvoisier cognac dating from 1942, the year he was born. Having
warmed ourselves with the brandy, we talk.

*Why do you think people who have issues with Russia are again gathering
in Britain? Is it coincidence or is there an explanation?*
There are two aspects to that. Of course, mostly it is just chance.
Akhmed is stranded here for the simple reason that he was invited to
England by Vanessa Redgrave and, under our European laws, a person
is returned to their country of departure. (In October 2002 it was from
Britain that Zakayev travelled to the World Chechen Congress in Copen-
hagen, where he was arrested after Russia demanded his extradition.
He was tried by a Danish court, released on December 3, and returned
to Britain.)

It was less random in the case of Boris [Berezovsky]. He is a finan-
cier, and it is generally acknowledged that we offer the greatest freedom
in the world for financial operations. Also, I told Boris, "You are
requesting political asylum, which Britain has already granted to Sasha
Litvinenko. Your case is directly linked with his. By legal precedent,
the Litvinenko case will be aggregated with yours, and he has already
received asylum. That means that no other verdict in your case is
possible: if they gave him asylum for refusing to kill you, they are quite
certain to give it to you, because it was you the Russian state authorities wanted to kill. That is an established fact."

In other words, it is both coincidence and for good reason that
Russians are gathering here. In today's Europe, out of the members

of the European Union (and I emphasise that, because Norway and Switzerland are not members, and they are even more free) Britain is the best country for getting things done. It keeps its distance from the European Union, and there is obviously still a great deal of freedom here.

Do you think that the concentration here of political refugees might seriously impair relations between Britain and Russia, or Europe and Russia?
As far as Britain is concerned, definitely not. Blair will continue to love Putin in spite of Zakayev, purely as a matter of political expediency. No matter how many émigrés accumulate here, Britain never alters its relations with anyone. Such is the tradition. For us in Britain, granting asylum is not a political but a legal decision, no matter what the Soviet – excuse me, Russian – Ministry of Foreign Affairs and the Kremlin lot think. Political asylum decisions are taken not by the Government but by the courts. The Government can make only an initial decision and any person has the right to an appeal, which is heard in court. Accordingly, the Government always bears in mind that its decision may be reviewed in court, and tries to second-guess how the courts are likely to rule. That gives a judicial guarantee of protection.

I couldn't help smiling at the protest by the Russian Minister of Foreign Affairs, Mr Ivanov, over the fact that an English policeman released Zakayev from Heathrow Airport on Friday night. [. . .] It demonstrates how professionally incompetent they are – they just don't understand how things work here. The English policeman did not ask the Prime Minister what to do about Zakayev. He simply thought it would cause less trouble if, since he had confiscated Zakayev's passport, he released this person into England. Zakayev couldn't leave the country anyway, and if the policeman's superiors wanted to change that decision they could do so tomorrow themselves. In other words, as a policeman on night shift, he was doing nothing that might harm Britain, and that was his main concern. It was his decision, not the British Government's. By delivering a completely unnecessary broadside at the British Government, Minister Ivanov merely caused offence and made it even less likely that Zakayev would be returned to Russia.

Nevertheless, the general European climate is clearly worsening because of the Zakayev affair. The European Parliament's delegation was not allowed into Chechnya, and this was expressly linked to Zakayev.
Yes, but that has no bearing at all on Britain's position. On the general European position, yes, in the sense that this is beginning to irritate people in Europe, but what is irritating them is not that the Chechen problem is fundamentally insoluble, but the way Russia is dealing with it. Listen, the European Parliament is an extremely neutral organization. If it is not Orwellian, it is certainly in the mould foreseen by Huxley. Yet it took the initiative of passing a special resolution approving Denmark's action in releasing Zakayev, whom they describe as "an outstanding Chechen politician," and they are giving him a so-called "Passport of Freedom" for Europe. That is very significant.

They passed the resolution, but they have been made to pay for it.
I have many friends in the European Parliament and they are simply laughing. The European Parliament has no great need to travel to Russia. It is Russia which needs that.

But this Commission visit was eagerly anticipated in Chechnya by people who have no other hope. They may well be laughing in Brussels but Europe now has no eyes and ears in Chechnya.
That is a different matter. By refusing to allow them a presence in Chechnya, Russia did not hurt the European Parliament in the slightest. Their presence is important for Chechnya and for Russia, but not for the European Parliament. The Russian authorities don't seem to understand that.

You are well known as a contemporary political Nostradamus. What do you think, will the Kremlin decide to assassinate Maskhadov?
Of course. They are searching for him right now and want to kill him. Europe would not react even to that. As far as the future resolution of the Chechen crisis is concerned, assassinating Maskhadov will make it practically impossible to achieve any ceasefire agreement, and all the Chechens' efforts to establish their own state will have come to nothing.

For Russia this will mean a perpetually festering wound in the South which nobody will be able to treat. An intelligent person does not allow such situations to develop. He tries to impose a measure of control in order to bring a conflict into at least minimally civilised bounds. Russia is giving no thought to that and is acting in a completely absurd manner. It is an insane policy calculated to obtain short-term advantage but which completely fails to take account of the interests of the vast majority of Russia's population. It is a criminal policy. You really should negotiate with people who are willing to negotiate, rather than kill them.

Why do you think Europe, which does not seek merely short-term advantage, is so unconcerned about trying to preserve the lives of witnesses of war crimes in Chechnya? If there is to be any prospect of an international tribunal like the one Milošević has been subjected to, their testimony is essential.

Milošević's presence in the Hague is illegal. He may deserve the gallows, but the charges against him are ludicrous. This was all got up by the New Left in Europe, who were flexing their muscles just at that moment. The NATO operation against Serbia was a crime and an act of aggression as defined by the United Nations. It was entirely without foundation, and was a vile political act of self-affirmation by the new elite in Europe. Nobody was fighting to get Milošević put in prison or to expose war crimes. They simply made up the crimes. They told us a minimum of 500,000 people would die if we did not intervene and Milošević remained in power. In fact, when the dust settled and the graves were opened, they contained 6,000 bodies, and they were from both sides, including victims of the NATO bombing. It was no more than a policing operation. They raised a tremendous hue and cry, comparing what was going on to the Holocaust – a criminal abuse of that historical example. News management. The world has gone mad, like a hammer head flying off its handle. We have idiots here and idiots over there. Do not imagine that the situation now is black and white. It was black and white in my youth: back when there were communists and democrats and it was clear who was the world's enemy.

What is the situation today then – universally grey?
Everything is shit-colored. Today we are dealing with varying hues of shit.

How do you envisage the end of the Second Chechen War?
If it ever has an end. One of the most likely outcomes is that there will be no end, everything will just drag on for decades. New groups of desperate young people will continue carrying out senseless acts of terrorism, sacrificing their lives for some cause but achieving nothing. A better outcome would be to stop military operations right now. Just stop them, and never mind if we can't resolve the political questions at present. Stop it, and at least start looking for local solutions to the very smallest, local social problems.

So why is Europe so inactive in Chechnya? The number of humanitarian organizations working in the zone is nothing like what there was, for example, in the Balkans.
The world context is that Europe sees Muslims as terrorists. There are friendly nations and enemy nations. All that matters is the global "war on terror," an idiotic concept, but in that context no practical politician can do anything at the moment: only cover his ears and wait.

It is strange to hear you say that. After all, in a past, far worse time you did not by any means sit around covering your ears, waiting for something to happen.
I'm not talking about myself but about the world. I am not covering my ears. In Europe I am currently in conflict with the Establishment. I am one of those who oppose the European Union, and I am trying to organise a large coalition to put an end to it. From my viewpoint, the European Union is little different from the Soviet Union; they don't yet have a Gulag but there are already signs of one. The first arrests for political jokes have been made. For example, in Britain one well-known television presenter joked at a country fête that he would like to have the same civil rights as a pregnant, one-legged Negro woman with a drugs problem. Political correctness here has reached absurd

heights; he was arrested. At least Parliament threw out a law on hate speech because comedians rebelled and said that if they couldn't make jokes they would be out of a job. But the European Union plans to have this law adopted throughout Europe! We are entering a totalitarian period. Many of my old friends are laughing now and say I've been settled for too long and am getting fretful, that I've decided to take up the cudgels again. Believe me, I have no wish to do that at all. I am an old man, I would like to live out my life with my cat, in my garden. I have done everything I wanted to do, but you can't live the way we are asked to live.

How, in your view, should a decent person live in today's Russia?
It is impossible for a decent person to live in Russia today. All the decent people are doing everything they can to get out as soon as possible. Those who remain do so because they can't leave. But there are still a few people capable of protesting: Andrey Derevyankin is in prison and has been forgotten, but this man went to the military base in his native town of Engels in Saratov Province and held up a placard reading "End the War in Chechnya!" For this he was given several years in jail. I understand where he is coming from. I also recognised when I was living in Russia that, under a dishonorable regime, my place was in prison. So when I was arrested I was happy.

BEREZOVSKY

January 20, 2003

Boris Berezovsky is the other magnetic pole, along with Bukovsky, of the new Russian political émigré community in Britain. Here he is straightforward, friends with everyone. Back in Russia, his reputation remains that of a demonic genius. Not here. What Boris most resembles here, in his cream jacket, is a perky sparrow with light-colored plumage.

It is easy to insult an oligarch in exile but far less easy to understand one. Consider what he was in the past. The man who manipulated Yeltsin, the Mr Fix-it of Chechnya, the man who made a fortune out of oil, Zhiguli cars, and Aeroflot. And then it was the turn of Vladimir Vladimirovich Putin, Berezovsky's most ambitious project. It was Berezovsky who backed Putin as the future of Russia, and so far he has lost hands down, which, admittedly, takes some of the sheen off his image as a demonic genius. It also makes him seem more human, what with the creature of his "Second President of Russia" project sitting comfortably in the Kremlin while Berezovsky is banished to the Lanesborough Hotel. Of course, this is a high-end hotel, in a top-of-the-range city, with Hyde Park outside his windows. Neither is he lonely; the Lanesborough is where the *crème de la crème* stay, and you can meet them in the foyer without their bodyguards. Oligarchs Deripaska, barefoot in jeans in the morning, Potanin and Berezovsky with their wives and children. And there's the Library Bar, the best place on the planet for the world's Establishments past and present to relax. The armchairs in the library are just like the ones you aren't allowed to sit on in the Hermitage, only here you are allowed to sit on them and even put your feet on them if you like. They are splendid, but all the same the Lanesborough is not the Kremlin.

Why did you choose Britain for your exile?
It was chance. I just happened to be here in October 2002 when I learned that the Prosecutor-General's Office wanted to arrest me on an allegation of embezzling Aeroflot funds. That's when I decided to stay, but that was not the only reason. I had lived in the South of France for a year but, in spite of the lush climate, I found it difficult to work there. The environment is debilitating. Britain is quite different. I find the climate here phenomenal and it suits me very well. The only thing I miss is the snow, but last week there was even some of that. It fell for the first time in 15 months – I felt quite at home. I have lived in France, Germany and America, and can say without hesitation that if I had to choose somewhere to live other than Russia, then this is the most comfortable place to be. Another thing is London itself. The city is super-international. You are left in peace entirely, although at the same time you are not allowed to bother other people. In spite of all the difficulties of my situation – and I am a thorn in the flesh of the

Russian Government – nobody has so much as hinted to me that I might not be welcome.

My status in Britain is rather unclear. I have not yet been granted permanent residence and have been waiting for the decision of the British Home Office for over a year, which is a bit disturbing. But imagine this situation in reverse: suppose I am a British citizen and a furious opponent of Blair (and I make no bones about the fact that I am conducting a campaign against the Russian authorities from here), and I am living in Russia; assuming Putin was on good terms with Blair, and Blair says, "Volodya, you have this character living in your country who is such a pain in my neck. Send him back to Britain, would you?" I have no doubt that the very next day, caged and in hand-cuffs, I would be on a plane back, because in Russia there is no justice and no protection of rights, and that goes not only for foreign citizens, but, for heaven's sake, even for their own. Britain, in contrast, is a country where the law is tremendously respected. Another significant aspect is that nobody who is here now – Zakayev, Litvinenko – came here of their own free will. They would like to go back to Russia. America is 10 hours' flying time from Russia. That's a long way, and communications are difficult, while here you are living in the same information environment as Russia. People emigrate to America who don't want ever to go back.

How do you see Europe's current position on the Chechen crisis, after the Zakayev affair has put an end to the peace process which was developing in Europe through him? Does Europe really want to stop the war?

Let us first of all consider the place that events in Chechnya occupy among the political and social concerns of the West. We have to admit they do not have that high a priority. The British have plenty of problems of their own. Number 1 is Iraq and whether there is going to be a war there. But, more generally I would say attitudes have changed radically, and not in Russia's favor. Serious matters such as the arrest of Zakayev have played a role in this, but also ephemeral things like Putin's ill-judged remarks at a press conference in Brussels about circumcising a journalist who asked him about Chechnya. Sad to say, the fate of a human being like Zakayev and a stupid remark made by an uneducated man seem to carry roughly the same weight here in the scales of public opinion. The Brussels outburst was simply crude, and people here react strongly to primitive behaviour. For a long time in the West they were asking, "Who are you, Mr Putin?", and now they think they have the answer.

These things coincided. The Zakayev affair infuriated Putin; he had lost the argument. Denmark's decision outraged him. Headlines started appearing in the leading Western newspapers equating Putin with Milošević. "Why should we accept Putin and roll out the red carpet for him when he is a state criminal?" Before the Zakayev affair you didn't hear that kind of remark. Although European governments are forever trying to maintain good relations with Russia, which is understandable from a pragmatic viewpoint because they need Russia's support in the impending war in Iraq, a chasm has suddenly opened up, between the logical behaviour of the upper echelons of European governments, and opposition politicians who have begun to criticize Putin and Russia harshly. There is also now a clear divide between the upper echelons and public opinion which, as a rule, is articulated by the press. The result is a change of attitude towards the Chechen War which may be important, although not decisive, for stopping it. That decision is one for the Russian Government to take. I would just like to quote what Zakayev once said: "Russia has the right to start a war with Chechnya, and it has the right to stop it."

What do you mean by "important, although not decisive"?
Europe's new position will seriously irritate the Russian Government, and push it towards a solution which will only result in its being constantly reminded of this irritant. Putin is very sensitive to personal attacks, and the terminology the West is adopting undermines him psychologically. He does not understand the real nature of the objections, and takes them personally. How the West reacts to Putin as an individual and his personal standing with the Russian public is one of the main sources of his power. After Brussels and Zakayev, the West is never going to view him as a friend because it sees that he does not

share ideas which are fundamental to Western society. He does not believe in them, and in the West he is now considered a hypocrite.

The Zakayev incident was a fiasco. Zakayev is one of the most admirable figures in Chechnya. I have no hesitation in saying that. I know him not only from hearsay. I conducted extremely difficult negotiations in Chechnya, and never had any doubt that Zakayev wanted peace or that he was constructive in that respect. Zakayev's role is plain for everyone in the West to see. There is not a single fact suggesting that he wishes to prolong the war, while there are many which testify to his having consistently defended the idea of a peaceful way out of this slaughter.

I consider that 2002 has been the most damaging year for Russia since 1991, when the Soviet Union collapsed. There aren't enough fingers on one hand to list the defeats. The most important landmark is a qualitative change in the situation in Chechnya. If before 2002 I was sure that we could find a solution ourselves, negotiate peace between the belligerent sides, I consider that is now impossible. 2002 has been a watershed: the hatred on both sides has reached such heights that without international mediation – including involvement of countries outside the former Soviet bloc and the use of force – we can no longer resolve the conflict. This is Russia's greatest setback. The country has lost its sovereignty in the sense that, without the intervention of external forces, it is incapable of settling its internal conflict. Russia has now suffered a devastating defeat in the Second Chechen War, considerably more serious than in the First, and the defeat is precisely that we have lost our sovereignty.

Russia's second political defeat has been Kaliningrad [the Russian enclave between Poland and Lithuania]. We shouldn't have gone on so foolishly and at such length, trying to tie everything down in terms of flight paths, access corridors and high-speed rail links. We should have approached the matter in terms of integration into Europe. We should have said, yes, we accept the option involving visas, but only so as to have guarantees that the whole of Russia will become part of Europe's borderless Schengen zone within a specified number of years. This discussion never took place for the simple reason that for many centuries the Russian political elite has deeply mistrusted its own powers. Russia does not believe it is capable of taking a bet on what will happen in five or ten years' time. Russia does not believe in its own strength. We want to be in Europe, but are afraid of that.

In the post-Soviet territories we have also suffered a complete rout. The Commonwealth of Independent States no longer exists as a unified political and economic community. That is a *fait accompli*. There are American troops in Central Asia and Georgia, the Baltic Region is in NATO. Relations with Belarus have only got worse. As regards more distant borders, the most striking example is Iraq. We are losing it. We took a serious step away from Iraq and lost political and economic influence in the region. I recollect the games played in 2002, manipulating a $40 billion co-operation deal as if it was just a game of "Now you see it, now you don't." The Kremlin is occupied by a bunch of sleight-of-hand spivs who think that if they tear up a $40 billion contract the Americans won't invade Iraq, or will pay us back afterwards.

In addition, Russia has suffered a huge moral reverse. Most people in the West are increasingly coming to the view that Russia is not a democratic country. It is not following a liberal path, but exactly the opposite, destroying the fundamental mechanisms of democratic statehood.

Afterword

And that was all. On that note my tape ran out. It was time to come back to Moscow. It can happen that even demonic geniuses make mistakes, and if they get it wrong once then what guarantee is there that they will not get it wrong again? It has to be said, though, that however things actually turn out, people think devilishly freely in London. The Kremlin it isn't.

THE MADNESS OF TRIBALISM, OR THE LAW OF THE CONSERVATION OF EVIL

March 18, 2004

Late information: first, a letter delivered by post to the Office of the Prime Minister of France threatens terrorist acts and is signed by Movsar

Barayev, leader of the terrorists who took captive the audience of the *Nord-Ost* musical. In the letter he styles himself as the leader of an organization called "The Servants of Allah."

Next, a reference to unnamed sources in the FSB. The FSB has a hand in the projected explosions in France, for which 200 kilograms of explosives was transported some time ago by diplomatic bag to the Embassy of the Russian Federation in Paris, where it is now stored.

Except that Barayev is dead, despite numerous tales that he "was allowed to escape" from *Nord-Ost*. No less certainly, the diplomatic post cannot be used for transporting 200 kilograms of compounds which every frontier dog in the world has been trained to sniff out.

This is the madness of tribalism. It is a modern, virulent disease which causes more and more people to want to commit acts of retaliative terrorism against someone or something. The prognosis for eliminating the disease is not good. The madness of tribalism is set to spread.

Islamophobia is being ratcheted up, with Muslims viewed as outcasts and pressure put at every opportunity on the Islamic world both generally and at a local level. "Everything is their fault," because the more we give them a hard time, the more they will return the favor. This is the long-familiar Law of the Conservation of Evil.

The incompetence, inefficiency and perfidy of Russia's secret services is becoming increasingly evident. They are partners in an international coalition which they cherish and, as we have seen, the more acts of terrorism there are, the more financial resources and power the secret services demand for themselves, including the right to take measures of an extra-judicial character. Their excuse is the need to catch another al-Qaeda cell, but in this they are usually unsuccessful, yet another terrorist act occurs, and everything is repeated. Those who demanded the extra resources and powers are not retired for failing to do their duty. In Russia they expect medals. They continue to furrow their brows and pretend they are doing a great job.

And yet, are the numbers of those wishing to cause explosions being reduced? No. They are increasing. Very few still believe the myth that we have only to catch bin Laden to be able to live in peace.

Increasingly, it occurs to people that the secret services find the hullabaloo about international terrorism highly profitable, and that the secret services themselves are part and parcel of what is sometimes the war against terrorism, and at other times just terrorism plain and simple.

We live in times when non-state terrorism is in a deadly embrace with state terrorism, the one complementing the other, and both of them targeting us. There is nowhere to hide. We are equally defence-less against our own secret services and against the growing number of those seeking revenge – for religion, for themselves, for their country, for their beliefs. There is no shortage of causes.

We run round in circles. The general fear of terrorist acts encour-ages a loosening of control over the secret services, who are suppos-edly doing what is needed but are in fact doing exactly as they please, and accordingly nothing useful. Who can be trusted in these circum-stances? Nobody. The contemporary total lack of faith in the state authorities only strengthens the madness of tribalism.

Judge for yourselves: the lunacy of the notion that the FSB could be involved in the anticipated terrorist acts in France and the trans-porting of explosives to Paris by diplomatic bag seems clear. One might be tempted to laugh at this latest nonsense someone has put on the Internet. Standing between drivel on the Internet and us, however, are recent events in Qatar. In Doha, agents of the Russian secret services blew up Russia's enemy Zelimkhan Yandarbiev [a former Acting President of the Chechen Republic of Ichkeria]. The agents failed to cover their tracks, were caught, and now have confessed to assassination.

What needs to be added? The Doha bomb proves, quite apart from anything else, that Russia has returned to the Soviet period in the sense that it is not only practising political terrorism within its own borders, in Chechnya, but is also exterminating people wherever it pleases. After Yandarbiev's assassination, it is not so easy to laugh off the idea of diplomatic explosives.

We now know that for "our people" exploding a bomb in France is merely a matter of technique, not permissibility. Some in Russia support the tactic of political terrorism which came in with Putin, while others are categorically opposed to it. Be that as it may, the tribalism of the FSB (or GRU) is real. Everything is permitted.

We again face that question of who to trust. Who can you trust as you go down into the Metro, as you take your seat in a suburban train, on a steamer or plane, or fall asleep in your own home?

Nobody. This total lack of trust will sweep away the very governments which have sown it – be sure of that. But, as we already know, it is a royal path to ideological radicalism when some, in order to forget everything, join the skinheads; others are Islamic murid devotees seeking enlightenment or jihadists; others again are something else. It is impossible to predict what a brain infected with the madness of tribalism will dream up tomorrow.

The world must start coming to an agreement about our collective survival rather than continuing its coalitions for extermination and destruction. The race between different kinds of madness we are witnessing will, of course, bring this about sooner or later. The question is only, at the cost of how many victims?

HOT MONEY UNDERLIES THE KREMLIN'S SUPPORT FOR CHAOS IN GEORGIA

September 20, 2004

As we know, in the days immediately following the Beslan nightmare, Messrs Putin and Ivanov (the one who is Minister of Defence) were unable to come up with anything more original than imitating Bush and the gentlemen closest to him, and promised to conduct pre-emptive strikes against the bases of terrorists and the terrorists themselves no matter where they might be found. It was clear to everybody that they were talking about Georgia which, without Eduard Shevardnadze,* is increasingly slipping out of Kremlin control. More precisely, about the Pankisi Gorge, the territory contiguous with Chechnya.

*Soviet Foreign Minister under Gorbachev, then President of Georgia until unseated by the Rose Revolution in November 2003.

Why should the Kremlin so hate Georgia? Why does Georgia so vehemently resist Kremlin control? And why does the Kremlin react so over-sensitively to Georgia's opposition? What is there now about this country and its foremost representatives that makes the Kremlin think it can bomb its way through their territory? Is Russia's war against Georgia a predictable result of our foreign policy, or is it an instant excuse generated by the Kremlin's political imperatives? A post-Beslan, post-traumatic stress syndrome?

In seeking answers to these questions, let us go from the simple to the complex, bearing in mind that the underlying causes of many inter-state cataclysms (and a war between Russia and Georgia would be precisely such a catastrophe) should be sought in elementary matters which lie on the surface.

Of course, Mikheil Saakashvili is a very clever boy. Moreover, he is handsome and a favorite of journalists all over the world. Clever boys, handsome men and other people's favorites have for a long time been systematically removed by Putin from his entourage. But what about the Georgians' court? What do Putin and his entourage see and hear when they meet Saakashvili?

Our approach to the President of Georgia begins today with his Senior Adviser.

"Daniel Kunin," he introduces himself in English, and Daniel's smile is wholly American, as if you are his best friend. He is very likeable and very young, he's not wearing a jacket, and his tie has slipped to one side. He has his shirt sleeves rolled up. Daniel doesn't speak Russian, although he turns out to be a descendant of the anarchist Mikhail Bakunin. Savour this: in emigration Bakunin's family dropped the first syllable of their surname in order not to be identified with their revolutionary kinsman, and now Kunin, with American citizenship, is the adviser to the Georgian President and has his salary paid by the US State Department. The source of his salary is no secret. Daniel himself tells me about it, and very humorously. When "Misha" invited him to become a senior aide, he agreed in principle and immediately sorted out all the details. The miserly salary Georgia could offer was not enough, so Misha organised him a salary in the USA.

Daniel is a very influential figure in the Georgian state civil service, where everybody now speaks English. This is *comme il faut* here, as it was *comme il faut* under the Tsarist regime to speak French. Even the President, Mikheil Saakashvili, and Prime Minister Zurab Zhvaniya, and the Speaker of Parliament, Nino Burdzhanadze, and the Deputy Defence Minister, Vasil Sikharulidze, and of course the Minister of Foreign Affairs, Salome Zurabishvili, are keen to be interviewed in English. Of course, that is their right if they find it more convenient.

One can imagine how, in this atmosphere of insistent Westernisation, members of Putin's Administration must feel, accustomed as they are to seeing everybody in the Commonwealth of Independent States at their feet.

"What language do you usually use when you're talking to your boss?" I ask Bakunin's descendant.

"Usually English," Daniel replies easily and cheerily. "Only during negotiations, when it's important nobody else should understand us, do we talk in Georgian. I have taken private lessons, and used to work in Georgia in an NGO."

An "NGO" is what they they call voluntary organizations.

"And you moved from an NGO straight into the position of a senior aide of the President of Georgia?"

"Yes, the entire government administration here is now made up of ex-NGO people," Daniel laughs.

A bureaucratic apparatus composed of charity workers? One can imagine what our statist President, who hates all these NGOs, must feel when he is obliged to deal with this kind of new Georgian officialdom. And also when this American live wire, Kunin-Bakunin, in the presence of Putin, gives advice in his Anglo-Georgian patois to the recalcitrant Saakashvili.

"What does being an American aide of the Georgian President involve?" I ask Daniel, and he replies:

"Offering new ideas 24 hours a day – morning, noon and night. To have dozens of options and proposals on every issue which interests Misha."

My diagnosis of today's official Tbilisi is that it has adopted the characteristics of American workaholic management, exactly as portrayed in American films: hamburgers, no deference, with everybody cheery, optimistic and life-affirming. The managers of the country are totally orientated towards the West, without any nuances. No helmsman to the north-west, none of the political unpredictability in which today's Kremlin court is mired. Georgia under Saakashvili is manifestly anti-byzantine, anti-bureaucratic, anti-hierarchical. It is an anti-colony rejecting the presence of a governing metropolis. The Kremlin, however, is the exact opposite: neo-Soviet byzantinism, archhierarchy, nostalgia for an empire which flows over into practical action to subordinate and suborn former colonies, of which the latest example is the $800 million tax gift to Ukraine and Belarus for supporting a quasi-Soviet status quo. And the politics of provocation.

Mikheil Saakashvili really is charming and smiles a lot. He is direct and precise in what he says:

"We asked the Russians, 'What have we done wrong? Why do you so dislike us?' We promised to pay pensions and salaries to state officials in South Ossetia. What's wrong with that? The Russians did not reply and began provocative exchanges of fire. We have American troops here, but we play it down. We say, 'We do not want an armed conflict,' and the Russians increase the pressure. But we will not allow the same thing to be repeated as happened here in 1992 [when a four-man Military Council which included Shevardnadze took power]. That stopped reforms. We want to make Georgia attractive. What's wrong with that? But frankly it is very difficult to tell what Russia wants from us. All its actions in Georgia are irrational. We asked the international community to organise a conference on South Ossetia, on its status, to suggest a political solution. The UN, OSCE and the European Union supported the idea. The Russians turned it down."

When did you last talk to Putin?
When I phone they don't put me through. I have sent two letters to Putin. I have had no reply. (A brief, impromptu meeting took place

only on September 16 in Astan, Kazakhstan at a summit meeting of
the Commonwealth of Independent States.)

*How did you react to the statement by Putin's Chechen favorite, Ramzan
Kadyrov, that he would send thousands of his troops to South Ossetia and
"solve the problem"!*
"Fuck him!"

On this high point we pretty much concluded. And now about the
atmosphere in the Georgian President's office, which was not spelled
out in words and sentences but which was very striking. He is completely
in love with his people. He speaks of the death of Georgian soldiers
as a catastrophe: "When 16 people were killed, I had to take a decision." And he took it: to withdraw the Georgian divisions to a safe
distance, so that no more Georgian soldiers would die.*

I emerged staggered by the contrast. In Russia not 16 but 16,000
soldiers can die and nothing would induce the President to save the
rest by moving units back to a safe distance. It is not Russia's size
which is at fault here, not its millions of inhabitants, but its mean-
spiritedness. Saakashvili's love for his people must, one supposes, be
completely baffling to Putin, who has persuaded himself that he is
reviving an empire and must not hesitate to squander lives. Once
the supposed road to empire has been embarked upon, colonies
must prostrate themselves, and anybody who is not with us is against
us. These are the irrational causes of the Kremlin's spat with Tbilisi,

---

*In the summer of 2004 the Georgian Government tried to put an end to the smug-
gling through the Roki tunnel, the border between Russia and Georgia. First they took
control of the tunnel, only for South Ossetian nationalist slogans immediately to ring
out claiming independence. The Georgian Government continued to attack and one
day closed down the Ergneti market. The Roki tunnel mafia had a heart attack. Where
were they to sell their smuggled goods? At this point the "right of nations to self-
determination" came in very handy, and South Ossetia started making a fuss about it,
openly supported by Russia. A war began which lasted from August 12 to 21, 2004,
and when 16 Georgian soldiers were killed, President Saakashvili withdrew his units
from the commanding heights they had previously occupied in order to defend Georgian villages from bombardment. [This note is taken from an article Anna wrote after
her assignment in Tsinkhvali, Sukhumi and Tbilisi.]

but there are other, entirely rational financial and economic, reasons for it.

What are modern Russia's interests in the territories beyond the Caucasian mountains? What has Putin's bureaucracy got to fight over in the region? In the first place, Russia wants to strengthen its so-called "Christian (Ossetian) axis" in the Caucasus as a counterweight to its "soft Islamic underbelly" (Chechnya, Ingushetia, Karachayevo-Cherkessia, Kabardino-Balkaria, Dagestan and Adigeya). These axes have a long history and are real enough. There genuinely is a territorial imperative which makes it logical for Russia to focus on South Ossetia, a tiny scrap of land on the other side of the mountains from North Ossetia.

In the second place, Russia has an interest in Abkhazia, a strip of land on the Black Sea coast, which it needs if it is to have overland access to Armenia, the Kremlin's sole remaining partner in that region (the others all having deserted Russia) where the US does not yet have a strategic presence.

The aims of South Ossetia and Abkhazia are also understandable. They have nowhere else to go. South Ossetia makes no secret of the fact that it would like to be united with North Ossetia, which is impossible without Moscow's involvement. For its part Abkhazia sees no possibility of returning to the bosom of Georgia and, since it needs someone to snuggle up to, turns to Moscow.

In practice, however, both these conflicts, frozen in Soviet times, have now turned into black holes, and although the political map of the world shows both territories as part of independent Georgia, both Abkhazia and South Ossetia are de facto zones without taxation, without transparent budgets, without legitimate government institutions, without budgetary resources and all the other things which fundamentally differentiate a law-governed territory from a lawless one.

Why does the Kremlin need black holes? For internal puposes, mainly; for a straightforward way of injecting covert funds where they are needed; to facilitate all kinds of plots. Russia's claims to support the rule of law are just so much hot air. In reality there is still a policy of supporting territories which can be used for injecting or extracting large amounts of money that don't need to be accounted for. Such zones are needed for covert operations and missions where nobody is accountable to anybody else, or even has to sign a form.

Russian policy continues to be one of cash under the counter. Without it nothing happens. Cash under the counter is a cornerstone of every branch and institution of the Government. Externally supported chaos in place of order and defined norms is essential for such games to succeed.

To have black holes beyond your own borders is extremely convenient, far more convenient than offshore funds, where at any moment somebody may sniff you out and you have to devise elaborate multi-layered structures for purposes of concealment, only increasing the probability that information will leak out. In Abkhazia and South Ossetia nothing like that is needed.

In Soviet times, certain African regimes served this purpose. The Politburo presented them as centers of "national liberation," pumped in Party funds, and got on with its dodgy financial operations. In Russia Chechnya provided a domestic black hole for a while. The failure to develop a normal banking system there was entirely deliberate, and Chechnya has none to this day. Chechnya, however, is within the Russian Federation and that was a snag. There was always the risk of official inspections, Audit Commissions, even an honest Prosecutor popping up. In any case the appetite of Ramzan Kadyrov and his comrades keeps growing.

Abkhazia and South Ossetia have so far operated without a hitch. You can do many things there which you can't elsewhere. You can send in money, arms and drugs – and that does go on. You can also pull it back out, and that too occurs. There is no inventorising or stocktaking; you just have to feed the undemanding local regimes and spread a bit of propaganda around about "defending Russian citizens." It's as easy as that.

In his first term Putin successfully pressurised Shevardnadze to the point where he, a Soviet oligarch who knew exactly how and why such black holes are needed, caved in and handed over a third of

Georgia's territory as an ask-no-questions zone for Russian dealings. Under the new President business slumped; Saakashvili almost immediately announced a policy of thawing out the frozen conflicts – for example between Georgia and Abkhazia, Georgia and South Ossetia – and thereby became Russia's Enemy No. 1. Putin let Saakashvili have Adjara back without too much fuss because it was in any case working more in the interests of its own Prince Abashidze than of Moscow, but for the black holes of Abkhazia and South Ossetia he decided to fight.

Russia's Transcaucasian game calls for severe punishment of the Westernising President Saakashvili, by bombing him, for example, as he openly aligns himself with the USA and tells the old colonial power to "fuck off." As a result, with every day and hour that passes, we Russians are losing Georgia as a good neighbour, when it is crucial that we should enjoy close and friendly relations with it.

The Putin regime's current policy of trying to annex two Georgian territories is completely counter to the strategic or indeed any other sensible interests Russia has in the Caucasus.

Finally, a word about love. In the twenty-first century clever rulers do not incite citizens they love and respect to bloodshed. The problems begin if the citizens are unloved, and the rulers a bunch of hopeless dunces.

CHINA ON THE MOVE

July 4, 2005

In June, at an international conference on security in Paris, the well-known Russian sinologist, Professor Vilya Gelbras, read a sensational report about Chinese migration into Russia. Here he replies to questions from *Novaya gazeta*.

Vilya Gelbras, Professor of Economics, Doctor of Historical Sciences, one of Russia's top sinologists, teaches at the Institute of Asian and African Studies of Moscow State University. He conducts research at the Institute of World Economics and World Relations of the Russian Academy of Sciences.

In recent years you have written two ground-breaking books about Chinese migration into Russia. What is their principal theme?
People have been talking about Chinese migration, to the effect that China is virtually seeking to take over the whole of Russia, for a long time. With the aid of my students, I systematically conducted large-scale research into this issue. The first study was in 2001, and for it we selected Moscow, Vladivostok, Khabarovsk, and also Ussuriysk, where the greatest numbers of Chinese shuttle traders get off the train, and from where they head for lucrative markets. This material provided the basis of the first book.

For the second book we selected Irkutsk and again the cities of Moscow, Vladivostok and Khabarovsk. Irkutsk interested us because migrants had already settled there. In addition, a Chinese plan came into our possession which had been considered worthy of the attention of the Politburo of the Central Committee of the Communist Party of China. In it, Irkutsk was allocated a special role. The plan proposed organised settlement of Chinese throughout the territory of Russia via Amur Province. Retaining control of their commodities, they would concentrate at junctions of the trans-Siberian railway all the way to Moscow, and thus radiate their influence outwards. Irkutsk is important to the Chinese because it is central to the movement both of goods and of people from Kazakhstan and into the Altai, including Buryatia. At the time of our research a Chinese consulate had already been opened in Irkutsk.

The resulting book painted a curious picture. We presented a panorama of the enterpreneurial activity of the Chinese in Russia, what they were doing with their money, how it was transferred to China, how goods came in from China and how, on Russian territory, they were converted into money. We also wrote a more substantial special report for the United Nations.

How much money do you calculate we are today transferring to China in this way, and how much are we spending on purchases from the Chinese?
I don't think we can say very accurately how much we are buying and selling. There is a massive black market, and blatant corruption.

On the part of the Chinese?
No, it is Russian corruption surrounding Chinese trade. For instance, Chinese delegations have recently turned up in the European part of Russia seeking contracts for lumbering timber. Is there no wood in Siberia? We discovered that along the railways in Siberia the Chinese have been allowed to fell the forests so completely that we are in danger of losing larch altogether.

Do the Chinese particularly prize larch?
It is an extremely precious wood. Larch emits a fragrance in perpetuity. It is a delight to live in a house built of larch.

It is surely not because of the fragrance that the Chinese are cutting it down here?
They use it in all kinds of ways, the oil, the seeds and the cones. Everything is processed. They are no longer felling their own forests. From an ecological viewpoint, if a territory has less than 12 per cent of forest cover, natural disasters are inevitable. China has barely 13 per cent, and that is why rarely a year goes by without torrential rain followed by flooding. It is a result of their having stripped their forests in the past.

Was the plan you spoke of approved by the Politburo?
That is unclear. Much is classified in China. My friends there tried to persuade me not to say anything on the subject. They were afraid of leaks, but now it is clear that there is a second similar plan to move via Heihe to Blagoveshchensk and via Suifenhe to Amur Province and beyond. Heihe and Suifenhe are major population centers. The plan provides for the inflow of both migrants and goods. If in 1998–9, even in 2000, these flows were spontaneous, today major Chinese companies have sprung up which give people precise instructions to sell particular goods.

So you're saying this is already political?
It was political from the outset. Now, my Chinese sources tell me, if a man marries a Russian woman in Russia, he is paid for it.

Who pays him?
The Chinese Government, for putting down roots on our territory. With their policy of birth control (couples are allowed just one child, and preferably a boy) the Chinese have unbalanced the natural reproduction of the sexes. In some districts there is a huge bias in favor of men. Forty to fifty million of them have no prospect whatsoever of finding wives, and now their leaders are looking for palliatives.

What has been the increase in Chinese living permanently in Russia between 2001 and 2004?
It is impossible to say, because the Chinese immigration is forever ebbing and flowing. At present we are talking about half a million or more. Hotheads say two to three million, but that is premature.

What kind of person is the modern Chinese who has settled in Russia?
In the main it is town dwellers, because they are the most literate.

What do the Chinese understand by literacy?
Mostly a Chinese coming to Russia can sign his name. He can read and count, and he is shrewd, able to think quickly in the market. There are only a few peasants in the overall total, and they will have been invited specially. To grow vegetables, for example.

And are they completely illiterate?
It is difficult to say. The Chinese world is such that the foreman speaks for everyone.

And who is the foreman?
The person who assembled the brigade. Nobody will talk to you without his agreement. On many occasions we had to make great efforts to get people to fill in questionnaires themselves. The first surveys were useless because all the questionnaires were filled in by the brigade leader, so they were identical. In agriculture and construction the brigade leader is completely in charge. It is different in trade, where he is more of a supervisor. Very often now in Moscow and Nizhny

Novgorod a brigade leader will hire Ukrainian and Russian traders. If the goods are poor quality you find Ukrainians, if they are a bit better, Russians, but they are working under the supervision of a Chinese.

Are these senior figures mafiosi?
It would be wrong to say they are all mafiosi. Many are hard-working people who earn a living by the sweat of their brow. Mafiosi do not usually actually work. Under an ancient Chinese tradition, they protect the traders for a certain payment.

A kind of protection racket?
They negotiate with our militia and Customs officers. Their job is to shift goods across the border.

The Chinese use Russians for "patronage"?
Of course. The Chinese have nothing against militiamen. I have seen that myself. Let me offer one striking example: the Russian press is always publishing figures about the volume of trade between Russia and China based on – Chinese statistics. Do we not have our own? Of course we do, but the Chinese figures are higher. As soon as goods cross the frontier, there are more of them, by many billions of dollars each year. And that continues year in, year out.

Where does this difference come from?
The black market. Ours is a corrupt economy. Mr Vanin, the Head of our Customs Service, is starting to say we need to impose order. It's not so much the Chinese mafia who are active as our own, and that is what makes it best to use Chinese statistics. The Chinese figures include both the grey economy and the black market. The second factor accounting for the differences is that in Russia the Chinese engage in forms of trade that would never occur to us. For example, they collect frogspawn. It is greatly valued, and they resourcefully collect kilograms of it at a time.

Where do they get licences for harvesting frogspawn?
Why, bless you, what licences?!

Well, what documents do the Chinese show at the border?
I have no idea, but in the forests of the taiga they live very much on their own, very secretively, busily milking frogs. It is a very gruelling form of poaching, and it will backfire on us.

Timber, frogs, marrying Russian women – are these the results of the new policy China calls "going out"?
Yes. This approach started in 1996–7. They came to it by thinking about conquering world markets. All the academic institutes were brought in, including natural science institutes. It was accepted that indigenous geological discoveries would be a long and very costly endeavour, and the Chinese wanted something quick that would change the situation in the country. They decided to break into world markets by producing cheap goods by the billion. And they have succeeded.

Why did the Chinese need to "go out"?
The majority of Chinese in China are peasants. In all ages they have served as a source of revenue, but 500 million Chinese peasants are not what is needed today. After the XVIth Party Congress, in 2000, when the leadership of China changed, they concluded that the economy had no internal mechanisms encouraging increased production. China has 20 per cent of the world's population, but they account for very little in the way of production: about 80 per cent of peasants earn less than one US dollar a day; about 60 per cent, less than half a dollar a day. What can someone in that situation aspire to in the market? What interest does he have in innovation? No, it was calculated that they needed to leave 150–170 million peasants in the rural economy, and to take 250–300 million out of the villages. Where to? That is how the era of Chinese expansion came about, "going out." The peasants were allowed to leave the villages. For China that was a revolution. All towns and provinces which produce goods for export now have mini-townships where peasants live and work. That is why they are so cheap. A new migratory phenomenon appeared: China began as it were to split into two parts, one moving towards our border, to Xinjiang, and the other towards the coast.

Are they moving physically?

Yes, that is where the work and the money are, but the Chinese cannot completely abandon their ancestral lands. The peculiarity of the situation is that a proportion remain behind, and those who leave return later. We still know very little about the basis of family and social relations in China. There are families which emigrated to the West, to America 100–150 years ago, but each New Year have to return; in Russia kinship ties were quickly destroyed after the revolution, but that didn't happen in China.

Where are these 250–300 million peasants who were to be taken out of the countryside?

Everywhere and nowhere. Some here, some there. The catch is that most of them have not settled. Some are milking frogs in Russia.

8. The Other Anna

Anna Politkovskaya has been described as "steely." She was not; she was matter-of-fact. These articles show her humanity, a sensitive conscience, a willingness to engage with the unfamiliar, and regret that her homeland was not a more enjoyable place to live.

PASSION ON TIPTOE THAT MAKES YOU QUIVER: MOVEMENT AS AN ALLOTROPE OF LOVE

March 30, 2000

In London the performances of the internationally renowned Buenos Aires company Tango Por Dos, directed by its creator and invariable principal dancer, the breathtaking Miguel Angel Zotto, have played to consistently full houses, raising sighs and gasps from a habitually reserved audience. In the Peacock Theatre on Kingsway, the visitors have been presenting a two-act performance of *Tango Argentino*. Almost three hours of bewitching stage action with never a word spoken, only music, dancing and emotion. By the finale the exceedingly well-balanced, phlegmatic, and even apathetic British audience had been roused to a peak of frenzied enthusiasm, wanting more. Know how to live and you can have a life!

There is pure passion on the stage, nothing else, performed by six couples. Naturally, there is no sex, which I mention for Russian ignoramuses yet to learn the distinction between passion and bed. All the dancers are middle-aged, not babes in arms or adolescents, expressing more than just climactic ecstasies. These are adults who know all about losing, and winning, and hoping. Their intensity is magnificent and mind-blowing. No grinding of teeth, no rending of raiment, no biting of lips, not even any crying out. It is a presentation of oblivious passion.

There is such heat generated by the show that from time to time you see couples quietly sneaking out of the auditorium and the theatre. The theatre's regulars assure you that they leave to make love to each other themselves. Rumors are swirling around London that this always happens during *Tango Argentino*: the men and women watching the dancing, in which nobody is topless, there is no striptease, not a hint of *Playboy* titillation, can't sit it out to the finale. They want to do it themselves, to experience this eternal reality. Such a torrent of libido floods from the stage that unless you are made of stone you succumb to it. If you came on your own, you would feel amorous towards whoever was sitting next to you. If only for a couple of hours, you can imagine yourself to be a dazzlingly inventive lover, capable of anything.

Do not suppose that this is a gourmet spectacle for the cognoscenti, or even for those accustomed to imbibing cocktails of passion. Nothing of the sort. Everything is very simple, even primitive. Six couples demonstrate every type and variety of tango, such as might grace a ballroom, or be seen at a rustic dance (in Argentina, of course), or in a seaside café to the accompaniment of a small, artless dance band. And that's pretty much it. What is striking about the performance is not what they are dancing but how: every womanly cell breathes desire, but it is not the kind of desire squandered in the Metro, on a trolleybus, or in the drunken cafés and dives of Russia. It is a desire trained to draw in to a happiness – possibly a transient and ephemeral happiness – every atom of the man beside you.

Tango Por Dos is both an Argentinian show and the name of the dance company. It was created in 1989 by Zotto and Milena Plebs, the best tango dancers in Argentina. At that time they were also in love and, for almost 10 years, touring constantly, they projected their private emotion from the stages of the world in dance steps and poses with unbelievable power.

In Argentina the couple were known as "our Romeo and Juliet." They had met in 1985 when Milena was already a famous ballerina and, moreover, the well-educated daughter of a prominent family. Zotto was her inferior in every respect. He was born the son of an amateur actor and had no popular following. Who trained him? Only "life itself," and the tango in the streets and nightclubs of Buenos Aires.

It was then Milena decided that Zotto was completely irresistible and would be magnificent in the tango. She abandoned her ballet career and, for the sake of her man, defied family and friends, even breaking off relations with many of them, just to be with Zotto, touring the world. In due course, living out their own love on stage, in front of an audience, they were transformed into a legendary couple in their own right and were crowned king and queen of their genre. People who saw Milena and Miguel dance maintain that the sparks they emitted every time they danced the tango could give members of the audience a heart attack.

Alas, three years ago Zotto and Plebs split up. Zotto announced that he wanted to be alone, and Milena said she would never dance again, despite an abundance of offers. The end of their *pas de deux* came when Zotto refused Milena, by then 36, a child, both for career and personal reasons. He refused to be burdened with a family and children.

There were other reasons. In 1992 he had lost his father, who died an agonising death from cancer. Plebs later said she had sensed that this was the beginning of their own last act. She continued to look after Miguel in his anguish, but suddenly discovered that her inconsolable partner had someone else wiping away his tears. In 1995 Milena had to recognise that, apart from the tango, they no longer had anything in common.

Milena Plebs is an amazing individual. She avers that the tango is a dance of passion which can be danced only by a couple who are in love. Anything else is a profanation which will not captivate the audience. "When you love a man," Milena has said, "that is the tango. The tango means being together, hoping for a child. When all that is in the past for Zotto and me, I no longer wish to dance." She lives in Buenos Aires and teaches choreography, sometimes directing a performance herself. But she doesn't dance, and she hasn't had a baby.

Today Zotto obstinately refers to himself as an incurable romantic, while continuing to dance without Milena, and doing so outstandingly well. He does not need to love the partner he twirls in the tango. Oh well – that's men. But Milena – that's also what women are like.

This show has toured the world but has never come to Russia. I suspect there is good reason for that. Zotto has circled almost the entire globe with his dancing, and more than once. He has performed in such lands disinclined to overt displays of passion as China, Thailand, and heaven knows what other places remote from Latin culture, from the salons of Europe, the cafés of Argentina, and the reality of Latin America. So why has Russia been denied the opportunity of sipping from this spicy chalice?

Love has, of course, taken root here, and often, but we entirely lack any culture of passion. Yes, it looms large in Dostoevsky, Leontiev or Tolstoy, both love and tears, but alas, it hardly figures in the everyday lives of people like us in the twenty-first century. We have become habituated to quiet love, to understanding another person to the depths of their soul. We pity the unfortunate and the alcoholics drinking themselves to death because their souls have been defiled. We have a tradition of making do with love on a shoestring, of living in hope as the years go by, of washing his feet and drinking the dirty water. But passion as a short-lived, all-consuming fire – forget it! We are incapable of a month of passion (even just the one, but sweet, devastating, and luring us towards madness), or even of a passionate break-up to shake our whole organism to the core even though it is obvious that this is the end, so let's end with a burst of passion. As an experiment, just try suggesting to your gentleman friend parting at the peak of your amorous relations. He will shy away in horror. For us, breaking up means divorce and walking out with all our belongings and all the ancient dust which has settled on them.

Our pro-Soviet love is nothing but rummaging around in ourselves, not a desire to take from our partner every last drop of the happiness he can give, even if these are our final hours together, and to give him in return the same, even though we know the pillow will be empty tomorrow. Passion Russian-style is a trip from A to B. At A we kiss, and at B we saw away at the bed-frame. It is great good fortune if the trip is direct, and awful if the path is tortuous, which it all too often is. But why go on? As if we don't already know this only too well.

Perhaps the accommodation shortage has put paid to our scope for passion. There's no doubt it can have that effect, but passion is not only about square metres of floor space, and it is vital not to be dwelling on how they might be divided if something goes wrong. Passion does undeniably require money, and our men have withered decade after decade because they have been penniless. Even when recently some of them have become rich, they have rushed away from their wives to prostitutes or other readily available women, to strip clubs and massage parlours – anywhere, just as long as they don't have to prove themselves.

These last years have been a complete disaster for passion. Following in the footsteps of teenagers and racketeers, the rest of society has even adopted the terminology "screwing." Anybody who has a relationship is "screwing," and that is how they and those around them refer to it. [The poet] Sergey Yesenin claimed elegiacally "not to regret, invoke the past, or shed a tear." Neither do modern couples in Russia – instead they screw. Bankers screw, their children screw, retired engineers screw, homeless people screw, and so do musicians and poets. Can we be bothered with the storms of passion, the paroxysms of a last farewell, our knees giving way at a chance meeting? Well, no, actually we can't. A quick screw is all we need. If you should regrettably find yourself engulfed by passion, the put-down of the Russian male, long adept at screwing, will be like a bucket of cold water: "Don't put me in a difficult situation. For heaven's sake, we are grown-ups."

In our culture you must either control or conceal your passion, and then people will find their way to you. It makes you sick! You are expected to be modest, not to have pretensions, not to give yourself airs, not to be different . . . and then you will be graced by happiness "just when you least expect it." What nonsense! What garbage! What a pathetic excuse for promiscuity! You should be emotionally open only at home, and then only if you are lucky enough to have someone who appreciates it!

We ladies, however, are not much better. We expect little and, as has long been known, it is women who reflect their men, never the other way round.

So why on earth would we need an Argentinian tango for two in Russia? It would just cause a lot of upset for no good reason.

"The Lord went forth to test the people's love." So wrote Yesenin, who knew the meaning of passion. That line belongs here if only because there is a quotation in large print in the program of Tango Por Dos from Isadora Duncan, who danced the tango and was Yesenin's lover. Alas, her spirit has not been passed on to us.

If you find yourself in London, escape Russia at the Peacock Theatre. If you miss the show there but still want to be lashed by someone else's unreasoning passion, you can catch it in Milan, Turin and Lyons where Tango Por Dos will be touring in April. But not in Moscow.

THE JOY OF PARIS

June 1, 2000

So much has been said about Paris that it is embarrassing to join the chorus. But it can't be helped, I really want to. This city has such powerful magic that your tongue, that wretch which betrays your innermost feelings, is untied and puts to sleep protesting reason. You want to shout that you too have been happy here. Even if it's banal, cliché-ridden, even if it's already been done to death by everybody, including the greatest and most brilliant people on the planet, you still want to say it your way, even though you recognise the pointlessness of the enterprise.

So, I'm in Paris, it's late May and the chestnuts are in bloom. The next five days are mine, all mine.

The reason for being here is that a collection of reports from Chechnya and Ingushetia, published in *Novaya gazeta* between September 1999 and April 2000, are being published here. This is very pleasing because it puts our regular readers, from Chukotka to Kaliningrad, ahead of the Parisians, those legislators on every aspect of fashion. The publisher who has lavished so much loving attention on *Novaya gazeta* (not without the prompting of Alexander Ginsburg, former political prisoner and dissident, who is today a champion of human rights, friend of Solzhenitsyn, and a Parisian), is not only very large, popular, and well known in Paris, but boasts the aesthetically pleasing name of Robert Laffont. There, in just those two words, those four syllables which flow into each other, France is rendered into sound. The uvular trill of the "r," twice. The lily-like "la" where a tender "l" merges with a kiss from lips delicately forming that special "a" to produce a sound close to the la-la-la of a toothless babe.

However, the imposing Robert Laffont was not until tomorrow morning. My first night in Paris was to be spent in a café. Where else? But how are you to pluck the very finest pearl from such a gleaming pile? In Paris, a city of freedom and a certain frivolity, the only way is to advance boldly and see what happens. The very first Parisian café we managed to select entirely at random ("Should we go in here?" "Oh no, much too crowded!" "OK, then, down the street there to the right?" "How about this one?" "Let's find a seat") was called by coincidence "Le Select."

It was perfect. We found ourselves in the center of Montparnasse, both the district and the Boulevard, and accordingly in a haven where the artistic elite of the entire world came to alternate resuscitation with inspiration. As we soon found out.

If we had known where we were headed, we might have been more circumspect. At the next table was a boisterous party of stereotypical Parisians: quasi-actors, quasi-artists, of differing ages but all with a suggestion of the eternal student at their greying temples. They were having a great time, oblivious to the joys or sorrows of anyone around them. There was little space between the tables and the rooms were very narrow, the furniture ancient. The interiors were perfectly preserved from the early 1920s. It is wholly impermissible to make any changes to the historical appearance of Parisian cafés. They are museums of the spirit of Paris.

The atmosphere, too, had been preserved. A young girl-artist, very proud of herself – like all Parisian girls – and instantly tipsy, eager to find happiness with a young boy-artist sitting some distance away, headed rapidly towards him through a historic, narrow space and sent a bottle on our table flying. There was water everywhere, in my hand-bag, on our clothes, in our shoes. So what did this select, impulsive fledgling of Montparnasse do about it?

Well, actually, nothing. Women in Paris are very proud indeed and have their noses in the air while managing simultaneously to seem entirely available. Our artistic mademoiselle politely, but not too politely, cooed "Pardon" and quickly found the joy she had fluttered in here to find, in the company of her Pierre, who was perhaps an as yet undiscovered Derain, or Matisse.

The names, of course, are deliberately selected. Derain, Matisse, and indeed Picasso, Cocteau, Max Jacob, Henry Miller, Scott Fitzgerald, and Hemingway himself had sat at these same little tables at which the early twenty-first-century Montparnasse avant-garde had given us a good soaking.

What more could a former Soviet citizen want in order to be happy? At this moment in life, nothing, unless to feel their backside in contact with the tattered armchair which had been scuffed by the threadbare trousers of the young Hemingway as he sipped the same cocktail as you. He was select, and you are select.

The waiters of Le Select, incidentally, are men of advancing years, if not just plain old. And yet, how proud they are, standing out even among the proud Parisian crowd. In vain will you seek to attract their attention, for you are no Picasso. Your predicament, however, is that you don't want to rise irately from your seat and storm out, having lost patience with the arrogant *garçon*. For some reason you understand and forgive, for you are still only in the foothills.

The waiter eventually deigns to come over to you, a débutante here still far from conquering Montparnasse. He brings you the water you requested long ago, naturally in a 1920s tumbler. The glass is thick and coarse, without a hint of gentility, and openly proclaims its primary function as being not to get broken too soon. The clientele have always been a bit rowdy. Give them half-decent glasses and you would have been permanently in debt, even if some of them did go on to become Nobel Prize winners, the *crème de la crème*, champions of the world.

You have to sympathise with the glasses. As he bangs mine down on the table, the waiter does not favor his non-regular customer with so much as a glance. The party next to us are "his." He and they belong here, guffawing, flirting, twining themselves around each other, even though one brings the coffee and another pays for it. Naturally the *garçon* can only look down on me.

He is haughty, but not actually rude. He even appears partly to forgive me for being a nobody in Montparnasse. You get a strange feeling from your mute contemplation of this old Parisian professional's game. You catch yourself trying to be noticed by him, supercilious though his glance will be, and are glad when you see he has forgiven you. You want to jump up straight away and pursue the bluebird, to stand out from the crowd, if only for an hour, but most certainly to be a hero. Such, they say, are the antics provoked by Montparnasse. We may not be the greatest on its slopes but neither are we going to be the least.

But now, farewell, proud Le Select! You may not have known it, but in fact we were not such nonentities. Tomorrow we too would begin our conquest of Paris. The "pre-publication marketing" of our book was about to begin. What in Russia we would call the hype. How was it? Bruising. Russian public relations firms have no idea: from an early breakfast to a late supper inclusive there were press conferences, interviews, parties, presentations, conversations. By evening I was hoarse, and the next morning everything began all over again. There was a whirl of journalists who for some reason were interested in the book, some of whom had even found time to read it. The timetable was rigorously adhered to: I was whisked from one interview to the next, with no deviations from the agreed program. Between meetings with journalists there was an orientation talk with my publisher Malcy Ozonna about things I must under no circumstances forget to say. Marie Gigault from *Le Monde* was to be told one thing, Thierry Brandt from the Franco-Swiss newspaper *Le Matin* something else, the magazine *Elle* something else again.

For all that, the frenetic pace did not dissipate the emotional charge. Everywhere kind words cascaded down, love, warmth, admiration, respect – a positive tsunami. Life was suddenly something to enjoy, surrounded by interested people. These were feelings long unfamiliar in Russia where people do not love you for your articles. On the contrary, most hate you for them.

The French intellectuals involved in promoting the book were clearly puzzled by my increasingly obvious embarrassment as this carousel of kindness continued. "Isn't it just the same in Russia when some-body has written and published a book?" "It is not at all the same in Russia." "What do you mean? Has your book not been published in Russia?" "Of course not!"

They were amazed. They shrugged their shoulders. For the first time they looked at me uncertainly, unable to believe it. I did not try to explain. What would be the point? These were trivial details. I looked about me instead, taking in what really mattered – how the Parisiennes were dressed.

You have only to stand in the bustle of Place de la Madeleine for ten minutes to understand that there is no answer to this question. The essence of Paris is that the women dress as they please. The men too. And they think as they choose to, and put on their make-up in the morning as they see fit. This kind of life is called freedom. Liberty. You live as you please, however you like.

Moscow had been only a transit airport on my flight to Paris. The starting point of the journey which brought me to the capital of France was Ingushetia and Chechnya: refugee camps; foothills; forests; soldiers desperate to go home; hungry people crying; the routine horror of life in our homeland where everybody lives as best they can, just trying to survive. That is why "my" Paris seemed such a sweet, heavenly treat. It was like the taste in your mouth after wormwood, when a single chocolate has the impact of kilograms of honey.

"'Why are you not sleeping?' 'Paris will not let me sleep.'" Some-times we hum that song to ourselves as we struggle towards the light through the routine austerity of life in Russia. And do you know what? It wasn't true! I slept very soundly in Paris, for the first time in all the months of the war, without sleeping pills, without shivering. Nobody was yelling at me, goading me, telling me I was a traitor. Everybody liked me. Everybody admired me. May you enjoy the same experience.

That was the joy of Paris, the private property of one Russian journalist who dares to testify to it. It was a joy all the more poignant because immediately before it I had to dare to do quite different things. My book will go on sale in the bookshops of Paris on June 4, 2000. Its publishers have decided to call it *Journey to Hell: A Chechen Diary. The Daring Testimony of a Russian Journalist.*

A Lighter Postscript

Simultaneously with the collection of articles from *Novaya gazeta* about Russia during the Chechen War, another book on the same topic will be published in France in early June.

It has the eye-catching title of *Chienne de Guerre, A Bitch of a War.* Its author is a Parisian journalist, Anne Nivat. Our books are not thought too similar, although they tell the same tale. But now, let's consider some parallels. Is it mere chance that the books are appearing together? The French emotionally assured me that it was a complete coincidence. That might seem hard to believe, but to confirm it, here is a story.

Anne Nivat is not just a brave French journalist, she is also the daughter of Georges Nivat, today a professor at the University of Geneva, and a very famous Slavist in France. Georges Nivat is not just a famous Slavist, but the same person who came as an exchange student to Moscow in the early 1960s and very soon found himself in the house of none other than Olga Ivinskaya, the last love of Boris Pasternak. Georges did not merely drink cups of tea in her house, but fell in love with her daughter, Irina. He even moved in with them, and their impending marriage was blessed by Pasternak himself. More than that, Pasternak and Georges spent a lot of time together, talking. Pasternak helped him to make sense of Russian life, with all its trials. Later he was booted out of Russia thanks to the efforts of the relevant agencies. And Irina? She ended up in one of the labor camps in Mordovia.

Gradually everything fell apart between Georges and Irina. First he got married in France and began bringing up his children in the ascetic spirit of strict Protestantism. Little Anne Nivat crawled through the mountains with her Papa. That is how she was brought up, learning to grit her teeth. Less than 30 years would pass before these lessons in survival came in very handy as Chechnya burned. She was to crawl through the mountains of Chechnya, well able to grit her teeth. But let us return to the story of that love in the middle of the last century. Learning that Georges had got married in France, Irina too fell in love with a prisoner in the neighbouring camp for men.

The marriage of Georges and Irina, to which Pasternak had given his blessing, never came to pass, but the love he had encouraged did flourish in a house in the very road where *Novaya gazeta*'s offices are situated. The house is still there, and so is their apartment.

We are all closer to each other than we know. Our world is a strange place and more intricately connected than we imagine in our wildest dreams. Paris and Moscow are almost the same.

COME WITH THE WIND: MOSCOW CHAMPIONS OF A BETTER RUSSIA MEET GEORGE W. BUSH (AT HIS REQUEST)

May 25, 2002

It is not only the Kremlin that gets to enjoy the Bushes' company. Over 100 of us, officially classified as "Russian social, parliamentary, and religious opinion-formers" and highly diverse in terms of our socio-political make-up, also got invited to meet the US President. On May 24, 2002, from 2:15 p.m. Moscow time, immediately after a presidential lunch in one of the Kremlin dining halls. The venue was Spaso House on Old Arbat, the renowned residence of the American Ambassador.

A fashionable function is good because nobody is responsible to anybody for anything. It is pure entertainment. While the Bushes were being catastrophically late arriving from the Kremlin, the rest of us in Spaso House were also enjoying ourselves. First, everybody was entertained by Boris Nemtsov of the Union of Right Forces, who appeared sporting such an amazing milk-chocolate tan that he eclipsed even Valentina Matvienko. Madame Matvienko is a Deputy Prime Minister in the Russian Government, and has lately been making increasingly strenuous efforts to mutate into a social lioness. Anyway, she was amazing too at the crush in Spaso House, displaying a tan worthy of the Caribbean and Seychelles.

"Well, I got mine in Sochi," Nemtsov said defensively. "I always go there in the spring."

An hour and a half passed in disputation and the consumption of aesthetically irreproachable canapés. Still Bush didn't appear, but no nervous anticipation was observable among the guests.

Jewish administrators, eternally indebted to America, sauntered around and the Chief Muslims of Russia in exotic costumes smiled sweetly at them. The A-team from the Moscow Patriarchate's Department of Foreign Relations, the whole lot of them, drifted in looking pleased with themselves. One of the last to appear was Gleb Pavlovsky, our principal Presidential Privy Counsellor, looking grumpy.

This provoked a minor stir. "What's *he* doing here?" echoed around the room with its laden tables. Most of those present evidently felt that Bush's definition of social, parliamentary and religious opinion-formers would not include, to put it mildly, supporters of Putin. "He probably bought the invitation," the crowd decided, whispering this explanation from ear to ear. "How much for, do you think?" novices in these matters mouthed at the cognoscenti of the political netherworld. "About $5,000," those versed in such matters muttered out of the side of their mouths.

Congregated around a large tray of fruit, Russia's best-known civil rights activists, Oleg Orlov, Tatiana Kasatkina ("Memorial") and Svetlana Gannushkina ("Citizens' Aid"), modestly dressed, discussed the course of the Second Chechen Campaign in funereal tones. Not three steps away from them the same topic was being discussed by official "representatives of the Russian people" Mikhail Margelov and Dmitriy Rogozin, chairmen of the Foreign Relations Committees respectively of the Soviet of the Federation and of the Duma, resplendent in the latest Parisian male fashions. They were studiedly pretending not to have noticed the human rights activists, and were discussing when they would next be obliged to return to Strasbourg to defend Russia from another attack by the human rights camp.

At last we were called through to the sumptuously decorated hall, solemn, bravura symphonic music flowing from the amplifiers, such as accompanies cosmonauts en route to a launch.

The President of the United States of America was manifestly not a hundred miles away. It was time for his speech. We were directed to our seats. Democrat Grigoriy Yavlinsky analysed the principles behind the allocation: "Those seated closest to Bush are those most persecuted." And indeed, Pavlovsky was awarded a seat right at the back, while *Novaya gazeta* merited the third of approximately 30 rows, between Yavlinsky and the head of the Russian Mormons. In front of me was the broad back of Yevgeny Kiselev, sacked director of the now closed NTV television station; Jews, Muslims and Catholics made up the first row, and were accordingly those deemed to be suffering most under the present regime.

A clipped command was issued to "fasten the cordon," and we were enclosed around the perimeter. It would not be permissible to go out, we were advised, even to the toilet or to smoke, until the presidential motorcade had departed from Spaso House. His back to the podium, a young man from the American security services stood facing the social, political and religious leaders of Russia, his eyes looking simultaneously in every direction. "He's checking for al-Qaeda," Yavlinsky quipped.

Another half-hour passed until finally there was a rustling behind the curtains and several men wearing black suits simultaneously brought in identical "nuclear briefcases." This was apparently a traditional ploy to confuse any possible enemy, who would not know which was *the* briefcase.

Condoleezza Rice was in the same group. The omnipotent National Security Adviser was wearing less than perfectly tailored black trousers and a rather chilly yellow jacket, with black piping along its imaginary pockets and real sides. She had no perm, something that Matvienko would never countenance in public.

"There's Condo-Liza Petrovna," the Soviet of the Federation quipped somewhere behind, in accordance with the sense of humor they have there.

Laura Bush was announced next, Secretary of State Colin Powell, and the ambassadorial couple, Lisa and Alexander Vershbow. Proud and serene, not even carrying a handbag, Laura came out in a grey suit with white buttons and black open-toed sandals. Powell sat down and crossed his legs. Glory be, he got away with it: unlike the socks of Russian men, which are invariably too short, Powell's were magnificently long. Unfortunately, something seemed to be annoying him and he sternly viewed the "Russian opinion-formers" as if they'd done something to upset him. By contrast, Lisa Vershbow beamed enchantingly, and the Ambassador glanced benevolently out at all of us from under his eyebrows.

The great moment arrived. A rather gorgeous Afro-American in a chocolate-brown three-piece suit, the President's personal bodyguard, materialised and, almost immediately behind him, Bush himself appeared, relaxed, smiling, and flushed. He landed on his chair, assumed the pose of a citizen of the greatest power on earth, and casually crossed his legs. (Well done, Laura: he too was wearing very long socks.) He was soon invited to speak and began, not by apologising for being more than two hours late, but with a paragraph in praise of his wife, the former librarian of a rural school who at one time had no interest at all in politics, but now found herself married to such an important political figure.

He spoke for perhaps another half-hour, about freedom and universal human values. Powell frowned periodically, Condoleezza was inscrutable, the black suitcases whispered about some manifestly practical matters, and the First Lady listened to her husband with the practised pose of all American First Ladies: her back straight, her head proudly raised a little, turned three-quarters towards him. Her faced expressed a calm, steadfast love which had stood the test of time, and unshakable admiration. For the entire half-hour.

All she allowed herself was an occasional nervous tapping of her right leg when something her husband was saying apparently did not impress her.

Bush enjoyed being at the lectern. He only occasionally squinted at the papers, previously arranged by his speech writers, and appeared to be speaking largely off the cuff. When he had finished, he walked directly towards us for handshakes. He had a slightly strange manner of exchanging a few brief words with one person while already extending his right hand to the next, with a gesture which suggested you were supposed to take it yourself. He is a simple man.

Nevertheless, Bush's grip was firm and his hand was not clammy, which was something. Russia's leaders melted, almost all of them, standing there with hands outstretched in anticipation.

The hand-shaking ceremony took another half-hour before the President and his retinue left the room. We were kept in our enclosure for a further 15 minutes, and then set free to go with the wind.

A SICK DOG IN THE BIG CITY

September 2005

Last summer our dog died. He was very, very old. Our loyal Dobermann, Martyn, was 15, exceptionally long-lived by Dobermann standards. He was a remarkable dog who loyally protected us through the long years of the chaos of perestroika, the total gangsterism of the three years of "primary accumulation of capital," and today's dissolution of freedoms, when life is again not without risk. Shielded by Martyn we felt safer than we would have behind a posse of bodyguards. He adored us and our friends, and unerringly identified and ruthlessly chased away anyone ill-intentioned. But he never bit anyone. In Martyn's presence we quarrelled and did not always manage to make up; we met and parted; and through it all he loved us unreservedly, even, on one occasion, swooning with love. Only during the last 45 minutes of his life was Martyn not there to serve us, when he lay down and lapsed into unconsciousness. Then it was we who served him, cupping our hands beneath his heart until it stopped beating.

Six months later we were missing him terribly. Life without Martyn was like living without an intravenous drip of love. We realized that he had been a powerful drug, a *perpetuum mobile* generating and projecting joy at us. Even as he was dying Martyn did not forget, occasionally raising his eyelids, to wag his stump of a tail and smile. After he died, two cats and a wonderful parrot moved in, so we had little to complain about. Yet every evening we were conscious that, although they were great, we were suffering acute emotional deprivation without a dog.

Then the children found a remarkable offer on the Internet. He looked nothing like Martyn, which was a must. He was not long-haired, which was also important because that was what we were used to. As far as we could tell from the information, he was friendly. A bloodhound puppy, a kind of basset hound on long legs, with eternally sad eyes and long ears.

We went to see the breeder. She kept saying, "He's simply wonderful, the best pup in the litter." Maybe, but he was peeing incessantly, every time he looked at us. On the other hand, here was an ocean of affection. He flirted with us: take me, please. That did it. He really wanted us to.

"Four months old. He still has every right to pee," the breeder insisted.

When we got home we renamed him van Gogh instead of the idiotic "Hagard" inflicted on him by the breeder, and we settled down to live together. It very soon became apparent that van Gogh didn't just pee all the time, he was a non-stop urination machine, and the strange thing was that he had only to catch sight of a man for there to be a puddle. We stopped letting men into the house, apart from our own, supposing that it was a phase he was going through. We never dreamt of shouting at him – of course not, heaven forbid – but we could not even slightly raise our voices for fear of an immediate flood. As soon as he made a puddle, he would rush around in despair, hiding away or, even more awful, trying to lick it up so we wouldn't see it. As for going for a walk, we soon found out that van Gogh hated going outside. He disliked everything about it, and his happiest moment was when we came back to the entrance of our block, got into the lift, and went up to the flat. His tail joyfully sprang to attention as soon as we were home. Our house had clearly become his castle, and he would prefer never to leave it.

At the vet's they told us straight away that the claim he was four months was nonsense. He was at least five months old, and they invited us to guess why the breeder had understated his age.

"Go on, then, why?"

"To get you to take him. People don't like taking older dogs because somebody has already been training them and there's no guarantee it has been done properly."

That turned out to be true, and the vets also found sand in van Gogh's bladder. Finding the sand cost over 25,000 roubles, and the antibiotics another 2,000 because he had an acute inflammation. Permanent damage. That was our first clue, as it became ever clearer that van Gogh was positively clinging to us as if we were his last hope. He became increasingly nervous of visitors. His fear of other people grew as he grew, and his inclination to hide behind us, his family, was becoming insane. Imagine the scene: somebody approaches us in the street, and this great big dog with huge paws cowers behind my back. He doesn't bark or growl, just looks at the stranger with such abject terror that you feel scared yourself.

Eventually we realized he was afraid someone would come and take him away. His first owners had been men who took him away. Men, sadly, had become his lifelong enemies.

Clearly we had acquired a dog with serious psychological problems. He was not going to protect us; we were going to have to protect him. Less than ideal.

I rang the breeder: what had happened to the dog in the past? I wasn't ringing to complain, I just wanted to know so I could help both the dog and myself. The breeder gave in. Before us van Gogh had twice been rejected, though what had gone on was nothing to do with her. But he had been beaten, by men, and they had done something else to frighten him, and then kicked him out.

That seemed credible. We would need to find an animal psychologist and a trainer who worked with dogs individually. Animal psychologists, we discovered, charged $50 a visit if you were lucky. For your $50 you were advised to take a holiday, take the dog to the countryside, let him rest, change your flat, your environment, your town, your country. Nor was all this imparted in a single consultation. Each separate piece of advice cost another $50.

Ouch! No way could we afford that.

So we rushed to find a personal trainer for him. Katya, at 500 roubles an hour from a company called something like "Clever Dog" or "Faithful Friend" informed us that she only worked with dogs of the elite (not elite dogs, but dogs belonging to the rich), and that she was fully booked. She did, nevertheless, find time for us. At 7:00 a.m. Katya arrived. She stuck her hands in her pockets and started giving me commands: "Go there! Do this!" There was nothing elite about it.

Fifteen minutes before the end of the session Katya, despite her anti-globalist garb of black pullover, trainers, and bandanna, entirely capitalistically demanded 500 roubles. We didn't invite her back. The second and third personal trainers were identical in respect of the quality of their exercises, but proved even pricier at 700 and 900 roubles for the same truncated hour.

We decided to stop throwing money down the drain, the more so since van Gogh's bladder continued to require thousands of roubles. Life went on as before. He was scared stiff of anything and everything, and I stood between him and the unfamiliar – screeching garage doors, squealing car tyres, and men walking past.

As he grew older, the problems intensified. In order to get to a dog-walking area in our neighbourhood, you need to cross a main road at a crossing without traffic lights. That is, you have to weave between cars not in the custom of reducing speed when approaching a zebra crossing. As we neared it van Gogh would collapse, prostrate with fear. I had to half carry him, half drag him like a sledge, 40–50 kilograms of resisting live dog, between the cars. One walk over the crossing and back guaranteed a rise in blood pressure. It was plain, however, that a dog with a dysfunctional metabolism, sand in his bladder and problems of social interaction simply had to be taken for a walk in the company of his fellows.

In the end I started loading van Gogh into my Lada 10 and driving him across the road. In the walking area he runs about anxiously among the other dogs, not playing with them often, but sometimes at least. He exercises, he sniffs, he gets used to them. His main occupation there, however, is standing by the fence gazing longingly at our Lada. The minute I open the doors, van Gogh jumps into the back seat.

Being driven, or even just sitting in the car, is the one thing he really loves. A small, contained space separate from the rest of the world, just him and his owner, that is the best place on earth for van Gogh. He immediately calms down, looks out of the windows at the world with pleasure, and his gaze becomes steady. He can fall asleep like that, all his fears forgotten. He jumps out of the car and heads straight for the the entrance, runs to the lift, and can't wait to get back into the flat.

For now my blood pressure has returned to normal, but what next? The vets are telling me unambiguously I should have him put to sleep. Friends and colleagues concur. Why give yourself such a hard time? A dog is not a human being. Give him away. That is only their polite way of saying the same thing: have him put down. Who else would put up with him, other than those already wholeheartedly attached to this long-eared, sad-eyed creature who is guilty of nothing?

Nobody. It is the lot of sick dogs in the big city to be put to sleep if their owners do not have large amounts of money for treating and supporting them. A world which has become heartless towards unfortunate people (the disabled, orphans, the sick), has become equally heartless towards animals. Naturally. What else could we expect? Quite how feral money makes us is something you understand when you have a sick dog. I am not a crazy dog-lover, a category of people as large as that of crazy dog-haters. Crazy dog-lovers differ from the rest of us in loving dogs more than people. When all is said and done, I love people more than dogs.

But it is not in my nature to abandon him, a sentient being who would not survive being rejected again. He would die without me. He is completely dependent on me, to the last hair on his long silky ear, and he would be equally in the power of anybody else in whose hands he found himself. The world of the rich has produced such a numerous, ever increasing caste of abandoned dogs, van Gogh's brothers. These people buy van Goghs as toys, play with them, tire of them, and kick them out. If they're lucky they are returned to the breeder who sold them and don't just find themselves on the street. They have no monetary value, and no one values a living soul devoted to you to its very depths.

I understand that not everybody who has money is bad. Not all vets are rip-off merchants. Of course not. Only why do we have packs of abandoned pedigree dogs sniffing around our gates?

It is evening once again. I turn the key in the door and van Gogh hurtles to greet me from wherever he is, every time. No matter how his stomach may be hurting, no matter how soundly he might have been sleeping, no matter what it was he was eating. He is a radiant perpetual motion machine of love. Everyone may abandon you, everybody may take umbrage against you, but a dog will never cease to love you.

I take him, I lead him to the car, I drive him over the road. I leap alongside him to get him to jump about with the other dogs in the square. I show him how he ought to play with them. I run the obstacle course with him to help him overcome his fear, and I take him over to other men. I take their hands and stroke van Gogh's ears with them, and try to persuade him they are not dangerous.

WHAT YOU SEE AT THE END OF THE WORLD

June 2006

I was recently in Australia at the annual Sydney Writers' Festival and couldn't resist a little tourism. Having failed to resist it, I now can't keep quiet about what I saw. The following are just the jottings of a tourist.

I have never seen a chapel or a naval base like these, although I have seen plenty of both. I had been told I must see a really curious place of worship, only it was in a naval base. Admittedly, it was an old Australian base, but still . . . So there I was at the checkpoint with my knees knocking, long conditioned to the knowledge that checkpoints are bad news. You don't get through them, or, if you do, only under guard.

In the goldfish bowl sat a cheery, suntanned officer who glanced casually at our passports and did not stick a rifle in our backs and tell us to get out. He was delighted that somebody was interested in visiting his base. "Have you come to see the chapel?" he asked. "Do you know how to get to it? You want to drive there? Of course. No probs."

He groped somewhere behind him and let us through. A recently democratised Soviet citizen's brain had difficulty coping with such free and easy behaviour: how could we be admitted to a naval base without having the car inspected, without even a look in the boot? What if it was packed with explosives? You even get checked nowadays if you want to drive into the Luzhniki Sports Complex in Moscow, just to relax and smell the flowers. This Australian officer, so woefully lacking in vigilance, continued whistling to himself, loafing in his chair, his body language totally at variance with my expectations.

At last we reached the chapel. Picture it: Australia is at the end of the world, you can't go any further, and this naval base is right at the end of the end of the world, on a stunning, high promontory jutting out into the Pacific Ocean. It hovers above it. Our chapel was at the very end of this end of the end. When you enter you are suspended above the ocean, and moreover the chapel's far wall, behind the altar, is made of glass. When you look at the altar it is like praying to the expanse of the ocean and the lofty, amazingly blue sky above the sea. Your prayer is to that great Ocean of Peace to protect and preserve you. A chapel in a naval base is built not for open-mouthed tourists, of course, but for those putting out to sea, and sometimes never returning.

This is a chapel which discriminates between faiths no more than the waves, which are wholly indifferent to the religious affiliation of those they swallow. Red-headed, fair-haired, curly-haired, hook-nosed, the Pacific engulfs them all impartially.

No doubt the chapel has a nominal affiliation, and I can probably guess which, but as you stand before the altar looking out to the end of the world, this place feels pagan. All those ingenious interventions placed between man and nature, this sect, that cross or another, or no cross at all, dissolve and become meaningless. You are communing with the sea, even if out of habit you call it the Almighty. You ask it not to take you, and there is no philosophy beyond that, not a hint of that universal human error of recent times, the belief that we are the all-conquering rulers of the earth.

Otherwise, the chapel is simple, like a plainly constructed hut. In addition to the rear wall, the façade is glass, and if you spin around you feel that both you and this cliff jutting out into the ocean are floating in the sky. The chapel is furnished with benches, their cushions embroidered with naval insignia, and on the walls are lists of those who did not return, and a cross. I was going to ask the officer at the checkpoint about the denomination but thought better of it. What do the specifics of faith matter?

The cheery sentinel waved us goodbye, and our incursion on to the territory of a military site was over. I am no uncritical admirer of the West who imagines that everything is better and purer there than in Russia, but I have to admit that it is far more common there to encounter something warm and human.

Sydney is a mixture of a city, which makes it seem strange by comparison with anywhere else. The center appears on the one hand to be pure London, but on the other pure New York. With that wonder of the modern world, the Sydney Opera House, looking out towards the harbour like the open lid of a shell, the central area resembles New York; with the exception of the Opera it is a concrete jungle of skyscrapers with narrow avenues between them. Fairly comfortless, highly urban, as linear as anyone could wish.

But it is only superficially New York. When you start reading the street names you are amazed: everything is just like in London: Hyde Park, King's Cross, the station and the adjacent district. There is a Paddington, and even an Oxford Street, and it too is very long. The names of London streets and places have been transplanted, with only a light admixture of local exoticism. King's Cross Station in Sydney, for example, is located in Woolloomooloo, an Aboriginal name Londoners could not imagine in their worst nightmares.

The Aborigines, admittedly, are in short supply. Woolloomooloo there may be, but Aborigines, the indigenous inhabitants of Australia, there are not. Search as you may, you will find none in the streets of Sydney.

Australia was born in tears and did not hold out the prospect of an easy life. In the late eighteenth century there was a crime wave in

London, and England, running short of prisons, hit on the idea of finding an island on the other side of the earth where it could dump its criminal elements, with the Exchequer bearing only transportation costs. Once the criminals were there they could be left to survive as best they could, a way of thinking similar to the Tsarist regime's view of the island of Sakhalin.

Captain Cook was given the commission by his government and duly performed it. Soon convict ships were sailing to the distant land he had discovered, the convicts were disembarked, and their survival was then very much up to them. There were already people on the island who bore little resemblance to Captain Cook, strange, dark-skinned people talking mumbo-jumbo. They named them Aborigines and set about brutally exterminating them, regarding them as little better than animals. Later they began sending the younger sons of lords to the British island, allotting them enormous territories in Australia to cultivate for next to nothing. Some Aborigines considered that these territories belonged to them, by the grace of Mother Nature and not of the minor aristocracy.

The offspring of the British upper classes accordingly took to destroying anybody who tried to defend his lands. There were occasional truces which held for a time, and Aboriginal women had babies by the younger sons and the British staff who served them. It was accepted that half-castes were taken from the Aboriginal women and brought up as British.

Those times are, of course, long gone, and today's Australians try their utmost to right the historical wrongs of their conquering forebears, but if they have had much success it is not very noticeable: I didn't spot a single Aborigine in Sydney. People told me to wait because one elderly Aborigine sometimes played his didgeridoo at the central harbour.

"One?"

"One."

In all the evenings of my visit not even that one Aborigine appeared. On the harbourfront Chinese musicians played passionate Latin American music which flowed out into the tourist shops, and there were heaps of Aboriginal bits and bobs: gift boomerangs, knick-knacks made of kangaroo hide, paintings in traditional colors and motifs on a variety of surfaces. Alongside sat photographs of the artists: smiling Aborigines. So many photographs, so few live Aborigines. One wondered anxiously whether they had all died.

There is a permanent exhibition of Aboriginal art in the National Art Gallery of New South Wales in Sydney with some 200 works dating from the 1950s to the present day, a period when there were no longer any conquerors, and the descendants of those cruel people were trying to atone for their sins. For all that, the most common subject of Aboriginal painting is conquerors killing Aborigines. Another is the family trees of Aboriginal tribes, certifying their right to their lands. The Aborigines draw all this in a unique manner: everything appears to be viewed from above, and the impression is that there are multiple visual planes. The kangaroos are flattened too, as if they are dead and have been dissected. The same goes for lizards, and koalas, and Aborigines themselves.

If you stand at the harbour waiting for the Aborigine to play his didgeridoo, you will observe a remarkable scene. White-collar workers, business people who work in the city center, stream out into it straight from the ferry at the harbour quays. Here people come to work in the morning, and in the evening go home on the little ferries and steamers. A ferry moors in the morning at Central Quay, and city workers in dark suits and clutching laptops pour from it as if an underground train had just come in. The city is built around the harbour, with people living on the shore and working in the center. The roads around the harbour are narrow and suffer from traffic jams, but nobody has yet devised a way of causing traffic jams in the Pacific Ocean. What's more, the ferry is cheap, and always arrives on time.

I naturally boarded the ferry, and it set off. The first stop, still in the city center, was the Rocks. That is the name of a district, and is the point where Captain Cook landed. There he stands today, a statue by his own toy-like house, which is built of the typical reddish-beige local sandstone.

The ferry takes us further, to the quays in the dormitory suburbs.

Such-and-such Street, only it is a quay. Rose Street, only that is a pier. There are signs like we have at bus stops, and a shelter in case of rain. Around the quays low houses grow into the cliffs, small stores and completely wild countryside. Ten minutes on the morning ferry takes you to New York with its soul-destroying pace of life, but on the way home you can meditate on the water flying by the side of the boat, the crests of the waves, the seagulls, the surf, and you must already be feeling better. Psychotherapists cannot be much in demand in Sydney, where the citizens have the ocean, and the major urban transport arteries lay themselves over it. There is nothing to build, and nothing to constantly maintain. What would Moscow's Luzhkov find to do if he were Mayor of Sydney?

You can also take the ferry to the theatre, the museum, and the colonial-style Governor's residence.

The ferry also takes you to the zoo, which in Sydney is called Taronga Zoo. Who or what was Taronga? None of the local people could give me an answer. Well, fair enough. The main thing is, I saw an echidna, a funny little animal, quiet and retiring, with a long nose and quills. Not the world's most beautiful animal, perhaps, just as not all people are Apollo Belvederes, but why do Russians say damningly, "You are not a mother – you are an echidna"? I observed the ways of the Australian echidna for a long time but couldn't work that out. It just snuffled everything around with its long nose and did nobody any harm.

In Taronga, naturally, there are a lot of koalas. They look like little cuddly bears, almost completely grey, but with a beige shimmer, and they sleep 20 hours out of 24 in trees, according to the sign, in uncomfortable postures: the back of their furry neck pressed against one branch, their backside against another, and the rest of their body dangling down. They sleep sweetly, so that must be how they like to be. How important it is not to impose our own ideas of comfort on other people.

And then, of course, the kangaroos. How could one visit Australia without seeing a kangaroo? Unfortunately, the kangaroos seemed rather unfriendly. They were probably afraid. They would look at you, but very anxiously. You could go into their pen and they would hop alongside, not agile bipeds but on their two rear paws, and not too close. Along with the kangaroos, an insolent beauty lives in Taronga: the emu. She sashayed over and promptly pecked the back of my head, which was at just the right level, with a beak the size of a small shovel. She was clearly asking for food, but all the signs in Taronga shout: Do Not Feed The Animals! So we parted with the emu not on the best of terms.

The cockatoos in the Sydney zoo are very handsome, striking, multi-colored, and friendly. They are almost the size of eagles, but the best cockatoos live on the Sydney central embankment, enormous, white with black patches, and move in flocks over short distances, from one of the enormous trees which surround the opera to another, kicking up a fuss among themselves, like our crows, and paying no attention at all to people.

Well, that is it. After the zoo I had to fly for 22 hours, for the most part over seas and oceans, with two stops, in Singapore and Dubai. In total it took over 24 hours to get back to Moscow. It wasn't much fun, but I don't regret it. To have been to the far end of the earth, which you always knew existed, is very invigorating and a good inoculation against the great-power mentality drummed into us in Russia. How can we be the epicenter of everything if you can fly for 24 hours from Moscow and still find there is more world to see?

9. The Last Pieces

Anna Politkovskaya's last articles continued her protest against the brutality unleashed by Yeltsin and Putin when they agreed to reignite the Chechen War. In "A Pact Between Killers" she passes on to a wider audience a report she believed important and illuminating.

A PACT BETWEEN KILLERS

September 28, 2006

A conference was held recently in Stockholm devoted, amongst other things, to the problems of the North Caucasus. Political analysts, journalists and human rights activists were invited. We publish below excerpts from one of the papers read at the conference.

Vakha Ibrakhimov, Researcher, Chechnya:

A significant number of local people regard the actions of Chechen squads as far worse than what was typical of the federals before them. "Those were Russians, but these are our own people. How can they treat us like this?" Such is the half-rhetorical question I heard repeatedly. Even so, those critical of the Kadyrovites, people who hate them, would not want to go back three or four years to when the Republic was totally under the control of Russian soldiers and agents of the intelligence services.

Why? Simply because the members of pro-Moscow detachments, being themselves Chechen, do not treat other inhabitants of the Republic in a racist manner. Their enemies are not "all Chechens without exception," and not even genuine separatists, but particular families and people with whom they have personal scores to settle. For a majority of Kadyrovites, Yamadayevites, Kakievites, and the followers of other warlords, the decision to fight on the side of the federal forces is not politically motivated but a convenient means of resolving their own problems with the backing of a state which ensures their security and, for a time, provides for them materially.

The members of these detachments are involved in exactly the same abductions, murders and torture, and long ago caught up with the death squads of regular officers of the Russian intelligence agencies in terms of brutality, but at least their actions are selective. Civilians who are not personally resisting either them or the federal authorities (who come a distant second) are usually left unmolested.

Who is in these detachments? The press, encouraged by the Government, represent them as former resistance fighters who, "having recognised the futility of continued resistance," have joined the Russian side. This is far from the truth.

One of the mainstays of Russian policy in the region is the blood feud. This custom continues to be observed in Chechen society and, until recently, even had a stabilising function. To commit murder was not something a criminal would undertake lightly, because a murderer who failed to obtain forgiveness was doomed. His only option was to flee. In periods when the Chechen state has been weak, such individuals often joined armed groups and put the heat on their pursuers from a position of strength. Some of the most troublesome armed groups when Maskhadov was in power also consisted of people bearing blood guilt.

It was, however, the Russian political leaders who saw an opportunity of basing their policy on them. A considerable number of today's so-called security agencies in Chechnya include, and are under the command of, people guilty of premeditated murders and kidnappings. Immediately after the occupation of the Republic, for example, Movladi Baisarov's group went into service with the Russian Army. Its leader was a member of a gang led by the recidivist criminal, Ruslan Labazanov, who was defeated by the Chechen security forces in summer 1994. Between the two wars he and his lieutenants specialised in kidnapping and ransom.

One of the first to transfer allegiance to the federal authorities was Suleyman Yamadayev. According to data from the Prosecutor's Office, his group also engaged in kidnapping but was subsequently legalised as a special company attached to the military commander of Gudermes District. The Vostok (East) Battalion has now been created on this basis as part of the 42nd Motorised Rifle Division of the Ministry of Defence of the Russian Federation. Said-Mahomed Kakiev's detachment has been incorporated in the same division, as the Zapad (West) Battalion. Kakiev too was a member of Ruslan Labazanov's gang and was accused of committing a number of criminal and terrorist acts.

The civilian population's most serious complaints are about the activity of the Kadyrovites. The detachments nominally identified in this way grew out of Akhmat Kadyrov's Security Service and to this day are commanded by his former bodyguards. These individuals now also occupy all the key posts in Chechnya. Ruslan Alkhanov, for example, is the Interior Minister, and Adam Demilkhanov is the Deputy Prime Minister in charge of the security agencies.

Originally, several dozen people were members of this service, and in the main they were close relatives or fellow villagers of the Republic's former Mufti (Kadyrov Senior). As they grew in number, members of criminal gangs emerged from the underground and were added. These were initially "anti-terrorist centers," and more recently mutated into the North and South Battalions, the Second Regiment of the Militia's Patrol and Checkpoint Service, and the like. They have been co-opted and now rank among the security agencies of the Russian Federation. Both then and now, people who have committed murders and kidnappings are the backbone of the Kadyrovite groupings. These are the people appointed as commanders, and responsible for recruiting new members.

The history of Lema Salmanov is typical. Born in the village of Mairtup, in November 2002 he shot two fellow villagers in his own courtyard who had come by prior arrangement to collect money for a truck he had bought from them. The relatives of the murdered men declared a blood feud on Lema, but the authorities intervened on the criminal's behalf. He was appointed commander of a detachment of Kadyrovites in the village, and thereafter of an anti-terrorist center which was being formed in Kurchaloy District. His powers now virtually

unlimited, he set about persecuting his sworn enemies, their immediate relatives, and anybody who might even hypothetically exact
vengeance on him at some time in the future. Some of these went off
to join the resistance fighters, others hid with friends. The friends
were also subjected to repression for giving them refuge: they were
beaten, tortured and killed. Several families were drawn into the
conflict, certain episodes of which were represented in the press as
being part of the struggle against terrorists. On Russian Militia Day,
2005, Lema Salmanov, who six months earlier had shot his elderly
great-uncle for trying to talk sense to him, was awarded a government
medal.

To the present day this individual remains one of the most powerful
Kadyrovite commanders, although one might wonder what use he has
been to the Russian authorities, since his activity has resulted in the
killing of his personal rather than the state's enemies, and dozens of
people have taken to the hills to join the fighters.

It would appear that this is precisely the aim of Chechenisation,
and that it was from the outset devised as a means of pitching Chechen
against Chechen, not allowing the conflict to die down, and fanning it
to the level of civil war. Clearly, if such a policy is to be implemented,
it is best to seek the support of those who, having committed one
crime, will not hesitate to repeat it in the future. There are no plans
to combat the tradition of the blood feud in Chechnya and, given
that retribution may be visited on a culprit even after many years, it
binds such people to the Russian authorities more firmly than any
ideological views.

This policy also serves the purely propaganda task of showing the
world local inhabitants fighting on the side of the federals, and hence
undermines the idea that the conflict has separatist roots.

There have always been Chechens who favored keeping the Republic
within Russia. They organised movements and armed detachments
and, for example, hundreds of people opposed the separatists back in
the early 1990s under the command of Bislan Gantamirov. At the
beginning of the Second Chechen War, even before Akhmat Kadyrov's
Security Service was created, vigilante detachments appeared in a

number of districts and enabled Russian troops to take control of the mountainous part of the Republic without serious losses.

The members of these detachments and their commanders refused, however, to participate in security sweeps, hostage-taking and summary executions. Emphasising their loyalty to the Russian authorities, they nevertheless showed a determination to protect the civilian population, if necessary from the Russian Army.

From early summer 2000, the Russians began to rid themselves of these "unreliable" allies. The vigilante group of Vedeno District, for instance, was first dissolved and most of its members subsequently either abducted or killed. The Rifle Company of the Shatoy District Commandant's Office was disbanded. It consisted mainly of men who had rallied to the Russian banner on intellectual grounds and had later refused to merge with the West Battalion, which consisted largely of criminals.

In other words, Chechenisation is not simply the transfer of power to institutions consisting of local inhabitants, but an encouragement and legitimisation of the activities of those who are prepared to participate in punitive operations against their own population. Chechenisation is a policy for expanding the scope of the war, and the result of the policy has been a replacement of the genocide practised directly by Russian agencies in the early stages of the conflict by today's reign of terror by criminal and semi-criminal gangs supported and directed from Moscow.

A POSTSCRIPT: FRAGMENTS OF TWO ARTICLES ANNA WAS WORKING ON AT THE TIME OF HER DEATH

Editorial Note

People ask whether we believe Anna Politkovskaya's murder was related to an article about torture which she was preparing, and which she had announced on Radio Liberty on Thursday, October 5, two days before her death. We are here publishing fragments from two items which our columnist did not complete.

The first contains eyewitness accounts of the use of torture, which is confirmed by medical reports. The second consists of a video which would have formed the basis of an article that was never written. The disk in Politkovskaya's possession (and we would ask whoever passed her the recording to contact us), shows unidentified citizens being tortured. The torturers themselves took the video and appear to belong to one of the Chechen security agencies.

WE ARE DESIGNATING YOU A TERRORIST

Novaya gazeta, No. 78 (October 12) 2006

Dozens of files come my way every day which contain copies of materials from criminal cases against people imprisoned or under investigation in Russia for "terrorism."

Why put "terrorism" in quotes? Because the overwhelming majority of these suspects have been designated terrorists. Now, in 2006, this habit of designating people as terrorists has not only displaced any genuine attempt to combat terrorism, but is of itself producing potential terrorists thirsting for revenge. When the Prosecutor-General's Office and the courts fail to uphold the law and punish the guilty, and instead merely act on political instructions and connive in producing anti-terrorist statistics to please the Kremlin, criminal cases get cooked up like pancakes.

A conveyor belt for mass-producing "voluntary confessions" works faultlessly to ensure targets are met in the so-called struggle against terrorism in the North Caucasus.

Here is what a group of mothers of a number of young Chechens, found guilty by the courts, have written to me:

"For convicted Chechens the corrective labor colonies have effectively become concentration camps. They are subjected to racial discrimination and kept permanently in solitary confinement or punishment cells. Almost all of them have been sentenced on the basis of fabricated court cases without credible evidence. Confined under cruel conditions, their human dignity is violated and they learn to hate everything. Here is a whole army which will be returned to us with their lives wrecked and with a warped outlook."

Their hatred frightens me. It frightens me because sooner or later it will burst its banks and everyone will become an extremist, not only the investigators who tortured them. These cases of designated terrorists constitute a battlefield on which two ideological attitudes towards what is being perpetrated in the "zone of the counter-terrorist operation in the North Caucasus" confront each other. Do we combat lawlessness with the law? Or do we try to bash their lawlessness with our own?

These two forms of lawlessness clash and fire dangerous sparks into both the present and the future. The end result of this process of designation is a growing number of people who are not prepared to put up with it.

Ukraine recently extradited to Russia Beslan Gadayev, a Chechen arrested in early August when documents were being checked in the Crimea, where he lived as a displaced person. These lines are from a letter he wrote on August 29, 2006:

"When I was extradited from Ukraine to Grozny, I was immediately taken to an office and asked whether I had killed a member of the Salikhov family, Anzor and his friend, a Russian truck driver. I swore I had shed no one's blood, neither Russian nor Chechen. They stated as a fact, 'No, you killed them.' I started denying it again, and when I repeated that I had never killed anyone they immediately began beating me. First they punched me twice in the right eye. While I was recovering my senses, they pushed me down and handcuffed me. They pushed a pipe behind my legs so I could not move my hands, even though I was already handcuffed. Then they grabbed me, or more precisely this pipe they had attached me to, and suspended me from two nearby cabinets which were about a metre high.

"As soon as they had done that, they attached wires to the little fingers of both my hands. A couple of seconds later they turned on the current and started beating me with rubber truncheons wherever they could. I couldn't stand the pain and started yelling, calling out the name of the Almighty and begging them to stop. In response, so as not to have to listen to my shouting, they put a black hood over my head. How long this went on I can't accurately remember, but I began to lose consciousness from the pain. When they saw that, they took the hood off and asked if I would talk. I said I would, although I did not know what to say to them. I said whatever they wanted so as to avoid the torture at least for a while.

"They unhooked me, removed the pipe, and threw me on the floor. They said, 'Talk.' In reply I said I had nothing to tell them. In response they hit me with the pipe I had been hanging from, again on my right eye. I fell sideways and, almost unconscious, felt them again beating me wherever they could. They hung me up once more and repeated what they had done before. How long it went on I do not remember. They kept drenching me with water.

"The following day they bathed me and rubbed something on my face and body. At about dinner time an officer in civilian clothes entered and told me some journalists had come and that I was to admit responsibility for three murders and robbery with violence. He threatened that if I did not agree they would do it all again, and also would shame me by degrading me in a sexual manner. I agreed. After I had given the journalists the interview, they threatened me with the same degrading treatment if I didn't testify that all the beating I had had, which they had inflicted on me, had occurred while I was supposedly attempting to escape."

Zaur Zakriev, the lawyer defending Beslan Gadayev, informed the members of the Memorial Human Rights Center that this physical and psychological duress had been inflicted on his client in the Grozny Rural District Office of the Interior Ministry. According to the lawyer, the defendant did indeed admit to committing robbery with violence in 2004 against members of the law enforcement agencies. However, the agents decided to obtain further confessions relating to a number of crimes he had not committed in the village of Starye Atagi in their district.

The lawyer states that the brutal violence inflicted on the defendant left visible signs of physical injury on his body. The Medical Section of Pre-Trial Detention Facility No. 1 in Grozny, where Gadayev is currently held under Article 209 of the Russian Criminal Code on a charge of robbery with violence, has issued an official medical certificate listing evidence of systematic beating, physical injury in the form of welts, scratches, bruises, broken ribs, and damage to internal organs.

The defence lawyer has lodged a formal complaint about these gross violations of human rights with the Prosecutor's Office of the Chechen Republic. [. . .]

Politkovskaya's text breaks off here, incomplete. The editors are seeking to establish what further episodes were to be included.

*   *   *

A video shows what appear to be members of one of the Chechen security agencies who have apprehended and are torturing two young men. One of those detained is sitting in a car, bleeding. A knife can be seen stuck in the region of the victim's ear. The other seems to have been thrown out of the car on to the tarmac. The torturers are not themselves visible, and only Chechen speech (Melkhi dialect) can be heard, interspersed with swearing:

Verbatim text:

"Putin said it. 'View it from every angle,' he said."

"He should know!" (Addresses the victim insultingly) "This bitch just won't die, [. . .] fucking goat, bastard . . . , fucked up queer. Doesn't he look handsome? I couldn't live without you."

"Croak, pal, croak, you shit! For God's sake, know what I'm saying? Do it . . ."

"Is he done? Is he done now?"

"Yeah."

"OK, we're leaving. Over here!"

"Hey, move your asses, take up positions, take up positions. Close observation of the surrounding terrain."

10. After October 7

ABC, *Spain*

There is only one way to dispel suspicions that her murder was planned: to establish the circumstances of the crime, to arrest those responsible, and make them answer in court for it. If Russian society does not demand the maximum penalty for those who were involved intellectually and materially in this crime, it can only be said that Russia is in serious danger.

Having murdered Anna Politkovskaya, they have not only deprived a woman of her life, but have sent a message to the whole country, threatening anybody who is thinking of doing what she did. Politkovskaya has paid with her life, but Russian society will pay with its freedom if it does not now manage to react courageously.

The Chicago Tribune

More than any other Russian reporter, she illuminated the plight of Chechen civilians driven from their homes, tortured and at times summarily executed by Russian troops and pro-Moscow Chechen forces.

Along the way, she received threats from all sides of the conflict – Chechen fighters as well as Russian troops. She fled to Vienna in 2001 after receiving threats from a Russian officer angered when she wrote about his involvement in war crimes.

In 2004, while she was on a flight to Beslan to cover the school hostage crisis there, she became seriously ill after drinking tea on the plane. She and many colleagues believed she was deliberately poisoned.

Igor Yakovenko, General Secretary of the Russian Union of Journalists, called the slaying "a kind of new and very black page in Russian history." "For the first time in several years, Russian journalism has been hit in its very heart," he told Interfax. "A tragedy has happened in our profession that is impossible to make up for because there is and will be nothing like Anna Politkovskaya."

El Correo, *Spain*

Russian institutions should make investigation of the unjustified murder of Anna Politkovskaya an absolute priority if they want to demonstrate to the international community, which demands elucidation of the circumstances of the crime, that Russian justice is capable of rising to the level of the democracy which they claim to defend. It needs to be established who shot this defender of human rights and an independent press and why, at the entrance to her home, when she had warned of threats to her life and was preparing to publish an article about torture in Chechnya.

Le Figaro

Anna Politkovskaya has been murdered. Does this mean that the famous journalist, whose pessimism many of our experts considered exaggerated, bearing in mind the tempo of Russia's economic growth, was right? It would seem that very important strategic partner, Vladimir Putin, has not succeeded in returning this "great country" to a normal life. Yet again we find that we have taken what we would like to believe for reality.

The Guardian

The fear now is that Russia's already fragile independent press could crumble without its talisman . . .

For years Politkovskaya, a mother of two, was a hero to the liberal opposition . . .

But her main enemy was Putin, the man who gained political capital on the back of the Russian Army's second bloody charge into Grozny in late 1999, and the man she said she hated "for his cynicism, for his racism, his lies, for the massacre of the innocents that went on throughout his first term as President" . . .

Yesterday brought an apparent paradox: while Politkovskaya's death served a bleak warning to the independent press that the price of dissent is death, newspapers were their angriest for many months. Predictably, opposition dailies such as *Kommersant* and *Novaya gazeta* were filled with fury about the murder. But the pro-Kremlin press was also in high dudgeon. *Rossiyskaya gazeta*, the official newspaper of the Russian government, praised Politkovskaya for "standing against war, corruption, demagoguery and social inequality." Even the usually loyal mass-market tabloid *Komsomolskaya Pravda* was happy to publish a conspiracy theory suggesting Politkovskaya was killed as part of a complex plan to lever Putin into the presidency for an anti-constitutional third term.

The Independent

Anna had more courage than most of us can begin to imagine, and her death is a reminder of the violent state she exposed so vividly in *Putin's Russia.*

International, *France*

Anna Politkovskaya was the conscience of Russia. In a country which increasingly is being enslaved by fear, self-censorship and cynicism, this journalist succeeded in retaining her civic courage. At a time when most of the Russian media prefer to remain silent, *Novaya gazeta* became, thanks to her, one of the last bastions of free speech. The principled position which she maintained to the last raises her to the ranks of such Soviet dissidents as Alexander Solzhenitsyn and Andrey Sakharov.

Libération, *France*

The impunity which the murderers of journalists enjoy, the protection which is extended to the tormentors of the Chechens, have as their aim to train the Russian people once again in the ways of silence and fear.

Anna Politkovskaya wanted to compel to think those people whose wish to know was greater than their fear. It is time to ask European politicians whose messages they are prepared to listen to: those of Vladimir Putin or of Anna Politkovskaya.

The New York Times

Her murder has made her a symbol of what Russia has become, but it was only the latest in a series of them. She was 48; the freedoms that she used to make her post-Soviet career, to write openly and critically about the deeds of a new Russian power, are much younger. And, it would seem, equally fragile . . .

Ms Politkovskaya's funeral, in fact, displayed the deep divisions in today's Russia between those in power and those not. The mourners included her family and friends, colleagues and politicians, though almost all from outside the center of power, and several foreign diplomats, including Ambassador William J. Burns of the United States, whose governments have denounced her killing far more forcefully than Mr Putin or any other senior government leaders here.

Le Nouvel Observateur

Her caustic position was something the Kremlin never liked, but she was one of the most respected journalists in the country, who moreover was given innumerable foreign awards.

Oleg Panfilov, Director of the Centre for Extreme Journalism: "Every time people asked if there was an honest journalist in Russia, the first name to come to mind was almost invariably that of Politkovskaya."

The Observer

Politkovskaya, 48, was a constant critic of the Kremlin and her murder will throw suspicion on the security services and the pro-Moscow regime in Chechnya . . .

In an anthology *Another Sky*, due to be published next year by English

PEN, a writers' group campaigning against political oppression, Politkovskaya chillingly predicted yesterday's events: "Some time ago Vladislav Surkov, Deputy Head of the Presidential Administration, explained that there were people who were enemies but whom you could talk sense into, and there were incorrigible enemies to whom you couldn't and who simply needed to be "cleansed" from the political arena. So they are trying to cleanse it of me and others like me."

On a visit to Chechnya she alleged that the former President of the Chechen Republic Akhmad Kadyrov vowed to assassinate her . . .

She remained defiant in the face of repeated threats but admitted she felt shaken by what she was convinced was a poisoning on a flight to cover the Beslan school hostage crisis in 2004 . . .

Toby Eady, her London literary agent, told *The Observer* he had recently tried to persuade Politkovskaya to leave Russia because of the threats. "She said she would not leave Russia until Putin was gone. She actually asked, with deeply dark humor, what would happen to her advance if she was killed."

There seemed little doubt that the journalist was killed for her cutting reportage from Chechnya . . .

El Pais, *Spain*

Anna Politkovskaya, like all journalists criticising the Government in Russia (and there are very few of them left), was subjected to intimidation by all the state institutions, official and semi-official, and was constantly called an enemy, particularly by the puppet government established by Putin in Chechnya. There are only two credible explanations of her murder: either it was committed on the orders of the Russian state authorities, in their central or Chechen hypostases, through the agency of the security services (which is most probable); or it may have been the work of people infected by the nationalist discourse encouraged by the state authorities.

Putin sought legitimacy through the blood of Chechnya, on the basis of which he built his neo-authoritarian regime, and now all the threads of power (executive, judicial, legislative, and also of the economy and mass media) run not only back to the Kremlin, but directly to the President's Office.

That is the Russia which Putin is building with the aid of oil as a strategic weapon, in order to enforce respect for his enormous country, with the connivance of Western leaders who whitewash all his crimes in exchange for energy supplies . . .

The cause, which European political figures both of the left and of the right have mentioned to me in private conversation, is quite objective – it is fear of Russia. The Soviet Union was a time bomb which, if it had exploded, could have turned the whole world upside-down. Putin proved capable of bringing order and avoiding chaos.

. . . But what is more dangerous for the West – the chaos which it is said Putin has succeeded in avoiding, or the authoritarian regime which he has built and which, as the world already knows, has at its disposal oil and weapons of mass destruction?

And here are the results: the execution of inconvenient people for the benefit of the Tsar and the motherland.

. . . When indifference and fear are instilled, when everything is justified as a part of a struggle against the enemy, when politics, judicial power and money accumulate in the hands of a single person, democracy is weakened and the venal feel strong and free. And when the world flirts, as now, with doctrines of ethnic homogeneity and an apologia of general unitarianism, any deviation is deemed a threat to all. Politkovskaya reminded us of this a million times, and nobody took her seriously. She has died, and Russia is profoundly ailing.

Die Tageszeitung

In an instant it is back again: the image of an unpredictable and incomprehensible Russia. Anna Politkovskaya, an indomitable journalist, has been shot in broad daylight at the entrance to her home. The whole world rubs its eyes in disbelief. What is going on in Russia where it is becoming clear that critically minded journalists are game to be hunted down? Is this country in fact not the bulwark of stability, developing democracy and economic flowering that the Kremlin's emissaries and the representatives of expensive PR agencies proclaim to the whole world?

CONDOLENCES AND RESPONSES FROM CITIZENS AND OFFICIALS

Novaya gazeta, October 23, 2006

Alu Alkhanov, President of the Chechen Republic

Russian journalism has suffered a great loss. The tragic death of Anna Politkovskaya has not only been a shock for Russian society but a blow to the ongoing democratic processes in Russia, including glasnost, one of the most important achievements of the changes in the country. We did not always agree with Anna Politkovskaya's point of view regarding the situation in the Chechen Republic, but we all understand that criticism is an important part of life and is a counterbalance to totalitarianism and the fostering of a personality cult at the helm of power. We respected the professionalism of Anna Stepanovna, the civic courage of a journalist, the principled position which she expressed strikingly in her publications. I express my sincere condolences to the relatives, friends and colleagues of Anna Politkovskaya.

Anna, a Student from Moscow

On Sunday, nine days after the murder of Anna Stepanovna, I lit a candle and put the lights out. I had seen her only twice, at meetings, but Anna Politkovskaya suddenly became somebody very close to me.

Artyom, Moscow

I saw her once in a shop on Myasnitskaya. I thought she was someone I knew, and then realized it was Politkovskaya. Simply, for some reason, I felt she was a friend. And when she was killed, I felt the blow very keenly. Anna, I will never forget you. Putin, I will never forget what you have done, no matter what drivel you utter.

Ruslan Aushev, Hero of the Soviet Union, Chairman of the Committee for Internationalist Soldiers' Affairs

A talented journalist has been taken from us before her time, an extraordinary and striking individual, an uncompromising fighter for truth and justice whose outstanding reports were exceptionally important and courageous. This is an irreparable loss.

Karl Bildt, Foreign Minister of Sweden

Her battle for human rights and freedoms was an important part of the work for a better Russia and a better Europe. I sincerely hope that the Russian authorities will make every effort to arrest the guilty and get to the bottom of this crime.

Vladimir Bukovsky, dissident, Cambridge

She was a courageous person who wrote a lot about war and its victims. She was well known in the West. The reasons for her murder are obvious. One cannot pretend it was due to her financial or business interests, because she had none. Her only enemy was the corrupt Russian system which, most likely, is what killed her.

George W. Bush, President of the USA

Like many Russians, Americans were shocked and saddened by the brutal murder of Anna Politkovskaya, a fearless investigative journalist, highly respected in both Russia and the United States. We extend our sympathy and prayers to her family and her friends.

Born in the United States to Soviet diplomats, Anna Politkovskaya cared deeply about her country. Through her efforts to shine a light on human rights abuses and corruption, especially in Chechnya, she challenged her fellow Russians – and, indeed, all of us – to summon the courage and will, as individuals and societies, to struggle against evil and rectify injustices.

We urge the Russian Government to conduct a vigorous and thorough investigation to bring to justice those responsible for her murder.

Jacques Chirac, President of the Republic of France

Letter of condolence to Ms Vera Politkovskaya and Mr Ilya Politkovsky [Anna's daughter and son]

> Dear Ms Politkovskaya,
> Dear Mr Politkovsky,
> The vile murder of Anna Politkovskaya has shocked me, as it has shocked all French people and all who defend freedom of the press. As a friend of Russia and of the Russian people, I know how angered your country has been by this particularly shameful murder of a passionate journalist whose professionalism and courage have been universally acknowledged, especially in her investigations into the situation in Chechnya.
>
> You know that France attaches enormous importance to the fact that everything needful should be undertaken to ensure that justice is done, and the murderers of your mother found and punished.
>
> In the tragic ordeal which has befallen you, I express to you my deepest and most sincere condolences, and pay the tribute of my profound respect to the memory of Anna Politkovskaya.
>
> I ask you to accept, dear Ms Politkovskaya and Mr Politkovsky, this assurance of my sympathy for you and your family. With heartfelt emotion and sympathy in this hour of your tragic ordeal, Jacques Chirac

Terry Davis, Secretary-General of the Council of Europe

I am shocked by the news that Anna Politkovskaya was found dead in Moscow today, and I am deeply concerned about the circumstances in which she has lost her life. She was a journalist of exceptional courage and determination, and her reporting on the conflict in the Chechen Republic provided the Russian public and the entire world with an independent insight into the fate of ordinary people caught in this conflict. We have all lost a strong voice of the kind which is indispensable in any genuine democracy. It is essential for the circumstances to be clarified quickly and in a convincing manner.

Bertrand Delanoë, Mayor of Paris

I have been deeply shocked to hear of the vile assassination of Anna Politkovskaya. An angry woman, as she once called herself, she knew she was under threat, but as a committed journalist never gave up in the face of intimidation, remaining indignant and determined to inform and reveal the truth.

Nicola Duckworth, Director of Amnesty International's Europe and Central Asia Program

Amnesty International is appalled by the murder of Anna Politkovskaya. We believe she was targeted because of her work as a journalist, reporting on human rights abuses in Chechnya and other regions of the Russian Federation. Russia has lost a brave and dedicated human rights defender, who spoke out fearlessly against violence and injustice, and campaigned tirelessly to see justice done. Amnesty International calls on the Russian authorities to investigate her murder thoroughly and impartially, to make the findings of the investigation public, and for suspected perpetrators to be brought to justice in accordance with international law.

Zainap Gashayeva

Anna was very close and dear to me. We often met in the course of the Chechen War and understood each other well. We were together when she was detained by Russian soldiers in the village of Khotuni.

She has left a profound impression in the memory and hearts of many people with whom she came into contact during all these years. Forgive us, Anna, it hurts so much and it is so difficult to believe you are no longer there, but no one can forbid us to continue to love you.

Thomas Hammarberg, Commissioner for Human Rights of the Council of Europe

Anna Politkovskaya was one of the most important human rights defenders in Russia today. Her dedicated work exposed grave human rights violations in the North Caucasus region, thereby allowing the world to understand that hidden corner of the globe. Having known her well and respected her enormously, the news of her death has made me very sad and angry. Her death is a great loss for Russia, and a great loss for the cause of human rights . . . While not everyone agreed with her views, no one questioned her professionalism, courage, and personal dedication to revealing the truth about controversial political issues. Ms Politkovskaya's murder signals a major crisis of free expression and journalistic safety in Russia. The Russian authorities have already failed in investigating previous murder attempts and death threats. They have no excuse now not to investigate the circumstances of her death thoroughly, and to punish those who committed this deplorable crime.

Ramzan Kadyrov, Prime Minister of Chechnya

I was not bothered in the slightest by what Politkovskaya wrote. It did not influence my work or my actions but, on the contrary, helped me, and I had no cause to want to persecute her. She was a woman, and I have never lowered myself to trying to settle scores with women. If even a gas canister explodes somewhere, they look for Chechen involvement, for "Chechen fingerprints." We are used to that, but I believe we should get over this practice of making baseless accusations.

Garry Kasparov

One of the few whose free voice was to be heard in the Russian press, Anna was a fearless journalist, well known for her reporting of the Government's atrocities in Chechnya. Those who knew her knew her responsiveness. She deeply felt the sufferings of others and carried that attitude over into her work. She collected documents about the crimes of the Russian security forces in the North Caucasus, about the brutalities perpetrated by Ramzan Kadyrov and other Kremlin placemen in the region. She indefatigably investigated what the Government was concealing about the terrorist acts in Beslan and *Nord-Ost*, where hundreds of civilians died. She took on the most sensitive stories, the most awkward topics. By her example she inspired others, because it was impossible to intimidate her. She never wrote a single line in which she did not believe implicitly. And on Saturday, the 54th birthday of President Vladimir Putin, Anna Politkovskaya was murdered. The killers made no attempt to conceal the nature of the crime, made no attempt to represent it as anything other than a political killing. Even Russian politicians who always spoke against Politkovskaya's reporting and tried to belittle its significance, are calling what happened a political murder.

Nadezhda Kevorkova, Special Correspondent of Gazeta: Live Like a Soldier

The world's most famous Russian journalist has been murdered. Actually, the only famous journalist on today's most famous Russian newspaper. Young foreigners interested in our country know about Russia through Anna Politkovskaya's books, and not through Mikhail Leontiev, Yuliya Latynina, Sergey Dorenko or Oksana Robski. Fine words have already been said about a blow struck at the very heart of Russian journalism, that the profession, free speech, and indeed the very lives of decent people are under threat. It is all lies.

You have to earn such a death. Observers of Kremlin life, chroniclers of the President's meetings, uncompromising critics of the Government, those mercilessly exposing economic politics, gossip columnists – all belong to the same guild but have differing destinies.

"She lived and died like a soldier," one of her colleagues said. No more than that.

Those who respected, loved and protected her have nothing to say because their facial muscles fail them. Everybody else's are in full working order. Some have used muscles to put up posters, others to speak about an "irreparable loss."

Novaya gazeta never left out a report by Politkovskaya, except once, on April 1, and once in an anniversary issue.

For seven years its editor, Dmitriy Muratov, printed everything his bloody-minded and unaccommodating columnist wrote. Colleagues in the journalistic guild spat behind her back, poured filth over her, debated whether she had some psychological proclivity to describe atrocities. They didn't like her style, her turns of phrase were questionable, and there was a certain lack of humor.

Even on NTV before the state takeover, TV–6, and Echo of Moscow radio she was an infrequent guest. She did not like generalisations and long-winded discussions about the Wahhabi Internationale or al-Qaeda's cash. In her presence you could not indulge in calling the Chechens or the federals brutes, Chechnya a dump, or Russia a whore.

Muratov was her unshakeable support, defending her from both friends and foes.

Why? Because this woman had put in the legwork on all her reports; because people came every day to see her; because officialdom feared her; because officials believed her even while they were excoriating her; because the *zindan* punishment pits she discovered really did exist; because she could not be bribed or intimidated, although she could be afraid, and was on more than one occasion; because she went to Chechnya not during the First War, when only the laziest Moscow journalists didn't get out there. She went there during the Second Chechen War, whose beginning the liberal politicians Chubais and Nemtsov described as bringing Russian society together again, and marking the rebirth of the Army.

People brought her photographs and clips of atrocities which made men feel sick. She was asked why she went on writing when it was producing no reaction, and replied that it was her duty to write, and she was doing it.

She was on the side of the humiliated. The powers that be she found equally repellent, whichever side they were on. She was not seduced by the interest taken in her by Zbigniew Brzezinski or people from the US State Department, and her report on the reception for the "esteemed democrats of Russia" by Bush and Rice at the US Ambassador's residence was written in the vein of light political satire.

It is not true that there was no reaction to her writing. Back in the days of Kadyrov Senior, one of his henchmen angrily shouted at the local and Moscow journalists, "Politkovskaya writes in a way that makes people believe her, but you . . ." He dismissed them contemptuously.

Mikhail Khodorkovsky

Friends and family of Anna! Please accept my profound condolences.

Marina Kostenetskaya, former People's Deputy of the USSR from Latvia (1989–91), Riga

I do not know whether the Orthodox Church will canonise Anna Politkovskaya, and neither do I care. For me Anna was a saint. For me she is still alive, because I often go to her memorial website and meet there a circle of people who think and feel as I do. With these people Anna generously continues to acquaint me. They helped me to survive, and accordingly it is precisely Anna who helps me to live worthily the fragment of life's path allotted me by fate.

Thank you, Anna, for having been among us. Neither Putin, nor his evil henchmen, nor your pro-Kremlin journalist colleagues have been able to kill you. In this undeclared war of honor against dishonor you have come out the winner for eternity. May your name be revered!

Vytautas Landsbergis, Member of the European Parliament for Lithuania

They have killed Anna Politkovskaya.

She stood selflessly, squarely, and looked the new, or perhaps merely reawakening, Russian fascism straight in the eye. They tried to kill her earlier. She stood up for the humiliated and insulted, against untruths and arbitrariness. The fewer such champions remain, the brighter does their example shine in the night and the more clearly is their voice heard, which is so unwelcome to gross ears. One cannot pass over in silence either the weakness of the Russian democrats or the indifference of Western democrats, all of whom are complicit in her death. But who will fill this new yawning breach for Russia?

Galina Starovoitova once told her Russian democratic comrades-in-arms, "If men are cowards, a woman will lead." In January 1991 in Moscow she led a 100,000-strong demonstration, despite the warnings of the Armed Forces, under the slogan of "Freedom for Lithuania!" She was later murdered in just the same way, in her stairwell, and in this instance too those who took out the contract will not be found. But will men be found capable of standing up for the entrancing star of decency and freedom? That would be a worthy rejoinder.

From Lithuania, condolences to the family of this woman who died for truth and to the last remaining Russian democrats.

Yevgeniya Lyozina, Student

Anna Politkovskaya: I saw her only a few times, and never met her personally. A young, good-looking woman. Born in 1958, the same year as my mother. Very composed and self-assured. It is impossible to forget people like her, because your first impression when you meet them is that they are real human beings, and that is how you remember them. Like many others, I can see that this murder was committed because Anna Politkovskaya's activity gave no peace to those in our country who are violating all the laws of truth.

I am still not very old and, looking at the example of this courageous woman, I want to live my life honorably, as she did. For that, as I understand it, I must be sure always to stay close to the truth. As regards Anna Politkovskaya, truth was undoubtedly and always on her side.

People kill, or more precisely take out contracts for the killing, of those they fear. Those who rode to power in our country on anti-Chechen chauvinism, on their willingness to "burst into the latrines and snuff out" their supposed enemies, fear most of all that the truth should become known about what this bravado of theirs has turned out to be. They are afraid of the truth about Beslan and *Nord-Ost*, about the deaths of civilians, tortures, security sweeps, a war which has lasted many years. We all know, as they do themselves, that in recent years it was primarily Anna Politkovskaya in *Novaya gazeta* who told the truth about this. She spoke intelligently and professionally, which was important in getting her message heard. It was heard in Russia, as always, however, only by those who had ears to hear, and by those beyond its borders. During my recent visit to London it was amazing to see Anna Politkovskaya's books on the shelves of all the bookshops. They are bestsellers there, people read them! And of course, that annoyed "them." It annoyed those who unleashed and supported the war in Chechnya. The truth Anna told was a slap in the face for those who constantly lie to us, trying to treat us as useful idiots.

In recent times every day has seen the feeling of shame grow in me for Russia and for all of us, its citizens. I am ashamed to live in a country where those in power have no conscience or intelligence. This is mainly because I believe that any people gets the government it deserves.

On the other hand, hope grows in me when I remember that there are still some in Russia like Anna Politkovskaya. Such stars shine apparently unpredictably, perhaps once in a lifetime, but in the surrounding darkness you are dazzled by the unexpected light they radiate. I know for a fact that, having once encountered such a star and having understood her significance, it is impossible to carry on living as you did before. The encounter makes the darkness only too depressingly obvious, and the light from such a star is imprinted in the memory and provides eternal guidance. It can even provoke a feeling of envy.

Lyuba, Nord-Ost

Anna was umbilically attached to the *Nord-Ost* tragedy. These last four years she has been the mouthpiece of *Nord-Ost,* supporting those of us who had lost our friends and relatives in that gas chamber. She helped us to prevail in the unequal battle with a lying government. She was not allowed to attend the court hearings into *Nord-Ost*; the investigators and judges of the Basmanny court were afraid of her. They were afraid of her truth and irreconcilability. How fearsome the truth about crimes must be and how dangerous for those complicit in them if, in order to silence it, they have to resort to the gun. "What are we going to let them get away with tomorrow?" Anna would say when we assembled on the anniversaries of the tragedy. Alas, we are again too late. We have allowed them to kill Anna, perhaps the most loyal friend of those she tried to save, persuading terrorists to let children and adults drink, whom the Government had condemned to a monstrous death. She will not be there at the anniversary on October 26. We have been orphaned.

Memorial Human Rights Centre

It is almost impossible to believe. We all feel that we have lost someone close to us. Anna Politkovskaya was a much greater champion of human rights than many of those who apply that description to themselves. She took to heart the problems of those who work in Chechnya as closely and passionately as her own. Now we can reveal that in the Caucasus Anna Politkovskaya worked constantly with members of Memorial, travelled together with them throughout the Republic, stayed in their homes. She constantly used materials from Memorial, sometimes referencing them, sometimes not, in order not to set anybody up. She herself appeared to live a charmed life, but it was a principle to publish everything, irrespective of the possible consequences. Only bullets could stop her. Will those bullets stop her cause? That now depends on the living.

Angela Merkel, Chancellor of Germany

It is essential to find the culprits if there is to be any possibility of living in democratic conditions.

Niotkuda

A completely weird sense of emptiness, of loss, and powerlessness. It is dreadful to live in a country where crudity and barbarism reign. It is dreadful that nothing can be changed. I am 20. I am studying to be a journalist. I often read Politkovskaya's articles. Actually, she was the reason I bought *Novaya gazeta*. I do not know what kind of journalist I will turn out to be, but I will most certainly follow Anna's example. Revered be her memory!

Ursula Plassnik, Federal Minister of Foreign Affairs of Austria

This vile and shameful crime. There have been too many unsolved murders of journalists in Russia. If Russia wants to be a democratic law-governed state it cannot intimidate independent journalists or silence them. Without freedom of the press and criticism from their direction, the democratic system of values cannot exist.

Polina, England

Lord, how full of sadness I am! How dreadful! I am studying to be a journalist in England. I read Anna's book, *Putin's Russia*. What a shame that it is not available at home, in Russia, because my family do not know English very well. When I heard the news, many of my foreign friends tried to console me by saying that she had taken the blow on herself, that by her death she would force world public opinion to to take action, that now all the newspapers would bring pressure to bear on Russia, but how can I explain to people who have not lived there that our country does not care about world opinion? I sincerely hope that my friends are right. How can I express the pain and fear, and

how are we to live without such journalists as Anna Stepanovna now?
May you rest in peace.

A Priest of the Russian Church

It is a great pity that there is so little room in present-day Russia for
an honest person. I did not take much interest in politics, thinking it
was not my business, but now I understand that Anna did everything
in her power to avert the triumph of evil in our country. I thank her
for opening my eyes to many things, and pray for the repose of
her soul.

Vladimir Putin, President of the Russian Federation

[Dresden, October 10, 2006, at a joint press conference with the German
Chancellor, Angela Merkel]

Right, if you will permit me, I will also say a couple of words on
this topic. First of all I would like to note that no matter who
committed this crime and no matter what motives these people had,
we must confirm that this is a crime of vile brutality. And of course
it should not be . . . should not remain unpunished. The motives
may be highly diverse. Yes indeed, this journalist was a harsh critic
of the present authorities in Russia, but I think that journalists
should know this, at least experts are well aware of this, the extent
of her influence on political life in the country, in Russia, was
extremely insignificant. She was known in journalistic circles, in
human rights circles, in the West. I repeat, her influence on political life in Russia was minimal. And the murder of such a person,
the cruel murder of a woman, a mother, it was directed of itself also
against our country, against Russia, against the current government
authorities in Russia. And this murder of itself inflicts on Russia
much, and on the current government authorities both in Russia and
in the Chechen Republic, where she was active professionally recently,
inflicts on the current government authorities a far greater loss and

damage than her publications. This is an absolutely obvious fact for everybody in Russia. But I repeat, no matter who this was and no matter what motives these people were guided by, they are criminals. They must be found, unmasked and punished. We will do all that is required for this.

The United States Secretary of State Condoleezza Rice is Interviewed by Novaya gazeta

Condoleezza Rice: Thank you very much. First let me say that I am very much saddened, as was the entire world, by the brutal murder of Anna Politkovskaya. She was a heroine to many people.

She stood for what is best in independent journalism, a willingness to try to get to the truth at whatever cost. And if I may just say to you, Ilya, that while I know the world has lost someone who was a symbol, you have lost your mother and we are very saddened by that. But her work goes on, and *Novaya gazeta* is a fine publication that I think represents a very good independent voice here in Russia.

The role of the independent press is extremely important in society, particularly for democratic development. And it's important not just because it is an important value to have an independent press, although it is one of the most important values of democracy. But it also is important to the proper functioning of government in democracy.

People need information in order to hold their government accountable. And only through an independent press can that information be developed and communicated. And whether it is in fighting corruption or questioning government policies or communicating to the Government the concerns of people, an independent press plays an extremely important role.

I want to encourage you to keep working. It is extremely important work, and we are very supportive of the role of independent media here in Russia. We know it has not been easy, but it is an important path – an important road – even if it's not an easy one . . .

Dmitriy Muratov: Madam Secretary of State, we will of course continue our work, but this is our newspaper's third terrible loss in the last six years. In 2000 Igor Domnikov was killed by hitmen, who are presently on trial. He was murdered because of his professional work, and the contract on him was taken out by a corrupt official who is the Deputy Governor of one of Russia's provinces. Three years ago the Deputy Editor of *Novaya gazeta*, Yury Shchekochikhin, Deputy of the State Duma and Chairman of its Commission for the Struggle against Corruption, also died in mysterious circumstances. The case has yet to be investigated. Now Anna has been murdered. Is this not too high a price to pay for the right to do your job?

Condoleezza Rice: You have recalled for us a very sad history of the last six years and one with which I am familiar. There have been many tragedies for *Novaya gazeta*, and you must feel it very personally. We have told the Russian Government that these murders and the murders of other journalists must be thoroughly investigated and people must begin to understand that those who have done this will pay the price.

It's hard for me to answer your question because I know these have been great personal losses. It's difficult to step back and give an abstract answer to a very personal human question. But I think that if you look at history and struggles in many different countries under many different historical circumstances, there have been people who sacrificed on the basis of principle, people who sacrificed for a cause and those sacrifices are never in vain because ultimately freedom will win out.

In particular, investigative journalists are very often in danger because by their very nature they expose the truth. Very often they run afoul of those who have a lot at stake and a lot to lose if the truth comes out. I recognise that it's a very dangerous profession, but without investigative journalists who are willing to seek the truth, it's very hard for a democracy to function.

If it is any comfort at all – at a personal level I'm sure that it's not – at a professional level if it is any comfort you should know that these murders have received world-wide attention. People are watching. People are pressing for a full investigation and for punishment of those who have committed these crimes. You are not alone in your struggle.

Novaya gazeta: How important is it for a politician to have strong emotions? By that I mean feelings of kindness and openness.

Condoleezza Rice: It is important for people who are engaged in politics to have human emotions, compassion, and most importantly to have principles. I watch very carefully the influence and tremendous effect that political leaders can have on the lives of ordinary people, and they need to be people who understand their impact.

It's very important for politicians, particularly in democratic societies, not to lose touch with the people that they represent. Even the President of the United States leaves the White House and visits with schoolchildren, or goes to a retirement home and sees the effects of our policies on older people. I think it's very important for politicians, and I know that when the President does this it has a big effect on him.

Ultimately I think a politician has to lead people and not be led by them, and that very often means making difficult, sometimes unpopular decisions. People expect their leaders to do exactly that. If the job were only to make easy decisions, anyone could do it. Because it's often a matter of difficult decisions, I think it takes a very special person to be a politician in a democracy. I admire very much our people who have entered political life. I admire people who want to serve their country in that way. It's not easy because you're very often making difficult, unpopular decisions for the good of a large number of people.

Novaya gazeta: So, politics is not just a form of business?

Condoleezza Rice: No, it's not. It's a form of service. [Politicians have] different values than those who go into other professions.

Dmitriy Muratov: Yesterday we read a report from Reporters Without Borders [*The Worldwide Press Freedom Index for 2005*] which shows Russia in 138th place in the world in terms of free speech, but the United States is in 137th place in respect of reporting on events in Iraq.

What is this – self-censorship by journalists or state policy? Fear or patriotism?

Condoleezza Rice: It's certainly not government policy. But I'll tell you something, I watch our reporting on Iraq every day, and our reporters in Iraq are very tough on the US Government. It was the American press that exposed the very bad events at Abu Ghraib. That came out first in the American press. I don't know what study you're talking about, but the US press reports exactly what they think, and they try to do it accurately. With press reporting – with freedom of the press – goes responsibility. It's not just reporting anything you hear or anything someone tells you. The American press tries to be accurate in what they are reporting, but they report in the very toughest of circumstances.

There is one circumstance that sometimes the American press will not report: if it is going to put our soldiers in danger. Then they may decide that they do not want to report on something that might cost American soldiers their lives. That's another part of press responsibility. The Government can't force the *New York Times* not to print something, but the *New York Times* can decide if something is potentially dangerous to the lives of American soldiers and not print it.

Zoya Yeroshok, Andrey Lipsky, Dmitriy Muratov, Ilya Politkovsky

Elena Romanovna, Philologist, Translator

From a radio behind a grille outside a shop I heard snatches of a report: "Militia and ambulances in front of the entrance . . . journalists waiting for the body of Anna Politkovskaya to be brought out . . ." I stopped and looked about me, at people's faces. It was as if nothing had happened. Had they not heard? I ran home, turned on Echo of Moscow radio, and stood numb with shock by the door. Eight years ago I felt the same blow when I heard Galina Starovoitova had been murdered, and the same sense of emptiness, except that now it felt more like a vacuum which makes it impossible to breathe or go on living.

I went to the Metro station to buy *Novaya gazeta*. There were several people in front of me also buying newspapers and magazines. I looked hopefully over their shoulders, but no. A glossy crossword magazine, *Sport, Vedomosti, World of Crime*. I hunched up against the cold, feeling lonely and ill at ease in my own town. And now also frightened. I looked at the mothers walking placidly by with their prams. Were they not afraid? Apparently not. They probably really believe that life in Russia has improved, that per capita income is rising inexorably, and that we are the best and strongest superpower in the world. They probably believe that Russia's democracy is in great shape, only ours is a special kind, "sovereign" democracy which is completely different from what they have in the West. From developed socialism to sovereign democracy! Any day now they will blow the dust off the old history textbooks, and today's schoolchildren will sing a slightly adapted Soviet national anthem in patriotism lessons, under a portrait of little Volodya (only now not Ulyanov but Putin), and will solemnly promise to do their duty to their Great Motherland and learn to inform on each other.

Where now are all those who huddled round their radios to listen with bated breath to the speeches of the Democrats at the First Congress of Deputies, who collected signatures for the Sakharov Constitution, and rejoiced when the Berlin Wall came down? The years of my youth were those of perestroika. How avidly we read *Dr Zhivago, Gulag Archipelago*, Dudintsev's *White Clothes*. Could I have dreamt then that very soon we would recoil, back to the times of the Soviet regime but repainted now with the dubious values of consumerism, pseudo-religion and fascism? In those days the process of democratisation seemed irreversible, but how wrong we were. How short our memories are. Here we are, wanting back under that yoke, wanting a return to the repressions, wanting the Gulag. History teaches us nothing.

I am ashamed today to be Russian because of Chechnya, the anti-Georgian campaigns, and the Russian nationalist processions. I am ashamed to be Russian Orthodox because the Church made no attempt to protect its brother Georgians, and because it will never canonise Anna Politkovskaya who, in its stead, comforted and interceded for the helpless. I am ashamed to be a native of St Petersburg because those 200 people who came to the meeting in memory of Anna Politkovskaya were even fewer than the number of journalists murdered in the post-Soviet period, and also because the courts of Petersburg acquit the killers of "non-Russians." What does that leave? It leaves just one thing: to continue to be a human being. "Not to bow down before the times, but to be the brains of your age, to be a human being," as the poetess Sofia Parnok wrote in an equally hopeless era in the last century.

Today it is 40 days since Anna died, and I will again light candles. Anna Politkovskaya had the strength and courage to be a human being. May I be able to do the same!

Vladimir Ryzhkov, Deputy of the State Duma

I am shocked. It seems unbelievable. At this moment in time Politkovskaya was probably one of the best-known journalists not only in Russia but in the entire world. She received numerous international awards for her work. In its repercussions this murder is comparable with the murders of Yury Shchekochikhin and Vlad Listiev.

I find the motives completely obvious. All these years Anna Politkovskaya concentrated principally on Chechnya, Beslan and *Nord-Ost*, that is, the topics most disagreeable to Russia's rulers, the FSB and the Army. Any of these organizations might have commissioned this crime. I frankly do not believe it will be solved, because those with an interest in her death are precisely the people who are to conduct the investigation. I hope nevertheless that a miracle will occur and that the killers will be found.

Russia is becoming an ever more dangerous country for independent journalists and opposition politicians. None of us is immune to a similar fate.

Mikheil Saakashvili, President of Georgia

She was one of the greatest friends of our country. In recent years she wrote excellent articles about Georgia. In Russia many decent people have come forward to protest at her killing, the first time that has happened on such a scale. I am filled with admiration and thank those people.

Gennadiy Seleznyov, Deputy of the State Duma

I grieve together with the *Novaya gazeta* team at the death of Anna Politkovskaya. For us she was a highly professional journalist, an honest person and a great colleague. I had the privilege of being closely acquainted with Anna, and I know she was a true citizen of our country. It is patently obvious that she was killed for telling the truth, because of her conscience, and her desire to change our life for the better.

Liza Umarova [Chechen singer], with profound sorrow, on behalf of the Chechens and Ingushes

On October 7 a disgraceful, cynical and cowardly shot from round the corner was fired at a woman from whose writing we learned the truth. Anna Politkovskaya! This fine, proud name we, Chechens and Ingushes, always pronounced with more reverence and admiration than any other name we had spoken for over 50 years. She represented the honor and conscience of Russia, and probably nobody will ever know the source of her fanatical courage and love of the work she was doing. She was a journalist like no other working today. She loved Russia so much that she turned down the opportunity of going to live and work in America, in security, in peace and quiet. "*Novaya gazeta* still needs me," she said. On this holy Muslim festival of Ramadan, we Chechens and Ingushes pray for you and your soul. We will dedicate our lives to the cause you began. No one can replace you, but we will try to fight as you did to enable people to live honorably in Russia.

The Union of Journalists of Russia

The dozens of assignments in the North Caucasus she survived, but now, in the entrance to her home, in the lift . . . A person of extraordinary courage and inflexible will, she was and remained to the end an example of the fact that in all circumstances a journalist can (and should, as she herself believed and demanded of her colleagues) write at the dictate solely of their conscience, with no nod to prevailing circumstances and no submission to them. She, just like her colleague Shchekochikhin, "was careless about the enemies she chose," and the more powerful, shameful and vengeful those enemies proved, the more heedlessly and furiously she attacked them. She brooked no compromises in the struggle for what she considered the truth, and tried to demonstrate that truth to all who read or heard her. For this she was hated, threatened and hunted, on one occasion in the most literal sense of the word.

And today, when we must try to ensure that the killers and those who ordered the killing are found and punished, let us remember what Politkovskaya wrote about: *Nord-Ost*; Beslan; abductions and torture of people in Chechnya; violations of human rights; despotism and government crimes. Let us say straight out: there could have been no other reason why she was killed. That is why it is so important that the answer to the question of who did it should be obtained by society, to enable it to decide how to react.

Sergey Uralsky, Consultant in Jurisprudence of the Supreme Court of the Russian Federation and Retired Federal Judge

I express my profound condolences in connection with the murder of Anna Politkovskaya . . . We are losing so many people. The state authorities promise to detect, to track down, to bring to court, to give a proper assessment, but on their faces what we see is not real grief, only a mask. There are a lot of these masks. Now yet again no less a person than the Prosecutor-General of the Russian Federation has taken the investigation under his absolutely and completely personal control.

IS JOURNALISM WORTH DYING FOR?

What does "personal" mean in this context? Why "control" and not
"supervision"? Why not individual, collective, corporate, or some other
kind of nonsensical "control"? What help has it been in the past? What
help is it going to be now? Why should Mr Yury Chaika feel the need
to faff about, to control, to involve himself in the detail of conducting
a murder inquiry? He does not need to "control" the investigation, but
to find the killers. Some hope there is of that. It is really all just too
much trouble for them.

Torture. They are no longer capable of doing anything without
torture. How could they possibly conduct an investigation or bring a
case to court without torture? And when the accused protest that they
have been tortured – physically, with cold, and hunger and vile forms
of degradation – they reply that this is just criminals slandering our
agencies, trying, together with journalists, to discredit the system.

They could not believe that this frail woman would stand up and
say torture in their torture chambers was unacceptable. They couldn't
conceive that there were still people in Russia who cared about that
sort of thing! And so they killed her.

The Voice of Beslan Association

It is difficult, intolerable to have to say of her, she is dead. We grieve
together with the whole world. The life of a writer has been cut off, a
journalist at the very peak of her talent. Courageous, brave, Anna lived
a special life without compromise, and for the people of the Caucasus
there was still hope. Frail and seemingly defenceless, by the power of
her limitless courage she was the hope of many living here, ordinary
people who wanted to live in peace. She was a spokesman, from
whom society learned about the monstrous misconduct of the state
authorities towards their own citizens.

Anna was not only a famous journalist, but also a civil rights
defender, and the pride of all of Russian society. The cause of this
crime was her courage and the crystalline purity of her conscience. In
Russia it is the defenders of human rights who pay for the thuggish
policies of the authorities.

There is no doubt that this was a political martyrdom. Anna simply could not take no interest, although she surely knew better than anybody that there would be no pity for her either. She did not retreat, she rushed to try to save the children of Beslan, and would have saved many if she had not been poisoned. In Beslan they were afraid of her fearlessness.

She took part in the investigation of the tragedy in Beslan, in *Nord-Ost*, exposed the crimes in Chechnya, Ingushetia and Dagestan. The authorities of every stripe feared these exposures, because it was simply impossible to silence Anna.

Who has dared to commit this dreadful, infamous act?

One way or another, the murder of Anna Politkovskaya is a consequence of the lawlessness of the government authorities and their immoral policies, which increasingly betray their true nature. It is a matter of honor for the law enforcement institutions to investigate this villainy thoroughly and to name the names of the murderers.

But if this crime is not solved, if the crime is not investigated properly and the murderers are not put in the dock, it will be clear in whose interests the murder was committed. Behind the invariable failure to investigate and solve such major crimes stand the authorities, whose limitless irresponsibility gives birth to them.

Voice of Beslan offers its condolences to the family and friends of Anna Politkovskaya, to all who knew her and worked with her, including the *Novaya gazeta* team.

Anna always was and will remain for us an example of amazing purity and courage.

Lech Walesa, Founder of Solidarity, Nobel Peace Prize Winner, 1983, President of Poland, 1992–5

I did not know Anna Politkovskaya personally, but heard about her work, the work of a journalist who tirelessly defended the rights of those deprived of freedom, and who stood as a sentinel for truth and freedom of speech. She knew she risked paying the highest price for her activity. Her murder is a dreadful crime and a violation of free speech. It is a stain on the honor of the representatives of the free world, and also on my own.

When talking to the Russian government authorities, people in the free world should not talk only about oil, gas, or the conquest of space. We should speak also about the problems of guaranteeing freedom, tolerance and respect for the views of others. This needs to be done if only to prevent a repetition of such crimes in the future.

For my part, I pray for Anna Politkovskaya in the words of an old Polish prayer, "Send her Thy eternal peace, O Lord." Some day we will meet in another, better world.

Grigoriy Yavlinsky, Leader of the Yabloko Political Party

The Yabloko Party considers the murder of Anna Politkovskaya to be political. Direct political responsibility for her murder is borne by those in charge of the country who condone the physical extermination of their political opponents. Her journalism was a profession not of the word, but of deeds, action. For the publication of facts and evidence of crimes committed by the government authorities and in their name, she was hated by people who did not trouble to conceal their hatred. Her striving to be in the most difficult situations in order to intervene, to help, to tell the truth, elicited active counter-measures. She was prevented from reaching Beslan in September 2004. What she has been kept away from now she can no longer tell us. She was a very well-known, internationally renowned political journalist. For a murder of this kind the President bears personal responsibility. For the murder of a well-known, outstanding political journalist who was systematic in her opposition, the state authorities bear full responsibility. Russia, having lost a journalist of this calibre, has been diminished by another major figure.

Yegor Yeremeyev, Omsk

On behalf of the students of the Physics Faculty of Omsk State University I offer condolences to the family, colleagues, and everybody who knew Anna Politkovskaya. I appeal to Anna's colleagues and very much beg them to continue to work, to write, and to tell the truth about our lives.

Victor Yushchenko, President of Ukraine

The news of the murder of Anna Politkovskaya, well known as a journalist and human rights defender, has been received in Ukraine with a sense of great sorrow and disquiet. Please accept my sincere condolences on the occasion of this irreparable loss. People in Ukraine will remember Anna Politkovskaya as a courageous person and professional who defended the high ideals of democracy and freedom of speech. I hope that those guilty of committing this terrible crime will be found and justly punished.

Akhmed Zakayev, Minister of Foreign Affairs of the Chechen Republic of Ichkeria

The Chechen people has been outraged to learn of the vile contract killing of Anna Politkovskaya who has been a fearless witness of its torments of recent years. Motivated by human sympathy and a sense of professional duty, Anna never succumbed to fear, or to the official anti-Chechen hysteria. She was one of the few Russian journalists who systematically, year after year, exposed the crimes against humanity which the Russian military machine visited upon the defenceless civilian population of the Chechen Republic.

The memory of this great Russian woman, who shared the tragedy of the Chechen people and did everything she could to convey the truth about it to the world community, will forever remain in our hearts and will, in the course of time, be perpetuated in the Republic of Chechnya.

TRIBUTES AND RECOLLECTIONS BY COLLEAGUES FROM *NOVAYA GAZETA*, FAMILY AND FRIENDS

Anna's Mother Discharged from Hospital

Novaya gazeta, November 16, 2006

[Anna's mother, Raisa Mazepa, went into hospital shortly before the death of her husband. She was in the Clinic of the President's Management Board and was being prepared for an operation.]

"We kept her husband's death from her for two days," Alexander Altunin, manager of the surgical department recalls. "Then we decided to tell her, after first giving her a sedative injection. She bore her grief with great dignity, and even agreed to stay in hospital. We performed a major operation on her. Raisa Alexandrovna was anaemic and we had to give her many injections of drugs, nutrient solutions and blood substitutes. She took it stoically. Her daughters visited her constantly. For something like that suddenly to happen . . ."

When news of the murder came out, the television and telephone were switched off in Raisa's ward. For the first day the family concealed Anna's death from her, but they realized they could not continue to do so for long: reports of the murder were in every edition of the news. At any moment Raisa might go out into the corridor and see a television or talk to one of the patients.

"Yury and Lena phoned me and said it was probably best that she should be told," Alexander Altunin recalls. "I phoned the cardiologist, Raisa was given a cardiogram, and we established that her heart was in good order. In the morning she was given a sedative and then her daughter Lena came with her husband. Physically Raisa bore her grief reasonably well, partly, no doubt, because of the sedative. I spoke to her the day after the murder. She was very stoical, told me about herself and her work in the USA, and then said that her daughter's death was like a stab in the back."

When Raisa was discharged from the hospital, she was feeling well, walking steadily, and her family sent her off to convalesce. She is recovering from the operation rapidly now.

"During the whole time she was in hospital Raisa Alexandrovna never once showed her grief. She is a very reserved person, and very brave."

Contact through Prayer
Alexander Politkovsky

> Lord, make me an instrument of your peace.
> Where there is hatred, let me sow love.
> Where there is injury, pardon.
> Where there is strife, harmony
> Where there is error, truth
> Where there is doubt, faith.
> Where there is despair, hope.
> Where there is darkness, light
> Where there is sadness, joy.

The Unpublished Letters of Marina Tsvetayeva is how it all began. As a student in the Faculty of Journalism I sat in the kitchen of Anna's flat. She was a schoolgirl then, and while my fellow students were taking notes, she and I dissected the gossamer of the poetess's idiosyncratic punctuation. Prof Rosenthal did not cover such matters in his lectures. The banned Tsvetayeva book had been brought from America by her father, who worked at the United Nations.

And then she herself became a student in the Faculty, following in the footsteps of Yelena, her elder sister. I was a four-storey-high Moscow lout who had earned his first money as a child doing odd jobs between excursions with my mum to the Conservatory, and graduated from a School for Working Youth. She had graduated from a specialist school and was living in accordance with the principles of classical literature. A tempestuous romance and immediately a devoted relationship. A trainee summer writing letters to each other. The slightly bitter smell of her sandalwood perfume, a student wedding in a one-roomed Khrushchev-era flat. A flower in my cap and a bottle of Moskovskaya vodka in a string bag with some black bread, such was the manner in which the bridegroom collected his bride. Her diplomat family did not appreciate the humor. Afterwards, socialist poverty and the joy when a new life is created.

My son entered the world and my student friends congratulated me: "Well done! Now you'll have someone to send out for beer in the morning." Instead, I remember rushing round the chemists' shops of Moscow looking for dill water to soothe colic.

Then, a daughter. Hurrah. She was called Vera.

Later, a nationalistically challenged moron of a schoolteacher with a straggly little beard gave my daughter a hard time in drawing lessons because of her surname, which he thought was Jewish. I wanted to treat him to a knuckle sandwich, Anna was sure that was the wrong approach and firmly protected the teacher's teeth. Her more humane approach triumphed. We explained at length to Vera that the teacher was barking up the wrong tree, but she should not demean herself by putting him right, just grin and bear it.

Anna gained her degree. Of course, her dissertation was on Tsvetayeva, and brilliantly defended. The plume of our student romance dissipated and the outlines of our relationship were fine-tuned, both matrimonial and professional. My first TV assignment in Rustavi. The agony of my first script. That evening Anna read the children a story remembered from her own childhood about a brave little tin soldier, or from mine, about Little Gavroche in *Les Misérables*. Having put the children to bed, she came to help me out. ". . . and thus the myth of seven-league boots came partly to be embodied in the idea of the internal combustion engine." That was Anna writing about motorbike racing. It was terrible, but it was used in the broadcast. Years later we laughed at ourselves in the kitchen on Herzen Street.

By now the flat was ours, and we were joined by Solly Zeus Smile or, more simply, Martyn the Dobermann. He wasn't at all Doberman-nish. In our crazy flat we had a growing dog with a fearsome bark but as affectionate as a kitten. He had some doggy sixth sense for identi-fying (infrequent) enemies. When he was a year and a half old, Anna saved his life by giving him injections every two hours. My friends offered to take the dog to the children's hospital where they worked, insert a catheter in a vein, and save us a lot of trouble. Anna was appalled. "We really couldn't do that. Alexander and I will take it in turns to get up."

Relations with my mother were difficult. Of course, we had arguments, mainly about how to bring the children up. Dr Spock was Anna's bible: "Teach them to swim before they can walk," and all that. The main bone of contention was finding a good nursery. It was impossible to get the children into one. I was a junior editor at a sports publishing house. I got a job teaching Asian martial arts, but in the early 1980s all that sort of thing was banned. There was no money for winter boots. In the mornings I ran barefoot in the snow in the courtyard so my feet didn't feel the cold on the way to work in Ostankino. The children followed behind me with their sniffles and coughs and upsets. Arguments.

After fairly wild evenings, I wrote in the kitchen at night. Anna herself very much wanted to write. Just 100 metres from where we lived were the offices of the railway union's newspaper, *The Whistle*. She went in but returned in dismay. The director had suggested she should begin her article with the words, "How's it going, railway worker?" You just can't write like that! There were tears in the evenings at the grey web of everyday routine.

She was surprised I only wrote for work, never for myself. I told her about how, when I was doing my Army training, the sergeant had pulled my diary out of my locker. He read it out loud to the entire unit. Now, I explained to Anna, I kept all my thoughts in my head where no buffoon in epaulettes could grope around in them. I never saw her keep a diary after that. Her diary was her articles. Writing what you think and not what pays is like keeping a diary.

We often had visitors, and there were theatres and the Conservatory near by. "I am my own independent creative unit!" she would say a little sadly, but with a smile, a phrase adopted from some journalism textbook. Everybody who visited us on Herzen Street remembers it, but nobody realized the extent to which it was to become her guiding principle.

She systematically investigated the theatres around us. All her friends and neighbours knew by heart the play, *Lunin, or the Death of Jacques* at the theatre on Malaya Bronnaya. The ideas of the Decembrist revolutionaries of 1825, and especially of their wives, were discussed passionately in our home.

Marina Goldovskaya, my journalism lecturer, made a film about our family for America. The film is mainly about Anna. Marina several times asked permission to show it in Russia but Anna was always opposed to that. Our friends have their own ideas about the film. In it I come across like the Red Commander of the civil war, Vasiliy Chapayev, only on the barricades of perestroika, saving the Fatherland. Anna is Anka the machine-gunner, lugging shells up to me and guarding the rear. It was just what an American audience wanted, but in Russia it was an embarrassment because of its unintentional support of the reformers' myth-making. In this film, *A Taste of Freedom*, the machine-gunner, dissatisfied with her fate, talks publicly about divorce for the first time. Our favorite scene in *Chapayev* is the suicidal attack. The White Guards advance and are sprayed with machine-gun fire. "A fine advance," and back comes the contemptuous plebeian reply, "Intelligentsia!"

My heroes are visiting. The entrepreneur Artyom Tarasov is telling us something about residual oil. We don't understand his diagrams too well, but in the evening talk together about Russia, and an oil glut which will stand everything on its head. It is plain that the so-called Democrats are already dragging their weary bones to Millionaires' Row on the Rublyovskoye Highway, closer and closer to Stalin's favorite haunts. Corrupt officials are receiving state awards, and Anna is shocked when she sees the son of 1960s icon Vladimir Vysotsky handing an award named after his father to the Minister of Posts and Telecommunications, Nikolai Aksenenko. The FSB, Interior Ministry and Ministry of Defence wouldn't dream of celebrating their anniversaries anywhere other than in the Kremlin. In the midst of a crime wave, the cops, using the money of taxpayers who are afraid to go out in the evenings, churn out television programs about how brilliantly they are fighting the criminals. The worse it is for some, the better it is for others. Perhaps an oil glut will give us a breathing space; otherwise portraits of our beloved leader would already be hanging not just in every office but in every home. Anna says, "It's lucky Martyn's tail was docked when he was a puppy. He doesn't chase it the way we do." We talked about the "sovereign business" run by the wives of officials who make speeches about the struggle against corruption.

Anna's first real victory was on the program *Vzglyad* ["Viewpoint"]. Volodya Mukusev and I came back from Minsk where we had been earning money by doing meetings with viewers. Anna turned out the pockets of my anorak before putting it in the wash. "Have you read this?" she asked. It was an urgent appeal for help, in a woman's handwriting, in red ink, about the Belarussian Children's Haematology Center. "This is addressed to you because of your Chernobyl," Anna exclaimed. "We must phone immediately!" A week later I returned to Minsk. Blurred filming with an amateur video camera which can be taken anywhere without being conspicuous. The truth is being concealed. We dig out information. Parents' tears.

I was away in a different part of Russia when Andrey Razbash edited the story, which swept Europe. In a short time millions were collected for the clinic. Anna insisted I should go back for an "inspection" trip to Minsk, and later to Germany where Russian doctors were being trained up. Raisa Gorbacheva visited the children's hospital. Within a few years the doctors were no longer Russian, and the Haematology Center was the best in Eastern Europe. Anna was delighted to see the situation so radically altered. Before the program went out more than 80 per cent of the children there were dying. Only a few years later, roughly the same number were being cured and the remainder were in remission.

She sat distraught and frozen in my car next to the house where journalist Vlad Listiev had just been murdered. We had never been close, but a year before she had arranged an amazing party at our house. It was very crowded, another attempt to bind together something that was falling apart.

International Women's Day, March 8, 1995, wasn't the obvious day to choose. Vlad did not drink, went away to offer good wishes to the women of the world live on air, and came back to the party. Everyone had had plenty to eat and drink and was in a good mood. Anna noticed a slight whiff of money. "You didn't once mention Ivan Kivelidi. He gave you the start-up capital for your television company. You won't last long at this rate." That same year the charming Ivan Kivelidi was mysteriously poisoned.*

Sitting in that car, neither of us yet realized that an oil bonanza would send everyone into moral hibernation, that the mass media would glamorously and expensively expire in the hands of "natural monopolies," whose naturalness was not obvious. I often heard on my assignments, "What a fearless namesake you have working at *Novaya gazeta*." I was glad people could see that, and were aware of her commitment to her guiding principle. There were threatening signs. At home pistols were left in parcels at the door of our flat. Another time the fire hydrant in the attic above was turned full on. That was unambiguously directed at her.

By 1996 the whiff of money had become a stench. The mysterious "box of Xerox paper" containing half a million bucks for Yeltsin's election campaign. Wealthy individuals who had built themselves mansions beyond the borders of Russia claimed that Russia was still their home. Anna was busy trying to save old people from a home in Grozny and told me on her return how a former friend of mine, by now a big official, had waited for ages by a corridor the old people were to emerge from, keeping well away from the gunfire like the coward he was, but well within range of the television cameras, in order to get himself filmed as their saviour and shown as such to the whole of Russia. To her great satisfaction, he failed, but it was symptomatic of a spreading web of vile behaviour. Anna always agreed with Dostoyevsky that you don't get at the truth through lies and trickery, even as a temporary expedient, as our recent history has shown.

We had a stint working as a husband-and-wife team. Anna was the first journalist in Russia to cover the topic of totalitarian sects and got hold of a unique video. I followed her with a program in the *Polit-*

---

*Ivan Kivelidi (1949–95) was Chairman of the Board of Rosbiznesbank. On August 1, 1995 an exotic poison was put in the telephone receiver in his office, and he died in hospital on August 5.

buro series on the same subject. We both came to the dispiriting conclusion that the Russian state was the biggest sect of all, using the people's own money to brainwash it. Very few were immune to the influence of all this garbage. We argued a lot. The Russian "market" was another name for individual greed. She was certain that greed could be managed, and that human beings were an end in themselves. They could be independent, creative units. I believed the individual could always be controlled. The genetic memory of a slave was in you whether you had a flashing light on top of your prestigious car and a bodyguard or whether you were a down-and-out on the status scrapheap. Anna was furious but had to agree. She had studied the experience of totalitarian sects only too closely. By definition, however, newspaper journalists delve deeper into their topics than television reporters, so I didn't always win.

Lazy celebrity TV presenters would often plagiarise her texts without even bothering to paraphrase them. Our home was a press room with an engrossing weekly review of the news programs, which we compared against her articles.

Anna came with me when I next decided to visit my beloved Kamchatka Province. We worked in parallel, examining the cheerless results of privatisation. She flew back on her birthday. Local friends laid on a birthday party at the airport before she flew out and wished her a happy longest birthday she would have in her life as she flew westward with the sun.

She sometimes seemed to move faster than the clock. In August 1991 our whole family was in Svetlogorsk. In the evenings we drank with Yury Shevchuk. He sang his new songs for us. In the mornings we tried to persuade the women to join a new party called the Hungovers. Anna invented a title for our top party functionary, "The Seventh Day Hungover." The holiday passed lightheartedly. On August 17 the season was to reopen at the Lenkom Theatre with Grigoriy Gorin's *Prayer of Remembrance*, in the last scene of which our son Ilya played the violin. I flew back to Moscow with Ilya only for us to find ourselves in the middle of the anti-Gorbachev putsch. I was relieved that Anna and our daughter Vera were far away, and that Ilya was staying with Anna's parents, out of harm's way. A day later I was astonished to hear from her parents that she was already in Moscow and preparing to take to the barricades in defence of democracy. Everywhere you heard Shevchuk's "Last Autumn." It proved not to be the last autumn, but only the beginning of things going wrong. Everything was about to become a business: management of the state, war, morality, elections, medicine, education. The real "Seventh Day Hungovers," the secret policemen, were only getting started in the cellars of Moscow's White House.

Two years passed and after another putsch I was asked to come to the Ministry by a certain highly placed official. The Minister himself came outside the building, gave me my documents, and warned, "Take care. Did you speak out against the shelling of the White House? Everything is just beginning." Back home I tried to persuade Anna to take out the American citizenship she was entitled to, because she was born there. She strongly objected to my suggestion. She hadn't much liked America after our trip there in 1991, but agreed to it after our daughter came home from school with the news that some of her friends were no longer talking to her. Society had split into people who were on side, and the others who weren't. It was only later that emotions cooled, people started using their brains again and realized they had been taken for a ride. I was no longer allowed to broadcast. Anna raged but, as tends to happen in Russia, our telephone rang less frequently. I tried to explain to the children that their surname might cause them problems. They didn't see that, and on the contrary were rather proud of the situation. They saw the point later, the first time they ran up against "on side" cops. When they casually mentioned it to their mother, she was furious.

In my worst nightmare I could never have imagined that the citizenship of the body in the coffin would be held against Anna by our "patriots," and used as a frightener by the "sovereign Russia" brigade. Her books, like the *Unpublished Letters of Marina Tsetayeva* all those years ago, are well known in the civilised world but not to be found on the shelves of Russian bookshops.

The main investor, receiver and allocator of favors in Russia is once again that well guarded fortress in the center of Moscow. Anna tells me how the fat cats fight for the right to a flashing light on their car, and how, if they decide to give it up, they make a major "democratic" fuss about their magnanimity. Celebrity brains do not function until hit over the head by a revived special operations militiaman.

Our marriage lasted 21 years. I managed to lose. We separated. Life under a permanent storm front came to an end. We separated but did not divorce, in order that our colleagues who work to get money from the bosses should not be given a news break. There were plenty of enemies. They didn't often sue because they knew what she wrote was the truth, but they pelted her with filth.

She was invited to a forum in Eilat devoted to the end of the century. It was our last tour. I accompanied her. In the bus our guide, an ex-Soviet, insisted that Judas was only acting his part in a play which had already been written. "That's rich!" Anna said, and laughed. We didn't take him to task.

We travelled through the Holy Land. Orthodox Christmas. Rain in Bethlehem. Anna and I stood next to the Temple. Everybody was pushed aside. Moscow cars with flashing lights. Did I imagine it? We squeezed into the building and there, sure enough, sitting in chairs in the middle of the Temple as if they were in a theatre, were Yeltsin, Chubais and Arafat. The service was being played out in front of them like a perform-ance. Had they come to beg forgiveness for their sins? It was totally monstrous. Horrified, we came out and heard in the repulsive drizzle a sweet voice. In the square we were confronted by another extra-ordinary sight. From our youth, like the brave little tin soldier, a wet Demis Roussos was rushing about on a stage in the almost deserted square. Not a single New Russian to be seen, only a few Israelis, and nobody was collecting cash, as they would be in Russia. "Goodbye, my love, goodbye." "He's taking the piss," Anna whispered. In the dark-ness we were surrounded by émigrés under umbrellas who wanted to ask us about perestroika.

It would have been good just to talk without them, and not about perestroika. We had to work on the perestroika of our family relations. We found it just as difficult to get unused to each other as to put up with each other in the same flat.

A few days later, the intimate meeting again in the church, at the funeral service, the dissipating gossamer of incense with its hint of bitterness. The priest pronounced the last word. I suddenly had the feeling that she was arguing with me again, and such a wretched emotion came over me that, as I remembered the tears I had caused this woman to shed, I couldn't proceed to the coffin to go through the motions of a helpful ritual. Whether it was the diary of the brave little tin soldier, or Gavroche going his own way and forced to spend nights in the ruined bowels of a monumental elephant . . . An independent creative unit. Tsvetayeva's noose. In the evening I remembered the first amazing words of the prayer, "Make me an instrument of your peace." Hers was my surname; how significant it was that I had taught the words of that prayer to a schoolgirl.

An Independent Creative Entity
Elena Morozova

MLAN (Masha–Lena–Anna): this remarkable association lasted long enough to celebrate its fortieth anniversary, but came to an end on October 7, 2006. The bullets fired from a Makarov pistol hit their target, the heart of the association, Anya.

We had been friends since childhood, and it was a friendship not directed against anybody else, as seems often to be the case nowadays: we just enjoyed each other's company and all that went with that. Friendship, especially if it lasts for many years, is a living organism. Like molecules in a cell, we were sometimes drawn to each other, sometimes repelled. Sometimes we existed quite autonomously, before again drawing close. We were forever asking Anna to write about us because so many interesting things happened; life threw up plots which the scriptwriters of soap operas might have envied. She did not take the suggestion seriously, and said she would think about it when she was old and sitting at home with her grandchildren. During the last decade, however, she never had time to sit anywhere. She periodically disappeared from our cosy, well-ordered life in the center of Moscow and went back again and again to a different, terrifying life where a war was being fought, people were dying, a life of pain and suffering.

She flew there to give help and hope, to rescue people and restore the truth. Protecting the peace of our families, we instinctively avoided letting that war into our hearts. We told her she only lived once, that she should think about her children and parents, that she shouldn't take such risks. Anna didn't even try to argue with us. She considered herself duty bound to relieve the pain of others. In the traditional photographs taken during our happy reunions in recent years, her eyes are always sad. That other life never completely freed her to return to our life in Moscow.

Anna was absolutely convinced of the rightness of her choice to fight for justice, and to defend the weak and the wronged. It is the way saints live but, as we know from history, their lives are unfortunately often short. She cannot write any more now. Now it is our turn to write about her.

The idea of forming our association came to us one time when, joining hands, we jumped off a garage roof into a deep snowdrift. Alas, I doubt there are any garage owners left who are so kindly disposed towards children. A few months before we had all been new pupils in Class 1B. We were all born leaders and a happy childhood intuition must have suggested to us that it would be better to join forces, to form a nucleus which would attract our classmates, rather than fight it out with each other to be the leader of this new pack. We were minded to do good, having been brought up on the edifying novellas of Valentina Oseyeva and Arkadiy Gaidar, and tales about heroic Young Pioneers.

Our first good deed was to help the class dunce, a boy called Volodya, to revise for a series of class tests and to improve dramatically on his disgraceful marks. We gathered at Anna's. She proposed an original incentive: for every mistake he made in the maths examples Volodya would have to eat several sugared cranberry sweets. Soon the sweets were all gone, but the mistakes persisted. Volodya did not come to school the next day. Sweet things disagreed with him and he came out in a terrible rash which took ages to clear up.

Our inclination to do good deeds evolved into a determination to catch criminals. Every day as we walked to school we passed a stand in the street which had photographs of people wanted for questioning by the militia. This inspired us to new feats. For several days we followed

close on the heels of a suspicious person who evidently lived somewhere nearby. Perhaps he really did have a criminal past. At all events,
he spent most of the day in the company of the local alcoholics or just
hanging around aimlessly. We were convinced that we had detected a
terrible saboteur and that the Motherland would be proud of us. We
were never to forget the militiamen seating us in a motorbike sidecar,
and with eyes ablaze and our Pioneer neckerchiefs flying in the wind
we were driven round the courtyards in search of our suspect. We do
not know to this day what the militia talked to him about, but for years
after that our hypothetical criminal crossed to the other side of the
road whenever he saw us.

We were good at our schoolwork, always organised the class concert,
edited the wall newspaper, bought presents for the boys on February
23, for Soviet Army Day, and took part in amateur dramatics and
dancing. We lived our lives to disconcert the foe and make our mothers
proud of us. Anna was outstandingly good in every subject for the
entire 10 years. Before tests and essays, her classmates would push
and shove to sit as close to her desk as possible, which ensured a good
mark. If Anna came into the class in the morning and said she hadn't
managed to do the homework, we knew for a fact that it was impossible. She was also successfully studying music, and had far less free
time than her classmates for playing outside. From childhood she knew
the meaning of discipline and hard work.

In her teens qualities became evident which were to be fundamental
to her personality. She was physically incapable of condoning unfair-
ness. She acknowledged no absolute authorities, and always told the
truth to people's faces, whatever the consequences. Anna was perfectly
capable of throwing down her exercise book on the teacher's desk if
she considered he had marked her unfairly. She even stood up to the
headmaster, who the teachers themselves were afraid of, if she felt
another pupil had been treated unfairly. She was a maximalist. When
she argued her cheeks would become livid, and she could be very
abrupt. "Ostap has got the bit between his teeth," we would joke, remembering the manic hero of Ilf and Petrov's *Twelve Chairs*. At first we
found her unyielding nature difficult, but later learned to ignore it and

tried not to bring her to boiling point, either giving way in arguments or changing the subject. We kept that habit going in later life.

Soon our friend's civic activism moved up a gear. Anna began doubting the fairness of "developed socialism," which is how society in the Brezhnev years was characterised. She was extremely sensitive to the sham values underlying it. We were baffled as to why she wanted to change the rules, and not just live in accordance with them like other people. It was obviously a lost cause, but she genuinely could not understand our indifference and lack of desire to improve society. Her first newspaper reporting was challenging and topical. She saw the main reason for working as a journalist as being to put right the situation she was describing, to identify and excoriate those responsible.

We grew up. Anna was the first to marry and the first to become a mother, while she was still very young. Her parents were upset that she had encumbered herself with all the trials of family life at such an early age. I will never forget her coming for a break at my dacha, holding her three-year-old son by the hand, with her year-old daughter in her arms, and simultaneously managing a folding pushchair, a potty, changes of clothing, baby food and books. All this she coped with without a car, travelling first by Metro and bus, then on the suburban train, and finally making it to the dacha on foot. It was not something every young mother could have undertaken, but Anna was never afraid of difficulties. In order to save up to buy a piano for the children, she took a second job as a cleaner at a studio on the ground floor of her apartment block. Soon a vintage instrument was bought which served not only for making music, but also as a bookshelf, a writing desk, an ironing board, and as a stand for the parrot's cage. In those days beginning journalists lived very modestly indeed. Preparing endless breakfasts, lunches and dinners; doing the laundry and tidying up; teaching the children music, drawing and general knowledge, Anna would periodically exclaim, "I am an independent creative unit." In fact, there was very little time for creativity, and she was able to write only at night after the children had been put to bed and the housework done.

We always joked that the more difficult her life became, the better she looked. She was naturally good-looking, and seemed to confirm the male chauvinist maxim that "hardship makes women prettier." She was never stumped for an answer, able in an instant to summon up her will, focus herself like a sportswoman preparing for a jump, and fling herself into battle against the latest vicissitude.

Throughout her life Anna made few demands on her surroundings. She had neither the time nor the money to furnish her new flat on Lesnaya Street, an address which has now unhappily become so famous. She dressed tastefully but simply and was uninterested in jewellery or expensive clothes. The handle of her favorite black bag, which went along on her numerous assignments in Chechnya, was bound round with sticking plaster, and immense efforts were needed to persuade her to buy a new one. There was a hole of unknown origin in the side of her beloved Zhiguli, but she did not want to buy a new car. She liked learning to cook new dishes and would scrupulously, step by step, carry out all the instructions in a recipe. Unfortunately, she had no time and could not be bothered cooking for herself. The only foods which were invariably to be found in her home were honey, cheese, rolls and tea.

We spent the whole of our lives within sight of each other, but it will remain a mystery to us how Anna managed to exist in two parallel worlds: in our familiar life, which is the life most women live, and in the life of an investigative journalist, writing mostly about politically sensitive matters, about society's imperfections, as responsive to the pain of others as to her own, making every effort to improve the lot of at least one person. In her "civilian" life Anna devoted a lot of time to her children and was a real friend and adviser to them. She often dropped in for a chat, and we would sit in the kitchen, drinking endless cups of tea and talking about everything in the world, but trying to avoid mentioning that other life. Anna was a marvellous conversationalist. She could tell a story vividly, and was an attentive listener. You could always turn to her for help. When my son was born she left the guests who had come to her birthday party to run over to the maternity hospital and leave me a note of congratulations. (It was before the era of mobile phones.) Anna could not bear irresolution and spinelessness. She greatly valued personal freedom. She was a complex person, but we always knew that we were living with an icon.

Anya was . . . It is impossible to become reconciled to that past tense. The pain of loss is something we have yet to come to terms with. For now it seems that Anna has again flown out on an assignment, and that soon our answering machine will pass on her favorite message, "Hello, this is Anya Politkovskaya. I live just across the road. Call me."

Unfortunately, there is no reaching her now by phone, but she is constantly in our thoughts. We miss you so much, Anna.

A Woman of Integrity
Zoya Yeroshok, Columnist for Novaya gazeta

We were not close friends, but when we met we talked at great length, usually after Anna returned from an assignment. She would tell me about the people she was describing at that moment. She spoke of them in great detail but very unemotionally.

Her office was a reception room for the whole of Russia, and there was invariably some person in trouble sitting there. Anna would listen to them for hours, questioning them, rescuing them from difficulties, giving them back their life. In Novaya gazeta's office I only ever saw her working, never just drinking coffee in the bar or chatting idly.

Anna was a pure, honest and fearless journalist, absolutely selfless and original. In the seven years she worked for Novaya gazeta she published more than 500 articles, and of these more than 40 resulted in criminal charges being brought or trials reviewed.

Her words had a different specific gravity from even the very best words in the very best order. They cast a shadow, probably because they had the power to redeem or expose. Mostly, they redeemed, despite her many critical articles, because Anna always remembered who she was writing for and what she was writing about. She never wrote just for the sake of it.

She was a journalist with raw nerves, for whom nothing was simple or easy – everything was serious and responsible. She was a very clear and intelligible journalist, never picking a fight for the sake of it. Rather, she had a tragic awareness that it was unavoidable. Anna wrote a lot about Chechnya, but her real concern was just ordinary people and the lives they were living. The attitude towards Chechens in our beloved Fatherland has long been not even to regard them as cattle (since cattle are sentient beings), but as matter, as inanimate objects. Many came to accept this attitude.

The poet Naum Korzhavin has written, "Is the law really an insane competition to see who can sacrifice whom for the good of the many?" Such a competition was indeed organised in Russia in the Stalin era, and it was a defilement. It is exactly what Pasternak describes: "I felt affinity with the poor ... but have been spoiled since the times were hexed and sorrow came to be reviled, and philistines and optimists perplexed." "Making optimists perplexed" refers to those who are invariably, unquestioningly cheerful in the face of other people's misery, who have no problem with living like that. They believe that living like that means they are in tune with the times, although even the most complex and intriguing of us are very, very ordinary in the eyes of God.

Anna never made a thing of her own exceptionalness, never made a thing about remaining true to herself. She was a sincere person, without cheap sentimentality, without touching sweetness, but she simply would not accept the idea that there might be people for whom you could feel no pity, who were expendable. When, in the name of the People, the state authorities were murdering people, Anna was not with the crowd who silently looked away. Her resistance to evil took the form of frankness. She openly hated evil and openly loved good. She never, ever came to terms with cannibals.

She was pained that the genuine links between people had been destroyed, that people were being divided according to nationality, or into the rich and the poor.

Anna carried on her shoulders and within herself a burden beyond the strength of even hundreds of journalists. Life made her resolute, and taught her to work ably and effectively, and only on behalf of and alongside ordinary people, the most vulnerable and the most forgotten.

She was no idol for the intelligentsia, and neither did she idolise the intelligentsia. That ordinary people living ordinary lives had no place in the New Russian life of the wealthy Anna blamed not only on the state authorities, but on all those "who only needed to promote solidarity." Even simple solidarity is something almost all the ordinary people have yet to see from the intelligentsia. The "common" people have been overlooked, they are "beyond the bounds of our sympathy," as Korzhavin once crisply put it.

Anna fought against the demagogy of social justice. She knew that justice is not something you introduce or attain: justice has to be worked on. She worked on it, sometimes completely alone. ("I wriggle between the elites of the sated and the scrubbed, pushing my own line and trying not to become part of any of them.")

Anna worked inside her own territory, one she had conquered. She was apart from everyone else, but she sought understanding, and failing that, then at least partial understanding.

She didn't try to shout anyone down, she merely invited people to hear and see each other. She tried desperately to find a modicum of enduring respect in society for the public and the personal.

Anna was a very Russian journalist. Today the pseudo-patriots splutter venomously about her American citizenship and cannot abide the fact that she was the daughter of diplomats and was born in America. Well, good luck to them. I will say only that Anna loved Russia. Russia was her life, and patriotism is love, not national egotism or a means of self-assertion. When Anna was invited to emigrate, she said, "*Novaya gazeta* still needs me."

She once told me about a brief note she had published. A family lived in Chechnya. One night people in uniform came and took away their 16-year-old son. The parents searched for him for a long time but did not find him. Then their house was bombed and they fled. They wandered through Central Russia, living in cellars. They had nothing left, not even their family photographs.

One day they came to Anna to tell her about their son, what kind of boy he was, what he liked, what books he read, the kind of smile he had.

Anna wrote about all that. Later they came to see her again, to thank her. The only thing they had left of their son was Anna's note in the newspaper, and now it hangs on their wall behind glass in a picture frame. "It's important to have something to hold on to, even if it is only in newsprint," his parents told her.

She did more than her duty.

Who Killed Anna and Why?
Vyacheslav Izmailov, Military Correspondent for Novaya gazeta

Thousands of people have died in Chechnya in extra-judicial killings. Not in battle: many of those killed had no involvement at all with the resistance fighters.

The victims of Major Lapin and his accomplices from the Khanty-Mansiysk Combined Militia Unit, assigned to the October District Interior Affairs Office in Grozny, died under torture; the GRU agents in Captain Ulman's gang shot and burned teachers from the Chechen village of Dai; Colonel Budanov, the Commanding Officer of 160 Tank Regiment, raped and murdered a 17-year-old Chechen girl.

The criminal charges brought against these scum in uniform were brought not as a result of facts revealed in Anna Politkovskaya's publications, but mainly as a result of the publicity she gave them by writing about them in Novaya gazeta. I have no doubt that, given the chance, these Lapins, Budanovs and Ulmans, and also some of their supporters, might well have settled scores with Anna Politkovskaya. Only, however, if they had the opportunity, and I do not believe that such an opportunity presented itself. Nevertheless, these possibilities, even though they have been looked at to some extent by Novaya gazeta's inquiry, should not be dismissed.

Anna wrote about torture, murder, and abductions in Chechnya. These monstrous deeds were perpetrated by representatives of all the security agencies: the Interior Ministry, the FSB, the Central Intelligence Directorate (GRU), and also the Kadyrovites, Baisarovites (Movladi Baisarov's men were operationally under the command of the FSB), the Yamadayevites (Suleyman Yamadayev is the Commander of the East Special Operations Battalion of the Central Intelligence

Directorate of the Ministry of Defence, the Kakievites (Said-Mahomed Kakiev is the Commander of the West Battalion), and resistance fighters.

Moreover, in order to divert suspicion from themselves, any of these organizations might employ the methods of their rivals and even enemies. All these kidnappers and murderers have so covered their tracks and so mimicked one another that sometimes they themselves could not tell who had abducted or murdered a particular person.

Sometimes, however, Anna's revelations were completely exclusive and presented, moreover, in the form of brilliant journalism. They discredited newly proclaimed "Heroes of Russia," and struck one living "Hero," Ramzan Kadyrov, who was making good money through criminal business dealings out of the memory of that dead "Hero," his deified dad, hitting him, as they say, not on the eyebrow but smack in the eye.

Until May 9, 2004 the Kadyrov family's opportunities for self-enrichment were relatively limited. In those days Ramzan's immediate entourage drove around not in Mercedes and Ferraris, as they do today, but in far more modest Zhiguli-99s and Zhiguli-10s.

After the death of Akhmat-hadji Kadyrov, his son Ramzan found he had considerably greater scope. In the first place, he was immediately promoted to the position of First Deputy Prime Minister, in effect crushing the Prime Minister, Sergey Abramov. In the second place, he set up the Akhmat-hadji Kadyrov Foundation, an organization for the laundering and uninhibited exploitation of resources amounting to many millions of dollars. Kadyrov Junior and his henchmen levied tribute on the entire population of Chechnya, from the humblest toilet cleaner to the highest state officials, including ministers, rank and file officers of the militia, and senior officers of the Chechen Interior Ministry.

In her article, "Ramzan Kadyrov, the Pride of Chechnya" (*Novaya gazeta*, No. 42, June 5, 2006), Anna proved that the A. Kadyrov Foundation obtained its funds in the main by extortion from the Chechen people. Anybody who refused to pay up was, at best, sacked. As a result of his legalised extortion racket, Kadyrov Junior became the richest man in Chechnya. He and his retinue now drive around in flashy foreign cars, build themselves palaces in Chechnya and beyond its borders, and buy expensive flats in Moscow.

Anna explained how journalists working on Kadyrov's image were generating a myth in Chechnya to the effect that the Republic's restoration was taking place at the expense of Ramzan Kadyrov personally and of his Foundation. She showed that of 27 projects, only six were being financed by non-budgetary resources. The other projects, amounting to billions, were being financed from the budget of the Russian Federation.

Having in spring 2000 become Prime Minister in the Chechen government, Ramzan Kadyrov was sucking at the breasts of two mothers, the Russian federal budget and his own Foundation's proceeds of crime.

Describing the Chechen beauty competition held at the Foundation's expense, Anna wrote, "After the jury had announced the name of the winner and many girls had been given cars, there was a celebratory dinner in a Gudermes restaurant. Kadyrov Junior and several dozen bodyguards arrived. The winners were commanded to dance for him and the others and, as the dancing continued, Kadyrov Junior ordered bodyguards who were not dancing to throw banknotes at the young ladies, hundred-dollar and thousand-rouble banknotes [. . .]

"Years will pass, all things will pass, and people will have no wish to recall any detail of these Hundred Days with their oaths of loyalty to the Kadyrov cause. But what of the girls who in May 2006 crawled around on that restaurant floor? What of the young journalists who put their signatures to a publication titled 'Kadyrov, the Peacemaker,' at a time when hundreds of people had been tortured to death in Tsentoroy? How will they live with themselves? I cannot imagine."

The mafia does not forgive such exposés.

I Remember, Anna and I were Talking . . .
Galina Mursalieva, Columnist for Novaya gazeta

I remember Anna and I were talking about the heroes of our times.

There had just been two tragic incidents: Private Andrey Sychev had been brutally mutilated in the Army, and another 20-year-old in Moscow, Alexander Koptsev, had himself done the mutilating when he took a knife into a synagogue and wounded those at prayer. Anna very scrupulously investigated the circumstances of the first tragedy, and I examined the highly dramatic fate of the second young man. Together we identified a phenomenon: she told me that money was being sent from different parts of the country to the mother of Private Sychev, and I told her that money was also being sent to the mother of Koptsev. She was extremely interested by this twist. People who knew her well remember her ability to home in on the essence of her topics, to empathise her way into them. You could almost feel it physically. Her whole being leaning forward, slightly hunched, one hand propping up her chin and the other at her brow like the peak of a cap – that is how she looked as she sat at her desk, thinking and concentrating.

"So those are the new heroes Russia has chosen," she said.

"I suppose so," I agreed. "If you discount the glitz, the gossip column celebrities, the show business personalities, then in effect we are left with just these two boys, symbolising two of Russia's horrors: the reign of the 'grandads' in the Army, and xenophobia. The popular mind seems to have no room for any other heroes."

Anna thought for a moment, and then said abruptly, "In other words, we have none."

I had to agree.

I also remember saying to her that nowadays no sensation lasted more than three days. She gestured dismissively, "They don't even last a day."

A certain solemn person said to me today, "Do you mean to say that you told Anna Politkovskaya, whose work was the most long-lasting sensation of recent history, who was herself a symbol of free, independent journalism and unquestionably a heroine, that there couldn't be any long-lasting sensations? You said that the only heroes can be people who evoke either pity or aggression? You said that to a saint after whom streets will be named?" Well, actually, yes.

These words were simply inapplicable to her in life. Depending on her mood she would either have burst out laughing in the face of anybody who spoke so pompously about her, or would turn away, having lost all interest in them.

I knew what she had achieved, I knew about the bronze presentation cases from award ceremonies, and I knew their recipient had never opened them. She not only never wore the mantle of the fine words which had been said about her, she didn't even try it on because that was not her style.

Of course I knew who I was talking to. I wasn't blind. I had seen the stream of people from every part of Russia coming to her, seeing in her their last hope of justice. I understood what she was doing, the risk she was constantly running. But as often happens, when you're in the middle of a professional conversation, you can't start viewing the person you are talking to as an icon, the more so when the icon herself never switches on her canonised look. You are talking to a colleague on a straightforward, everyday, down-to-earth, work level. I was just sitting too close to her, our desks side by side, for seven years.

I remember her coming back after receiving all sorts of amazingly prestigious awards. There was no celebration, no joy, only disappointment. There she was sitting, holding her column very close in front of her and reading out her own text. I came in and said in passing, "Anna, congratulations. That's super."

"But they don't want to understand anything. They won't listen! They are completely uninterested. It's not super, Galya."

"But it's a victory?"

"No!"

And at first I didn't understand. Why would they hand out these awards, how could they select and assess if they didn't want to understand? OK, perhaps it wasn't a victory, but surely an award was at least a demonstration of support?

"Yes, but it is support for a journalist and not for what he or she is doing. They not only don't want to get involved in helping with what I'm doing, they don't even want to try to understand it!"

If it had been anyone else, I would have suspected they were striking a pose, but the woman sitting there and saying this was so disillusioned, so weary, her expectations so clearly disappointed. The individuals on whom people's fates depended, who might have brought about a breakthrough in the situation, didn't want to lift a finger to help. It wasn't just Russia, it was the world. It just wanted to buy her off.

She was being left alone with a burden she could hardly bear. She had been fêted and blessed on her way, and in the process they had psychologically washed their hands of her. That was how I understood the situation.

But there were other people, a whole pack of them within Russia, who seemed to be on her side. I'm not talking about those who hated Anna – their position was clear enough and what more can one say about them? I'm not even talking about those who did not like her, because that too is not all that important. There were others, though, who didn't love her enough. They were agitated every time something terrible happened to her, when she was taken prisoner in Chechnya, when she was poisoned on her way to Beslan. Yes, they were upset, but when everything worked out all right, they didn't think it had been that big a deal. They were sort of beside her, and this gave them the right to snipe at her. They stood shoulder to shoulder with her, but in a casual sort of way, and looked on at someone who had assumed a burden which, without exaggeration, would have had a thousand people groaning under its weight. And they decided it wasn't that big a deal.

"It is as if she is living in a mortuary," one very well-known spin doctor informed me one time. "A normal person cannot be exposed to a constant torrent of deaths and describe it endlessly."

"A normal person cannot help feeling that in front of their eyes part of the country is being turned into a mortuary and cannot help wanting to do their utmost to hinder it. Even less can they adapt so completely to being in a mortuary that they wander in eating cake," I told him. "And this really is an endless topic. Who is more normal, the person who cries out in pain, or the person who pretends there's no problem? 'Ooh, you were quite right to stamp on my foot. It doesn't hurt a bit,

I'm enjoying it! Please go ahead and stamp on my other foot too, because . . .'" Well, because that way, even though you are powerless, you can still seem to be in control.

But you aren't in control, and it isn't normal! The world is topsy-turvy and, hanging down head first, you so much want to be included in the society of morally decent people. It wouldn't be decent to hate Anna, but you can not love her quite enough without losing face. Something is nevertheless hiding in there behind that "not quite enough," perhaps the way people feel about themselves, a feeling deep inside that the life they are living in Russian society in the guise of decent people is not close enough to really being alive. They tried so hard to live as good people, but somehow they weren't really; while once upon a time Anna did, and was, and that was not a fairy tale.

I remember once we were discussing some film with a lot of parts, something about special operations. It was one of those conversations fitted in while we were both busy with something else. We were checking through something on our computers and in the process exchanging comments about how disgusting this kind of false romanticisation was, abundantly spiced with racism and violence. We were going through examples which I no longer remember, and wondered what the people who created such a product would get out of it.

"Well nothing, I suppose, except a lot of money and some prizes," I said, not taking my eyes off the monitor.

"They will bring shame on themselves," Anna said with such conviction that I turned round and looked at her, uncertainly and with a half-smile at first: what was this? Did she really mean it?

"They will bring shame on themselves!" she repeated heatedly.

She had just been very decently brought up; that was the whole explanation. Of course, we all had explained to us when we were little what was good and what was bad. Everybody knows that. It's just that as we grow up, we tend to drop the heavy stuff, some to a greater and some to a lesser extent. Some unload it on to the scrap heap, others just relegate it to the cellar or the attic of their consciousness, because it is difficult to live wearing these penitential chains of morality, especially when most people have long ago chosen the easy way. In any

case, there are attributes of "merit" – like cynicism, or scepticism, or
that sure-fire winner, wit – which hardly weigh anything at all. With
wit you are received into the society of morally decent people, you turn
a caustic phrase and, even if there is no action behind your words, the
topic is closed. You are sharp. You are cool.

The quandary was formulated long ago: "To Be or To Seem?" If you
choose the latter, you will live long. Whereas Anna chose the former
and has been murdered.

I remember how I first heard the news, and to this day it is as if I
have a foreign body lodged in my brain: "Anna has been killed." It is
as if a red streamer flares up in my mind, and hurts, and gives me no
peace, and cuts into me and oppresses me. "Anna has been killed."
"They have killed Anna." "Anna . . ." It was exactly as if a fire had
engulfed a virtual space needed simply to take the fact in. I remember
those first hours, our friends ashen faced, the businesslike investigators, the television cameras. While you are answering their questions,
you feel you are going around with a watering can, putting things out,
trying to rescue what has not already been burned to a cinder, some
features. You move the markers they are already putting down in a way
that makes you rise up in revulsion and shout "No!" You say, "What
are you talking about? What sort of "iron lady" was she? You haven't
even read her! "Indefatigable soldier" – who are you talking about?
Anna? For heaven's sake, the minute she came into the office she could
tell me what perfume I was wearing. What kind of bloody soldier does
that? She dressed elegantly, stylishly. She was an amazingly devoted
mother to her children."

Our children grew up together not in front of our eyes but because
we talked about them. When you sit next to someone in a small room
for seven years, you know about every boil, every joy and torment, all
the enthusiasms and achievements of your colleague's children, and
she knows all about yours.

Anna treated her children with such care and respect, and such a
reserved tenderness came into her voice. You might not have heard her
say their names, but you could tell immediately from her tone of voice
that she was talking to one of them. There was so much pain when things

were not going well, and so much delight and pride when there was cause for celebration. "Galya, my son is now earning more than I do!"

Her tone was light, as if to say, "There, we've lived to see the day!" But the exclamation marks were dancing in her eyes: "I have lived to see my son completely grown up. I don't need to worry about him now. Everything is going well!"

And now, here we are.

I remember how much she loved coffee, and brought a coffee-maker to work. After she was poisoned on the way to Beslan she wasn't allowed to eat or drink anything she liked. She seemed to be sustained by air and work. I don't believe that people suddenly become mortal. There's nothing sudden about it. We just find it easier to believe that. If someone isn't dead then everything must be pretty much OK. We had used up all our reserves of concern for her, and that's always the way: as soon as you stop worrying, something bad happens.

She was edgy and run-down, and frequently in tears, but it was amazingly easy to comfort her. A long time ago I stumbled upon a method and thereafter used it shamelessly. She could be comforted like a child by distracting her attention. It was useless to start arguing with her or giving her advice when she was in that kind of state. You needed to hear her out, and then as if quite randomly tell her something amusing. The tears would still be flowing, but already there was a smile, so open, so genuine. And then that infectious laugh. Everybody who knew her remembers how she could laugh.

Anna was very much alive, a real human being.

Anna was? I remember the phrase, "He is a coward. He will kill someone if he is afraid of them." If she hated someone's acts she brought them out into the light, to be judged. They, furtively, sneaking along a wall, inside a lift, killed Anna.

I'm really not that interested in what happens to those cowards, I know it already. I believe the theory that we live several lives and I read an elaboration, I don't remember where, but it very much appealed to me. It was to the effect that in this life conscience makes things awkward for us. That's true, isn't it? It causes a lot of trouble. It's at the root of all our problems. It's like a hermit's chains, why deny it? In fact it really doesn't seem to serve any useful purpose. But if we imagine that a mother's womb is a different world in which the human embryo lives, and we know that it lives there for a long time with its little hands and feet, we can equally well ask: what does he need them for, in that life? They just get in the way. They don't serve any purpose. It's completely incomprehensible what they are for until the moment of birth, but if then you were born without them, it would be a disaster. You would be a cripple. In just the same way, perhaps, for us earth-bound embryos, conscience is an organ of that kind.

Anna has been born into that different world completely normal and perfect.

Her killers are heading the same way, and they will be monsters.

I remember . . .

A Healthy Dog in a Big City

Van Gogh the bloodhound joined the Politkovskaya family just over two years ago. The puppy had problems, and his need was not so much for food and injections (well, not only that), as for selfless and all-enveloping love. He wallowed in love, and gave as good as he got to his owners.

Anna related this extraordinary doggy history, which says no less about her as a journalist and a human being than her reports and investigations, in the pilot color issue of *Novaya gazeta* in September 2005. We reprinted the article (*Novaya gazeta*, No. 77, "A Sick Dog in a Big City") two days after the tragedy at Lesnaya Street. Readers responded with a barrage of phone calls asking what had happened to van Gogh. At our request, Anna Politkovskaya's daughter Vera updates us on van Gogh:

Van Gogh is fine. His mood seems to have returned to normal. At first, of course, he appeared rather lost, but he is feeling much better now. For the first week after October 7 it was as if he was waiting for someone. He was off his food and didn't play with his toys. Anybody with a dog will recognise the symptoms.

Now van Gogh is leading a normal doggy life. We take him to the vet regularly, but he is healthy now and does not need special treatment. My mother simply rescued him from a dire situation when he was a puppy. We despaired and did not know what to do, but she nursed him back to health and now he is over those problems and behaves quite normally, except that he is still afraid of people, especially men.

Van Gogh is living with us and enjoys all the blessings of a normal life. He and I have been friends for a long time: when my mother was away on assignments, she left me in charge of van Gogh, so we have loved each other for years. Nobody knew him better than Mother and I.

Van Gogh shows no signs of giving up old habits. You can say goodbye to any boots or shoes left unattended in the hallway. His preference is for leather shoes but recently, in the absence of such delicacies, he chewed his favorite toy to pieces. It is beyond repair. He used to bring it to everyone who came into the house if he wasn't afraid of them. It was his traditional way of showing he trusted someone, and since traditions should be respected we will find him a replacement toy.

He has a trainer who helps us when some particular aspect of his upbringing is beyond us, but we no longer have the earlier problems with him. He is a bloodhound, of course, a hunting dog, but two years ago we bought a puppy with the sole aim of having a friend living in our family.

ANNA POLITKOVSKAYA'S AWARDS

2000

January. Moscow. Golden Pen Prize of the Russian Union of Journalists for reports on the struggle against corruption.

2001

January. Moscow. "Journalists Against Corruption" Prize, Russian Union of Journalists with support from the Soros Foundation.

Special prize of the Russian Union of Journalists, "A Good Deed and a Kind Heart." For aid to an old people's home in Grozny. During bombing Anna managed to organise the evacuation of old and forgotten people to safe regions.

February. Moscow. Winner's Certificate in the Golden Gong 2000 competition, with a bronze statuette of the goddess Iris. For a series of articles from Chechnya.

April. Washington. Inaugural winner of the Artyom Borovik Prize for Investigative Journalism, established in the USA by CBS and the Overseas Press Club and awarded by the Pulitzer Committee. For detailed chronicling of the Chechen War.

July. London. Global Award for Human Rights Journalism, Amnesty International's highest award. For a series of reports on torture in Chechnya, and for many years of reporting from the Republic.

2002

London. Most Courageous Defence of Free Expression Prize from *Index on Censorship*.

October. Los Angeles. Courage in Journalism Award of the International Women's Media Foundation, and Crystal Bird symbolising freedom. [Awarded *in absentia* since Anna was obliged to return to Moscow in connection with the *Nord-Ost* hostage-taking.] For work in dangerous and difficult conditions and reporting on the war in Chechnya.

December. Moscow. Winner of the Andrey Sakharov Prize for Journalism as Action. For consistently defending the rights and freedoms of inhabitants of Chechnya and courage in exposing war crimes.

2003

USA. Europe's Heroes nomination by *Time* magazine.

February. Vienna. Prize for Journalism and Democracy of the Organization for Security and Co-operation in Europe. For courageous professional activity in support of human rights and freedom of the mass media, for publications on the state of human rights in Chechnya.

October. Berlin. Lettre Ulysses Award for the Art of Reportage, established by *Lettre International* magazine, the Aventis Foundation, and the Goethe Institute, for her book *Tchétchénie, le déshonneur russe,* published in France.

November. Darmstadt. Prize of the German PEN Center and Hermann Kesten Medal. For courageous reporting of events in Chechnya.

2005

January. Stockholm. Olof Palme Prize, the Olof Palme Foundation. For courage and strength when reporting in difficult and dangerous circumstances, shared with Ludmila Alexeyeva and Sergey Kovalyov.

April. Leipzig. Prize for the Freedom and Future of the Media, Media Foundation of Sparkasse Leipzig. For her contribution to developing freedom of the press.

October. New York. Civil Courage Prize of the Northcote Parkinson Fund [now the Train Foundation]. For steadfast resistance to evil at great personal risk. [John Train is the father-in-law of American journalist Paul Klebnikov who was murdered in Moscow.]

2006

October [posthumously]. Tiziano Terzani International Literary Prize. To mark the rare moral courage of Anna Politkovskaya, who paid with her life for criticising abuses of power.

December. Reporter of the Year, National Union of Italian Reporters, to Anna Politkovskaya who "died defending her right to bring the truth to the public, and people's right to obtain truthful and free information."

"Flouting the Law," annual prize for journalism, awarded by the Open Russia Foundation.

For Valour, special award from the Artyom Borovik Prize committee.

2007

Paris. UNESCO/Guillermo Cano World Press Freedom Prize. "Anna Politkovskaya showed incredible courage and stubbornness in chronicling events in Chechnya after the whole world had given up on that conflict. Her dedication and fearless pursuit of the truth set the highest benchmark of journalism, not only for Russia but for the rest of the world. Indeed, Anna's courage and commitment were so remarkable that we decided, for the first time, to award the UNESCO/Guillermo Cano World Press Freedom Prize posthumously."

July. Washington, DC. John Aubuchon Freedom of the Press Award, the National Press Club. "Anna Politkovskaya, who never let death threats deter her from her remarkable reporting of the conflict in Chechnya, deserves to be remembered and honored for her courage and commitment to journalism."

September. Washington, DC. Democracy Award to Spotlight Press Freedom, the National Endowment for Democracy. "Throughout her distinguished career as a Russian journalist, Anna was an outspoken advocate for human rights and an end to the devastating war in Chechnya."

October 7. The first Anna Politkovskaya Award "to recognise women who are defending human rights in zones of war and conflict" was presented to Natalia Estemirova, "a close friend and colleague of Anna as well as a courageous human rights defender and freelance journalist, working in Chechnya for the human rights organization, Memorial."

The Prize was instituted by Reach All Women in War, with the support of the Nobel Peace Prize winners Mairead Maguire, Betty Williams, Jody Williams, Shirin Ebadi, Wangari Maathai, Rigoberta Menchú Tum and Archbishop Desmond Tutu, as well as Elena Bonner, Tatiana Yankelevich,

President Václav Havel, Harold Pinter, The Hon. Zbigniew Brzezinski, André Glucksmann, Gloria Steinem, Sergey Kovalyov, Terry Waite, CBE, Susan Sarandon, Alexei Simonov, Gillian Slovo, Bernard-Henri Lévy, Marek Edelman (the last surviving leader of the Warsaw Ghetto uprising), Elisabeth Rehn, Mariane Pearl, Adam Michnik, Asma Jahangir, Sister Helen Prejean, Ariel Dorfman, Vanessa Redgrave, Michael Cunningham, Eve Ensler, John Sweeney, Jonathan Schell, Noam Chomsky, Marina Litvinenko, Lyudmila Alekseeva, Desmond O'Malley, Anne Nivat, Victor Fainberg, Lord Frank Judd, Lord Nicolas Rea, Lord Anthony Giddens, Lord Nazir Ahmed, Baroness Shirley Williams, Baroness Molly Meacher, Sir Nigel Rodley, Professor Yakin Erturk, Anna's sister, Elena Kudimova, Natasha Kandic, Caroline McCormick, Sister Marya Grathwohl, Heidi Bradner, Meglena Kuneva, Elizabeth Kostova, Esther Chavez, John D. Panitza, Dubravka Ugresic, Katrina van den Heuvel, Victor Navasky, Aidan White, Holly Near, Elizabeth Frank, and many others.

Natalia Estemirova said,

"I am proud to receive an award in Anna's name and honoring what Anna stood for. This award is extremely important for me and my colleagues, because it will enable us to continue our work for human rights in Chechnya and to further help the victims of this war.

"Freedom is not something given to a person. Freedom matters only if you feel free inside yourself. Anna was an absolutely free person.

"I would like to say to the people of Europe: please do not forget that Chechnya is in Europe. Please know that we are human beings like you, we want the same things as you do. And do not ignore our suffering in exchange for cheap gas and oil. There is no such thing as suffering that can be contained behind closed doors without eventually also affecting all of us. Please stand up to protect our lives and to restore our human dignity, because in doing so, you help preserve your own."

[Natalia Estermirova was abducted and murdered in Chechnya on July 15, 2009.]

Glossary

People:

Alkhanov, Alu: elected President of Chechnya in a much-disputed election in August 2004. He was dismissed by Putin in February 2007.

Basayev, Shamil: a leading commander of the Chechen guerrillas when Russia invaded Chechnya in 1994. Russian bombing killed 11 members of his family, after which he became a pitiless warrior. Accused of masterminding the hostage-takings at *Nord-Ost* and the First School in Beslan, both of which the Russian Government ended bloodily. Killed in an explosion in 2006.

Berezovsky, Boris: became an oligarch in the Yeltsin era and built a media empire that aided Yeltsin's re-election, only to fall out with Putin over his opposition to the Chechen War and support for liberal and democratic causes in Russia. Now living in London. Accused Putin of responsibility for the murder of Alexander Litvinenko, a close associate, in 2006.

Dudayev Djohar: local politician who rose by referendum to become President of the Chechen Republic of Ichkeria in 1991 and then unilaterally declared independence from the Soviet Union. He coordinated Chechnya's forces during the First Chechen War and encouraged the guerilla operations which followed that. Akhmat-hadji Kadyrov, whom he appointed Mufti of Ichkeria, declared *jihad* on Russia. Dudayev was killed in April 1996 by Russian missiles after his mobile phone was intercepted.

Fridinsky, Sergey: Deputy Public Prosecutor for the Southern Federal Region, in charge of the failed attempt to extradite Akhmed Zakayev from the UK to Russia.

Gorbachev, Mikhail: last General Secretary of the Soviet Communist Party (1984–90) and first executive President of the USSR (1990–1). His attempts to democratise the Communist regime led to its collapse.

Gryzlov, Boris: close ally of Putin and Interior Minister 2001–03, since when he has been Speaker of the State Duma.

Kadyrov, Akhmat: pro-Moscow Chechen Mufti, later "President" of Chechnya, assassinated the day after attending Putin's second-term inauguration in the Kremlin.

Kadyrov, Ramzan: fought against Russia in the First Chechen War of 1994–6. Changed to support Russia in the Second War (1999 to the present). Appointed Prime Minister after the assassination of his father, Akhmat Kadyrov. Heads a paramilitary force.

Khodorkovsky, Mikhail: formerly Russia's wealthiest oligarch and founder of Menatep Bank and Yukos oil company. Supported democratic opposition parties and proposed the introduction of transparent Western business practices. Fell foul of the Putin regime, was arrested in 2003 for alleged tax irregularities and sentenced to nine years' imprisonment.

Maskhadov, Aslan: foremost Chechen military leader in the First Chechen War; elected President in 1997 and signed a peace treaty with Yeltsin in the Kremlin, but was unable to prevent a split between secular nationalists and Islamic fundamentalists. Killed by the FSB in 2005, apparently while attempting to negotiate a peaceful settlement of the conflict. His body was not returned to his family for burial.

Mironov, Sergey: since 2001 Speaker of the Soviet of the Federation, the upper house of the Russian Parliament. Since 2003 Chairman of the Russian Party of Life, which merged in 2006 with the Rodina and Russian Pensioners' Parties to form the Russian Justice Party, which he leads. Pro-Putin.

Pamfilova, Ella: Duma Deputy in the 1990s and presidential candidate in 2000. Chairwoman of the Presidential Commission for the Development of Civil Society and Human Rights.

Putin, Vladimir: resigned from the KGB in 1991 with the rank of lieutenant-colonel. Director of the FSB (1998–9) and succeeded Boris Yeltsin as President of the Russian Federation in 2000. Re-elected in 2004. His term as President expired in 2008 and he now serves as Prime Minister.

Saakashvili, Mikheil: leader of the 2003 bloodless Rose Revolution in Georgia, which obliged Eduard Shevardnadze to step down after elections considered to have been rigged. Became President of Georgia in 2004. Successfully defused separatist confrontations in Adjara and Abkhazia, but still has serious problems with South Ossetia.

Surkov, Vladislav: foremost Kremlin ideologist and spin doctor, who held senior positions in Menatep and Alfa Banks during the 1990s. Public-relations director of ORT television company (1998–9). Deputy Head of Putin's Presidential Administration. Himself half-Chechen, Surkov is believed to be the main supporter within the Kremlin of Ramzan Kadyrov and the policy of Chechenisation of the war in Chechnya.

Yavlinsky, Grigoriy: author in 1990 of an unsuccessful program to transform Russia from a communist to a free-market economy in two years. Co-founded the Yabloko political party in 1995, which later attempted to impeach President Yeltsin. Refused to run for the presidency in 2004 on the grounds that Putin had rigged the 2003 parliamentary elections to ensure no Yabloko representation in the Duma.

Yeltsin, Boris: first President of the Russian Federation (1991–9). Succeeded in banning the Communist Party within the Russian Republic and dismantling the USSR in favor of a Commonwealth of Independent States. Believed to have started the First Chechen War in order to retain his personal power with Army backing, and to have handed over power to Vladimir Putin in 1999 to outflank his rivals' bid for the presidency in 2000.

Zakayev, Akhmed: Prime Minister of the separatist Government of the Chechen Republic of Ichkeria, hero of the resistance in the First Chechen War, representative of Chechnya in 1996 at peace talks which led to a Russian withdrawal, then Deputy Prime Minister, later Foreign Minister and Prime Minister. Wounded early in the Second Chechen War (1999 to the present), Zakayev left Chechnya in 2000 and became the most prominent representative of the Maskhadov government in Western Europe. Granted political asylum by the UK in 2003 and lives in London.

Zhirinovsky, Vladimir: outspoken populist and ultra-nationalist politician, and leader of the Russian Liberal Democratic Party. Commented on the poisoning of former KGB agent Alexander Litvinenko in London in 2006 that "a traitor must be eliminated using any methods."

Zyazikov, Murat: President of Ingushetia, a republic that borders and has close ethnic links with Chechnya. A member of the KGB in the 1980s, he was elected President (with heavy FSB involvement) in 2004.

Organizations:

Commonwealth of Independent States (CIS): established in 1991 and loosely binding all the former republics of the Union of Soviet Socialist Republics except for Georgia and the Baltic states of Estonia, Latvia and Lithuania.
Duma: the Russian Parliament, which, under the Yeltsin Constitution, replaced the Supreme Soviet in 1993. Consists of 450 elected Deputies.

FSB (Federal Security Bureau): the present domestic state-security organization; successor to the Federal Counter-Espionage Service.

KGB (Committee of State Security): the Soviet secret police, replaced in 1991 by the Federal Counter-Espionage Service after its involvement in the attempted anti-Gorbachev coup.

Liberal Democrats: the first opposition party to be registered, in 1989, after the breaking of the Communist Party's monopoly. A confusingly named, vociferous nationalist party led by Vladimir Zhirinovsky, believed to have been subsidised by Yeltsin to draw support from the Communist Party.

OMON (Special Operations Unit of the Militia): first established in 1979 to protect the 1980 Summer Olympics in Moscow from terrorist attack. Subsequently used as riot police, a unit is to be found in every territory of the Russian Federation.

Organization for Security and Co-operation in Europe (OSCE): the world's largest security-oriented intergovernmental organization which called in 1999 for a political settlement in Chechnya and was henceforth regarded with increasing suspicion by Russia.

Parliamentary Assembly of the Council of Europe (PACE): the oldest international parliamentary assembly, composed of democratically elected members and established on the basis of an intergovernmental treaty, its recommendations on human rights issues in particular carry weight in Europe.

Russian Federation: successor state, from 1991, to the USSR, but does not include the USSR's autonomous republics.

Union of Right Forces: liberal party formed in 1999 from a number of small parties dedicated to introducing free-market reforms and sharply critical of Putin's curtailment of democratic freedoms. Officially polled 4 per cent in the 2003 parliamentary elections, depriving it of Duma representation, which requires 5 per cent support, prompting widespread suspicion of electoral fraud by the Kremlin.

United Russia: party created in 2001 by the Kremlin to support Vladimir Putin; holds a constitutional majority in the Duma.

Yabloko: liberal party set up in 1995 in reaction to infighting within the democratic camp; speaks out against infringements of freedom of the press and of democratic political practices, supports Russia's ultimate integration into the European Union, opposes the war in Chechnya and has called for the removal of Putin's regime by "constitutional means."

Others:

Chechnya: situated in the eastern part of the North Caucasus and predominantly Sunni Muslim. Most of its economic potential has been destroyed in the two Chechen wars, together with huge loss of combatant and civilian life. According to the Russian Government, more than US $2 billion have been spent on reconstruction since 2000, though the Russian economic monitoring agency considers that no more than US $350 million were spent as intended.

Dagestan: located in the southernmost part of Russia, in the North Caucasus mountains. Ethnically very diverse.

Georgia: the first republic to declare its independence from Russia, shortly before the collapse of the USSR. Separatist problems with Abkhazia and South Ossetia in particular are fomented by Russia. Rich in natural resources, attractive to tourists and famed for its wine-making, Georgia is combating corruption, which holds back the economy.

Ingushetia: comprises mainly Sunni Muslims of various Sufi orders. It has many refugees from the war in Chechnya. Population of half a million made up of 77 per cent Ingushes, 20 per cent Chechens and 1.2 per cent Russians.

Rose Revolution: a series of protests in Georgia in late 2003 to early 2004 in response to massive rigging of the parliamentary elections of November 2003. President Eduard Shevardnadze's inability to cope with separatist problems and pervasive corruption caused him to lose the election to Mikheil Saakashvili. Shevardnadze claimed victory, but was forced to concede defeat after the Parliament building was seized by Saakashvili's supporters, bearing roses as a symbol of non-violence; elite military units sided with the protesters. The election was re-run in January 2004 and Saakashvili's party won by a landslide.

Ukraine: declared independence from Moscow in 1991, but was slow to implement free-market reforms; heavily dependent on Russia for energy supplies, which Russia has attempted to exploit for political advantage. Its population of 46 million is 78 per cent Ukrainian and 17 per cent Russian.

Wahhabism: the dominant form of Islam in Saudi Arabia, Qatar and western Iraq, which advocates a puritanical and legalistic stance in matters of faith and religious practice. Russian-speaking Wahhabi Arabs flooded Chechnya at the end of the First Chechen War, allowing the Russian Government subsequently to present Chechnya as a bridgehead of Islamic fundamentalism

Index